Smart CALL
Personalization, Contextualization, & Socialization

This book brings together some thought-provoking papers around the theme of "Smart CALL." The term "smart" nowadays means "connected to and exchanging information with other devices." The contributions in this volume focus on a more human-centered perspective, namely the definition of smartness in terms of three qualities or dimensions: personalization (adaptation to the learner and the teacher), contextualization (adaptation to the sociocultural, educational, and geotemporal context of the learner) and socialization (the extent to which CALL stimulates interaction and relatedness between the learner, co-learner, teacher, and other stakeholders). Contributing authors are established scholars coming from different continents, using different technologies, and representing different points of view. A smart initiative.

Jozef Colpaert teaches Instructional Design, Educational Technology and Computer Assisted Language Learning in the Faculty of Social Sciences at the University of Antwerp. He is editor-in-chief of *Computer Assisted Language Learning* (Taylor and Francis) and organizer of the International CALL Research Conferences. His ongoing research lines focus on transdisciplinarity, multimodal learning environments, natural language decoding, and motivational task design. He is currently working on the empirical and theoretical validation of *Educational Engineering*, a novel instructional design and research method.

Glenn Stockwell is Professor of Applied Linguistics at the Graduate School of International Culture and Communication Studies, Waseda University. He is author of *Mobile Assisted Language Learning: Concepts, Contexts and Challenges* (Cambridge University Press, 2022) and editor of Computer Assisted Language Learning: Diversity in Research and Practice (Cambridge University Press, 2012). He is editor-in-chief of *The JALT CALL Journal* and the *Australian Journal of Applied Linguistics* and associate editor of *Computer Assisted Language Learning*.

New Theoretical Perspectives on Technology and Language Learning

Series Editor: Regine Hampel

Colpaert & Stockwell (Eds.): *Smart CALL*

More information about titles in this series can be found at
https://www.castledown.com/academic-books/book-series/new-theoretical-perspectives/

Smart CALL
Personalization, Contextualization, & Socialization

Edited by

Jozef Colpaert
University of Antwerp

Glenn Stockwell
Waseda University

Melbourne – London – Tokyo – New York

www.castledown.com

4th Floor, Silverstream House, 45 Fitzroy Street Fitzrovia, London W1T 6EB United Kingdom

Level 9, 440 Collins Street, Melbourne, Victoria 3000, Australia

2nd Floor Daiya Building, 2-2-15 Hamamatsu-cho, Minato-ku, Tokyo 105-0013, Japan

447 Broadway, 2nd Floor #393, New York NY, 10013 United States

First published 2022 by Castledown Publishers, London

Information on this title:
www.castledown.com/academic-books/view-title/?reference=9781914291012
DOI: 10.29140/9781914291012

Smart CALL: Personalization, Contextualization, & Socialization

© Jozef Colpaert & Glenn Stockwell (Editors), 2022

All rights reserved. This publication is copyright. Subject to statutory exception and to the provisions of relevant collective licencing agreements, no reproduction, transmission, or storage of any part of this publication by any means, electronic, mechanical, photocopying, recording or otherwise may take place without prior written permission from the author.

Typeset by Castledown Design, Melbourne

ISBN: 978-1-914291-01-2 (Paperback)
ISBN: 978-1-914291-02-9 (Digital)

Castledown Publishers takes no responsibility for the accuracy of URLs for external or third-party internet websites referred to in this publication. No responsibility is taken for the accuracy or appropriateness of information found in any of these websites.

Contents

List of Contributors	ix
List of Abbreviations	x
Foreword	xi

Chapter 1   1
Smart CALL: The concept
Jozef Colpaert & Glenn Stockwell

Chapter 2   7
Exploring a Smart CALL environment through the critical lens of Affordance-Actualization Theory
Nobue Tanaka-Ellis

Chapter 3   29
New perspectives on computer-mediated communication research: A social network analysis approach
Ward Peeters

Chapter 4   55
Exploring the potential of Intelligent Personal Assistants on foreign language learners' communicative ability
Howard Hao-Jan Chen, Tzu Yu Tai, Christine Yang & Toni Wang

Chapter 5   82
Using artificial intelligence technology as a tutor for EFL speaking practice
Ming Li & Bin Zou

Chapter 6   101
Exploring the impact of AI on EFL teaching in Japan
Hiroyuki Obari, Stephen Lambacher & Hisayo Kikuchi

Chapter 7 126
Socialization in telecollaboration: The smart use of WhatsApp to develop social presence in the HI-UB project
Olivia Espejel, Pilar Concheiro & Joan-Tomàs Pujolà

Chapter 8 151
Socialization in language learning: Topic modeling and bibliometric analysis
Xieling Chen, Di Zou, Haoran Xie & Gary Cheng

Chapter 9 184
L2 learners' strategies for using machine translation as a personalized writing assisting tool
Sangmin-Michelle Lee

Chapter 10 207
Exploring the processes and products of collaborative multimodal writing in a French as a foreign language class
Miriam Akoto & Mimi Li

Chapter 11 233
Case studies, multimodal OERs and online collaboration: Enhancing undergraduate learners' source-based expository writing skills in context
Jia Li

Chapter 12 266
A first step to task design in computer-based L2 listening: Task characteristics elicitation
Mónica S. Cárdenas-Claros & Kimberley Dassonvalle

Chapter 13 293
F-Lingo: Leveraging Smart CALL for massive open online courses
Jemma König, Shaoqun Wu, Alannah Fitzgerald, Margaret Franken & Ian Witten

Index *320*

List of Contributors

Miriam Akoto, *University of Michigan*
Mónica S. Cárdenas-Claros, *Pontificia Universiadad Católica de Valparaíso*
Howard Hao-Jan Chen, *National Taiwan Normal University*
Xieling Chen, *The Education University of Hong Kong*
Gary Cheng, *The Education University of Hong Kong*
Jozef Colpaert, *University of Antwerp*
Pilar Concheiro, *University of Iceland*
Kimberley Dassonvalle, *Pontificia Universiadad Católica de Valparaíso*
Olivia Espejel, *University of Barcelona*
Alannah Fitzgerald, *The University of Waikato*
Margaret Franken, *New Zealand Ministry of Education*
Hisayo Kikuchi, *Aoyama Gakuin University*
Jemma L. König, *The University of Waikato*
Stephen Lambacher, *Aoyama Gakuin University*
Sangmin-Michelle Lee, *Kyung Hee University*
Ming Li, *Suzhou Foreign Language School Wuzhong Campus*
Jia Li, *The University of Ontario Institute of Technology*
Mimi Li, *Texas A&M University-Commerce*
Hiroyuki Obari, *Aoyama Gakuin University*
Ward Peeters, *Kanda University of International Studies*
Joan-Tomàs Pujolà, *University of Barcelona*
Glenn Stockwell, *Waseda University*
Tzu Yu Tai, *National Tsing Hua University*
Nobue Tanaka-Ellis, *Tokai University*
Toni Wang, *Taoyuan Municipal Qingpu Junior High School*
Ian H. Witten, *The University of Waikato*
Shaoqun Wu, *The University of Waikato*
Haoran Xie, *Lingnang University*
Christine Yang, *National Taiwan Normal University*
Bin Zou, *Xi'an Jiaotong-Liverpool University*
Di Zou, *The Education University of Hong Kong*

List of Abbreviations

AI	artificial intelligence
AR	augmented reality
ASLL	autonomous second language learning
ASR	automatic speech recognition
CAF	complexity, accuracy, and fluency
CALL	computer assisted language learning
CLIL	content and language integrated learning
CMC	computer-mediated communication
CMDA	computer-mediated discourse analysis
CMW	collaborative multimodal writing
CW	collaborative writing
CoI	community of inquiry
EMI	English as the medium of instruction
FL	foreign language
GA	Google Assistant
IoT	internet of things
IPA	intelligent personal assistant
ICALL	intelligent CALL
IMLL	instructor-manipulated language learning
ITS	intelligent tutoring system
LT	learning technology
MALL	mobile assisted language learning
MIM	mobile instant messaging
MOOC	massive open online course
MT	machine translation
MW	multimodal writing
NLP	natural language processing
NMT	neural machine translation
SLA	second language acquisition
SP	social presence
TBLT	task-based language teaching
UTAUT	unified theory of acceptance and use of technology
WTC	willingness to communicate

Foreword

Computer-assisted language learning (and teaching) has come a long way over the past decades, developing from programmes that allowed individual learners to engage in drill and practice activities (from gap-fill and cloze exercises to simulations) to more communicative activities with the computer to a more "normalized" way of using the computer for a range of purposes from role-playing games to virtual worlds and videoconferencing to mobile learning.

The latest developments focus on harnessing the smartness of the tool—with "smart" referring to the effective and practical use of intelligence in our daily lives rather than the computer having the kind of intelligence that we humans have. Thus the editors of this book take a human-centred approach, interpreting smartness in terms of three dimensions—personalization, contextualization and socialization—proposing that the higher the dimension the more effective the learning environment.

The chapters in this book bring together research on a wide range of tools and technologies that illustrate the way in which digital tools can help to create smart learning environments. They include Computer Mediated Communication (CMC), AI speech evaluation programs, digital personal assistants (also known as smart speakers), machine translation, Google Docs, multimodal open educational resources (OERs) to enhance peer collaboration, computer-based L2 listening environments, and tools such as F-Lingo (which can be used to promote smart CALL in massive open online courses).

The research that inspired the 12 chapters took place in universities and schools across the globe (including Asia, Oceania, the Americas, and Europe), with most of the participating learners based at physical institutions but using smart tools and environments to learn a language, often interacting with other learners (or speakers) of the language, and in some instances interacting with others across the globe. While most students were engaged in learning English, other languages also featured.

Students were engaged in a variety of tasks, including interaction with native speakers, collaborative multimodal writing, computer-based listening, vocabulary learning, flipped lessons, presentations, and self-evaluation.

The authors underpin their research with a range of theoretical approaches from both inside and outside CALL or SLA. They include interactionist approaches to second language acquisition, the noticing hypothesis, sociocultural theory, social constructivism, situated learning, language socialization theory, semiotics, affordance-actualization theory, and graph theory; frameworks such as the Community of Inquiry framework, and pedagogical approaches such as multiliteracies pedagogy, genre-based writing, task-based language teaching, and data-driven learning.

Methodological approaches include quantitative methods (e.g., surveys, social network analysis, pretest-posttest design, test scores, quantitative analysis of tool use) as well as qualitative methods (e.g., in-class discussions, interviews, focus groups, case studies, analysis of multimodal interaction data or of writing performance, observations, reflection pieces) and also mixed methods (e.g., quantitative content analysis and qualitative analysis of screen recordings). Some of the contributors also point to a lack of specific theories and methods to approach online language production.

This book will be of use to researchers who are interested in the ways in which smart tools can be used for language learning and teaching. It will also be of interest to teachers and institutions who want to find out more about smart tools and technologies that have the potential to enhance the way they teach.

Regine Hampel
The Open University

1
Smart CALL: The concept

Jozef Colpaert
Glenn Stockwell

Introduction

This volume brings together some thought-provoking papers on the theme for the XXIst International CALL Research Conference at Waseda University in Tokyo in July 2022. Despite being postponed twice due to the COVID pandemic, the theme remained the same: Smart CALL.

Given the evolution of Computer Assisted Language Teaching (CALL) research and development, most participants would have expected something in the line of "Intelligent CALL." Intelligent Tutoring Systems (ITS) have been around since the 1980s. Their main purpose was to "put the teacher in the machine," to take over typical teacher tasks such as providing immediate and customized instruction or feedback to learners. A dedicated CALICO Special Interest Group "ICALL" (https://calico.org/sigs/icall/) has been working on the topic for several years now. ICALL aims to integrate insights from computational linguistics and artificial intelligence (AI) into the language learning process. CALL systems that are able to analyze language automatically can provide individualized feedback to learners working on exercises, to (semi-) automatically prepare or enhance texts for learners, and to automatically create and use detailed learner models.

Will artificial intelligence (AI) live up to its current—rekindled—hype? Is it a myth that one day AI will inevitably equal or surpass human intelligence? Well, intelligence may be a misleading term, both from a technological and from a psychological point of view. Dancing (or soccer playing) robots are a good example: technologically speaking, the required algorithms (or software routines) are not that sophisticated and have not evolved that much over the years. The difference in performance is in the processor speed, the accuracy of sensors and the power of the mini motors. In other domains such as image recognition, speech recognition, and weather forecasting, the neural network technology has not evolved that much, but next to the obvious processor speed it is mainly the huge amount of available and accessible data that made the difference.

Many AI-based systems and applications are extremely useful and often life-saving. In some cases, however, the label "AI" is being applied to products in order to create exaggerated expectations, what Alan Cooper would have called "Dancing Bearware" (Cooper, 1999). Like someone posted on Facebook once: "It is not because I call my dog birdie that it can fly." Technology can create virtual spaces, avatars, augmented reality, and simulations, but in order for technology to become intelligent, as a teacher told me recently, it should be able to grade assignments, to prepare lessons, to detect my students' needs and to provide individual feedback. It should in principle meet the psychological needs and goals of learners and teachers. So what is exactly the difference between "intelligent" and "smart"?

> "Smart" and "intelligent" are words that are a part of our everyday language. At first glance, they might seem easily interchangeable. However, there is a difference between what we mean and how we use these words. In other words, the distinction is reflected in the context in which the terms are used. For example, when one refers to a friend as "intelligent," they do not necessarily mean that the friend is also "smart." When the term "intelligent" is used most of the time, it means someone has the brain processing power to solve problems, measured by evaluating the person's reasoning ability. When the term "smart" is used, it often means using intelligence effectively and practically in day-to-day life. (Moallem, 2022, p. xiii)

When applied to computer systems, the difference is not so obvious. Smart is of course well known as an acronym for Specific, Measurable, Achievable, Relevant, and Time-Bound. SMART is a recognized principle for goal-oriented management which may be relevant to language tasks and CALL activities. But there is another meaning that we will further expand upon here: smart devices exchange data. Phones, watches, fridges and even light bulbs become smart if they connect with other devices and exchange data through protocols such as Bluetooth, Wifi or 5G. The interconnection of multiple devices on a larger scale is called the Internet of Things (IoT).

The main difference in our vision is that smart devices can generate, gather, process, analyze, visualize and exchange data, but intelligent systems can make autonomous decisions and take initiatives. A smart lawn mower is controllable and traceable with a smartphone, but an intelligent lawn mower adapts its behavior depending on the weather. Within the domain of language learning and teaching, that would mean that smart devices would gather and exchange data while intelligent systems would adapt learning content, task type, feedback, evaluation based on an analysis of learner data from various (smart) sources.

Now we prefer to look at smartness from two different angles: the ecological dimension and the psychological dimension. Bronfenbrenner's Ecological Systems Theory (Bronfenbrenner, 1997) inspires us to look at the learning environment from a holistic perspective. The learning environment as an ecology which consists of the learner, the co-learner, the teacher or trainer, other stakeholders such as parents, policy makers and publishers, the learning content, the pedagogical model, the learning model, the evaluation model, and the available infrastructure, technology and media, all seen in their sociocultural, educational and spatiotemporal contexts (Colpaert & Cerpentier, forthcoming). A smart learning environment consists of interacting components within a coherent design. Smartness can be defined as a design quality of the learning environment. Smart learning environments ("dispositifs" in French) put the best possible support system at the disposal of the learner with a view to reaching the best possible learning effect.

This targeted learning effect also depends on our second dimension: psychology and, more specifically, motivation (Colpaert, 2010). Models and theories such as the Technology Acceptance Model (Venkatesh *et al.*, 2003) and the more extensive version UTAUT, Self-Determination Theory (Deci & Ryan, 2000), and the L2 self model (Dörnyei & Ushioda, 2009) point to crucial aspects such as mental acceptance, identification, and self-regulation. Agency, ownership and effort/reward ratio are frequently mentioned concepts in this respect. A smart learning environment reduces the workload and cognitive overload for teachers and learners, reduces their anxiety, increases their self-efficacy and satisfies their need for autonomy, relatedness and competence.

Based on theory and on our own experience, we believe that the main qualities of a smart learning environment are personalization, contextualization, and socialization, as is reflected in the title of this book:

Personalization is the extent to which technologies and learning environments are adapted to the specific profile and performance of the language learner and includes topics such as answer analysis and feedback, error analysis, diagnosis and remediation, automatic writing evaluation (AWE), prediction of performance, adaptive language testing, pronunciation training, and intelligent tutoring.

Contextualization is how technologies and learning environments can be adjusted to the specific contexts of the learner, and includes topics such as adaptation to the spatio-temporal location of the learner, adaptation to the sociocultural and educational contexts of the learner, Open Data for relevant content, augmented reality (AR), and mobile language learning.

Socialization is the way in which technologies and learning environments afford meaningful interaction, such as interaction amongst learners, interaction between the learner and the teacher, native speakers, content providers, or researchers, and tele- collaboration.

Our research hypothesis is that scoring as high as possible on these three qualities increases the effectiveness of a learning environment. Failure to do so leads to poor results. A concrete example is the poor performance of massive online open courses (MOOCs) with regard to the extremely high dropout rates, mainly due to the lack of socialization.

Available technology currently affords many more functionalities than we actually use while designing learning environments. The use of fascinating technologies such as Open Data, geotemporal locations and adaptive learning paths remains largely underexploited.

Smartness is less the property of a single device, application, system or tool. It is a transversal aspect we are all confronted with in our research and development in CALL. This is why we thought it is an excellent theme for the conference.

In this volume we have included a series of articles that highlight different intriguing aspects of smart CALL.

Tanaka-Ellis presents an exploratory-theoretical paper that attempts to determine the efficacy of the Affordance-Actualization Theory in contextualizing a CALL environment.

Peeters explains how educators and researchers can start to identify structures of interactional rules, procedures and conventions that govern Computer Mediated Communication (CMC) and to improve their understanding of how language students interact when they are part of an online community for learning, how they form bonds with others and how they exercise their agency within an online space

The study by Chen, Tai, Yang, and Wang investigates the impact of Intelligent Personal Assistants (IPAs) on L2 learners' communicative ability and perceptions of IPA-assisted language learning games/activities.

Li and Zou explore university students' use of AI speech evaluation programs for their individual speaking practice regarding their learning attitudes, user experiences, and learning outcomes.

Obari, Lambacher, and Kikuchi focus on utilizing digital personal assistants (also known as smart speakers) as a tool to improve English language skills by introducing two case studies.

Lee discusses L2 learners' strategies for using machine translation as a personalized writing assisting tool.

Akoto and Mimi Li present an empirical study on collaborative multimodal writing (CMW) which has recently attracted researchers' and instructors' attention following the social turn and visual turn in writing studies.

Jia Li describes a case-study approach to provide contextualized writing instructions by using and developing multimodal open educational resources (OERs) and peer collaboration throughout the reading-to-write process employing a cloud-based platform.

Cárdenas-Claros and Dassonvalle describe the first step for the design of a theoretically-and-empirically based framework for the design of tasks in computer-based L2 listening environments.

Finally, König and colleagues explore how F-Lingo can be used to promote smart CALL in massive open online courses.

We hope this volume lays the basis for an exciting conference, and for many new research activities in smart CALL.

References

Bronfenbrenner, U. (1979). *The ecology of human development: Experiments by nature and design*. Cambridge, MA: Harvard University Press.

Colpaert, J. (2010). Elicitation of language learners' personal goals as design concepts. *Innovation in Language Learning and Teaching, 4*(3), 259–274.

Colpaert, J., & Cerpentier, A. (forthcoming). Context and contextualization. In G. Stockwell (Ed.), *Cambridge handbook of technology in language teaching and learning*. Cambridge: Cambridge University Press.

Cooper, A. (1999). *The inmates are running the asylum. Why high tech products drive us crazy and how to restore the sanity*. Carmel, IN: SAMS Publishing.

Deci, E.L., & Ryan, R.M. (2000). The "what" and "why" of goal pursuits: Human needs and the self-determination of behavior. *Psychological Inquiry, 11,* 227–268.

Dörnyei, Z., & Ushioda, E. (Eds.). (2009). *Motivation, language identity and the L2 self*. Bristol, UK: Multilingual Matters.

Moallem, A (Ed.). (2022). *Smart and intelligent systems. The human elements in artificial intelligence, robotics, and cybersecurity*. New York: Routledge.

Venkatesh, V., Morris, M., Davis G., & Davis, F. (2003). User acceptance of information technology: Toward a unified view. *MIS Quarterly, 27*(3), 425–478.

2
Exploring a Smart CALL environment through the critical lens of Affordance-Actualization Theory

Nobue Tanaka-Ellis

Introduction

In designing a learning environment for second/foreign language (L2) learning and teaching, educators need to understand how the learning environment can facilitate achievement of the desired goals. However, this seemingly fundamental issue in teaching can be a complex matter to deal with, especially when a learning environment involves multitudes of factors that construct the learning context. This is especially true in recent years where technology has been incorporated into education in forms ranging from microlearning (Sirwan Mohammed, Wakil, & Sirwan Nawroly, 2018) to fully online language courses. In the field of CALL, there have been a number of approaches arguing how L2 skills should be taught involving technology. Compared to traditional language education as a research field, the history of CALL as a research discipline is indeed shorter; however, it has given birth to some major journals with decades of history; for instance, *CALICO* and *ReCALL* appeared in the 1980s, and *Computer Assisted Language Learning* and *Language Learning & Technology* in the 1990s. Not solely devoted to technology and language education, System has the longest history of publishing CALL-focused research papers, where the first issue dates back to 1973. Even after decades of advancement as a popular research field in language education, CALL still seems to suffer from its reputation of being theoretically unsound or perceived as a subcategory of second language acquisition (SLA). Perhaps it was a fair judgement in the past, as even CALL researchers once mentioned that CALL does not need theories specific to its field because SLA is able to fill in the role (Egbert, Chao, & Hanson-Smith, 1999). There was also a substantial body of research consciously relating CALL to SLA (e.g., Chapelle, 1997, 2009; Doughty, 1987) both in research (e.g., Chapelle, 2001, Egbert & Petrie, 2005; Garrett, 1995) and pedagogy (Chapelle, 1998; Kenning & Kenning, 1990). In defining CALL, Egbert (2005) claims CALL is a construct involving language learners, the target language(s), contexts, technologies, tasks, and stakeholders like peers and teachers. Unlike research conducted in a traditional language classroom, the extra component—technology—leaves the research field always in flux, diverse and dynamic as technology constantly evolves. Befittingly, CALL research has seen more diversity in theories in recent years. Among the expanding range of theories, Stockwell (2022a) claims that three potential theoretical domains may be applied to SLA from CALL publications in the last several years. According to Stockwell, these domains are social theories, the aid of technology in the learning process, and challenges in predicting the complexity of factors involved in the language learning process. Although this upward trend in taking up different theories, CALL is still in the midst of finding its own identity as an academic field. However, CALL deserves a position as an independent research field, not as an appendix to SLA, because technology has "the ability to change tasks, environments, and outcomes" (Egbert, 2005, p. 5). One of the functions that CALL research can offer to the research arena in language education is its unique insights into making sense of how language acquisition can be done from both SLA and educational technologist perspectives. As we have witnessed the rapid advancement in technology in recent years, CALL practitioners can now choose different learning environments to suit their purposes, depending on the types of technology available at the time of designing the course and if the environment affords the types of tasks that the course designers want to incorporate into the course.

In terms of learning environments, we have seen an increasing number of research papers related to, for instance, blended learning (e.g., Gleason, 2013; Gruba & Hinkelman, 2012; Neumeier, 2005) and ubiquitous learning (e.g., Jung, 2014; Ogata, Akamatsu, & Yano, 2005; García-Sánchez & Luján-García, 2016) with varying types of technology being used depending on the learning and teaching objectives. It is important to note, however, that the terms "blended learning" and "ubiquitous learning" are not to be used in describing learning environments that afford learners to use technology in any random manner. For example, using a mobile device without clear instructions or a purpose does not make a learning environment into a blended or ubiquitous learning environment. Another often confused term usage is that the term ubiquitous learning is used interchangeably with Mobile Assisted Language Learning (MALL) probably because mobile devices provide language learners ubiquitous access to learning materials. However, with ubiquitous learning settings, learning opportunities are offered anytime and anywhere, but not limited to learning through mobile devices (see Stockwell, 2022b). With the proliferation of mobile devices, learners are likely to already be in a context that allows them to access their learning materials whenever and wherever they want, even if the course or the tasks are not specifically designed for MALL or blended/ubiquitous learning. In such a case, the mobile device is usually introduced to learning by the learner, not by the course designer and, therefore, this type of mobile device use is performed outside of the educator's intention. Hence, it is important to understand if the use of technology in "blended" or "ubiquitous" learning environments is planned and intended by the educator and has a specific purpose towards teaching the target language. As the variety of technology available for language education widens, the environment that accommodates them can become highly complex and perhaps smarter in assisting learning contexts. As the affordances of complex learning environments can differ due to the types of technology employed, task types and pedagogy, identifying the factors for success or failure of a smart learning environment would be challenging—but necessary.

This chapter, therefore, attempts to evaluate a theory developed outside of CALL or SLA research fields, that is, Affordance-Actualization Theory, to see if it is suited in elucidating the characteristics that exist in a highly complex ubiquitous L2 learning environment—a smart CALL context. Thus, the current paper is theoretical and exploratory in nature in that it may contribute to further understanding of the smart CALL contexts we are seeing more in recent years.

Literature Review

The original and adaptations of affordances

In this section, the notion of affordance is revisited and discussed, then Affordance-Actualization Theory, developed and proposed by Strong, Volkoff, and their colleagues (Strong *et al.*, 2014; Volkoff & Strong, 2017) for Information Systems, is examined. The theory of affordances rooted in Ecological Psychology (Gibson, 1979) has widely been adopted in many research disciplines due to its applicability in analyzing various situations where humans and their environments are involved. The versatility of the concept is exemplified by the extensive collection of topics seen in academia, most of which are concerned with the relationship between humans and artefacts in their surrounding environments. For example, apart from Ecological Psychology itself, the construct is seen in human-computer interaction, robotics, communication, education, and music (see Conole & Dyke, 2004; Chemero & Turvey, 2007; Hutchby, 2001; Kennewell, 2001; Windsor & de Bézenac, 2012) and it is also not new to language education (e.g., see van Lier, 2002, 2004).

The concept of affordances was introduced by Gibson (1979) explaining various relationships between the animal (including humans) and the environment.

> The *affordances* of the environment are what it *offers* the animal, what it *provides* or *furnishes*, either for good or ill. (Gibson 1979, p. 127; emphasis in original)

In explaining the concept further, Gibson gave some examples of how the suffix "-able" with various verbs can illustrate the affordances of things in the environment in relation to organisms. For example, to explain the affordances of a terrestrial surface, he provided phrases *stand-on-able* and *walk-on-able*, and if the surface is not solid, *sink-into-able* and so forth. These descriptions of terrestrial surfaces are all relative to the animal, therefore, affordances cannot be measured as we do in physics (Gibson 1979, pp. 127-128). In this regard, affordances can be described as a formula of [*verb* + *-able*], which expresses the potentiality of the actions taken by the animal (or the perceiver) with the perceived support of the environment (Kono, 2009; Rietveld & Kiverstein, 2014; Scarantino, 2003). While many academic researchers have taken up this construct, it is not without criticism.

Some researchers in Gibson's own field of ecological psychology have voiced concerns that the theory is not well defined (Michaels, 2003; Oliver, 2005; Stoffregen, 2000a, Stoffregen, 2000b). For instance, it is unclear that affordances exist in the target environment with or without the observer's perception and if they need to be perceived (Heft, 2001; Stoffregen, 2000a). Other criticisms of the construct include if affordances are action-related or if they can be more general. Michaels (2003) claims that Gibson's *-able* related explanations of affordances are action-related, but in the latter section of the same chapter in his book, Gibson offered more examples that are nonaction-oriented to explain affordances, such as affordances of a snake and a cliff can be *danger* to the perceiver, while air affords respiration. These affordances do not prompt actions by the perceiver, which are different in nature from the earlier examples. Another problem in applying the concept, especially in recent years, was pointed out by Chong and Proctor (2020), arguing that affordance as a concept has deviated significantly from Gibson's intention, and the term has been overused. This is probably due to the popularity of the construct, which has been translated into different academic disciplines, but the label "affordance" was retained because the new usage is derived from the now-famous construct.

Turning to language learning, some concepts from ecological psychology, including affordances, have been introduced by van Lier (1993, 2004). According to van Lier (2004), language learning does not initiate with input but with affordances. The term input comes from a view that a language is a fixed code, and learning, therefore, is a process of receiving and decoding this fixed code like a computer. Affordance, on the other hand, is viewed as the first level of language awareness that learners need to recognize the target language as an object to be learned. In van Lier's (2004) translation of Gibson's affordances into the language learning context, the environment is explained that it is full of meaning potential with a rich semiotic budget, although this might not apply to all classrooms and learning materials. He also argues that "affordances are the relationships that provide a "match" between something in the environment…and the learner" (2004, p. 96). As affordance is a meaningful way of relating to the environment through perception-in-action, by actively engaging in language as the action, the learner is presented with opportunities for meaning-making that enables further action and interaction (van Lier,

2002). By rejecting Krashen's approach of providing the learner with comprehensible input, namely $i+1$, van Lier (2004) proposes replacing input with affordance by creating an environment where the teacher teaches grammar explicitly by "raising the learner's awareness of what they are trying to say and how they are saying it, and coming up with more efficacious ways of saying things" (p. 90).

Following on from van Lier's introduction of the ecological view to SLA, the notion of affordances has been widely accepted by language teaching scholars for their research. In Guerrettaz and Johnston (2013), affordances were used to investigate the role of the textbook in an English as a second language grammar class in an intensive English program at a university in the United States. They found that the materials used in the classroom had three main roles. The first role, *materials as curriculum*, is straightforward in that the textbook played a role in regulating the content to be covered in each class. However, the influence the materials had on the classroom discourse was more complex. There were three dimensions to the classroom discourse: *topic*, *type*, and *organization of the discourse*. The topic of discourse concerned the grammatical concept covered in class, and the type of discourse included elicitation and production of the target forms. With regards to the organization of the discourse, some topics elicited more student-initiated utterances than other tasks. In terms of the relationship between the materials and language learning, the learners' utterances sometimes digressed from the intended topic on the textbook, which shows that the activities can have different outcomes from the affordances that the textbook designers had in mind.

In another L2 study related to affordances, Thoms (2014) investigated how affordances may be constituted and used during whole-class discussions in a third-year intermediate Spanish course, *Topics in National Literatures/Cultures: Narratives of the Conquest of Mexico*, at a US university. The definition of affordance given by the author of this study was "any discursive move (or series of moves) involving a teacher and/or a student that emerged at particular moments in whole-class discussion that was intended to clarify a participant's contribution to the unfolding talk" (p. 729). The results showed that the teacher reformulated her questions to increase comprehension in three different ways: *access-creating*, *funnelling*, and *content-enhancing*. The most common type of affordance offered by the teacher was access-creating reformulation, in which the teacher rephrased or summarised student outputs when the messages were unclear to other students. The second most common strategy was funnelling, which emerged when the instructor noticed that a cognitively challenging first discussion question was not understood by the students, an easier and more specific question was asked. The last feature of affordances mentioned in the study, content-enhancing reformulation, was identified as the teacher correcting her students' utterances and acknowledging the content of the utterance to also move forward with the discussion.

In these studies, affordances were interpreted in different ways. With Guerrettaz and Johnston's (2013) research, affordances of the textbook were looked at from Gibson's "verb + -able" aspect; however, it is unclear whose point of view the textbook was analyzed from. The textbook can work as the curriculum from the teacher's point of view, but it might be viewed differently from the learner's side. What the researchers needed to ask to investigate the affordances of the textbook was if the teacher or the learners were aware that it was an object to be learned. Regarding the classroom discourse, the categorizations of *topic*, *type*, and *organization of discourse* do not qualify as affordances. The authors acknowledge that the fill-in-the-blank exercise did not elicit much talk, while the combine-the-sentence activity elicited more student-initiated talk. Thoms's (2014) study, on the contrary, focused on the teacher, and the class structure was not as constrained as Guerrettaz and Johnston's grammar class. Although the study had a clearer definition of affordance, the way the research was conducted did not need to employ the construct of affordances. For instance, the affordances presented in the paper were the presentation of teacher-specific teaching strategies and action or reaction prompted by the learners' behaviour. Since the teacher was not asked to use those strategies, and there was only one teacher in the study, claiming these strategies as affordances may appear misleading since the reformulations were not tested as affordances but were found and identified in the data. However, the teacher's reformulations seemed to highlight the gap between the correct form and the interlanguage, raising awareness of what needs to be learned in the semiotic budget. In both cases, the teacher was the one who facilitated in raising awareness of the object of learning by providing recast, repeat, and negotiation of meaning (Long, 2016; Lyster, 2018), while the roles of the textbook seem to give instructions of tasks and the materials to work on. In this study, the existence of the textbook is considered black-boxed. Different tasks in the textbook prompted different types of interactions meaning that the affordances of the textbook content, that is, the text, topics, and activities are needed to be analyzed separately. In other words, similar results may be obtained from using the interactionist view of SLA to analyze the discourse data from these data.

The adoption of the concept of affordances in the CALL research looks quite different from that of in the SLA research. That is, affordances in CALL research tend to focus more on technology rather than scrutinizing the environment as a potential meaning-making context as stated in van Lier's papers. Barrett and Liu (2016) investigated global trends and research aims for English academic oral presentations for learning technology. They searched papers on oral monologues in English for academic purposes (EAP) and CALL through academic search engines like Web of Knowledge, ScienceDirect, and JSTOR for the articles falling between 2000 and 2014. Of three dominant research themes, one of them was *pedagogical affordances of learning technology (LT)*, along with two other themes, *the learning process and attitudes toward the learning process* and *the final product*. They tabulated the papers under each category, and eight papers were listed for affordances. The category on affordances was explained as the paper "illustrates specific applications of LT that can assist language learners preparing for oral monologues. Subthemes include the role of multimodal resources for communications, how technology helps develop learner autonomy and skills, and how LT is used for peer or instructor feedback" (p. 1237). From the description, the term affordance is not defined as Gibson's or van Lier's definitions in choosing the articles.

In McNeil's (2014) paper on anxiety in an oral asynchronous computer-mediated communication (ACMC) and affordance, van Lier's view of affordances is discussed with an emphasis on the aspects of meaning-making and interaction. The affordances of the technology looked at in his study was a voiceboard (Voxopop) which allowed users to record their speech and review it before posting. Voiceboard activities were incorporated into a lower-intermediate level compulsory English communication course of 15 students at a South Korean university. The students were instructed to state their opinions on the textbook-related topics as homework once a week for eight weeks and encouraged to respond to their classmates' postings. The affordances of the voiceboard include the asynchronicity in communication that allowed the learners to enhance comprehension, and also monitor and review their speech. Also, the voice recording function afforded opportunities to practice using paralinguistic properties, such as intonation and stress. In the discussion, the author revisited Gibson and van Lier's affordance postulates and compared the observed affordances from the data. As affordances can be "good or ill," he argues that the re-recording function worked positively against the learners' anxiety as they could work on their pronunciation until they were satisfied before posting, however, the replay function made them feel uncomfortable as the students could compare their postings against each other.

Another study in CALL concerning affordance was reported by Haines (2015) about how two language teachers' perceived affordances on new tools (blogs and wikis) changed over 18 months. Unlike McNeil's paper, Haines's study does not concern L2 development or educational technology that studies the effect of technology in learning and teaching, therefore, she defines affordances as "the potential that teachers perceive in a particular technology tool that will support learning and teaching activities in their educational contexts" (p. 166). The researcher found that the two teachers became proficient users of both blogs and wikis through hands-on experience, and their perceptions of affordances became more attuned to their courses and students. From the study, perceptions of affordance are specific to the individual teacher, pedagogical experiences and intentions for the tools.

More recently, Li (2018) investigated affordances of a social network service (SNS) WeChat when it was used by two Chinese as a second language undergraduate students of two contrasting proficiency levels (i.e., beginner and advanced) during an intensive study abroad program in China. The collected data were WeChat activity screenshots such as messages posted to the WeChat public group, weekly surveys, and semi-structured interviews. According to Li (2018), four categories of affordances emerged from the data set. WeChat enabled the beginner-level learner to access native Chinese speakers for casual interaction and gave him a new identity as a competent Chinese user because of the ease of typing Chinese texts. For both students, WeChat also provided opportunities for meaning-focused communication outside of the classroom, such as asking for help with the target language, and more practically, organizing meetings with Chinese friends. The SNS also allowed both learners to access linguistic resources by asking their friends to translate English into Chinese and learning new expressions not taught in their language classrooms. Although these varying affordances were mentioned, the definition of affordance for Lin's study is somewhat unclear. In the paper, van Lier's version of affordance is briefly explained in the literature that affordances are perceived opportunities for L2 learning through the interaction between the learner and the environment. However, the paper does not go into detail to explain how the affordance construct was applied either as an analytical tool, nor does it indicate the boundary of the perceived environment. In this respect, it leaves some fuzziness to the process of how the results were yielded and categorized that if WeChat alone is the focal learning environment or if it includes a more extensive context like the study abroad trip.

These CALL papers show that affordances in CALL are more technology-oriented than focusing on actual L2 learning activities. Not surprisingly, the theory of affordances is widely used in applied science, especially in human-computer interaction. According to Nye (2012), the research into human-computer interaction employs affordances to help design a computer interface that is obvious to the intended functions. From this point of view, the use of affordances in CALL may be closer to the research in human-computer interaction. The criticism of CALL as an academic discipline may be due to this hybridity in research. From the researchers in SLA, the theoretical aspect in CALL may be too focused on the technological aspects than engaging in a deeper inquiry into L2 learning and teaching through technology. However, what CALL researchers want to embrace is that the best of both worlds. In order to achieve this, Affordance-Actualization Theory will be explored and applied to examine a complex L2 learning environment with technology to see what this theory might reveal for this context.

Affordance-Actualization Theory

Affordance-Actualization Theory was developed by Strong, Volkoff, Johnson, Pelletier, Tulu, Bar-On, Trudel, and Garber (2014) for Information Systems (IS) in order to fill gaps in the existing affordance literature. The current affordance view lacked the theory for the process of actualizing, explaining an affordance potential in an organizational context, and describing bundles of interrelated affordances. These factors, especially regarding the process and interrelated affordances, are also considered important for CALL in capturing the process of learning an L2 and analyzing the relationships between different affordances, as CALL contexts encompass both applied linguistics and applied science domains. In this paper, those two factors related to the process and multiple affordances are mainly looked at.

Affordance in Information Technology and IS is described as the possibilities for goal-oriented action provided by an artefact in relation to a goal-driven actor (Markus & Silver, 2008; Strong *et al.*, 2014; Volkoff & Strong, 2017). The perception relating to the role of actors in IT is problematic in describing the changing process since it only recognizes the actor's attitude or action at that instant. In a similar vein, Actor Network Theory (ANT) describes the relationship between humans and nonhumans. ANT assumes a symmetrical relationship between human and nonhuman actors (Callon, 1986; Latour, 1993). However, the core tenet of ANT has been criticized for its ambiguity in determining which symmetry between humans and nonhumans can be assumed—as humans afford intentions and nonhumans do not (McMaster & Wastell, 2005).

In forming an ally in a network or identifying an affordance in a context, relationships between humans and nonhumans cannot be conceptualized without a human perception, especially when the object is technology. Technology exists because of the intention that drives its developer to materialize it and its users' needs; therefore, the affordances of technology can be determined by the confluence of the developer/designer and the user's perspectives. In capturing affordances in transition, Strong *et al.* (2014) interviewed medical workers as the users of a newly introduced technology (in their study, electronic health record or EHR in medical organizations) to analyze the affordances of the technology and their influence over the users, the medical organizations, and the database. Affordances observed in their study are all described in "verb + ing" form, which are associated with the actions that may be taken by the EHR user to actualize the affordance. For instance, affordances of the medical database can be "inputting and archiving data about patients," or "accessing and using EHR information anytime, anywhere," and so forth. The identified affordances are categorized by determining the features of the technology and the characteristics of actors (users). These two elements are together called *elements giving rise to an affordance*. By identifying these factors, they looked at the interview data to look for *immediate concrete outcomes*, which are the outcomes of the actions taken by the users, however, they are regarded as separate from the organization's goals.

As affordances of technologies were assumed to change in some forms over time, potential affordances viewed by the organizations were identified, then the previously identified affordances were looked at to see if they were realized after a certain amount of time. The results yielded from the affordance-actualization analysis can then be used to adjust the actions and the features of the technology and the actor concerning *the elements giving rise to the affordance*. Through this cyclic process, the changes in the itemized affordances can be followed up on. For this model, they define actualization as "the actions taken by actors as they take advantage of one or more affordances through their use of the technology to achieve *immediate concrete outcomes* in support of organizational goals" (Strong *et al.*, 2014, p. 70). They further explain immediate concrete actualization as a specific expected result from actualization.

Strong *et al.* (2014) assert that in analyzing a context, multiple affordances can exist at the same time; however, these affordances are not likely to be actualized simultaneously, but they are likely to be interrelated with each other. They suggest that these different affordances can be mapped based on their dependencies with each other. Also, dependency can be strong or weak. With the EHR example, the database needs to be created before it is being accessed. The first affordance, thus, needs to be actualized before the second affordance can be realized. Therefore, a strong dependency can be observed between these affordances. In this manner, affordances may be mapped out and captured to grasp relationships between multiple affordances. In this paper, some affordances in one CALL context are selected to be analyzed through the lens of Affordance-Actualization Theory to see if it can be applied to a smart CALL environment where different types of affordances, that is, technology-related and language learning related, are embedded. However, the intention of this paper is to discuss different aspects of affordance-related concepts and attempt to assess the suitability of the Affordance-Actualization Theory as an analytical tool rather than to provide a full range of analyses. Therefore, the data presented here is selective and limited. With this in mind, let us turn to the context of the selected L2 ubiquitous learning class in the following section.

Application to Smart CALL

The class chosen for this chapter was a global leadership course offered in a highly complex context at a mid-sized private university in Japan from 2016 to 2018. The setting of the course can be perceived as content and language integrated learning (CLIL) that students learned about global leadership in their target language (i.e., English) in a combination of flipped and ubiquitous learning environments. The students enrolled in this course were from three different faculties with varying English proficiency and year levels (CEFR A2 to B2, and first to fourth-year levels, respectively). Although the content was taught in English, the language teaching component was not explicit as the university offered this course as a global leadership course. Another set of skills that the university aimed to cultivate was "21st-century skills." According to Griffin and Care (2015), 21st-century skills are a bundle of skills comprised of four skill sets: (1) *Way of thinking* (creativity, critical thinking, problem-solving, decision-making), (2) *Way of working* (communication and collaboration), (3) *Tools for working* (ICT and information literacy); and (4) *Living in the world* (citizenship, life and career, and personal and societal responsibility) (p. 7). In order to accommodate the university's requests and teach students with varying skills and backgrounds, a smart learning environment needed to be designed.

The university set up two elective leadership courses, *Current Affairs A* (the first semester) and *Current Affairs B* (the second semester), each had different learning objectives, but the learning context was identical. The curriculum coordinator selected the learning materials for these courses from FutureLearn, a Massive Open Online Course (MOOC) provider. The content for Current Affairs A was from the course entitled "Logical and Critical Thinking" offered by The University of Auckland, and "Developing Cultural Intelligence for Leadership" offered by Common Purpose was used for Current Affairs B. The MOOC materials were mainly comprised of lecture videos, reading articles, online quizzes, and discussion boards, which were five-week courses; however, they are reorganized to be spread over 14 weeks. The relevant MOOC materials from FutureLearn were uploaded by the curriculum coordinator to the content management app, Handbook. Handbook is an app for mobile devices, but it can also be accessed from desktop computers. In this way, all the learning materials, weekly assignments, and class information and announcements were centralized, making it easier for the coordinator to manage the content. The idea of using MOOCs as the course materials was to make the latest global knowledge available to undergraduate students in Japan and provide authentic English materials which were not developed for language learners. Due to the difficulty of the original content, the coordinator chose some of the videos and reading materials from the MOOC courses for the students to study at home before coming to the physical classroom.

In order to maximize learner support, facilitate the smart environment and improve the students' ICT skills, the university lent one tablet computer (a 9.7-inch iPad) to each of the registered students. Also, to replicate an international learning environment, some international exchange students from the U.S. joined these courses as volunteer tutors. Approximately one tutor was assigned to a group of three or four students to moderate their discussions in English and provide help with their target language. Both Current Affairs A and B had two classes running concurrently to achieve small class sizes of about 20 students each. The members of these classes, including the tutors and the teachers, regularly switched classes so that the students were exposed to various people and opinions. The students were frequently asked to conduct some research in groups on a topic related to the MOOC content and present it to their classmates for further discussion. They also had a debate as a midterm assessment and poster presentation as a final examination, both of which used the university-provided tablet computers. As these activities were typical in these courses, affordances of the tablet computer were decided to be investigated as the material to test out the Affordance-Actualization Theory. The data used in this paper were collected through two video cameras set at the front and the back of both classrooms, which captured the presenting students and the audience's activities.

Analysis and Discussion

Table 2.1 shows the analysis of affordances of the tablet computer in the CALL environment described in the previous section. The sections in the table numbered 1 and 2 are the *elements giving rise to an affordance*. For the cell where an artefact is put in, a tablet computer was put in. *Characteristics of actors* refers to the tablet users. *Example immediate concrete outcome from data* in the third column shows the examples of the immediate consequences after taking action in realizing the affordance. "Immediate" here only concerns what is on the video recordings because there were no screen recordings on the tablets when the students were using them outside the classrooms. Columns 4 and 5 show the actualization of the affordance described. Affordances are described in the light grey cell, for example, "Using a tablet computer for an in-class presentation." Columns 1 through 3 are the elements for this affordance potential, albeit "in-class presentation" was a task that had to happen, not a potential. Column 4 describes the actions to be taken to achieve the goals in the final column. The goals listed in the final column refers to the goals set by the curriculum coordinator, and the organizational context refers to the intentions that the university aims to achieve chosen from Griffin and Care's (2015) 21st-century skills. The curriculum coordinator was also one of the teachers for Current Affairs A and B, who also was a research collaborator for our previous research using this data (Tanaka-Ellis & Sekiguchi, 2019).

Table 2.1 *Affordances of the student tablet computer in a classroom environment.*

Elements giving rise to an affordance		(3) Example immediate concrete outcome from data	(4) Goal-directed actions needed to actualize an affordance	(5) Applicable goals and organizational context
(1) Tablet computer features	(2) Characteristics of actors			
Affordance 1: Using a tablet computer for an in-class presentation			**Actualization**	
• Enables Handbook access for learning materials and class noticeboard • Presentation app (Keynote) • All students have the same learning device (the same specs)	• Students know where to check the presentation topic on Handbook • Students know what app to use for presentation slides	• Students created a presentation file as group work • Students gave group presentations	• Understand the structure of the presentation • Be familiar with Keynote • Collaborate with groupmates on structure, design	Goals: • Improve ICT skills • Opportunity to present • Learn about effective presentation Organizational context: • Ways of thinking, ways of working, and tools for working
Affordance 2: Using a tablet computer for an in-class presentation (L2-related)			**Actualization**	
• Enables Handbook access for learning materials and class noticeboard • Presentation app (Keynote) • All students have the same learning device (the same specs)	• Students know how to get relevant information in L2 • Students know how to type in English	• Students used the specialized vocabulary relevant to the topic • Students gave coherent arguments • Students showed informative slides	• Understand the key concepts in tasks and content • Construct coherent arguments as a team • Conduct research on the assigned topic in the L2 • Put together relevant information on slides in L2	Goals: • Learn and show understanding of the MOOC topics • Convince and educate the audience in L2 • Provide coherent arguments in L2 • Answer questions from the audience in L2 Organizational context: • Ways of thinking and ways of working

The features of the device were the same, however, the characteristics of the actors changed as the students needed to have different sets of skills. This was particularly apparent in Column 3 where students used a range of vocabulary specific to their assigned topic, which was most likely as the result of studying the learning materials in the Handbook. Since the goals were then different from Affordance 1, the actions that the students needed to take to actualize Affordance 2 were different. From this sample analysis, it is evident that the same device could create two sets of totally different affordances from different perceptions. CALL research, therefore, needs to have both perceptions (i.e., technology-focused and L2-focused) in analyzing affordances of the same object in the same context. Since there are only two affordances listed in Table 1, it is difficult to picture how different affordances depend on each other. However, it is clear that the tablet computer cannot be the only focal point to look into, and in order to make sense of the learning context, other "things" such as the task itself or activities within a task will need to be analyzed for potential affordances from both non-L2 related and L2 related perspectives. When sufficient affordances are identified, possibly around a certain task, then the dependency of affordances can be mapped.

Conclusion

This paper explored affordances in both the original and later disciplines to see how they are defined, adopted and appropriated into each research area. In the process of appropriation, however, the tenet has drifted far from the original concept, and the current definitions became ambiguous (Chong & Proctor, 2020; Oliver, 2005). Apart from the criticisms of the original construct being vague in describing the perceptions of the object, the previous sections show that the definitions of affordance indeed vary across different research disciplines. This is probably unavoidable as each discipline needs to handle various issues from each other, and thus, it gave rise to diverse interpretations of the concept (e.g., van Lier, 2004).

Although the sample analysis of a smart-thus-complex CALL context using Affordance-Actualization Theory was extremely limited in the quantity of the data analyzed, the process revealed the complexity of the research field. CALL research needs to have both technology-related and language-related perceptions and the analytical tools that support them to fully grasp the affordances of the technology we use. Levy and Stockwell

(2006) state that CALL practitioners are "predominantly in the role of consumers as far as theory is concerned" (p. 139). This is true not only for CALL practitioners, in that most users of affordances have altered the construct to fit in their purposes. However, this should not be viewed negatively because research is based on the body of previous research and researchers should critique and alter previous research to build further knowledge. As CALL researchers and language teachers, we consciously need to look for theories, analytical tools, or a combination of both that serve and encompass technology and language learning aspects in analyzing pedagogically and technologically complex and ever smarter CALL contexts.

References

Barrett, N.E., & Liu, G.-Z. (2016). Global trends and research aims for English academic oral presentations: Changes, challenges, and opportunities for learning technology. *Review of Educational Research, 86*(4), 1227–1271. http://dx.doi.org/10.3102/0034654316628296

Callon, M. (1986). Some elements of a sociology of translation: Domestication of the scallops and the fishermen of Saint Brieuc Bay. In J. Law (Ed.), *Power, action and belief: A new sociology of knowledge? Sociological Review Monograph* (pp. 196–233). London, Routledge and Kegan Paul.

Chapelle, C.A. (1997). Call in the year 2000: Still in search of research paradigms. *Language Learning & Technology, 1*(1), 19–43. http://dx.doi.org/10125/25060

Chapelle, C.A. (1998). Multimedia CALL: Lessons to be learned from research on instructed SLA. *Language Learning & Technology, 2*(1), 22-34. http://dx.doi.org/10125/25030

Chapelle, C.A. (2001). Computer applications in second language acquisition: Foundations for teaching, testing and research. Cambridge: Cambridge University Press.

Chapelle, C.A. (2009). The relationship between second language acquisition theory and computer-assisted language learning. *The Modern Language Journal, 93*, Focus Issue, 741–753. http://dx.doi.org/10.1111/j.1540-4781.2009.00970.x

Chemero, A., & Turvey, M.T. (2007). Gibsonian affordances for roboticists. *Adaptive Behavior, 15*(4) 473–480. https://doi.org/10.1177/10597 12307085098

Chong, I., & Proctor, R.W. (2020). On the evolution of a radical concept: Affordances according to Gibson and their subsequent use and development. *Perspectives on Psychological Science, 15*(1), 117–132. http://dx.doi.org/10.1177/1745691619868207

Conole, G., & Dyke, M. (2004) What are the affordances of information and communication technologies? *ALT-J, 12*(2), 113–124, https://doi.org/10.1080/0968776042000216183

Doughty, C. (1987). Relating second-language acquisition theory to CALL research and application. In W.F. Smith (Ed.) *Modern media in foreign language education: Theory and implementation.* The ACTFL Foreign Language Education Series. Lincolnwood, IL: National Textbook Company.

Egbert, J., Chao, C., & Hanson-Smith, E. (1999). Computer-enhanced language learning environments: An overview. In J. Egbert & E. Hanson-Smith (Eds.) *CALL Environments: Research, Practice, and Critical Issues* (2nd ed.) (pp. 1–13), Second Edition. Alexandria, VA: TESOL.

Egbert, J.L. (2005). Conducting research on CALL. In J.L. Egbert & G.M. Petrie (Eds.), *CALL research perspectives* (pp. 3–8). New York: Routledge.

Gibson, J.J. (1979). *The ecological approach to visual perception.* Boston, MA: Houghton Mifflin Company.

Guerrettaz, A.M. & Johnston, B. (2013). Materials in the classroom ecology. *The Modern Language Journal, 93*(3), 779-796. http://dx.doi.org/10.1111/j.1540-4781.2013.12027.x

Evans, S.K., Pearce, K.E., Vitak, J. & Treem, J.W. (2017) Explicating affordances: A conceptual framework for understanding affordances in communication research. *Journal of Computer-Mediated Communication 22*, 35–52. https://doi.org/10.1111/jcc4.12180

García-Sánchez S., & Luján-García C. (2016). Ubiquitous knowledge and experiences to foster EFL learning affordances, *Computer Assisted Language Learning, 29*(7), 1169–1180. https://doi.org/10.1080/095 88221.2016.1176047

Garrett, N. (1995). ICALL and second language acquisition. In V.M. Holland, J.D. Kaplan, & M.R. Sams, (Eds.). *Intelligent language tutors: Theory shaping technology*. Mahwah, NJ: Lawrence Erlbaum Associates.

Gleason, G. (2013). Dilemmas of blended language learning: Learner and teacher experiences. *CALICO, 30*(3), 323–341. https://doi.org/10.11139/cj.30.3.323-341

Griffin, P., & Care, E. (2015). Chapter 1. The ATC21S method. In P. Griffin & E. Care (Eds.), *Assessment and teaching of 21st century skills: Method and approach* (pp. 3–33). New York and London: Springer. https://doi.org/10.1007/978-94-017-9395-7_1

Gruba, P., & Hinkelman, D. (2012). *Blending technologies in second language classrooms*. New York: Palgrave Macmillan. http://dx.doi.org/10.1057/9780230356825

Haines, K.J. (2015). Learning to identify and actualize affordances in a new tool. *Language Learning & Technology, 19*(1), 165–180. https://dx.doi.org/10125/44407

Heft, H. (2001). *Ecological psychology in context: James Gibson, Roger Barker, and the legacy of William James's radical empiricism*. Mahwah, NJ: Laurence Erlbaum Associates.

Hutchby, I. (2001). Technologies, texts and affordances. *Sociology, 35*(2), 441–456. https://doi.org/10.1177/S0038038501000219

Jung, H.-J. (2014). Ubiquitous learning: Determinants impacting learners' satisfaction and performance with smartphones. *Language Learning & Technology, 18*(3), 97–119. http://dx.doi.org/10125/44386

Kennewell, S. (2001) Using affordances and constraints to evaluate the use of information and communications technology in teaching and learning, *Journal of Information Technology for Teacher Education, 10*(1-2), 101–116. https://doi.org/10.1080/14759390100200105

Kenning, M.-M., & Kenning, M. J. (1990). *Computers and language learning: Current theory and practice*. New York: Ellis Horwood.

Kono, T. (2009). Social affordances and the possibility of ecological linguistics. *Integrative Psychological and Behavioral Science*, 43, 356–373. https://doi.org/10.1007/s12124-009-9097-8

Latour, B. (1993). *We have never been modern*. Cambridge, MA: Harvard University Press.

Levy, M., & Stockwell, G. (2006). *CALL dimensions: Options and issues in computer-assisted language learning*. Mahwah, NJ: Lawrence Erlbaum Associates.

Li, J. (2018). Digital affordances on WeChat: Learning Chinese as a second language. *Computer Assisted Language Learning, 31*(1-2), 27–52. https://doi.org/10.1080/09588221.2017.1376687

Long, M. (1996). The role of the linguistic environment in second language acquisition. In W.C. Ritchie & T.K. Bhatia (Eds.), *Handbook of second language acquisition* (pp. 413–468). San Diego, CA: Academic Press.

Lyster, R. (2018). Roles for corrective feedback in second language instruction. In C.A. Chapelle (Ed.), *The Encyclopedia of Applied Linguistics*. https://doi.org/10.1002/9781405198431.wbeal1028.pub2

Markus, L.M., & Silver, M.S. (2008). A foundation for the study of IT effects: A new look at DeSanctis and Poole's concepts of structural features and spirit. *Journal of Association for Information Systems 9*(10/11), 609–632. https://doi.org/10.17705/1jais.00176

McMaster, T., & Wastell, D. (2005). The agency of hybrids: Overcoming the symmetrophobic block. *Scandinavian Journal of Information Systems, 17*(1), 175–182.

McNeil, L. (2014). Ecological affordance and anxiety in an oral asynchronous computer-mediated environment. *Language Learning & Technology, 18*(1), 142–159. http://dx.doi.org/10125/44358

Michaels, C.F. (2003). Affordances: Four points of debate. *Ecological Psychology, 15*(2), 135–148. https://doi.org/10.1207/S15326969ECO1502_3

Neumeier, P. (2005). A closer look at blended learning — parameters for designing a blended learning environment for language teaching and learning. *ReCALL, 17*, 163–178. https://doi.org/10.1017/S0958344005000224

Nye, B.D., & Silverman, B.G. (2012) Affordance. In N.M. Seel (Ed.), *Encyclopedia of the Sciences of Learning*. Boston, MA: Springer. https://doi.org/10.1007/978-1-4419-1428-6_369

Ogata, H., Akamatsu, R., & Yano, Y. (2005). Computer-supported ubiquitous learning environments for vocabulary learning using RFID tags. In J.-P. Courtiat, C. Davarakis, & T. Villemur (Eds.), *Technology enhanced learning, Vol. 171 of the International Federation for Information Processing* (pp. 121–130). New York: Springer.

Rietveld, E. & Kiverstein, J. (2014). A rich landscape of affordances. *Ecological Psychology, 26*(4), 325–352. https://doi.org/10.1080/10407413.2014.958035

Scarantino, A. (2003). Affordances explained. *Philosophy of Science, 70*(5), 949–961. https://doi.org/10.1086/377380

Sirwan Mohammed, G., Wakil, K., & Sirwan Nawroly, S. (2018). The effectiveness of microlearning to improve students' learning ability. *International Journal of Educational Research Review, 3* (3), 32–38. https://doi.org/10.24331/ijere.415824

Stockwell, G. (2022a). Historical foundations of technology in SLA. In N. Ziegler & M. González-Lloret (Eds.), *The Routledge handbook of second language acquisition and technology* (pp. 9–20). New York: Routledge.

Stockwell, G. (2022b). *Mobile assisted language learning: Concepts, contexts and challenges.* Cambridge: Cambridge University Press.

Stoffregen, T.A. (2000a). Affordances and events. *Ecological Psychology, 12*(1), 1–28. https://doi.org/10.1207/S15326969ECO1201_1

Stoffregen, T.A. (2000b). Affordances and events: Theory and research [Reply to commentaries], *Ecological Psychology, 12*(1), 93–107. https://doi.org/10.1207/S15326969ECO1201_11

Strong, M.D., Volkoff, O., Johnson, S.A., Pelletier, L.R., Tulu, B., Bar-On, I., Trudel, J., & Garber, L. (2014). A theory of organization-EHR affordance actualization. *Journal of Association for Information Systems, 15*(2), 53–85. https://doi.org/10.17705/1jais.00353

Tanaka-Ellis, N., & Sekiguchi, S. (2019). Making global knowledge accessible to EFL speakers of an undergraduate leadership program through a flipped and ubiquitous learning environment. *Technology in Language Teaching & Learning, 1*(1), 3–20. https://doi.org/10.29140/tltl.v1n1.141

Thoms, J.J. (2014). An ecological view of whole-class discussions in a second language literature classroom: Teacher reformulations as affordances for learning. *The Modern Language Journal, 98*(3), 724–741.

van Lier, L. (2002). An ecological-semiotic perspective on language and linguistics. In C.J. Kramsch (Ed.), *Language acquisition and language socialization: Ecological perspectives* (pp. 140–164). New York: Continuum.

van Lier, L. (2004). *The ecology and semiotics of language learning: A sociocultural perspective.* Norwell, MA: Kluwer Academic Publishers.

Volkoff, O., & Strong, D. (2017). Affordance theory and how to use it in IS research. In R.D. Galliers & M.-K. Stein (Eds.), *The Routledge companion to management information systems* (pp. 232–245). Abingdon: Routledge. http://dx.doi.org/10.4324/9781315619361-18

Windsor, W.L., & de Bézenac, C. (2012). Music and affordances. *Musicae Scientiae, 16*(1), 102–120. https://doi.org/10.1177/1029864911435734

Ziglari, L. (2012) Affordance and second language learning. In N.M. Seel (Ed.), *Encyclopedia of the Sciences of Learning*. Boston, MA: Springer. https://doi.org/10.1007/978-1-4419-1428-6_901

3
New perspectives on computer-mediated communication research: A social network analysis approach

Ward Peeters

Introduction

Computer-mediated communication (CMC) is an online text-based interactive process that has increasingly become part of our personal and professional lives over the past three decades. The study of CMC is a topic of interest that heavily relies on a range of data-driven tools and methods to analyse and visualise digital discourse (Bou-Franch & Blitvich, 2018; Zourou, 2019). Meta-analyses on CMC in education (Domahidi, 2018; Liu *et al.*, 2018) have shown, however, that the ways in which language and interaction are analysed within online spaces vary tremendously across studies and "preclude an unequivocal answer to the question of the effectiveness of computer-mediated communication" (Lin, 2015, p. 86). The efforts that have been made often take established theories of mediated communication and aim to translate them to the new realm of digital discourse, but they often fail to recognise the affordances of the digital context, the wealth of user data that is available and the impact this context has on human interaction (Carr, 2020; Jacobs & Tschötschel, 2019).

It is imperative that we improve our understanding of CMC, particularly in a CALL context, by formulating and testing new, replicable methods for analysis, and use this knowledge to integrate and evaluate CMC spaces in education. In this chapter, the ways in which CMC has been analysed over the years will be elaborated upon. Next, new insights into CMC text analytics will be presented, using examples from a peer interaction project in which foreign language learners (N = 188) at a private university in Japan collaborated on a number of learning tasks through Google Classroom (Peeters & Mynard, 2019, 2021). The main goal of this chapter is to show how educators and researchers can start to identify structures of interactional rules, procedures and conventions that govern CMC. This way we can improve our understanding of how language students interact when they are part of an online community for learning, how they form bonds with others and how they exercise their agency within an online space (Peeters, 2020).

This chapter further emphasises the role of CMC text analytics in the context of Smart CALL. This context embodies a number of distinct features that revolve around 1) the ways technologies and learning environments can be designed and modified to suit the individual language learner, 2) the ways these technologies and learning environments can be adjusted to fit the context in which that learner is working, and 3) the ways in which they allow meaningful interactions between learners, co-learners, teachers and researchers to take place. Smart CALL can serve as a contemporary, comprehensive lens through which data-driven methods for text analysis can be contextualised and explained. Furthermore, it provides researchers and educators with a well-balanced approach for studying CMC that can provide a more unequivocal answer to the question: "how are online interactions for educational purposes organised and is there an identifiable structure of interactional rules, procedures and conventions that govern the use of CMC in this context?", as it takes into account the person that is learning, the context in which they learn and the socialisation processes they go through along the way.

Literature Review

Researching CMC in online language learning spaces

Philp (2016), in her epilogue on new directions for researching interaction in online spaces, has pointed out that there is no clear pathway to describe and analyse interaction in CMC contexts across a vast majority of studies, and urges to draw on cross-disciplinary research to fill this gap. When focusing on researching CMC in the context of language education, one of the major caveats that arise is that analyses and evaluations of language and interaction are often neglected in favour of measuring the outcomes of tasks and assignments (Balaman & Sert, 2017). In other words, research often singles out the end product of interaction or collaboration in CMC spaces—that is, whether the learner fulfilled the requirements to obtain a grade—rather than detailing the way in which that product was made, discussed, shaped or reshaped (Zourou, 2019).

Another factor that further undermines the possibility to provide a more systemic approach to analysing CMC, elaborated upon by Sato and Ballinger (2016), is that the ways in which many institutions choose to use and promote CMC spaces for interaction, collaboration and learning are ill-founded; with approaches for integrating CMC opportunities in education often lacking evidence-based design principles. With these gaps in mind, it has become apparent that both the research field of (applied) linguistics and the field of CALL are in need of a new framework to track and map human interaction online. The present chapter, therefore, aims to initiate a conversation to rethink CMC research in language education. This process involves describing and assessing methods for text analytics with a critical eye for the affordances of the online context, comparing results of previous studies and meta-analyses, and using this knowledge to form a new basis for evaluating and integrating CMC spaces in education. At the same time, there will be a focus on approaches that allow us to measure and visualise the features of Smart CALL (i.e., personalisation, contextualisation, and socialisation), how they take shape in online interactive spaces and how they come to the foreground in the interaction process.

Modus operandi

In his review of the state-of-the-art, Carr (2020) has argued that there has been a continuous strive for novel ontological approaches for studying and visualising the ways we interact in a virtual world. And yet, as Walther and Valkenburg (2017) have pointed out, the field lacks a thorough theoretical and empirical modus operandi to analyse online interactive processes. This lack of established context-specific theories and methods to systematically analyse online language production is problematic since CMC is omnipresent in our daily lives and has taken over as one of the main forms of interaction in our education systems (cf. special issue of SiSAL Journal, 11(3)).

One example of an existing approach under scrutiny is computer-mediated discourse analysis (CMDA). This method has taken a more interdisciplinary approach to CMC text analytics over the years, hinging on, among others, the description of structure, meaning, interaction management and social phenomena (Herring, 2004). Nevertheless, leading CMDA scholars have mentioned their struggles to keep up with accurately describing interaction within ever more complex, multimodal CMC spaces that have emerged over the years. This has raised the question among them "whether CMDA is still relevant in the age of multimodal CMC" (Herring, 2019, p. 28).

Carr (2020) proposes to focus less on the term "computer" in our analyses of CMC, and to, alternatively, focus on studying the ways in which technology has become part of our social fabric; thus studying how it is used to "mediate" communication. He further asserts that giving priority to mediation rather than to the devices, programs or spaces that facilitate communication, can help us realign the field and develop more robust modus operandi for CMC text analysis. Recently, more quantitative methods for CMC text analysis have emerged that focus on analysing and visualising mediation, where various linguistic or pedagogical aspects (such as recurring topics of interest or self-regulated learning features) are taken as structural units to analyse interconnectivity, interdependence and structural integrity of interactive groups online (Peeters, Saqr, & Viberg, 2020). In line with these recent developments, this chapter will further highlight some of the opportunities quantitative approaches provide for CMC text analytics in the context of Smart CALL.

Quantitative methods in CMC text analytics

The adoption of quantitative linguistic methods to analyse CMC text has provided new opportunities to synthesise research findings in recent years. A topic of interest that has come to the foreground, for example, centres around determining if interaction sequences follow a particular structural path in CMC contexts. It has been found that turns at talk, for instance, do not randomly follow each other, but cluster together so that they become "sequentially meaningful" (Farina, 2018). In other words, when people are sharing messages or posts online, they perform actions which can generate other actions, which give relevance to actions performed earlier, or which can trigger particular responses (Tudini & Liddicoat, 2017). Researching this type of "sequence organisation" in CMC contexts has rapidly gained ground (Farina, 2018) and has enabled researchers to identify overarching structures and analyse recurring patterns within text-based CMC. It has also allowed researchers to start and make predictions on the range of responses a certain message can trigger in a CMC text environment (Peeters, Saqr & Viberg, 2020).

Nevertheless, when dealing with big amounts of data, it becomes increasingly difficult to see and map the patterns that are arising. It is, therefore, necessary to bring together methods from (applied) linguistics, digital conversation analysis and mathematics to describe, calculate and visualise patterns within interaction sequences. In doing so, it becomes possible to empirically determine the behaviour and function of the different linguistic elements we observe, and do so across different data sets and corpora (Peeters, 2018, 2019).

One of the possible new pathways in the quantitative analysis of CMC, which coincides with current research on peer interaction and CALL, involves the use of quantitative measures—mostly integrated within mixed-methods approaches—to analyse the range and reach of language use, interaction and collaboration. Abe and Roever (2019), for example, found in their study on the development of interactional competence that foreign language learners in text-chats only use a narrow range of suggestions or "proffers" to find a solution in task-based activities. In doing so, the researchers have started to uncover how learners tend to give rise to and shape their online interactive process in a CMC space. Deng *et al.* (2019) and Yang and Farley (2019), furthermore, have designed similar studies in which they scrutinise the internal linkage, structure, and logic of online group discussions to determine how the online exchange leads to a range of solutions or outcomes to specific challenges or tasks.

While these studies rightfully employ new quantitative measures to categorise and synthesise the language that is produced in online spaces, they are not able to determine which of the elements that they have distinguished may affect prototypical sequencing, structure or logic in CMC. There is no mention of the linguistic elements that might cause substantial changes in the structure of the interaction thread, for example, and which elements might be peripheral in this regard. Having this information at our disposal, however, could change our understanding of online interaction and collaboration in a CMC space completely, especially if it enables us to determine which elements embedded within CMC text may cause fundamental changes in people's online communicative behaviour, for better or for worse.

The reason why these studies do not do this is because of a methodological caveat, similar to what can be observed in the CMDA tradition. Using linguistic and statistical analyses do not allow researchers to empirically determine how the elements that have been distinguished in CMC text are interconnected, nor if any of them affect the frequency or behaviour of other elements within the data set. As an example, it is unknown if there are certain topics that are predominantly used to initiate conversations in these studies. It also remains unclear whether certain messages prototypically generate more answers than others, whether those answers follow logically from the initial message, whether they commonly tend to generate sub-questions and sub-threads or whether they can cause communication breakdown.

To do so, these studies would have needed a method to model pairwise relations between the elements that they had described, as can be found in the mathematical branch of graph theory: social network analysis (Peeters, Saqr & Viberg, 2020; Scott, 2017). Applying the principles of graph theory to text-based data has become a new pathway to map language-in-use. In the present chapter, it is, therefore, proposed to apply this mathematical tool to CMC-text and analyse if it is a viable method to study, map and structure the patterns within online communication and determine whether it enables us to make new evaluations of the "effectiveness of CMC" (Lin, 2015) and, potentially, revisit, or reinterpret, earlier findings in the field.

Creating linguistic networks

In the humanities and social sciences, social network analysis methods have been applied to represent relationships between actors or entities, and to analyse the significance of any patterns that might emerge between them (Scott, 2017). In most cases, this involves analysing how people connect with each other, which includes how often they interact, how many people they interact with and how fast information can be shared among them. The interactions between users can then be drawn up as a network in which actors are represented by nodes and the interaction, or connections, between them as edges (Saqr & Nouri, 2020). However, depending on the corpus or data set, it is possible to branch out and analyse "what is said" rather than on "who is saying it." A focus on mediation, for instance—that is, a focus on the message, on how it is conveyed, and on how it fits within interaction sequences—might shed more light on the internal structure of CMC in this regard. In other words, social network analysis can be used to create linguistic networks in which linguistic elements and the relationships between them act as the main topic of research.

Just like any other network, a linguistic network requires actors, represented by nodes, and connections between actors, represented by edges. In recent research, self-regulated learning tactics have been used as a coding scheme for such a CMC analysis, where researchers distinguished a number of self-regulation activities (including planning, applying feedback and reflecting) in CMC text and analysed how these different activities interrelated and depended on one another (Peeters, Saqr & Viberg, 2020). In another study, network measures were used to decipher the structure of a self-regulated network for learning, highlighting the importance of activities such as social bonding and acculturation in groups of new language learners at university (Saqr, Viberg & Peeters, 2021). Next to learning activities, linguistic and discourse elements could function as data points as well. Topic analysis, sentiment analysis or agreement classifications (Cambria *et al*., 2013) could, for example, serve as input for further network analyses.

In order to show how such an analysis can be performed and which results it might yield, the present chapter provides an example case, using data from a study performed at a Japanese private university (Peeters & Mynard, 2019, 2021). The focus will lie on some key aspects of the social network analysis approach, including the need to incorporate time measures in such an analysis, as well as on some of the basic building blocks, including the creation of heatmaps.

Methodology

Context and participants

The data originated from a study at Kanda University of International Studies (KUIS), where a group of foreign language learners (n = 188) took part in an effective learning module at the Self-Access Learning Center (SALC), part of the institution. The modules were designed to help learners develop necessary skills to manage and regulate their language learning such as planning, managing resources and applying different learning strategies, making and following through on learning plans, working with peers, teachers and learning advisors, and evaluating their own progress (see Curry *et al*., 2017, for details). The modules were taught in English and ran for one semester, during which learners worked their way through a number of units in which they could systematically draft learning plans, reflect on their weekly activities and report back to their peers and to learning advisors. Google Classroom was integrated into the module to give learners the opportunity to consult with their peers at any given time. Google Classroom was chosen because it was already well-integrated into other courses of the language curriculum, which lowered the threshold for participation. Every two weeks, the module pack included a reminder to motivate learners to share their reflections or questions with their fellow students on Google Classroom. These small exercises to share their thoughts were optional and were meant to keep students aware of the online forum. No teachers or learning advisors were present in this Google Classroom. It functioned as a peer collaboration and peer review space.

Participants were first-, second- and third-year students at the university. The majority of them were part of the English department (Group 1, n = 78), while others were part of the department of Chinese, Spanish and Korean (CSK) (Group 2, n = 61) or the department of International Communication (Group 3, n = 39). Students participated voluntarily and were grouped into three Google Classrooms based on their departments. There were no requirements for students to interact with their fellow learners online and their participation online would not affect their mark for the module. Because all students are required to take English classes and achieve certain scores on international tests before they can graduate from the university, no matter the language major they follow, the language of instruction of the effective learning module is English. As a result, all interactions online were in English too. All students had Japanese as their first language. Students' English proficiency levels tended to range between intermediate and upper-intermediate when entering the module. Informed consent was obtained from all participants in the study before any data was collected.

Data and analysis

Students generated 697 posts on the Google Classroom forum (384 initial posts and 313 comments). CMC data was collected using an application programming interface through which textual data was downloaded, including metadata such as time stamps, user IDs and like counts. The data set was fully anonymized before any analysis was conducted. Using the annotation software NVivo, recurring topics that dealt with learners' effective learning process were listed in a code book through several coding phases (DeCuir-Gunby, Marshall, & McCulloch, 2011). In the end, a team of two coders compiled a code book with twenty-four recurring themes and motifs (see Appendix and Peeters & Mynard, 2021, for details) including, among others, discussing planning and timing, identifying learning strategies, reflecting on performance, reflecting on materials and resources, sharing personal stories and expressing gratitude (Figures 3.1 – 3.2).

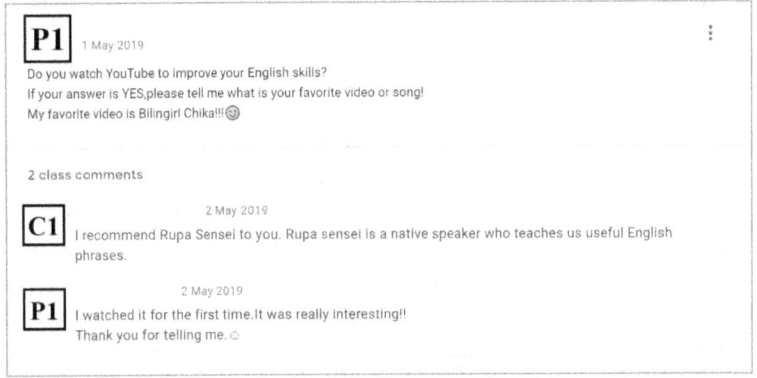

Figure 3.1 *Example of a conversation between two students (Group 1) in which they ask for information on learning strategies and resources, and share their recommendations, acknowledgements and expressions of gratitude. P1 stands for the student who made the initial post, C1 stands for the student who made the first comment.*

Figure 3.2 *Conversation between three students (Group 2) on Google Classroom in which they introduced themselves, discussed their learning goals and shared their personal stories.*

Using time stamps, an overview is presented of the number of posts and comments students in each Google Classroom shared each day. Using the coded data points, heatmaps were created using the technical computing program Wolfram Mathematica.

Results

In the results section, special attention is paid to a number of data visualisation approaches such as interaction heat maps that can help educators and researchers to start making sense of CMC. The information obtained can be used to improve our understanding of foreign language learners' online interaction and collaboration patterns, as well as improve the integration of CMC spaces in education. Two aspects, in particular, will be highlighted: the presence of burst patterns and the importance of temporality in CMC analysis on the one hand, and the relations that can be drawn between the coded data points in the CMC data set on the other.

Burst patterns in online collaboration

Within learner analytics studies, as well as in CMC text analytics, the time factor—that is, questions revolving around when and for how long actions and activities occur—has come to the foreground in recent years (Baker *et al.*, 2021; Saint *et al.*, 2020). Also in this study, taking into account temporal aspects of interaction and collaboration are key. The following timelines (Figures 3.3 – 3.5) illustrate why these temporal aspects matter when researching CMC in education. In all three figures, burst patterns could be observed with peaks at times when students were very active, and valleys where students were less engaged. What also could be observed for all three groups was that these bursts faded and lost power and intensity, meaning that students became less and less active as time went by.

Group 1 (English department) saw three major peaks, situated in the first half of the effective learning module (Figure 3.3). The weeks where there was a lot of activity correspond with the weeks where students were required to hand in reflections and where they were reminded that they could consult with their peers online. During the days between peak one and peak two, students remained active throughout the days. From peak two onwards, gaps started to occur. These gaps of inactivity became wider and wider as the module progressed. The same patterns could be observed for Group 2 (CSK department) and Group 3 (IC department).

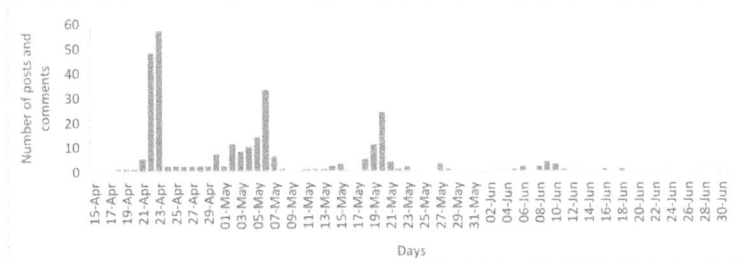

Figure 3.3 *Number of posts and comments made by students (English department) over a period of two and a half months.*

In Group 2, which had about the same number of students participating, the same bursts can be observed around the same time as Group 1 (Figure 3.4). The first burst in Group 1, however, reaches a higher peak, while the onset and offset of the first peak in Group 2 is more pronounced. The time between the first and the second burst in Group 2 sees one small gap of inactivity around the second week of the module. Peak two and peak three do not reach the same highs as the ones in Group 1. In comparison, there is little to no activity after the final peak.

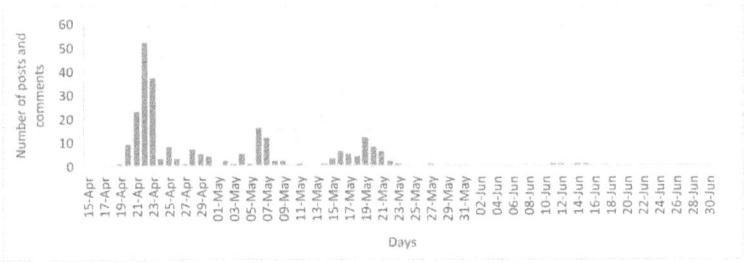

Figure 3.4 *Number of posts and comments made by students (CSK department) over a period of two and a half months.*

In Group 3, which had about half the student number compared to Group 1 and Group 2, the same burst patterns can be observed (Figure 3.5). Here the onsets and offsets of the peaks are also more pronounced compared to Group 1, while there are more gaps noticeable between the first, second and third peaks. There is still some student activity occurring after the third peak, relatively similar to Group 1.

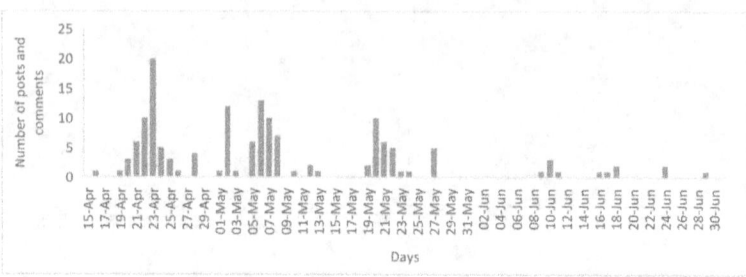

Figure 3.5 *Number of posts and comments made by students (IC department) over a period of two and a half months.*

These burst patterns show how periods of active engagement alternate with periods of inactivity in a CMC space. When analysing CMC through network analysis methods, it is, therefore, advised to integrate this information in the analysis. If not, nuance might get lost as interaction and interaction patterns that might change over time are not accounted for. For example, in the case of the present study, learners might address different topics or issues at different times as they grow accustomed to the tasks, their peers and the learning environment (Peeters & Fourie, 2018). Creating one overall picture (e.g., an aggregate network) could blur the lines between these phases, and between possible changes and developments. These burst patterns, therefore, can provide an indication of how to divide up the analysis, resulting in the creation of multiple networks dependent on active time intervals, rather than creating an aggregated picture.

Interaction heatmaps

An approach that can help educators and researchers to make sense out of CMC data is the creation of heatmaps. Heatmaps provide information on where most of the activity is concentrated in collaborative processes and can serve as the basis for the visualisation of more elaborate networks. When working with coded CMC data, like in the present study, all codes can be arranged on two axes, creating a matrix. Using simple "coding and counting principles," we can map the number of times certain codes are part of the same conversation thread in the matrix. In other words, these kinds of adjacency matrices provide information on how many times connections are made between codes. Looking at horizontal and vertical alignment (in which the vertical axis represents the "initial post" in the conversation thread and the horizontal axis represents the "comments"), we can start distinguishing patterns.

In Group 1, it can be observed that there are two major topics of interest that dominate in the comment section of conversation threads (Figure 3.6). These are "asking for acknowledgement" after giving or suggesting an answer to a posed question (n = 101) and "expressing gratitude" (n = 56). The lit-up columns also indicate that these comments can be linked to a variety of initial posts. "Asking for information on resources" (n = 64) and "discussing learning goals and objectives" (n = 57) were well-connected topics in the initial posts in conversation threads. In the comments to questions that revolved around "asking for information on resources", learners most commonly "share personal resources" or materials they have used themselves (n = 20). The links between these two topics were most common in the collaborative process. Interestingly, learners shared more personal resources than resources that were available through the university website or university library (n = 3).

In Group 2, "asking for acknowledgement" after giving or suggesting answers was also the most common comment in conversation threads (n = 141), followed by "expressing likes" (n = 124), which revolved around expressing how much learners liked using certain materials or resources in the learning environment or how much they liked comments or resources shared by others (Figure 3.7). While the column "asking for acknowledgements" is still lit up, we can also observe a cluster of "expressing likes" and "leisure talk" in the bottom right-hand corner, which designates comments that mention going on vacation, spending time on hobbies or talking about pastime. When looking at the initial posts these comments can be associated with, we can see that they most commonly appear in conversation threads in which the initial post revolved around the same topics of interest (i.e., "expressing likes" and "leisure talk"). This group seemed more focused on creating social bonds, compared to Group 1, as the topics in initial posts commonly revolved around "discussing personal stories / introductions" (n = 82) and "leisure talk" (n = 74).

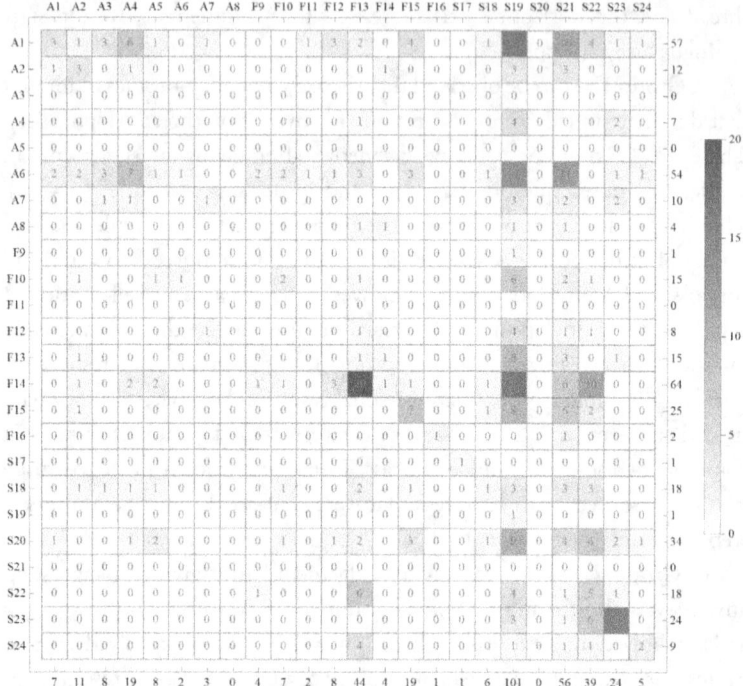

Figure 3.6 *Aggregate heatmap of the links between posts and comments made by students (English department) over a period of two and a half months.*

Lastly, Group 3 had less-defined hubs of activity (Figure 3.8). Overall, "asking for acknowledgement" (n = 14) was the most common topic of interest in the comment section, followed by "expressing likes" (n = 13) and "leisure talk" (n = 12). Most initial posts addressed "leisure talk" (n = 22) and "evaluating strategies" (n = 18), where learners reflected on their use of certain learning strategies and gave their assessment of how well it worked for them or how well it fitted their needs. A small hub can be observed, where posts on "leisure talk" received comments on "leisure talk" and on "expressing likes."

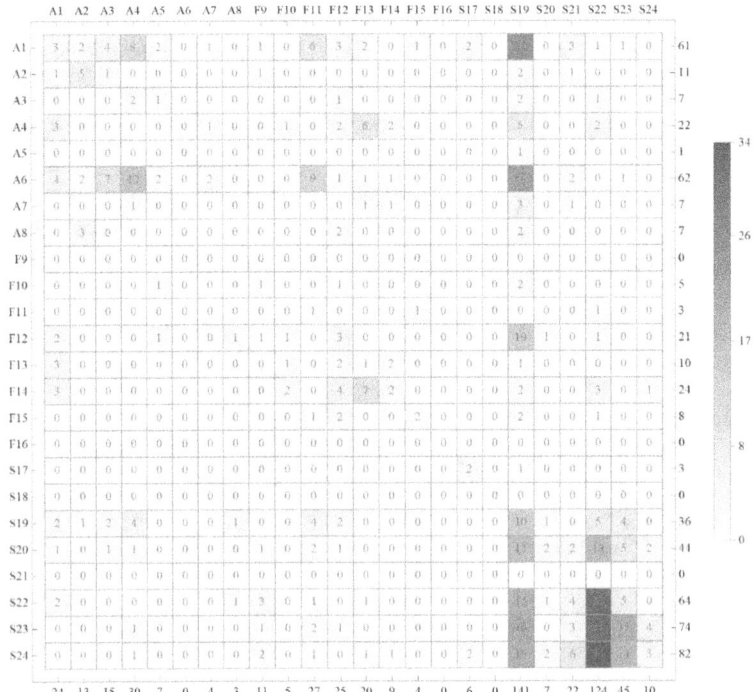

Figure 3.7 *Aggregate heatmap of the links between posts and comments made by students (CSK department) over a period of two and a half months.*

Time-bound heatmaps

As indicated in the literature review, the aspect of time can be a key factor in understanding CMC dynamics as well as collaboration within CMC spaces. In the present study, based on the burst patterns, we can distinguish three main periods in which students were actively engaging with the module, with the materials and with each other. For these three periods, three heatmaps were made, providing an overview of the hubs and the focal points in the interaction process at certain times. As an example, we will look at Group 1. For the first period (which corresponds with the first two weeks of the module), the heatmap shows 187 connections between different topics of interest (Figure 3.9). From the start, it becomes clear that the heatmap shows more variation, with different areas lighting up, compared to the aggregate heatmap (Figure 3.6). Similar to the aggregate heatmap, "asking for acknowledgement" (n = 41) and "expressing gratitude" (n = 29) are the most common topics in the comment section across a variety of interaction threads. "Discussing learning goals and objectives" (n = 41) and "evaluating strategies" (n = 39), however, are the most commonly found initial posts. This deviates from the aggregate heatmap, where "asking for information on resources" was most commonly found. The middle column "sharing personal resources" is also prominent, with the strongest link to "asking for information on resources," which is similar to the aggregate heatmap for Group 1 (Figure 3.6).

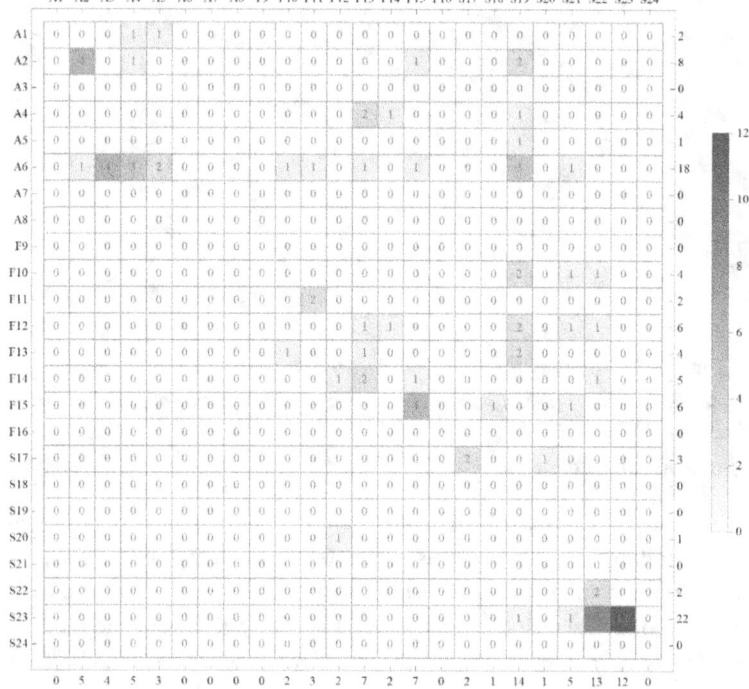

Figure 3.8 *Aggregate heatmap of the links between posts and comments made by students (IC department) over a period of two and a half months.*

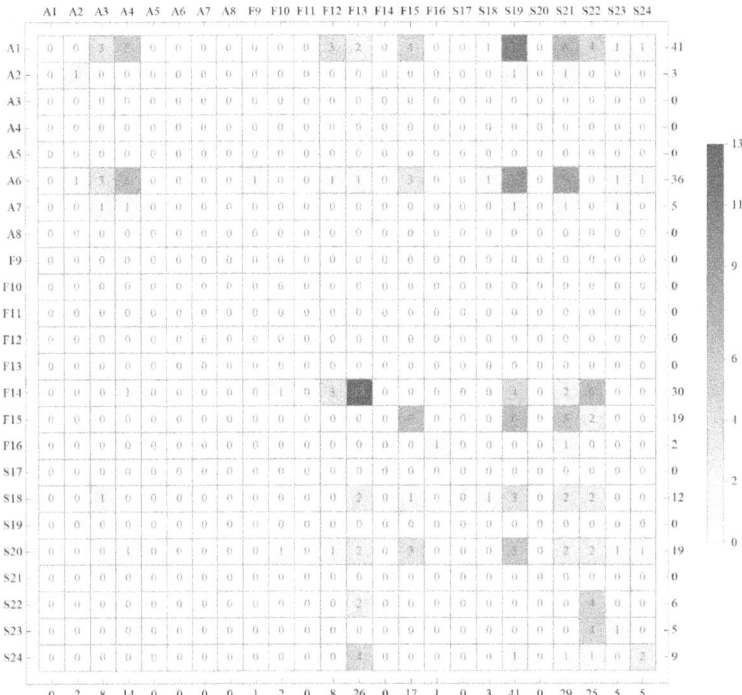

Figure 3.9 *Heatmap of the links between posts and comments made by students (English department) over the initial period of two weeks.*

Some notable similarities and differences can be seen for the second burst period of two weeks (Figure 3.10). Both columns of "asking for acknowledgement" (n = 24) and "expressing gratitude" (n = 19) are still lit up, but these two topics could now be found more often in conversations that revolve around "asking for information on resources". The strongest link here is "leisure talk", which was a prominent comment in conversation threads that followed posts on the same topic. It can be noted that, in the first period, there was little to no interaction on this topic. The strongest link in the first period (i.e., comments on "sharing personal resources" to posts on "asking for information on resources") had faded away.

In the final period of six weeks, the role of "asking for acknowledgement" (n = 36) holds strong, while "expressing gratitude" (n = 8) fades into the background (Figure 3.11). The strongest links could be found between "asking for acknowledgement" and "asking for information on resources" where students tended to give their opinions or remarks, followed by questions on whether or not these were useful or helpful.

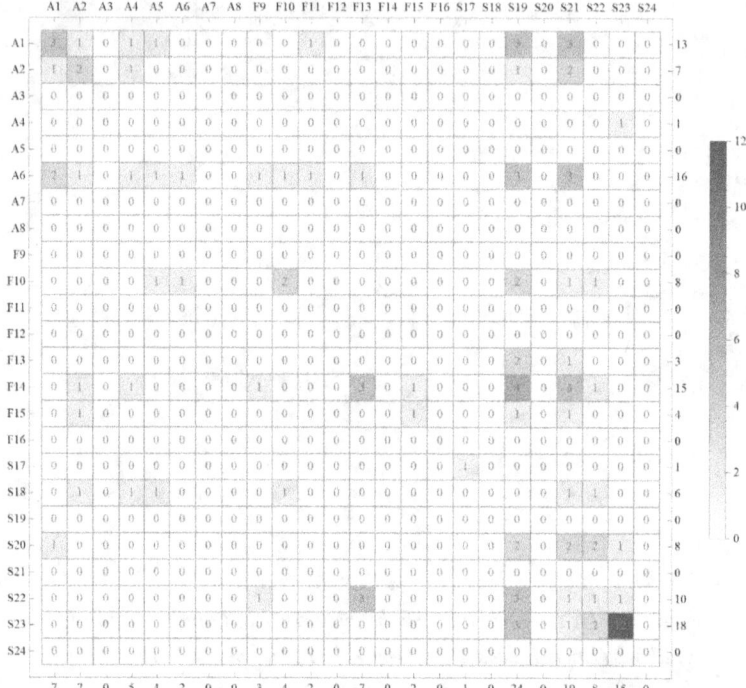

Figure 3.10 *Heatmap of the links between posts and comments made by students (English department) over the middle period of two weeks.*

Overall, these heatmaps better illustrate the dynamics that occured in a CMC environment for language learning. While the aggregate heatmap for Group 1 showed acknowledgement and gratitude as the most prominent responses to a variety of posts, we can see that over time, showing gratitude fell out of favour. It also became apparent that, during the first period, learners were more focused on discussing learning goals and strategies, while over time the focus moved to resource management. Interestingly, during the second period, social bonding came to the foreground very prominently, while during the initial and final periods of the module, this faded into the background. The discussion will focus on the importance of mapping these dynamics, paying special attention to how these methods can be applied to the principles of Smart CALL.

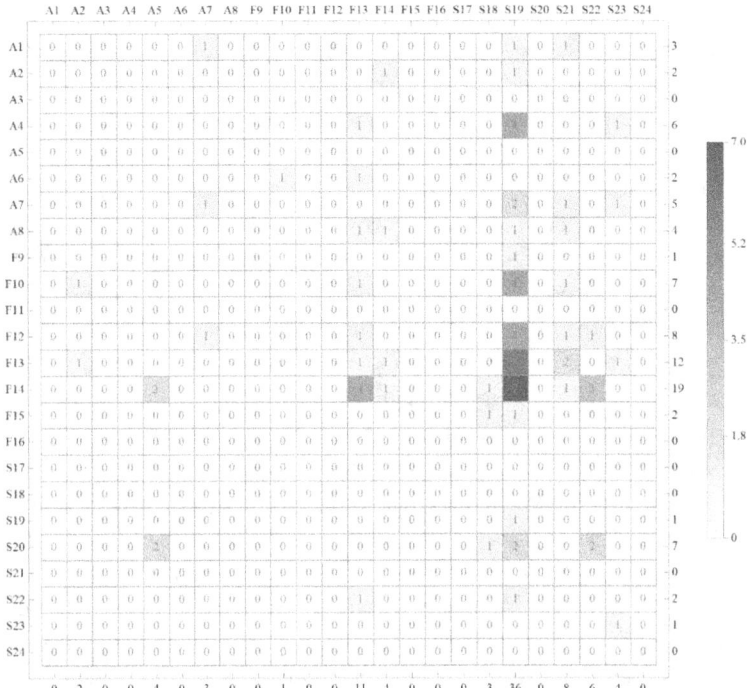

Figure 3.11 *Heatmap of the links between posts and comments made by students (English department) over the final period of six weeks.*

Application to Smart CALL

Mapping CMC dynamics within a number of time frames allows educators and researchers to distinguish between different processes and stages of the learning process. As a first step, it is vital to determine appropriate time frames for such an analysis (Gašević *et al.*, 2017) in order to organise activities and events into meaningful groups. The burst patterns that could be observed in this study and in similar studies in the field (e.g., Chen & Poquet, 2020; Saqr & Nouri, 2020) can serve as indicators to divide the interaction and collaboration process online into different clusters or cycles.

Heatmaps that follow these clusters or cycles provide more accurate visualisations of online collaborative processes in general, and the dynamics within CMC text in particular. These visualisations can assist educators and researchers to better observe learners' learning process, determining, for example, if they are able to meet pre-set requirements and, thus, can advance properly. This monitoring also allows them to assist and support students faster and more accurately (Peeters, Viberg & Saqr, 2020). In doing so, they can prevent students from bumping into avoidable hurdles by making them aware of the specific pitfalls they might encounter on their path. This kind of awareness raising can help students that might run into trouble in their learning trajectory to adjust, plan and reflect on their activities and actions better. Similarly, on a group level, it is possible to determine if group dynamics follow logical paths of connecting, negotiating and socialising with others (Peeters, 2018). Since the main reason for integrating online platforms into the language learning curriculum is to provide learners with an environment for support, collaboration and growth (Zourou, 2019), monitoring if all necessary components are present for interaction and learning to take place can form a key role in assessing the efficacy of CMC spaces in education.

In this regard, CMC text analytics can inform educators and researchers on the ways different aspects of socialisation within Smart CALL take shape in online groups. Socialisation refers to the ways in which technologies and learning environments afford meaningful interaction, such as interaction amongst learners. The coding methods applied in this study, as well as the methods applied for measuring the interrelation between the different codes through heatmaps, have created opportunities to visualise how learners of a foreign language can potentially expand their horizons, dialogically improve their skills and make use of the target language (Sato & Ballinger, 2016). These methods also form an opportunity to map how learners tend to gain experience in negotiating content, discover new resources and develop their critical literacy skills; all necessary components of becoming life-long learners.

As these approaches can enable us to see the links between the different elements of CMC text, we can start to determine how a successful peer network is built up and how interpersonal relationships are established over time when students try to form an online community for academic purposes (Peeters & Pretorius, 2020). Analysing key components of CALL, such as socialisation within CMC, in a structured, replicable way, therefore, is a much-needed next step in optimising the smart integration of online tools and platforms in language learning contexts.

This study is set up in line with earlier research which has shown the positive impact of socialising novice students in language learning contexts (Curry *et al*., 2017; Sato & Ballinger, 2016). What is new, however, is that the application of social network analysis principles to analyse and visualise the process of socialisation and information exchange in CMC text allows us a look into the wider semiotic contexts in which the learning process is taking place, which is a critical aspect of the pedagogical use of online platforms for language learning (Zourou, 2019). In the present case, it allowed us to determine how socialisation unfolds while students collaborate on a number of self-regulated learning tasks through Google Classroom. It also allowed us to see the interplay between different aspects of socialisation over time as the focus of interaction and collaboration changed from discussing learning goals to creating social bonds and, eventually, resource management. Given the context in which these learners were operating (i.e., in an effective learning module), it is both informative and educational for educators and researchers to be able to observe this shift between academic acculturation, identity construction, and organisation.

Conclusion

The first purpose of this chapter was to investigate if applying some of the principles of social network analysis to CMC text would allow us to describe and analyse interaction in CMC contexts in such a way that we can start making new evaluations of the "effectiveness of CMC" (Lin, 2015). Taking into account time measures in the analysis, based on the burst patterns that could be observed in participants' active engagement, proved to be a valuable first step in this regard. As a second step, adjacency matrices proved to be valuable sources of information to create heatmaps on the interplay between the different aspects of collaboration and learning that were found in earlier coding processes (Peeters & Mynard, 2021). These matrices can, furthermore, serve as the basis for more elaborate social network analysis measures such as the creation of weighted, directed networks.

For the purpose of creating opportunities to better understand CMC in the context of Smart CALL, this study has shown that the dynamics within interaction and collaboration online change over time and that accounting for these dynamics can enable educators and researchers to better map and observe processes such as socialisation. These methods, furthermore, can help to improve both the design of CMC spaces for education—as they provide an overview of the dynamics that are present or absent in a certain space—as well as the support mechanisms that educators can provide throughout the learning process of their students.

References

Abe, M., & Roever, C. (2019). Interactional competence in L2 text-chat interactions: First-idea proffering in task openings. *Journal of Pragmatics, 144*, 1–14. http://dx.doi.org/10.1016/j.pragma.2019.03.001

Baker, R.S., Gašević, D., & Karumbaiah, S. (2021). Four paradigms in learning analytics: Why paradigm convergence matters. *Computers and Education: Artificial Intelligence, 2*, 100021. https://doi.org/10.1016/j.caeai.2021.100021

Balaman, U., & Sert, O. (2017). Development of L2 interactional resources for online collaborative task accomplishment. *Computer Assisted Language Learning, 30*(7), 601–630. https://doi.org/10.1080/09588221.2017.1334667

Bou-Franch, P., & Blitvich, P.G.C. (Eds.). (2018). *Analyzing digital discourse: New insights and future directions*. Cham: Springer.

Cambria, E., Schuller, B., Xia, Y., & Havasi, C. (2013). New avenues in opinion mining and sentiment analysis. *IEEE Intelligent systems, 28*(2), 15–21. https://doi.org/10.1109/MIS.2013.30

Carr, C.T. (2020). CMC is dead, long live CMC!: Situating computer-mediated communication scholarship beyond the digital age. *Journal of Computer-Mediated Communication, 25*(1), 9–22. https://doi.org/10.1093/jcmc/zmz018

Chen, B., & Poquet, O. (2020). Socio-temporal dynamics in peer interaction events. In *Proceedings of the Tenth International LAK Conference* (pp. 203–208). https://doi.org/10.1145/3375462.3375535

Curry, N., Mynard, J., Noguchi, J., & Watkins, S. (2017). Evaluating a self-directed language learning course in a Japanese university. *International Journal of Self-Directed Learning, 14*(1), 37–57.

DeCuir-Gunby, J.T., Marshall, P.L., & McCulloch, A.W. (2011). Developing and using a codebook for the analysis of interview data: An example from a professional development research project. *Field methods, 23*(2), 136–155. https://doi.org/10.1177%2F1525822X10388468

Deng, S., Zhou, Y., Zhang, P., & Abbasi, A. (2019). Using discussion logic in analyzing online group discussions: A text mining approach.

Information & Management, 56(4), 536–551. https://doi.org/10.1016/j.im.2018.09.013

Domahidi, E. (2018). The associations between online media use and users' perceived social resources: A meta-analysis. *Journal of Computer-Mediated Communication, 23*(4), 181–200. https://doi.org/10.1093/jcmc/zmy007

Farina, M. (2018). *Facebook and Conversation Analysis: The structure and organization of comment threads.* Camden: Bloomsbury Publishing.

Gašević, D., Jovanović, J., Pardo, A., & Dawson, S. (2017). Detecting learning strategies with analytics: Links with self-reported measures and academic performance. *Journal of Learning Analytics, 4*(2), 113–128. https://doi.org/10.18608/jla.2017.42.10

Herring, S.C. (2004). Slouching toward the ordinary: Current trends in computer-mediated communication. *New media & society, 6*(1), 26–36. https://doi.org/10.1177%2F1461444804039906

Herring, S.C. (2019). The coevolution of computer-mediated communication and computer-mediated discourse analysis. In P. Bou-Franch & P.G.C. Blitvich (Eds.), *Analyzing digital discourse* (pp. 25–67). Palgrave Macmillan. https://doi.org/10.1007/978-3-319-92663-6_2

Jacobs, T., & Tschötschel, R. (2019). Topic models meet discourse analysis: A quantitative tool for a qualitative approach. *International Journal of Social Research Methodology, 22*(5), 469–485. https://doi.org/10.1080/13645579.2019.1576317

Lin, H. (2015). A meta-synthesis of empirical research on the effectiveness of computer-mediated communication (CMC) in SLA. *Language Learning & Technology, 19*(2), 85–117. https://doi.org/10125/44419

Liu, D., Wright, K.B., & Hu, B. (2018). A meta-analysis of social network site use and social support. *Computers & Education, 127*, 201–213. https://doi.org/10.1016/j.compedu.2018.08.024

Peeters, W. (2018). Applying the networking power of Web 2.0 to the foreign language classroom: A taxonomy of the online peer interaction process. *Computer Assisted Language Learning, 31*(8), 905–931. https://doi.org/10.1080/09588221.2018.1465982

Peeters, W. (2019). The peer interaction process on Facebook: a social network analysis of learners' online conversations. *Education and Information Technologies, 24*(5), 3177–3204. https://doi.org/10.1007/s10639-019-09914-2

Peeters, W. (2020). Peer interaction and scaffolded support on social media: Exercising learner autonomy. In J. Mynard, M. Tamala & W. Peeters (Eds.), *Supporting learners and educators in developing language learner autonomy* (pp. 118–152). Hong Kong: Candlin & Mynard. https://doi.org/10.47908/8/5

Peeters, W., & Fourie, C. (2016). Academic acculturation in language learning through Facebook: Passing the turning points. *English Text Construction, 9*(2), 292–316. https://doi.org/10.1075/etc.9.2.04pee

Peeters, W., & Mynard, J. (2019). Peer collaboration and learner autonomy in online interaction spaces. *Relay Journal, 2*(2), 450–458. https://doi.org/10.37237/relay/020218

Peeters, W., & Mynard, J. (2021). Supporting the development of self-regulated language learning skills online: Awareness raising approaches for computer-supported collaboration. *Language Awareness*. Advance online publication. https://doi.org/10.1080/09658416.2021.2018447

Peeters, W., & Pretorius, M. (2020). Facebook or Fail-book: Exploring "community" in a virtual community of practice. *ReCALL, 32*(3), 291–306. https://doi.org/10.1017/S0958344020000099

Peeters, W., Saqr, M., & Viberg, O. (2020). Applying learning analytics to map students' self-regulated learning tactics in an academic writing course. In H. J. So, M. M. Rodrigo, J. Mason, & A. Mitrovic (Eds.), *Proceedings of the 28th ICCE* (pp. 245–254). APSCE.

Philp, J. (2016). New pathways in researching interaction. In M. Sato & S. Ballinger (Eds.), *Peer interaction and second language learning: Pedagogical implications and research agenda* (pp. 377–3951). Amsterdam: John Benjamins. https://doi.org/10.1075/lllt.45.15phi

Saint, J., Gašević, D., Matcha, W., Uzir, N.A.A., & Pardo, A. (2020). Combining analytic methods to unlock sequential and temporal patterns of self-regulated learning. In *Proceedings of the Tenth International LAK Conference* (pp. 402–411). https://doi.org/10.1145/3375462.3375487

Saqr, M., & Nouri, J. (2020). High resolution temporal network analysis to understand and improve collaborative learning. In *Proceedings of the Tenth International LAK Conference* (pp. 314–319). https://doi.org/10.1145/3375462.3375501

Saqr, M., Viberg, O., & Peeters, W. (2021). Using psychological networks to reveal the interplay between foreign language students' self-regulated learning tactics. In M. Viberg, J. Mynard, W. Peeters, & M. Saqr (Eds.), *Proceedings of the 2020 STELLA Symposium* (pp. 12–23). CEUR.

Sato, M., & Ballinger, S. (2016). *Peer interaction and second language learning: Pedagogical potential and research agenda*. Amsterdam: John Benjamins.

Scott, J. (2017). *Social network analysis*. London: Sage.

Tudini, V., & Liddicoat, A.J. (2017) Computer-mediated communication and conversation analysis. In S. Thorne & S. May (Eds.), *Language, education and technology. Encyclopedia of language and education (3rd ed.)*. Cham: Springer. https://doi.org/10.1007/978-3-319-02237-6_32

Walther, J.B., & Valkenburg, P.M. (2017). Merging mass and interpersonal communication via interactive communication technology: A symposium. *Human Communication Research, 43*, 415–423. https://doi.org/10.1111/hcre.12120

Yang, H.H., & Farley, A. (2019). Quantifying the impact of language on the performance of international accounting students: A cognitive load theory perspective. *English for Specific Purposes, 55*, 12–24. https://doi.org/10.1016/J.ESP.2019.03.003

Zourou, K. (2019). A critical review of social networks for language learning beyond the classroom. In M. Dressman & R. Sadler (Eds.), *Handbook of Informal Language Learning* (pp. 369–382). Hoboken, NJ: Wiley-Blackwell. https://doi.org/10.1002/9781119472384.ch24

Appendix

Table 3.1 *Overview of the code book (Peeters & Mynard, 2021).*

Code	Strategies	Metastrategies	Strata	SARC
A1	Discussing learning goals and objectives, including personal goals	Planning	Meta-cognitive	Awareness of approaches to learning
A2	Discussing planning and timing			
A3	Identifying strategies	Orchestrating strategy use		
A4	Trying out strategies			
A5	Asking for information on the use of tactics and strategies for learning			
A6	Evaluating strategies	Evaluating		
A7	Reflecting on performance			
A8	Discussing the Module pack and reasons for taking the Module			
F9	Reflecting on materials and resources	Evaluating	Meta-cognitive	Awareness of facilities, roles and resources
F10	Discussing the content of materials and resources for the course	Obtaining and using resources		
F11	Sharing resources: spaces and people			
F12	Sharing resources: materials available at the institute			
F13	Sharing resources: personal materials			
F14	Asking for (info on) resources			
F15	Sharing experiences, tips and tricks about learning trajectory	Organising	Meta-social	
F16	Solving a practical or technical problem			
S17	Expressing emotions on performance	Evaluating	Meta-affective	Awareness of self
S18	Reflecting on (choices made in) learning trajectory	Monitoring		
S19	Asking for acknowledgement		Meta-motivational	
S20	Providing acknowledgement or positive reinforcement	Paying attention		
S21	Expressing gratitude			
S22	Expressing likes			
S23	Leisure talk		Meta-social	
S24	Discussing personal stories / introductions			

4
Exploring the potential of Intelligent Personal Assistants on foreign language learners' communicative ability

Howard Hao-Jan Chen
Tzu Yu Tai
Christine Yang
Toni Wang

Introduction

Communication in the target language has been considered to be the most difficult and anxiety-provoking language skill for second and foreign language (L2) learners due to rare input and output practice in an authentic context, limited class time, and personal factors such as anxiety, fear of making mistakes, and peers' negative feedback. Therefore, promoting L2 learners' communication ability has been an enduring challenge for L2 instructors (Moussalli & Cardoso, 2020). According to Goh (2014), learners should develop not only listening but also speaking skills in order to interact effectively with others.

Recently, with the emergence of artificial intelligence and automatic speech recognition (ASR), Intelligent Personal Assistants (IPAs; e.g., Apple's Siri, Amazon's Alexa, and Google Assistant) offer potential advantages in L2 communication. IPAs refer to the voice-controlled services connected to smartphones or smart speakers (e.g., Apple's HomePad, Amazon Echo, and Google Nest) that can perform concierge-type tasks or provide information based on a combination of user input, location awareness, and online sources. They may be used to engage learners as their conversational partner (Moussali & Cardoso, 2020; Istrate, 2019), provide more opportunities for input exposure and output practice in a stress-free environment (Dizon, 2020; Tai & Chen, 2020), allow for more focused personalized instruction and individualized feedback, and encourage autonomous learning (Istrate, 2019).

Given the aforementioned benefits, IPAs appear to be an attractive alternative for conventional L2 education. However, as Dizon (2020) indicates, IPA-assisted language learning research is still in a rudimentary stage. Among the few studies, they are exploratory, limited in scope and with small sample sizes, and yielded conflicting results. For example, in Tai and Chen's (2020) on EFL learners' willingness to communicate (WTC), they found Google Assistant increased the cognitive load on low-achievers and thus hindered their learning and WTC in English. Furthermore, much of the focus in prior research has typically been on IPAs with their associated smart speakers, which provide only audio feedback. The use of IPAs with multimodal presentation mode of feedback on screen has received relatively little attention from researchers and thus calls for further investigation (Wu *et al.*, 2020). In addition, prior research targeted adult L2 learners' perceptions toward the use of IPAs; nevertheless, few attempts have been made to investigate the adolescent L2 learners' attitudes toward IPA-assisted language learning. This study hence aimed to investigate how adolescent EFL learners perceive the potentials of the IPA *Google Assistant* for English learning.

Literature Review

Intelligent Personal Assistants in L2 Education

Santos *et al.* (2016, p. 194) define IPAs as "software agents that can automate and ease many of the daily tasks of their users." According to Goksel-Canbek and Mutlu (2016), IPAs use a combination of three technologies: personal context awareness, a conversational interface, and service delegation to function and perform properly. With the advance of ASR and automatic language processing (NLP), IPAs have increased their functionality, enabling them to do more complex tasks including controlling other internet-connected devices and accessing information from a variety of online sources to perform the required services. Furthermore, IPAs can communicate with users in human-like interactions (Moussalli & Cardoso, 2020).

Language educators are advocating their potential in assisting L2 learning (Bibauw, François, Van den Noortgate, & Desmet, 2022; Dizon, 2020). An assumption behind IPA-assisted language learning is that the meaning-oriented practice contributes to the development of learners' proficiency in that language (Sydorenko, Daurio, & Thorne, 2018). According to Carhill-Poza and Chen (2020), this idea finds a theoretical foundation in the interactionist approach of second language acquisition: through the dialogue, learners receive input, opportunities for output, feedback, noticing, and negotiation of meaning, which are all essential for L2 development (Long, 1996, 2017).

The Target IPA and Smart Speaker: Google Assistant via Google Home Hub

Driven by recent advances in IPA technology, numerous IPA platforms have emerged with varying levels of functionality. For example, learners can interact with Google Assistant (GA) via its smart speakers Google Nest Hub, providing audio input and a visual display of content on screen (e.g. text, pictures, and videos), and Google Nest Mini, providing audio feedback only. According to Mayer's (2017) multimedia principle, people learn better from words (i.e., in spoken or written form) and pictures (i.e., in the static or dynamic form) than from words alone because they have both auditory and visual channels activated and can achieve better understanding and learning. Given this, GA via Google Nest Hub, with multimodal screen-based feedback, was adopted in this study to take advantage of IPA platforms.

IPA-Assisted Language Learning Research

Research has been carried out to investigate the use of IPAs in assisting L2 learning. For example, Underwood (2017) investigated the impact of IPAs (i.e., Amazon's Alexa, Apple's Siri, and Google Assistant) on 11 primary EFL learners' English learning. The researcher observed that the learners were highly engaged in speaking to IPAs and spoke more English when using IPAs in group work. In addition, the learners were found to spontaneously reformulate or self-correct their utterances in order to maintain a smooth interaction with IPAs. Although the researcher highlighted adolescent EFL learners' strong motivation to speak to IPAs, he also identified some obstacles that the learners encountered when speaking to IPAs, such as learners' difficulty in responding to IPAs' utterances and IPAs' difficulty in successful voice-recognition when learners spoke at the same time. Similarly, Kessler (2018) highlighted that, with speech recognition systems, IPAs can provide L2 learners with ample opportunities to practice speaking.

Furthermore, Dizon and Tang (2019) examined how Alexa was used by two adult EFL learners in the context of Autonomous Second Language Learning (ASLL). After the four-week intervention, the researchers collected the participants' usage data and investigated their attitudes toward Alexa for ASLL through a survey. The learners still displayed a positive attitude toward the use of Alexa for ASLL and commented that Alexa could facilitate the development of L2 dialogue and pronunciation.

In Moussalli and Cardoso's (2016) study, they examined the use of Amazon Echo and its companion IPA, Alexa, with four adult EFL learners with intermediate English proficiency. The learners tried a variety of pre-set questions/commands and some self-generated questions to interact with Alexa, and reported that speaking with Alexa was an enjoyable experience. Alexa could be a useful tool for developing pronunciation and vocabulary; some learners, however, indicated that they encountered difficulties in being understood by Alexa. To better understand the extent to which IPAs understand and are understood by L2 learners, Moussalli & Cardoso (2020) continued to examine Alexa's ability to recognize 11 adult EFL learners' accented speech. They conducted a survey and interview to retrieve the learners' perception of how well they and Alexa understood one another. Results show that the learners generally perceived that they could relatively easily understand and be understood by Alexa. However, Alexa still has some problems in comprehending L2 learners' speech.

In addition to perception-based findings, empirical evidence also supports that IPAs can indeed facilitate L2 learners' language development. For example, Sing, Embi, and Hashim (2019) demonstrated that IPAs can enhance adolescent ESL learners' reading ability. They invited 10 primary ESL learners, who struggled with reading comprehension activities, to use Google Assistant in answering reading comprehension questions. Their findings show that, compared to traditional reading comprehension methods, the learners made more attempts to complete comprehension tasks and even gave more correct answers. The researchers thus concluded that IPAs like Google Assistant could effectively facilitate ESL learners' development of reading comprehension by increasing learners' motivation for better language performance.

Another empirical study was conducted by Dizon (2020), who examined the effects of in-class use of Alexa for listening and speaking development. Thirteen adult EFL learners received a 10-week in-class treatment of weekly interaction with Alexa for 12 minutes, and compared the post-test performances on listening and speaking between the treatment group and control group. He discovered that both groups made slight gains in listening development, yet no significant difference was found between the two groups. On the contrary, the treatment group made significantly more gains in their speaking development than their counterpart, which thus proves that IPAs can effectively develop L2 learners' speaking ability.

Review of previous studies on adult L2 learners' perceptions and learning gains have demonstrated that IPAs are perceived to be useful tools for language learning and are effective to enhance L2 learners' speaking ability. Despite the positive results found in these studies, IPA-mediated language learning does not always outperform conventional teacher-led training. For example, Dizon (2020) investigated the effects of IPAs on EFL learners' speaking and listening ability. The results revealed that IPAs only improved learners' speaking but not listening ability. Another example is Tai and Chen's (2020) study. They compared the impact of IPAs with different presentation modes (audio and audio and visual) of feedback. They found that Google Assistant benefited higher-achievers more but it increased the cognitive load on low-achievers and thus hindered their learning and willingness to communicate in English. Furthermore, as Dizon (2020) indicates, most of the literature is exploratory, limited in scope and with small sample sizes. Hence, more research is required to validate its usefulness for L2 learning. In addition, much of the focus in prior research has typically been on IPAs with their associated smart speakers, which provide only audio feedback. The use of IPAs with multimodal presentation mode of feedback on screen has received relatively little attention from researchers and thus calls for further investigation (e.g., Dizon, 2020; Moussalli & Cardoso, 2020; Sandeep, 2019; Underwood, 2017, for Alexa on Amazon's Echo). Thus, more evidence on the application of IPAs with multimodal presentation of feedback/responses is needed to capture a more comprehensive picture of IPA-assisted language learning.

To have a more comprehensive understanding of the role of IPAs in promoting L2 learning, this study thus aims to examine adolescent EFL learners' perceptions toward the use of IPAs for English learning. We specifically targeted learners' opinions about the use of GA via Google Home series. Three research questions were addressed in this study,

(1) What are the EFL learners' perceptions toward GA for promoting English communicative ability in a classroom environment?
(2) What are adolescent EFL learners' favorite functions/applications of GA?
(3) How do adolescent EFL learners interact with GA in a classroom environment?

Method

Participants

An intact class of 29 ninth-grade students (14 males and 15 females) from a public junior high school in Taiwan was invited to join this experiment. The participants' age was around 15 with Mandarin Chinese as their first language. They all have been receiving formal instructions on English since they were in third grade, and their English proficiency level was estimated to be around the CEFR A1-A2 levels. Informed consent form of all participants was obtained prior to the data collection phase.

Instruments

Google Assistant on Google Home Hub

To investigate the participants' perception toward GA for English learning, four Google Home Hub were purchased and installed in the participants' classroom. The reason for adopting Google Home Hub was that this device is equipped with a touch panel, which provides certain types of visual aid (e.g. subtitles, pictures, video clips). We thus decided to use Google Home Hub as the medium to observe how the participants would interact with the speaker and how this feature would influence the participants' perceptions toward the use of IPA for English learning.

Background Questionnaire and Google Assistant Language Learning (GALL) Questionnaire

To gather information regarding the participants' English learning experiences, a 5-point Likert-scaled background questionnaire (from 1 = strongly disagree to 5 = strongly agree) with eight items was made and administered to the participants before the experiment. A GALL questionnaire survey was conducted with the participants to measure their perceptions of the use of GA for English learning after the intervention. The survey consisted of 22 5-point Likert-scaled items (from 1=strongly disagree to 5=strongly agree) and included six dimensions on the use of GA for language learning: (1) learning motivation, (2) learning anxiety, (3) usefulness for language learning, (4) willingness to use, (5) mutual comprehensibility of learner-IPA speech, and (6) overall experience (see Appendix A). A Cronbach's α test was conducted on the survey and yielded a value of 0.959, showing that the items have high internal consistency. In addition to Likert-scaled items, one multiple-choice question of the participants' favorite activities and two open-ended questions of the perceived strengths and weaknesses of GA for English learning were also included in the survey.

In-Class Discussion and Focus Group Interview

To obtain the participants' feedback about the use of GA for English learning more thoroughly, in-class discussions and a focus group interview with 11 questions (see Appendix B) were carried out by the participants' English teacher. Five in-class discussions were held for the participants to freely share their feelings about using GA. After completion of the survey, two groups of students (10 students in total) were selected randomly for the focus group interviews. Two researchers, one for each group, participated in the interviews. Detailed communication was carried out before the interviews to determine the appropriate interview method and strategies. All interviews were recorded. The three group interviews were carried out simultaneously and lasted for 20 minutes. The interviews were conducted in Chinese, the students' first language. All interviews were audio-recorded. Then the researchers transcribed the audio of each interview into text, which was then sent to each interviewee by email for revision and supplementation to ensure the accuracy and completeness of the text.

Then, the researchers sorted all of the texts again to form the final interview text. The interview included 11 items (Appendix B).

Classroom Observation

Because the participants' English teacher was also their homeroom teacher, the teacher hence had opportunities to closely observe how the participants interacted with GA, and took notes on the participants' reactions as well as on behavioral changes. The teacher then summarized her observations into a short report for the researchers to better uncover the underlying reasons for the learners' responses to the survey items.

Data Analysis

A mixed-methods design (Creswell, 2003) was adopted in this study in which both qualitative and quantitative data were collected and analyzed. The GALL questionnaire was analyzed quantitatively. The researchers tallied frequency distributions for each survey item to determine consensus or discrepancy in opinion among participants. Then the qualitative data collected from focus group interviews were analyzed to substantiate and explain the quantitative findings.

Procedures

The study lasted for five weeks. All the participants were given a brief orientation on the goals of the study and the interaction activity during the intervention. Then, the teacher demonstrated some of the commands (e.g. "Hey, Google, play some music."; "Hey, Google, stop.") to the whole class. She distributed a user guide to the participants (see Appendix C), which included five types of interactive activities for the participants to experience during the 5-week intervention.

In the first week, the participants were required to ask GA various questions, including language related commands such as asking for word definitions and synonyms. In the second week, the participants asked GA to play music/songs or tell stories/jokes. In the third week, the participants played four interactive games that required the participants to talk to GA. In the fourth week, the participants could freely converse with three chatbots available via Google Home Hub. In the last week, the participants had to use two English learning apps developed by a Taiwanese research team, which are based on Google Dialogflow system of Actions on Google. One app is Cool English Taiwan Lessons, which contains various multiple choice questions in English about Taiwan. The other app is Cool English Coach, an English conversation app that requires the participants to role play in 10 different scenarios in English.

To allow the participants to have more interactions with GA, the teacher left the four Google Home Hubs in the classroom at all times, and encouraged the participants to take turns using these devices during their breaks and at lunch time. She also allowed the participants to interact with GA if they finished their classroom assignments early. At the end of the 5-week experiment, the researchers then administered the survey to all of the participants to measure their perceptions and conducted interviews with some of the participants to collect feedback and suggestions.

Results

Learners' Perceptions toward the Use of GA

For the dimension of learning motivation, the majority of the participants agreed that GA increased their motivation to improve their English communicative ability, including pronunciation (83%), speaking fluency (79%), listening comprehension (75%), and vocabulary learning (72%) (see Figure 4.1).

For the dimension of communicative anxiety (see Figure 4.2), nearly 80% of the participants agreed that they were more relaxed to speak with GA as compared to speaking English in front of their teacher. Sixty-nine percent of the participants agreed that practicing English by speaking with GA is less stressful than with their classmates. When compared to other in-class activities, the majority of the participants considered it to be less stressful to practice English listening (90%) and speaking (86%) with GA. Based on the figures, the participants considered that GA is a less stressful tool to practice English listening and speaking and that interacting with GA is even more relaxing when compared with other in-class activities and speaking in front of their teachers/classmates.

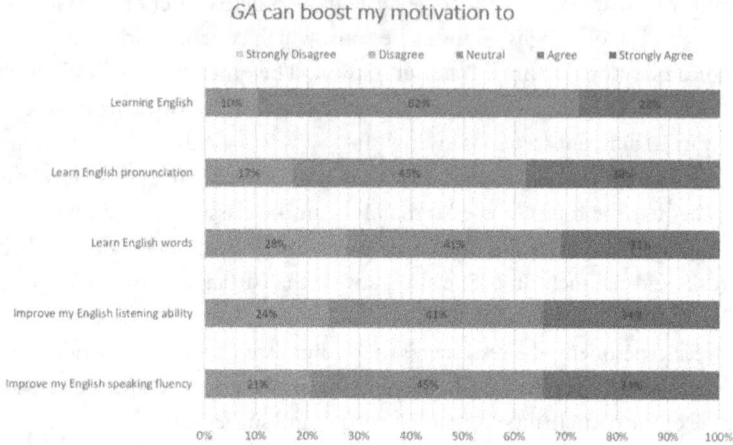

Figure 4.1 *Results of participants' perceptions of GA for increasing communicative motivation.*

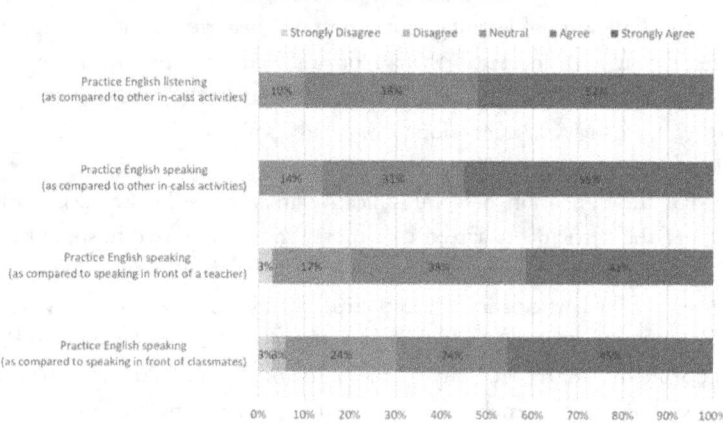

Figure 4.2 *Results of participants' perception of GA for reducing communication anxiety*

For the perceived usefulness of GA for language learning, nearly 85% of the participants held a positive attitude toward the potential usefulness of GA for language learning (see Figure 4.3). They considered GA a useful tool to increase their vocabulary size (87%), improve their pronunciation and speaking fluency (86%) as well as listening comprehension (83%). Regarding GA's usefulness for improving reading skills, 76% of the participants agreed that GA might be helpful.

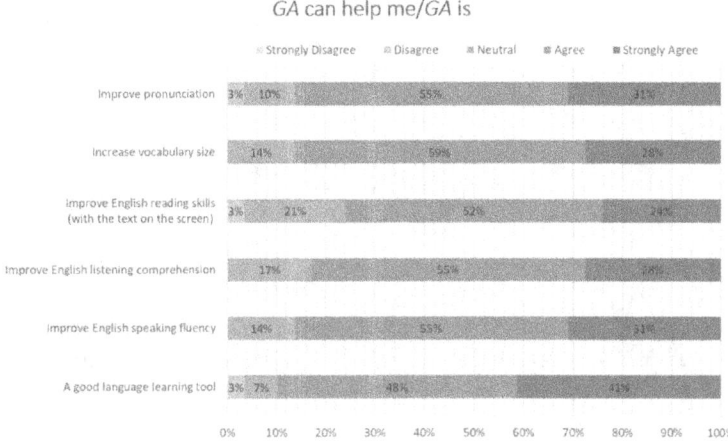

Figure 4.3 *Results of participants' perception of GA's usefulness for language learning.*

Regarding the participants' willingness to use GA for language learning, around 80% of the participants considered using GA to learn English pronunciation and other languages (see Figure 4.4).

Regarding the participants' perceptions towards how much they and GA understood each other's speech and how natural the pronunciation of GA was (see Figure 5), for the perceived naturalness of GA's pronunciation, 83% of the participants agreed that its pronunciation sounded natural. Nevertheless, the participants' responses to how much they comprehended GA's speech was less promising as only 69% of them agreed that they could understand GA's English. The participants also gave similar responses to how much they were understood by GA with 69% of them perceiving that GA could understand their English.

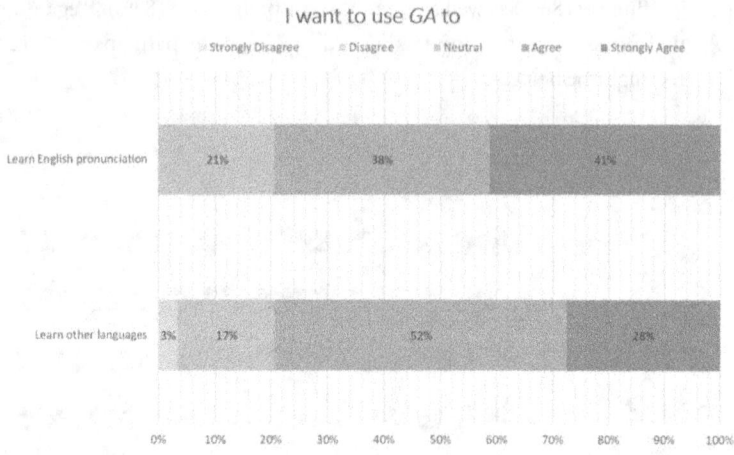

Figure 4.4 *Results of participants' willingness to use GA for language learning.*

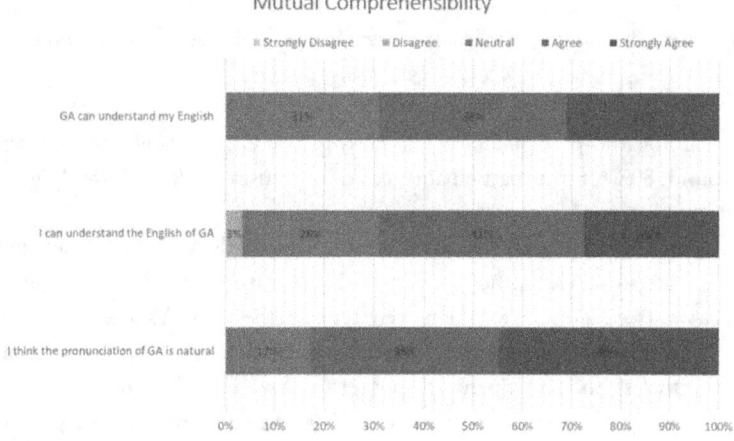

Figure 4.5 *Results of participants' perceptions toward mutual comprehensibility of IPA-learner interaction.*

As for the participants' overall experience of using, 79% of them agreed that they enjoyed their time interacting with GA, and 89% of them found this experience to be interesting (see Figure 4.6).

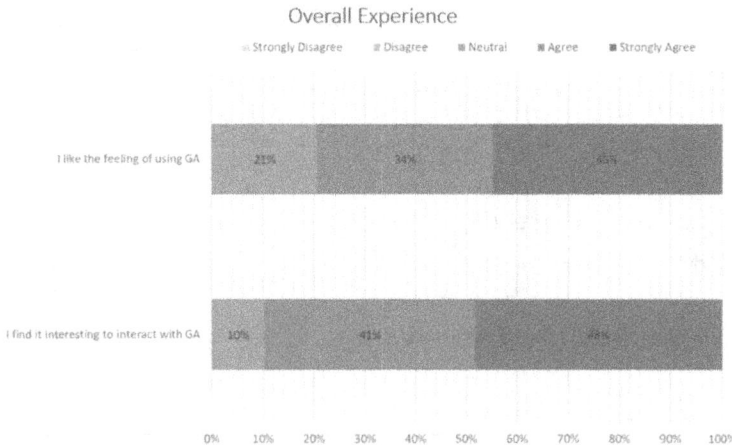

Figure 4.6 *Results of participants' overall experience in IPA-learner interaction.*

Regarding the participants' responses to the open-ended questions in the focus group interviews, their responses to the strengths of GA for English communication approximately echoed their perceptions revealed in the survey, which showed that GA would be especially useful to enhance their communication competence, including listening, speaking, pronunciation, and vocabulary. With the use of GA, some of the participants further indicated that they were more willing to speak English and had more chances to practice speaking.

As for their responses to the weaknesses of GA for English learning, many of the participants complained that GA sometimes could not correctly understand a given command/question and occasionally just did not respond to a question at all. For some of the participants, the speed of GA's speech was sometimes too fast for them to follow. A few of the participants reported that poor network connections at school sometimes hindered their interactions with GA. One participant suggested that Chinese should be allowed when interacting with GA. Table 4.1 summarizes the participants' responses to the interviewed questions.

Table 4.1 *Summary of participants' responses to the interviewed questions*

Category	n (%)
Strength	
Helpful to improve English speaking ability	11 (37.9%)
Helpful to improve English listening ability	11 (37.9%)
More willing to speak English	8 (27.6%)
Helpful to improve English pronunciation	6 (20.7%)
Helpful to increase English vocabulary size	6 (20.7%)
More chances to practice English speaking	3 (10.3%)
Interactive/Interesting to learn English	3 (10.3%)
Making English learning more fun	2 (6.7%)
Weakness	
Unable to correctly understand commands/questions	10 (34.4%)
Fast talking speed	4 (13.8%)
Unable to answer/respond questions	3 (10.3%)
Poor network connection	3 (10.3%)
Suggestion	
Inclusion of other languages (i.e. Chinese)	1 (3.4%)

In addition to results of the survey and open-ended questions, the teachers also provided a summary of the participants' feedback on the use of GA in the in-class discussions and interview. In her report, the participants showed a positive attitude toward GA's usefulness for English communication, ability to motivate their learning, and reduce communication anxiety. For example, the participants reported that, since GA could only understand English, they would consult with their classmates or online resources to check the correct English words/sentences that they wanted to say (Interview Q2). After interacting with GA, the participants felt more confident in speaking English (Interview Q9), and they believed that their English listening and speaking abilities would be greatly improved if they had their own GA at home (Interview Q5). In addition, the participants reported that they were motivated by GA to talk in English, because this innovative and highly interactive tool gave them instant, sometimes interesting, answers to their questions (Interview Q1). Participants also felt that talking to GA in English was not stressful, because they would not feel embarrassed when making errors/mistakes (Interview Q3).

For strengths other than language learning, the participants reported that they were quite satisfied with GA's sensitive speech recognition, natural pronunciation, and fast response time to information queries (Interview Q6). They commented that because GA could recognize their commands very quickly, they considered it to be very useful to search for information; however, they felt that GA could not converse in a natural manner, and it was thus difficult to have daily conversations with (Interview Q4). The participants further complained that they sometimes had to repeat their commands many times since GA failed to understand their speech, as well as mentioning that the talking speed of GA was a bit too fast for them to follow (Interview Q8). Furthermore, the participants considered GA's English to be too difficult for them to comprehend at times, and suggested that simpler English or Chinese subtitles should be offered (Interview Q11). The participants also identified some obstacles of using GA in a traditional classroom environment, such as the unstable networks at school and the interference caused by having the four devices receiving/responding to different groups of participants at the same time (Interview Q7).

Learners' Favourite Functions/Applications of GA

Each function/application involves IPA-learner interaction, similar to human-human interaction. In general, the participants prefer functions/applications which provide them with rich audio/visual input (e.g. songs, music, videos, stories etc.) and/or with interesting/interactive elements (i.e., the two games and the two English learning apps). For example, more than 80% of them liked to ask GA to play music for them. Around 50% of the participants liked to command GA to play specific artists' songs or videos. More than 40% of the participants liked to have GA tell them stories. In addition to songs, videos and stories, more than 30% of the participants enjoyed playing games (i.e., Akinator and Number Genie) and the English learning app Talk to Cool English Taiwan Lesson via GA. Finally, 10% of the participants reported that they liked using Talk to Cool English Coach via GA. Table 4.2 summaries the participants' responses to their favorite functions/applications.

Learners' Interactions with GA

In addition to the participants' feedback, the English teacher also observed how the participants interacted with GA and shared her findings with the researchers. The first thing she noticed is that the participants, including students that were not interested in English learning, were strongly motivated to chat with GA and would take the initiative to start the interaction. Once an interaction began, most of the participants would listen to its speech very attentively and were much more focused than they otherwise would be during regular listening tests. The participants would even discuss with others to piece together what they just heard. In addition to figuring out the content of GA's speech, the participants would also collaborate to resolve problems occurring in their interactions with GA. According to the teacher, the participants often would form small groups to interact with GA. When participants had difficulties with words/sentences produced by GA, they would work together and consult their textbooks to find the answers. Sometimes, participants would ask GA for help directly. This, to the teacher, is a great advantage since the participants were no longer pushed to learn by exams and/or teachers.

Table 4.2 *Summary of participants' responses to their favorite functions/applications.*

Functions/Applications	n (%)
Play (name of music)	24 (82.6%)
Play someone's song/album	14 (48.2%)
Play/Search (name of video)	14 (48.2%)
Tell me a story	13 (44.8%)
Play *Akinator*	10 (34.4%)
Talk to *Cool English Taiwan Lesson*	9 (31.0%)
Talk to *Number Genie*	9 (31.0%)
Talk to *Cool English Coach*	3 (10.3%)

In addition, the teacher also reported that GA was a very good tool for low achievers in English. She observed that some low achievers in her class were really engaged in their interactions with GA. The following details one distinctive case that she reported to the researchers:

> There is a student in the class who almost gave up studying English. He usually took the lowest mark in English in the class. However, he was very enthusiastic about talking with GA. Although his pronunciation was sometimes incorrect, he still showed a strong motivation in

speaking to GA. To get GA to answer his questions, he would keep asking his classmates about the correct pronunciation of words and sentence patterns he wanted to use. If GA could understand his expressions, he would become very happy and content about his own performances. I even discovered that he was more willing to speak simple English in class and more willing to join the group discussion during the period of the experiment.

The teacher's report on the participants' behaviors demonstrates that GA was a motivating tool for the participants and encouraged them to become collaborative and autonomous English learners in some way.

Application to Smart CALL

This study explored adolescent EFL learners' perceptions of IPA-assisted language learning. The results showed that the adolescent EFL learners generally considered GA a useful tool to improve their English communicative ability, including listening, speaking, pronunciation, and vocabulary. The findings corroborate with adult learners' positive comments on the usefulness of IPAs for L2 speaking in previous studies (e.g., Dizon, 2017, 2020; Dizon & Tang, 2019; Moussalli & Cardoso, 2016). Findings in this study and in previous research thus indicate that IPAs indeed serve as useful tools to enhance both adolescent and adult learners' language abilities regardless of their age.

The reason for IPAs' potential usefulness for language learning might be that they can motivate learners to use the target language(s). The participants recognized GA as a motivational tool to engage them in English communication. This result was also observed in Underwood (2017), whose observations of primary EFL learners showed high levels of motivation and deep involvement in speaking English with IPAs. Possible explanations for young learners' strong motivation for communicating with IPAs might lie in these tools' highly interesting and interactive features.

Furthermore, talking to GA in English was somewhat less stressful to the participants than speaking in front of their teachers/classmates or in-class activities, because they would not feel embarrassed when making errors/mistakes. The findings support Canbek and Mutlu's (2016) comment that IPAs can engage language learners in speaking activities and further uncover the reasons for language learners' strong motivations in communicating with IPAs in a foreign language due to the relaxed atmosphere created by these devices.

In addition, IPAs motivated learners to further improve English knowledge in order to have the interaction go smoothly. As pointed out in the interview and the teacher's report, the participants would consult with their classmates and/or textbooks for the correct pronunciation(s)/word(s)/sentences(s) that they intended to say, and then they would write down and practice these English expressions before talking to the IPA. Through these preparations and practices, the participants became more confident in speaking English and even more willing to use some of these expressions in class, as demonstrated by the low achiever's learning growth observed by the teacher. Via the use of GA, the participants became more active English learners. The findings are not only in accordance with Dizon and Tang's (2019) discovery of IPAs' ability to facilitate learners' autonomous language learning, but they further support Istrate's (2019) argument of IPAs' supportive function to foster learners' self-learning in the language classroom to enhance their pronunciation.

However, as Moussalli and Cardoso (2020) indicate, given the current technology on ASR, IPAs sometimes have recognition errors. Only 69% of the participants agreed that they could understand and be understood by GA, and this percentage was obviously lower than that of the participants' perceptions toward the naturalness of GA's pronunciation (83%). This indicates that what troubled the learners about comprehending GA's speech is not related to its articulation; instead, GA's fast talking speed and/or difficult words/sentence structures caused students more trouble in full comprehension, as revealed in the participants' responses to the open-ended and interview questions. As described in the method section, the participants' English proficiency was around the CEFR A1-A2 levels, which suggests that they might only be able to use and comprehend simple English at rather slow speeds. Because GA is originally designed for native speakers, its talking speed and words/sentence structures might hence be difficult for the non-native adolescent learners to follow. These findings further indicate that the English of IPAs might be somewhat difficult for lower level language learners to understand.

Furthermore, the fact that GA is made for native speakers could also explain why the adolescent EFL learners considered their interactions to sometimes not be correctly understood by GA. Many researchers have pointed out that most speech recognition engines of IPAs, which are based on native speaker speech models (Levis, 2007; Van Compernolle, 2000), often work better with native speakers (cf. Ehsani & Knodt, 1998; Pogue, 2004) than non-native speakers (cf. Coniam, 1999; Derwing, Munro, & Carbonaro, 2000) and hence are less tolerant of non-native speakers' accented speech. This therefore negatively affected GA's ability to comprehend the adolescent EFL learners' commands/questions. In fact, IPAs' deficiencies in fully understanding language learners' utterances had already been reported by prior research (e.g., Moussalli & Cardoso, 2016; Dizon, 2017; Pyae & Scifleet, 2019), whose studies on adult ESL/EFL learners with intermediate to high-intermediate English proficiency all demonstrated IPAs' difficulties in successfully comprehending their learners' speech. Based on the findings yielded in our study and previous research, it is possible to conclude that, at the current stage, achieving high mutual comprehensibility with IPAs is still challenging for less advanced language learners regardless of their age.

To respond to the current challenges faced by less proficient language learners, the researchers propose the following suggestions to both language teachers and CALL researchers. Language teachers should carefully select the applications with suitable content for second/foreign language learning. For lower level learners, teachers can introduce them to applications with simpler content/language and easier commands (e.g., the Akinator and Number Genie games used in the current study), so that these learners will be more willing to interact with IPAs and further use them for language learning. In addition, language teachers are suggested to explain the demanding/sensitive nature of IPAs' speech recognition engines to their learners. If learners are pre-informed that their accented speech and/or mispronunciation might cause difficulties for IPAs to understand, learners might be less frustrated/confused and even more willing to modify their output when IPAs fail to respond to their commands/questions.

As discussed above, various IPAs can contribute much to Smart CALL because they can provide rich, authentic input and interesting tasks to language learners and effectively motivate them to use the L2. However, IPAs clearly still have some limitations for second language learning. At present, IPAs in general have limited capacities in providing modified input, corrective feedback, and negotiated interactions. It is expected that in the future CALL and NLP researchers can make IPAs more interactive. IPAs can make great contributions to smart CALL if they can be made to accomplish the following goals: First, they can better understand L2 learners' input. Second, they can be programmed to modify their languages to L2 learners. Third, they can be supplemented with some mechanisms in correcting L2 learners' errors and providing relevant feedback. These three goals are not simple research tasks because these improvements can make IPAs become much smarter and perform more like human teachers. To make CALL smarter, we expect that more CALL researchers can work together to build more IPA applications which can meet some of these challenging goals. The enhanced IPA applications can be beneficial for many L2 learners.

Conclusion

This study aimed to investigate adolescent EFL learners' perceptions toward the use of IPAs for promoting English communication ability, and to further observe how learners interact with IPAs in a classroom environment. The results showed that learners generally perceived IPAs as useful tools to improve their communicative ability, including listening comprehension, speaking, pronunciation, and vocabulary. Compared to speaking in front of teachers/classmates or other in-class activities, practicing English speaking with IPAs was less stressful, because they did not feel embarrassed if they made mistakes. Furthermore, IPAs, acting as an interlocutor, an interviewer, an entertainer, a narrator, and a facilitator in interacting with learners, added variety to L2 interaction, engaged learners, and further motivated them to enhance their language abilities in order to maintain smooth communication. Overall, adolescent EFL learners consider interacting and learning with IPAs to be interesting, enjoyable and beneficial for their English communicative ability. Based on the above discussion, IPA-assisted EFL communication seems to meet the three main themes of smart CALL: Personalization, contextualization, and Socialization. For example, IPAs can be adapted to meet the learners' own interests and needs (personalization). It can create an authentic context for meaningful communication in the target language, which promotes learning via increased input and output practice (contextualization and socialization).

While adolescent EFL learners generally held quite a positive attitude toward the use of IPAs for language learning, some obstacles for learners to successfully use these tools were also identified in this study. For adolescent EFL learners, who were often considered to be less proficient English speakers, the talking speed and content of IPAs' speech posed some challenges for them to follow and caused difficulties for them to fully comprehend the speech of IPAs. In addition, learners' lower language proficiencies might also negatively influence the extent to which they are understood by IPAs. Most IPAs are designed for native speakers so the speech recognition engines of IPAs are hence less able to recognize accented speech and/or mispronunciations, which often occur in the utterances of lower level learners. The difficulties for adolescent EFL learners to understand and to be understood by IPAs might thus reduce the educational value of IPAs for foreign language learning, and measures should be taken to deal with these issues.

Although the current study identified both advantages and disadvantages of IPAs for adolescent EFL learners' language learning, there are still some limitations of the study that can be further addressed in future research. The first limitation of the study is concerned with the short intervention time. A related issue is the novelty effect. Thus, future research will need to have further detailed analysis of the long-term impact of IPA-assisted language learning. The second suggestion is to further examine how learners can benefit from the use of suitable language learning applications via IPAs. As discussed in the previous section, applications with suitable language learning content should be more useful for adolescent EFL learners. The two English learning applications introduced in this study are specifically made for adolescent EFL learners, which contain content and language that match the learners' language proficiency level; however, due to time constraints, the researchers had no chance to allow the learners to fully experience these applications and examine the language gains that they might acquire after extensive use. Future studies are thus encouraged to investigate the extent to how these learning apps can improve adolescent ESL/EFL learners' language knowledge and abilities.

References

Bibauw, S., François, T., Van Den Noortgate, W.V., & Desmet, P. (2022). Dialogue systems for language learning: A meta-analysis. *Language Learning & Technology*, *26*(1). Retrieved from https://serge.bibauw.be/publication/bibauw-et-al-2022-dialogue-systems-language-learning-meta-analysis/Bibauw_et_al_2022_Dialogue_systems_meta-analysis.pdf

Canbek, N.G., & Mutlu, M.E. (2016). On the track of artificial intelligence: Learning with intelligent personal assistants. *Journal of Human*

Sciences, 13(1), 592–601.

Carhill-Poza, A., & Chen, J. (2020). Adolescent English learners' language development in technology-enhanced classrooms. *Language Learning & Technology, 24*(3), 52–69. http://hdl.handle.net/10125/44738

Coniam, D. (1999). Voice recognition software accuracy with second language speakers of English. *System, 27,* 49–64. http://dx.doi.org/10.1016/S0346-251X(98)00049-9

Derwing, T., Munro, M., & Carbonaro, M. (2000). Does popular speech recognition software work with ESL speech? *TESOL Quarterly, 34*(3), 592–603. https://www.jstor.org/stable/3587748

Dizon, G. (2017). Using intelligent personal assistants for second language learning: a case study of Alexa. *TESOL Journal, 8*(4), 811-830. https://doi.org/10.1002/tesj.353

Dizon, G. (2020). Evaluating intelligent personal assistants for L2 listening and speaking development. *Language Learning & Technology, 24*(1), 16–26. https://doi.org/10125/44705

Dizon, G., & Tang, D. (2019). A pilot study of Alexa for autonomous second language learning. In F. Meunier, J. Van de Vyver, L. Bradley, & S. Thouësny (Eds.), *CALL and complexity–short papers from EUROCALL 2019* (pp. 107–112). Research-net.

Ehsani, F., & Knodt, E. (1998). Speech technology in computer-aided language learning: Strengths and limitations of a new CALL paradigm. *Language Learning & Technology, 2*(1), 45–60. http://dx.doi.org/10125/25032

Goh, C.M. (2014). Reconceptualising second language oracy instruction: Metacognitive engagement and direct teaching in listening and speaking. *AJELP: Asian Journal of English Language and Pedagogy, 2,* 1–20. https://ejournal.upsi.edu.my/index.php/AJELP/article/view/1096

Goksel-Canbek, N., & Mutlu, M.E. (2016). On the track of artificial intelligence: Learning with intelligent personal assistants. *International Journal of Human Sciences, 13*(1), 592. http://doi-org/10.14687/ijhs.vl3il.3549

Istrate, A.M. (2019). The impact of the virtual assistant (VA) on language classes. In *Conference proceedings of» eLearning and Software for Education «(eLSE)* (Vol. 1, No. 15, pp. 296–301). "Carol I" National Defense University Publishing House.

Kessler, G. (2018). Technology and the future of language teaching. *Foreign*

Language Annals, 51(1), 205-218. https://doi.org/10.1111/flan.12318

Levis, J. (2007). Computer technology in teaching and researching pronunciation. *Annual Review of Applied Linguistics, 27*, 184-202. https://doi.org/10.1017/S0267190508070098

Long, M.H. (1996). The role of the linguistic environment in second language acquisition. In W. C. Ritchie & T. K. Bhatia (Eds.), *Handbook of research on language acquisition* (pp. 413-468). New York: Academic Press.

Long, M.H. (2017). Instructed second language acquisition (ISLA): Geopolitics, methodological issues, and some major research questions. *Instructed Second Language Acquisition, 1*, 7–44. https://doi.org/10.1558/isla.33314

Mayer, R.E. (2017). Using multimedia for e-learning. *Journal of Computer Assisted Learning, 33*, 403–423. https://doi.org/10.1111/jcal.12197

Moussalli, S., & Cardoso, W. (2016). Are commercial 'personal robots' ready for language learning? Focus on second language speech. In S. Papadima-Sophocleous, L. Bradley & S. Thouësny (Eds.), *CALL communities and culture–short papers from EUROCALL* (pp. 325-329). Research-pusliching.net. https://doi.org/10.14705/rpnet.2016.eurocall 2016.583

Moussalli, S., & Cardoso, W. (2020). Intelligent personal assistants: can they understand and be understood by accented L2 learners? *Computer Assisted Language Learning, 33*(8), 865–890. https://doi.org/ 10.1080/09588221.2019.1595664

Pogue, D. (2004). Speaking naturally, anew. *New York Times.*

Pyae, A., & Scifleet, P. (2019). Investigating the role of user's English language proficiency in using a voice user interface: A case of Google Home Smart Speaker. In *Proceedings of Extended Abstracts of the 2019 CHI Conference on Human Factors in Computing Systems* (pp. 1–6). https://doi.org/10.1145/3290607.3313038

Santos, J., Rodrigues, J., Silva, B.M.C., Casal, J., Saleem, K., & Denisov, V. (2016). An IoT-based mobile gateway for intelligent personal assistants on mobile health environments. *Journal of Network and Computer Applications, 71*, 194–204. https://doi.org/10.1016/j.jnca.2016.03.014

Sing, P.B., Embi, M.A., & Hashim, H. (2019). Ask the assistant: Using Google Assistant in classroom reading comprehension activities. *International Journal of New Technology and Research, 5*(7), 39–43. https://doi.org/10.31871/IJNTR.5.7.6

Sydorenko, T., Daurio, P., & Thorne, S.L. (2018). Refining pragmatically-appropriate oral communication via computer-simulated conversations. *Computer Assisted Language Learning*, *31*(1-2), 157–180. https://doi.org/10.1080/09588221.2017.1394326

Tai, T.Y., & Chen, H.J. (2020). The impact of Google Assistant on adolescent EFL learners' willingness to communicate. *Interactive Learning Environments*. https://doi.org/10.1080/10494820.2020.1841801

Underwood, J. (2017). Exploring AI language assistants with primary EFL students. In K. Borthwick, L. Bradley & S. Thouësny (Eds.), *CALL in a climate of change: adapting to turbulent global conditions–short papers from EUROCALL* (pp. 317–321). Research-publishing.net. https://doi.org/10.14705/rpnet.2017.eurocall2017.733

Van Compernolle, D. (2001). Recognizing speech of goats, wolves, sheep and non-natives. *Speech Communication*, *35*(1-2), 71–79. https://doi.org/10.1016/S0167-6393(00)00096-0

Wu, Y., Rough, D., Bleakley, A., Edwards, J., Cooney, O., Doyle, P.R., Clark, L., Cowan, B.R. (2020, October). See what I'm saying? Comparing intelligent personal assistant use for native and non-native language speakers. In *MobileHCI '20: 22nd International Conference on Human-Computer Interaction with Mobile Devices and Services* (pp. 1–9). Oldenburg, Germany. https://doi.org/10.1145/3379503.3403563

Appendix A

Post-treatment questionnaire

Please select the option that best reflects your perception of using GA, based on your experience with it after this experiment.

1. GA can boost my motivation to learn English.
    Strongly Disagree   Disagree   Neutral   Agree   Strongly Agree
2. GA can boost my motivation to learn English pronunciation.
    Strongly Disagree   Disagree   Neutral   Agree   Strongly Agree
3. GA can boost my motivation to learn English words.
    Strongly Disagree   Disagree   Neutral   Agree   Strongly Agree
4. GA can boost my motivation to improve my English listening ability.
    Strongly Disagree   Disagree   Neutral   Agree   Strongly Agree
5. GA can boost my motivation to improve my English speaking fluency.
    Strongly Disagree   Disagree   Neutral   Agree   Strongly Agree

6. Compared to other in-class activities (e.g., role-playing, recitation, and group cooperation), using GA to practice English listening is less stressful for me.
   Strongly Disagree   Disagree   Neutral   Agree   Strongly Agree
7. Compared to other in-class activities (e.g., role-playing, recitation, and group cooperation), using GA to practice English speaking is less stressful for me.
   Strongly Disagree   Disagree   Neutral   Agree   Strongly Agree
8. Compared to speaking English in front of a teacher, using GA to practice English speaking is less stressful for me.
   Strongly Disagree   Disagree   Neutral   Agree   Strongly Agree
9. Compared to speaking English in front of my classmates, using GA to practice English speaking is less stressful for me.
   Strongly Disagree   Disagree   Neutral   Agree   Strongly Agree
10. GA can help me improve my pronunciation.
    Strongly Disagree   Disagree   Neutral   Agree   Strongly Agree
11. GA can help me increase my vocabulary size.
    Strongly Disagree   Disagree   Neutral   Agree   Strongly Agree
12. With the text on the screen, GA can help me improve my English reading skills.
    Strongly Disagree   Disagree   Neutral   Agree   Strongly Agree
13. GA can improve my English listening comprehension.
    Strongly Disagree   Disagree   Neutral   Agree   Strongly Agree
14. GA can improve my English speaking fluency.
    Strongly Disagree   Disagree   Neutral   Agree   Strongly Agree
15. GA is a good language learning tool.
    Strongly Disagree   Disagree   Neutral   Agree   Strongly Agree
16. I will learn English pronunciation by using GA.
    Strongly Disagree   Disagree   Neutral   Agree   Strongly Agree
17. I want to use GA to learn other languages.
    Strongly Disagree   Disagree   Neutral   Agree   Strongly Agree
18. GA can understand my English.
    Strongly Disagree   Disagree   Neutral   Agree   Strongly Agree
19. I can understand the English of GA.
    Strongly Disagree   Disagree   Neutral   Agree   Strongly Agree

20. Do you think the pronunciation of GA is natural?

    Strongly Disagree   Disagree   Neutral   Agree   Strongly Agree

21. Overall, I like the feeling of using GA during the hands-on session.

    Strongly Disagree   Disagree   Neutral   Agree   Strongly Agree

22. Overall, I find it interesting to interact with GA.

    Strongly Disagree   Disagree   Neutral   Agree   Strongly Agree

Appendix B

Interview questions

1. Do you like talking to GA? Why?
2. Would you like to learn more English words or sentences in order to talk to GA?
3. Compared with talking to your classmates and teachers, do you think speaking English with GA is less stressful?
4. Do you think GA is smart/stupid? Why?
5. If you are given a Google Home Hub at home, do you think the device can help you improve your English?
6. In your opinion, what are the advantages of GA for English learning?
7. In your opinion, what are the disadvantages of GA for English learning?
8. What difficulties do you encounter when using GA on Google Home Hub?
9. What do you like the most when using GA on Google Home Hub?
10. Do you feel more confident in speaking English in class after interacting with GA?
11. Do you have any suggestions for GA and Google Home Hub developers?

Appendix C

User guide for interacting with GA

Tasks	Activity
Orientation	Get familiar with *Google Home Hub*

Task 1	**Questions**
	1. Ask as many questions as you want, such as "what's the weather like today?" and so on…
	2. Try some language commands like:
	    What is the definition/the meaning/a synonym of ____ ?
	    How do you spell ____?
	    Translate ___ into [LANGUAGE].
	    How do I say ____ in [LANGUAGE]?

Task 2	**Music/songs & jokes/stories** 1. Sing me a song. 2. Play some music from Spotify. 3. Play [SINGER's NAME]'s song. 4. Tell me a joke/short story.
Task 3	**Games** Play *Strangest Day Ever / Jungle Adventure / Number Genie / Akinator*
Task 4	**Chatbots** – try to talk as long as you can Talk to *Pandora Vince / Good Robot / Julie Chatbot*
Task 5	**Talk to *Cool English Taiwan Lesson*** This app tests your knowledge about Taiwan, and you need to choose the right answer.
Task 6	**Talk to *Cool English Coach*** There are 10 lessons. In each conversation, you need to respond to various questions. Please ask for help if you cannot answer the questions.

5
Using artificial intelligence technology as a tutor for EFL speaking practice

Ming Li
Bin Zou

Introduction

Educational programs supported by AI technology help learners obtain many essential skills, which are relatively necessary in the 21st century, through offering learners a number of services, improving students' motivations and learning interests, as well as extending learners' conventional learning framework to the digital world (Wekke *et al.*, 2017). More importantly, it brings much positive influence on language learning activities, particularly in the field of learning English as a Foreign Language (Hamuddin, 2016). Utilizing AI in foreign language learning has developed to be a practical and helpful choice because of the increased reliability, practicality, and affordability characteristics of AI technology (Abad, 2013). In the early 2010s, AI began to recognize speech successfully and automatically, while computers started to accurately deduce the "meaning" of words in context and piece together the complex expressions of language with its infinite variabilities (Lewis & Valente, 2009). AI programs may help students achieve tailored learning schedules and cultivate their independent learning skills (Kim *et al.*, 2013). Among the technologies used in AI, the intelligent voice recognition technology develops swiftly in the language learning market in terms of voice input technology, voice recognition technology, speech synthesis technology as well as natural language processing technology. In particular, the occurrence of speech-assessment technology may provide diverse opportunities by utilizing AI technology in assessing speaking assignments and tests of learners (Chen, Wu, & Li, 2019). Meanwhile, using AI technology could enhance the autonomous learning of students and integrate language learning outside the traditional classrooms (Zou *et al.*, 2020).

Although AI technology has been widely used in many fields, research has rarely paid attention to AI's influence on EFL learners' English-speaking practice (Maftoon *et al.*, 2012; Solano *et al.*, 2017). Moreover, many of the studies seen in the literature have been conducted under a western-education background, and there is a paucity of research exploring AI for speaking practice in other regions such as China. Meanwhile, since there are many apps incorporating AI that target young children, much attention to AI has been laid on the primary and secondary schools' students rather than university students (Hamuddin *et al.*, 2018). Therefore, this paper aims to explore learners' perceptions of using AI for English speaking practice study, especially in researching the use of AI speech evaluation programs, including both benefits and existing problems. It seeks to identify AI's features in helping learners' speaking skills, mainly targeting their pronunciation, oral fluency, oral rhythm, grammar accuracy, idea-organization skills, reading aloud, and presentation skills. Students from an EMI (English as the Medium of Instruction) university in China were selected as the focus of this study to investigate whether AI speech evaluation programs can have an impact on EFL learners' speaking performance.

Literature review

Luckin *et al.* (2016, p. 14) defined AI as "computer systems designed to interact with the world through capabilities and intelligent behaviors that are essentially human." AI can be interpreted as an efficient system for performing specific tasks and solving diverse problems (Wang, 2019). According to Burn *et al.* (2022), AI applications may be classified as having weak intelligence or strong intelligence. Weak intelligence mainly focuses on one specific task, whereas a strong intelligence system needs to solve more complicated tasks and problems. A strong AI system can gather and process huge amounts of statistical data and utilize problem-related knowledge to tackle many challenging issues (Stewart *et al.*, 2020), and it is these strong intelligence systems that are used for evaluating English speaking abilities in educational settings. Currently there are diverse AI evaluation programs on the market for learners to use, and these have been broadly described as AI tools, AI programs, AI products, and AI applications. Such AI technologies may be used on a variety of platforms ranging from computers through to smartphones, making them easily accessible to a wide range of users.

Technologies have been broadly used in language teaching and learning for some time (see Debski, 2003), but the worldwide spread of the COVID-19 pandemic has contributed to teachers turning to technology to support them in contexts where online classes have become the primary teaching method. Under this situation, an increasing number of learners use their mobile devices to practice foreign languages, which has sparked an interest in exploring tools using these devices. Given that AI has the potential to provide activities and spontaneous feedback that are tailored to individual learners' needs with (Luckin *et al.*, 2016), it is not surprising that AI tools have emerged as a means supporting language learning as well.

Learners of English, whether as a foreign language (EFL) or as a second language (ESL), often encounter many speaking issues, ranging from linguistic aspects to psychological reasons. Linguistic reasons include pronunciation, vocabulary, discourse, and grammar issues (Rahman & Sangaji, 2019; Shen & Chiu, 2019). At the same time, psychologically, they may be nervous, lack confidence, and are afraid of making mistakes (Shen & Chiu, 2019). Besides, learners' initiative can also impact upon their speaking performance, which is usually influenced by their activeness in speaking practice activities and teachers' feedback. Needless to say, one-on-one contact time with teachers is usually quite limited for students (McArthur, 2015), meaning that many are lacking opportunities to interact orally in English. Therefore, AI with speaking applications can meet learning demands as a useful complementary tool by providing learners with rich speaking materials, instant feedback, and flexible learning experiences (Damio & Ibrahim, 2019). AI speech evaluation programs can provide scores and feedback for users' speaking performances in pronunciation, fluency, content, vocabulary and grammar so that learners can learn how to improve their speaking skills (Fouz-González, 2020; Zou *et al.*, 2020).

Previous studies have found that students have increased motivation for autonomous learning when using apps for pronunciation practice with AI speech evaluation in learning foreign languages (e.g., Choi, 2016; Liakin, Cardoso & Liakina, 2014). According to Fouz-González (2020), using AI-based apps for pronunciation exercises can develop and improve EFL learners' pronunciation abilities and increase their vocabulary range. Similarly, some AI speech recognition apps for speaking skills can enhance learners' independent study because the learner can practice repetition in these AI pronunciation-training programs as supplemental tools (McCrocklin, 2016, 2019). In spoken language learning, AI products have rich libraries of voice resources, with ample examples of reading aloud and leading students to read, repeat and correct their pronunciations and other functions (Kim *et al.*, 2018; Wang, 2019). According to Meyerson (2018), learners are likely to improve their English pronunciation and other spoken skills through an app that uses AI in terms of speech recognition technology to assess pronunciation errors and provide efficient feedback and phonetic hints. Similarly, an empirical study conducted at one vocational university in Tokyo confirmed an AI application is a useful tool for students to practice English after in-depth interviews, especially for learners of lower-level English proficiency to increase their learning confidence of English speaking. Therefore, AI offers excellent opportunities to improve college students' oral English. Bao (2019) conducted a one-month controlled pilot study among one large financial institution's staff in East Asia where one group used an AI chatbot while the other did not. The results showed that AI was widely endorsed by the subjects as an interlocutor that positively enhanced respondents' confidence and improved the individual components of IELTS speaking, such as pronunciation, fluency, and coherence. In addition, the author addressed the fact that AI chatbots possess an important promise in terms of reducing users' speech-related anxieties. By analyzing two qualitative cases of chatbot technology (an AI speaking-learning program), researchers at Polish universities (e.g., Hill *et al.*, 2015) found that chatbots develop learners' technical and programming capabilities and provide a high possibility of improving their linguistic expertise. However, the sample size of this study is limited since they only discuss two cases of higher education applying AI in Poland. In another discussion of AI and its implications for higher education institutions, the authors support the positive improvements brought by AI in the personalization of learners' requirements and abundant forms of human interactions in language learning (Ocaña-Fernández *et al.*, 2019). However, it only reviews several trends of AI technology in higher education by illustrating facts without providing any quantitative and qualitative research data to prove the statements.

However, there are also opposing views of using AI for learners' speaking practice. A common issue of the existing applications is that they cannot provide real-time feedback for learners' speaking performance and give limited evaluation due to the problem of the prosodic system, which provides guidelines on users' pronunciation. In the meantime, most AI evaluation programs for speaking practice do not easily cater to different accents (Zou *et al.*, 2020). As a result, it is notable that learners may sometimes obtain incorrect feedback from speech recognition when they learn from these programs (Hubbard, 2019). Accordingly, how these AI evaluation programs influence learners' speaking practice need to be further explored and discussed.

As described above, the aforementioned studies regarding the use of AI technology have mostly been done in western countries, and few have been done in China, not to mention under Chinese higher education. Therefore, in this chapter, the researchers seek more comprehensive insights and more valid and ample research data of Chinese learners' learning experience of AI technology, especially targeting AI evaluation programs in their spoken English. By using these AI evaluation programs, learners can practice English words, paragraphs, articles and other rich speaking resources. The significance of the paper is that it can provide details of Chinese university learners' attitudes towards using AI technology in their English-speaking practice. This paper was guided by the following two research questions:

1. What are EFL learners' perceived benefits of AI speech evaluation programs in practicing their speaking skills online?
2. What are user perceptions of existing problems in using AI speech evaluation programs for speaking practice?

Methodology

This research used a quantitative research method, namely a survey, to collect data. Students from an EMI (English as the medium of instruction) university in China were selected as the research subjects of this research, specifically first- and second-year undergraduate students. The reason for choosing the target research group is twofold. First, this university provides regular EAP classes for the freshmen and sophomores, and they have a formal speaking test at the end of every semester. Meanwhile, they have many informal and formal presentations among their school assessments.

Compared with students from other grades, the target group has more needs to practice their spoken English at an early stage, and they are more likely to use different speaking apps, including AI evaluation programs in their English academic study.

The survey was circulated to the target group through convenience sampling and snowball sampling. The snowball sampling method was adopted as it can effectively widen the desired characteristics among the target respondents (Malhotra, 2015). These two sampling methods were combined, and data collection took place over nearly ten days. In total, there were 101 valid questionnaires with 43 males and 58 females, five of which were international students. Nearly 71% of the participants were first-year students, and the remaining 29% were in their second-year. The majority of participants (81%) were 18–19 years old, and the remainder were over 19 years old. Meanwhile, they came from a wide range of majors, such as Business Administration, Mathematics, English-related majors, Electronic Information and so on.

The questionnaire explored the user experience and feedback using AI speech evaluation programs for English speaking practice including Liulishuo, EAP talk, YaSiGe, Duolingo, and iSpeak, all of which are popular in China. It includes questions about their learning platforms, learning frequency, learning time, the number of recordings they record each time, overall satisfaction of the AI speech evaluation programs and diverse sub-factors, and the reasons they liked or disliked the AI speech evaluation programs. These AI speech evaluation programs usually included a wide range of functions, and the most two prevailing functions were the learning content of "reading aloud" (i.e., reading the text of articles aloud) and "presentation" (i.e., delivering mini presentations). Then students receive scores from the applications about their recording from diverse angles, such as speaking fluency, pronunciation, and grammar accuracy.

In the questionnaire, there were six sub-factors of learning satisfaction with the AI speech evaluation programs: learning efficiency, learning effectiveness, convenience, access, motivation, and institutional efficiency. These six factors were chosen from Hubbard's (2019) influential framework. These are the meaningful areas that are thought to positively influence learners' language learning. Every factor in the questionnaire was clearly explained using simple language adapted from the original framework. For instance, learning efficiency is introduced by "I can improve my speaking skills faster or with less effort by using AI technology compared with the traditional class taught by teachers."

In the meantime, detailed questions of AI speech evaluation programs were also included. One question focuses on the content and the scoring system of AI speech evaluation programs, and the other item discusses the specific factors of speaking skills, such as oral fluency, pronunciation, oral rhythm, grammar accuracy, idea-organization skills, reading aloud, as well as presentation skills. These questions are presented as levels of agreement, namely from strongly disagree to strongly agree. For example, "AI technology is helpful in improving my oral fluency," then subjects can choose from 1 (strongly disagree) to 5 (strongly agree). These specific questions in the level of agreements or satisfactions are helpful to generate and gain more direct and important research data (Johnson, Onwuegbuzie, & Turner, 2007) about learners' attitudes toward using AI speech evaluation programs.

At the end of the questionnaire, there were two open-ended questions considering the problems and suggestions students had in their use of the AI speech evaluation programs. Although as Hyman and Sierra (2016) point out, using close-ended questions is easier to answer with a speedy response for the respondents and data can be coded and analyzed quickly, the responses may potentially be limited and mask underlying issues that were not considered by the researchers in advance of the study.

Results

The findings showed that respondents indicated that they had used all of the AI speech evaluation programs that were listed in the survey to improve their English speaking, namely Liulishuo, EAP talk, YaSiGe, Duolingo and iSpeak. Data shows that their preferred device to use AI speech evaluation programs was the laptop, followed by mobile phone and iPad, with the desktop computer being the least used. This suggested that these younger learners favored mobile devices to learn the language. Meanwhile, they mostly preferred to use apps to engage with the AI speech evaluation programs, followed by websites, and the WeChat Applet in turn. For learning frequency, 18% of respondents reported they used AI speech evaluation programs several times a day, and in total more than half of them used it within a week. In comparison, 33% said they did not have the habit of using AI in their daily study. In addition, nearly one-third of subjects reported they used AI for more than 15 minutes each time, and 8% said they used it for more than 30 minutes. For those respondents who used AI in their speaking, 16% recorded six to ten recordings every time, and 13% recorded more than ten times. They showed nearly the same preferences of "reading aloud" and "presentation," which were the two primary functions of the AI speech evaluation programs.

When respondents were asked whether they liked to use AI speech evaluation programs to practice their English speaking, 62% selected "Yes, I like it," while 8% disliked it and 29% said it was hard to answer the question. The top five reasons of those who liked to use the AI speech evaluation programs to practice speaking English were: first, AI speech evaluation programs provided customized learning materials (73%); second, they could use AI in a judgment-free learning environment (65%); third, it provided immediate feedback (48%); fourth, it could be used after/outside of class (46%); fifth, it is more fun than other methods (29%). In comparison, the most important reason for those who disliked AI in language learning is its limited feedback (38%), followed by high costs (35%), poor internet connection (23%), limited content (21%), and inconvenience to use (19%). Two subjects added that it lacked a clear explanation of the scores they received. Moreover, 34% of subjects did not feel familiar with these AI speech evaluation programs. In general, 31% of the respondents believed that overall it is good to use AI speech evaluation programs in terms of improving their speaking skills, 5% thought they were "very good," and 53% of respondents held a neutral view. These findings suggest around half of learners were willing to use and have positive attitudes toward AI speech evaluation programs in their daily language study, while there are still many subjects who are unfamiliar with AI speech evaluation programs and many existing problems need to be improved in the current programs.

Regarding the learning efficiency of AI speech evaluation programs compared to the traditional class taught by human teachers, 21% of the respondents agreed, 24% strongly agreed, and 5% took a neutral view because they could improve their speaking skills faster or with less effort with the teacher. Regarding learning effectiveness, 28% strongly agreed, 27% agreed, and 35% were neutral, for the learning effectiveness because they could pick up the targeted knowledge and keep knowledge of speaking skills longer or learn more of what they need. Similarly, more than half of the respondents agreed or strongly agreed that using AI speech evaluation programs is convenient as they could improve their speaking skills anywhere and anytime, such as learning outside class on mobile devices. Out of the six factors (Figure 5.1), the highest percentage of "strongly agree" lay in the convenience of the AI speech evaluation programs (37%). Similar results are also found with access, motivation as well as institutional efficiency. These three factors correspond to the ease of obtaining abundant learning materials and experiencing interactions more easily; enjoying the learning process; and requiring less space, less teacher time or less expensive materials for respondents, respectively. The Kaiser-Meyer-Olkin (KMO) value of these six factors was 0.904 (p=0.00), and the value of Cronbach alpha was 0.936, which shows that these factors are applicable to use factor analysis and have excellent internal reliability and validity. Thus, it could be seen that the majority of subjects had a positive attitude towards the use of AI speech evaluation programs from these six factors compared with class teaching.

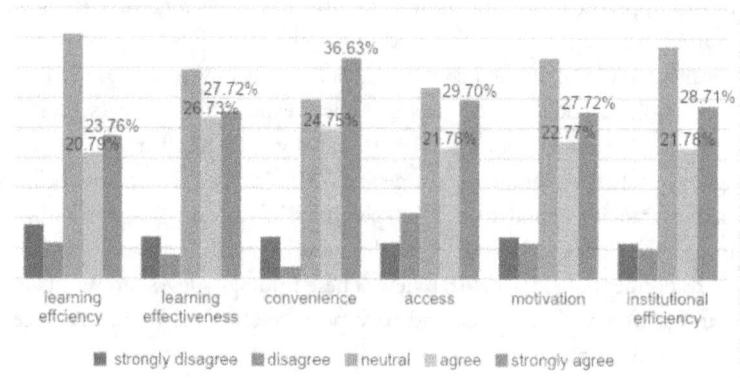

Figure 5.1 *How would you evaluate the AI technology in your learning of spoken English regarding the following aspects?*

According to the data, about three-fifths of the respondents agreed or strongly agreed with these AI evaluation programs' settings. Respondents reported a similar extent of satisfaction of AI evaluation programs from the content to the scoring system, specifically in the content of "reading aloud" and "presentation" sections; and the feedback, accuracy, comprehensiveness, and practicability of the scoring system (KMO=0.899, p=0.00, Cronbach's alpha=0.95). However, 11% of subjects were dissatisfied or strongly dissatisfied with the comprehensiveness of the scoring system, and

9% and 8% respectively of practicability and the accuracy of the scoring system, which suggests the scoring system of AI evaluation programs needs to be improved from diverse angles. Concerning each aspect of English-speaking skills (KMO=0.940, p=0.00, Cronbach's alpha=0.974), approximately 60% agreed that AI technology is helpful in improving their oral fluency (M=3.80; SD=1.03), pronunciation (M=3.80; SD=1.07) and idea-organization skills (M=3.82; SD=1.03). 57% believed it helps improve their oral rhythm (M=3.76; SD=1.07), read-aloud skills (M=3.78; SD=1.02) as well as presentation skills (M=3.77; SD=1.03), and 55% said it is useful in their grammar accuracy (M=3.70; SD=1.08). The above data reveals that more than half of the subjects agreed that AI technology helps their detailed speaking practice, especially their idea-organization skills.

Apart from the above results, it was also found that the various content provided in the AI speech evaluation programs correlated with those in detailed speaking skills. Table 5.1 shows six factors of the content and score feedback of speaking practice in these AI programs, for example,. 1 represented "Content of 'reading aloud' practice" and 4 stood for the "Accuracy of the scoring system" to evaluate learners' speaking for "reading aloud" and "delivery of presentations." This correlation test was conducted by using nonparametric Spearman correlations because all the variables are ordinal data. The results are shown in detail in Table 5.2 with factors 1 through 6 in Table 5.1, mainly by illustrating the correlation coefficients (r=value of Spearman's rho) combined with two-tailed p values.

Table 5.1 *The meaning of each of the variables represented by 1 through 6.*

Number	Variable
1	Content of "reading aloud"
2	Content of "presentation"
3	Feedback from the scoring system
4	Accuracy of the scoring system
5	Comprehensiveness of the scoring system
6	Practicability of the scoring system

Table 5.2 shows that subjects' speaking improvement (e.g., oral fluency, pronunciation, or presentations) were strongly correlated with the design of the content and scoring accuracy (factors 1–6 in Table 5.1) in the AI speech evaluation programs. In other words, respondents' improvements of oral

fluency, pronunciation, oral rhythm, grammar accuracy, idea-organization, read-aloud, and presentation skills correlated strongly with the content and the scoring system of the AI speech evaluation programs. According to Cohen (1988), the correlation effects among these factors are strong because the R-values are all above 0.7, and the p-values are significant. This means that when respondents were more satisfied with the design of AI technology, they were more likely to have better improvement in terms of their specific speaking skills. This suggests that AI evaluation programs should pay more attention to the programs' design, especially to provide more plentiful content and effective scoring systems to attract more learners in the future.

Table 5.2 *Correlations between AI evaluation programs design and subjects' improvement in various speaking skills.*

Variable	1	2	3	4	5	6
Oral fluency	.724**	.753**	.800**	.736**	.770**	.807**
Pronunciation	.797**	.802**	.782**	.761**	.722*	.760**
Oral rhythm	.759**	.758**	.771**	.731**	.788**	.771**
Grammar accuracy	.762**	.760**	.767**	.776**	.784**	.810**
Idea organization	.747**	.752**	.764**	.767**	.790**	.791**
Read aloud	.742**	.741**	.773**	.664**	.665**	.726**
Presentation	.726**	.770**	.760**	.705**	.775**	.774**

* $p < .05$ ** $p < .01$

The chi-square test was also used in exploring the relationship between two nominal variables of the questionnaire. As such, it was found that the learning frequency of subjects by using AI was significant with their satisfaction of access by using AI speech evaluation programs ($\chi2=39.13$, $p=0.03$, Cramer's V=0.31). In other words, learners with a higher learning frequency of AI are more satisfied with the ease of access brought by AI programs compared to classroom teaching. The learning frequency also positively correlated with subjects' willingness to use AI and the number of recordings they record each time. Furthermore, the results revealed that when subjects used AI more frequently, they were more willing to practice English speaking at a greater frequency than before, and this correlation approaches a strong relationship ($\chi2=24.89$, $p=0.00$, Cramer's V=0.496).

Similarly, these significant positive relationships are also found between learning time and willingness to practice speaking more frequently; learning time and subjects' fondness for using AI speech evaluation programs, and the number of recordings. In addition, the number of recordings is also positively correlated with subjects' grades ($\chi2$=12.92, p=0.02, Cramer's V=0.36). Specifically, the second-year students were more likely to have more recordings than the first-year students. One noteworthy finding here was that the number of recordings had a medium significant relationship with "AI can replace the teacher in terms of speaking practice" ($\chi2$=31.06, p=0.01, Cramer's V=0.39), which suggests the more times the subjects record, the more likely they are to feel that AI could replace the position of a human teacher in their speaking practice (25%). Meanwhile, 40% believed AI speech evaluation programs could replace the teacher in speaking practice after class, while nearly 20% reported AI speech evaluation programs could only take some part of the teacher's role outside of class.

By asking the open-ended question of learners' suggestions, some valuable ideas were put forward. Firstly, subjects reported that the current AI speech evaluation programs had some common problems. Specifically, respondents cited the limited content, inaccurate and limited feedback, lack of fun, lack of emotion, poor internet connection, difficulty to use, inability to recognize non-native speakers' accents, and that some of the programs required payment to use them. As a result, the common suggestions are summarized below. The AI speech evaluation programs could increase the feedback's accuracy and content, and have more topics, more downloadable resources, and more information related to IELTS. Simultaneously, participants suggest these programs should be more fun and interactive.

Application to Smart CALL

Using the AI speech evaluation program as an intelligent tutor

This section discusses using AI speech evaluation programs as a manifestation of Smart CALL for its personalization, contextualization, and socialization (see Chapter 1). The results showed that participants believed there were a number of benefits to using AI speech evaluation programs as intelligent tutoring for their spoken English practice. Two-thirds of the respondents reported that they developed the learning habits of using AI speech evaluation programs in their daily study, and they put effort into recording and practicing their speaking skills individually. As such, they perceived that they improved their speaking skills through the time they devoted to practicing and the feedback they received from the AI speech evaluation systems. The findings indicated that the majority of subjects perceived the benefits of AI speech evaluation programs from learning efficiency, learning effectiveness, convenience, abundant access and high motivation. These findings are consistent with studies by Choi (2016), Liakin, Cardoso and Liakina (2014), and McCrocklin (2016, 2019) in learners' motivation in using AI for speaking practice. Compared with a traditional class taught by human teachers, subjects could have more opportunities, resources, and more freedom to practice English speaking individually due to the fast development of AI technology into language learning. This individualization can be considered as personalization. Furthermore, respondents' user experiences of the AI technology are largely based on the evaluation programs' design and scoring system. Meanwhile, respondents are generally satisfied with the content of both reading aloud and presentation sections and the design of the feedback and the scoring system of these AI evaluation programs. This result echoes Wang's (2019) study that learners generally hold positive attitudes towards the diverse functions of AI speech evaluation programs for their speaking practice. In fact, the content and score system in the AI speech evaluation programs can be considered contextualization because the AI programs provide specific contexts including sources of "reading aloud" and "delivering presentation" for students to practice their speaking skills. In addition, the AI speech evaluation programs provide learners with individual socialization, that is, practice speaking with an interlocutor—in this case, the AI system. As suggested by Luckin *et al.* (2016), AI is designed to interact with people, and AI systems have the potential to serve that purpose.

Moreover, the results reported that subjects' learning frequency, learning time, and numbers of recordings using AI could contribute to their learning motivation and their willingness to use AI evaluation programs to improve their speaking skills. Subjects were more prepared to practice English speaking with a higher frequency after utilizing AI technology because they had observed their improvement and gained more confidence in speaking English from the feedback in the AI intelligent tutoring system. Meanwhile, the findings suggested that AI evaluation programs may replace some part of teachers' role outside of class for students' speaking practice. This situation could be explained by the fact that AI technology has the potential to act as an intelligent tutor to provide immediate feedback to the users to lead them to discover problems and make corrections, and as such, it may make it possible to move some parts of teachers' roles from in class to out of class. This is consistent with McArthur (2015), Luckin *et al*. (2016), and Wang's (2019) in that by using one-to-one tutoring, AI can provide spontaneous and immediate feedback for learners based on their individual learning pace and learning activities. Thus, respondents may benefit from AI technology in obtaining customized and targeted learning materials, which was selected as the most important reason for choosing to use AI by respondents in the survey. This is consistent with Ocaña-Fernández *et al*.'s (2019) claim that AI can provide a customized study plan for learners according to their learning needs. Moreover, the findings illustrate that learners can learn anytime and anywhere they want by using AI, providing them with more learning freedom and confidence.

One interesting finding in the paper was that second-year learners seemed to have a higher motivation to record their voices than the first-year learners in the survey. This might be explained by the fact that they have more complicated speaking tasks than first-year students, and this motivates them to take advantage of AI technology to improve and practice English speaking. The results show that subjects used both reading aloud and presentation sections nearly equally in their study. This finding might be supported by the respondents' EAP classes in this EMI university, which required them to practice English speaking using read-aloud materials and pay attention to presentation skills. The findings also illustrate that subjects practice through diverse topics and learning materials, which could help them improve their varied specific speaking skills, ranging from oral fluency, pronunciation, rhythm, and read-aloud capabilities to organize ideas, focus on grammar accuracy and acquire presentation skills. This finding is also supported by Bahi and Necibi (2020) that AI can help learners improve speaking skills from various aspects. Among these diverse skills, the idea-organization skill received the highest average score among respondents, which shows that AI technology may assist learners to cultivate logical thinking and present their ideas clearly and logically when speaking in English.

However, there are also some problems raised by subjects in their study of AI evaluation programs. The biggest problem is the limited feedback of the scoring system of these programs. A certain number of respondents showed their dissatisfaction with the scoring system, specifically regarding its accuracy, practicability, and comprehensiveness. This situation is connected to Hubbard's (2019) findings that the accuracy rate of current voice recognition technology is limited, and sometimes AI provides incorrect feedback. This has immediate implications for the design of AI evaluation programs, making it clear that there is a need for further development of speech recognition technology, and that more detailed feedback that is not limited only to providing a score but also more tangible interactions with users to emulate a human teacher, who is able to carry out a more specific analysis of the learner's mistakes and give suggestions about how correct the mistakes and improve their speaking skills. In addition, subjects also reported that some programs were too expensive to afford, that they did not function properly if there was a poor internet connection, that some programs were not able to recognize non-native English speakers' accents. These points suggest that these systems need to be usable even in the absence of a stable internet connection, and that more data of diverse accents should be included in the AI speaking programs' databases in order to improve the user's experience. While there is obviously a need for developers to recover costs from creating the AI evaluation programs, at the same time this needs to be balanced with users' affordability. Moreover, given that nearly one-third of subjects showed they were unfamiliar with AI evaluation programs, it is evident that the popularity of using AI technology in university students' speaking study is still relatively limited. This may be in part due to the interface of the programs, indicated by the fact that respondents thought the AI programs could be designed to be more enjoyable, colorful, interactive, and convenient.

Conclusion

This study explores the general perceptions of university students in an EMI university in China towards using AI evaluation programs for speaking practice. The results suggested both benefits and problems in using these programs as a part of students' language learning. The majority of respondents appreciated the various benefits of using AI, as evidenced by their learning habits using the AI evaluation programs, such as learning frequency, learning time, and how they use the functions of the programs In addition, while the acknowledged that there were limitations, most of them also reported improvement in various aspects of their speaking as a direct result of using the AI programs, and they were more willing to practice their spoken English on their own after using them.

The study was not without limitations. Due to the time constraints, this study lacked any real qualitative research methods. The sample size of this study was limited, in that it targeted first and second-year university students, and it could involve a greater number of participants from different backgrounds. Moreover, there is no comparison between experimental and control groups and between pre-test and post-test groups using AI evaluation programs, and data about language development is limited to self-reported perceptions. Despite these limitations, this study has shown preliminary evidence of university students' attitudes towards using AI for their speaking practice, suggesting that AI can serve as a means of improving Chinese EFL learners' speaking performance. Based on these preliminary observations, it is possible to have some indication of the next steps needed for AI to take on a more central role in language teaching—and particularly speaking—in the future.

Acknowledgements

This research is supported by KSF-E-16 at XJTLU.

References

Abad, J.V. (2013). Pedagogical factors that influence EFL teaching: Some considerations for teachers' professional development. *Profile Issues in Teachers' Professional Development, 15*(1), 97–108.
Bahi, H., & Necibi, K. (2020). Fuzzy logic applied for pronunciation assessment. *International Journal of Computer-Assisted Language Learning and Teaching, 10*(1), 60–72.
Bao, M. (2019). Can home use of speech-enabled artificial intelligence mitigate foreign language anxiety – Investigation of a concept. *Arab World English Journal, 5*, 28–40. Retrieved from https://ssrn.com/abstract=3431734
Burn, E., Laskowski, N., & Tucci, L. (2022) What is artificial intelligence (AI)? Retrieved from: https://searchenterpriseai.techtarget.com/definition/AI-Artificial-Intelligence
Chen, Y., Wu, K., & Li, J.N. (2019) The automatic scoring system of Chinese learners' spoken English - a new system to assess oral English proficiency. *China Academic Journal Electronic Publishing House, 185*, 72–77.
Choi, I.C. (2016). Efficacy of an ICALL tutoring system and process

oriented corrective feedback. *Computer Assisted Language Learning, 29*(2), 334-364.

Cohen, J. (1988). *Statistical power and analysis for the behavioral sciences (2nd ed.).* Hillsdale, NJ: Lawrence Erlbaum Associates.

Damio, S.M., & Ibrahim, Q. (2019). Virtual reality speaking application utilisation in combatting presentation apprehension. *Asian Journal of University Education, 15*(3), 235-244.

Debski, R. (2003). Analysis of research in CALL (1980-2000) with a reflection on CALL as an academic discipline. *ReCALL, 15*(2), 177-188.

Fouz-González, J. (2020). Using apps for pronunciation training: An empirical evaluation of the English File Pronunciation app. *Language Learning & Technology, 24*(1), 62-85. https://doi.org/10125/44709

Fryer, L., & Carpenter, R. (2006). Emerging technologies: Bots as language learning tools. *Language Learning & Technology, 10*(3), 8-14.

Hamuddin, B. (2016). Using blog to promote English skills for EFL students: The students' perception. *ELT-Lectura, 3*(2), 22-27, Doi: https://doi.org/10.31849/elt-lectura.v3i2.481

Hamuddin, B., Kurniawan, K., Syaifullah, S., & Herdi, H. (2018). Detecting major problems in learning English through blog-based class. *Journal of Education and Learning, 12*(3), 529.

Hubbard, P. (2019). Five keys from the past to the future of CALL. *International Journal of Computer-Assisted Language Learning and Teaching, 9*(3), 1-13.

Hyman, M., & Sierra, J. (2016) Open- versus close-ended survey questions, *Business Outlook, 14*(2), 1-5.

Johnson, R.B., Onwuegbuzie, A.J., & Turner, L.A. (2007) Toward a definition of mixed methods research. *Journal of Mixed Methods Research, 1*(2), 112-133.

Kim, I.-S. (2006). Automatic speech recognition: Reliability and pedagogical implications for teaching pronunciation. *Journal of Educational Technology & Society, 9*(1), 322-334.

Kim, D., Rueckert, D., Kim, D.J., & Seo, D. (2013). Students' perceptions and experiences of mobile learning. *Language Learning & Technology, 17*(3), 52-73.

Lewis, J.W., & Valente, A. (2009). Tactical language and culture training systems: Using AI to teach foreign languages and cultures. *AI Magazine, 30*(2), 72.

Liakin, D., Cardoso, W., & Liakina, N. (2014). Learning L2 pronunciation with a mobile
speech recognizer: French /y/. *CALICO Journal*, 32(1), 1–25.

Luckin, R., Holmes, W., Griffiths, M., & Forcier, L. (2016). *Intelligence unleashed: An argument for AI in Education*. London: Pearson Education.

Maftoon, P., Hamidi, H., & Sarem, S.N. (2012). The effects of CALL on vocabulary learning: A case of Iranian intermediate EFL learners. *BRAIN: Broad Research in Artificial Intelligence and Neuroscience*, 3(4), 19–30.

Malhotra, N.K. (2015). *Essentials of marketing research*. London: Pearson PLC.

McArthur, J.A. (2015). Matching instructors and spaces of learning: The Impact of space on behavioral, affective and cognitive Learning. *Journal of Learning Spaces*, 4(1), 1–16.

Meyerson, D. (2018). The future of the future of learning. *Training & Development*, 47(3), 16–17.

McCrocklin, S. (2016). Pronunciation learner autonomy: The potential of automatic speech recognition. *System*, 57, 25–42.

McCrocklin, S. (2019). ASR-based dictation practice for second language pronunciation improvement. *Journal of Second Language Pronunciation*, 5(1), 98–118.

Ocaña-Fernández, Y., Valenzuela-Fernández, L.A., & Garro-Aburto, L.L. (2019) Artificial intelligence and its implications in higher education. *Propósitos y Representaciones*, 7(2), 536–568.

Rahman, Z., & Sangaji, S. (2019). A study on the university students' speaking difficulties. *Journal of Linguistics, Literature, and Language Education*, 2 (1), 1–8.

Shen, M., & Chiu, T. (2019). EFL learners' English speaking difficulties and strategy use. *Education and Linguistics Research*, 5(2), 88–102.

Solano, L., Cabrera, P., Ulehlova, E., & Espinoza, V. (2017). Exploring the use of educational technology in EFL teaching: A case study of primary education in the south region of Ecuador. *Teaching English with Technology*, 17(2), 77–86.

Stewart, J.C., Davis, G.A., & Igoche, D.A. (2020). AI, IoT, and AIoT: Definitions and impacts on the artificial intelligence curriculum. *Issues in Information Systems*, 21(4), 135–142.

Takahashi, Y., & Vate-U-Lan, P. (2019). Toward understanding the impact of artificial intelligence on education: An empirical research in Japan. In P. Griffiths & M.N. Kabir (Eds.), *Proceedings of the ECIAIR 2019 European Conference on the Impact of Artificial Intelligence and Robotics* (pp. 433–438). Red Hook, NY: Academic Conferences and Publishing Limited.

Wang, P. (2019). Defining artificial intelligence. *Journal of Artificial General Intelligence, 10*(2), 1–37.

Wekke, I.S., Yandra, A., & Hamuddin, B. (2017). Learning strategy in class management: A reflection from Manado Case. *International Conference on Environment and Technology, 97*(2017), 012053. https://iopscience.iop.org/article/10.1088/1755-1315/97/1/012053/pdf

Zou, B., Liviero, S., Hao, M.Y., & Wei, C.Y. (2020) Artificial intelligence technology for EAP speaking skills: Student perceptions of opportunities and challenges. In M. Freiermuth & N. Zarrinabadi (Eds.), *Technology and the psychology of second language learners and users* (pp. 433–463). London: Palgrave Macmillan.

6
Exploring the impact of AI on EFL teaching in Japan

Hiroyuki Obari
Stephen Lambacher
Hisayo Kikuchi

Introduction

As has been described in earlier chapters (see Chapters 4 and 5), artificial intelligence is intelligence demonstrated by machines, unlike the natural intelligence displayed by humans and animals. It is an interdisciplinary field focusing on the simulation and reproduction of human intelligence, thinking processes, and problem-solving (Popenici & Kerr, 2017). AI describes machines or computers that mimic or approximate cognitive functions associated with the human mind, such as learning and problem solving (Russell & Norvig, 2009). Top AI textbooks define the field as the study of "intelligent agents" and the use of any device that perceives its environment and takes actions to maximize its chance of successfully achieving its goals (Kessler, 2018). This chapter explores the impact of AI on EFL education by evaluating the use of digital personal assistants (also known as smart speakers) as part of a blended-learning (BL) environment in improving the English proficiency of native Japanese undergraduates. Following a brief introduction to artificial intelligence, the basic capabilities of personal assistants/smart speakers are discussed, along with specific examples of their use in educational and L2 learning environments, before the key findings of three case studies are presented.

Literature Review

Basic features of personal assistants/smart speakers

Emerging technologies such as virtual reality, augmented reality, and voice interaction have transformed people's experiences and interactions and reshaped the personalization, contextualization, and socialization of their digital experiences. Thanks to advancements in cloud computing, AI, and the Internet of Things (IoT), voice control is the next step in the human-machine connection (Terzopoulos & Satratzemi, 2020). Due to the widespread use of smartphones and the growing popularity of smart speakers, cloud-based, intelligent personal voice assistants have emerged, such as Apple's Siri, Google's Assistant, Microsoft's Cortana, and Amazon's Alexa. Voice assistants deliver services to consumers using voice recognition, speech synthesis, and natural language processing (NLP). Voice assistants are already available in millions of households, thanks to cloud platforms.

AI smart speakers are wireless devices with artificial intelligence activated through voice commands. Voice assistants rely on a cloud-based architecture because data must be transmitted back and forth to centralized data centers. Because a smart speaker is designed to be simple, most of the computation and artificial intelligence processing occurs in the cloud rather than on the device itself. Smart speakers are the most common device with voice assistants, and they have recently begun to be utilized contextually within schools and institutions of higher-level learners. The user issues a request through their voice-activated device, which is subsequently broadcast to the cloud, where the voice is transformed into text. The text request is then sent to the backend, which processes it and responds with a text response. Finally, the text response is sent to the cloud, where it is converted into voice and delivered back to the user (Terzopoulos & Satratzemi, 2019).

AI interacts in the form of a virtual personal assistant, such as Amazon's Alexa and Google's Home Mini. Its capabilities can be enabled to develop new, personalized skills. The focus of the current chapter, Alexa, has "skills" that are the programs or commands that "she" can execute (much like the apps on a smartphone) which can be executed through smart speakers as a smart home hub. A smart speaker, such as the Amazon Echo Plus, can connect to wireless protocols to operate smart home gadgets. The smart speaker uses Wi-Fi, Bluetooth, or other wireless protocol standards to operate home automation equipment such as lights, thermostats, coffee makers, and televisions (Smith, 2020).

Voice assistants are simple to use, which is why there are millions of devices with them in homes today. The Alexa platform is currently the most popular, with more than 70% of all intelligent voice assistant-enabled devices (other than phones) running on it. According to Canalys (2018), there were 320 million expected smart speaker users by 2022. Smart speaker sales now outpace smartphones and tablets, with one-third of owners using it to perform tasks that were done before on smartphones. Nearly a quarter of US households own a smart speaker, and more than half of those who do have two or more, with 55% of households expected to have one by 2022 (Juniper Research, 2017; Richter, 2020). Bunyard (2019) explains the complex reasons IoT technology has become integrated and contextualized into people's daily lives. The fundamental reason is that the technology provides convenience by removing the need for users to cope with time-consuming and stressful tasks. Below are some of the more common smart speaker usages:

- provide news and weather
- perform web searches: 50% done by voice command
- listening to music
- ordering products (e.g., flowers)
- checking recipes
- calling uber rides
- checking PayPal balance and paying bills
- playing games and telling jokes
- making hotel reservations
- controlling other smart devices (e.g., lights, locks, thermostats, vacuum cleaners, switches)
- hearing marketing messages (e.g., I love Nike -- Alexa)

Application in education

Even though smart speakers are now standard in many homes, their use in schools for educational purposes has been limited due to privacy settings and data collection concerns (Terzopoulos & Satratzemi, 2020). However, the Echo can have a wide range of capabilities in the classroom when integrating and setting it up with English as the primary language. At its most basic level, the Echo can set a timer in the classroom. The timer may be paused, and it will tell you how much time is left if you ask it. Alexa can also choose an activity or a student from a group (Davie & Hilber, 2018). Google Assistant had over 18,000 voice applications by the end of 2019 (Kinsella, 2020) whereas there were over 100,000 Alexa apps available during the same period (Schwartz, 2019). A few of these voice apps can help students learn a new language. For example, Word of the Day Quiz Game and Magoosh Vocabulary Builder can assist students in improving their English vocabulary. To augment the socialization of learning environments, Alexa includes socialbots with which users can have open-ended conversations in the L2, providing language students with opportunities to converse in the L2 (Dizon & Tang, 2020).

Smart speakers, as they are currently used in homes, can also be used as a source of knowledge in schools, according to some studies (e.g., Terzopoulos & Satratzemi, 2019). Instead of asking the teacher, children can direct their queries to the devices and verify their answers. The devices force students to ask their questions correctly and understandably by allowing them to grasp the fundamental principles of human-computer interaction. The learning experience is personalized and socialized as smart speakers respond to questions based on who is asking them and mention their names in their responses. Voice assistants and smart speakers can be used for more than just providing information. Students are encouraged to seek out information on their own.

The integration of AI speakers in educational environments can assist students by providing timely and accurate information. "ProblemPal" is an Alexa skill that allows teachers to generate practice content automatically through voice commands (Trivedi, 2018). Any topic can be used to produce practice questions using APIs from Wikipedia, Wolfram Alpha, and Khan. The created queries can be posted to Google Classroom and shared with students, which can help teachers save time and be valuable for students.

Application of AI smart speakers in L2 learning contexts

Due to technological breakthroughs in natural language processing and automatic speech recognition, dialogue-based CALL has been increasingly crucial in interactionist research in recent years (Dixon, 2020). In contrast to computer-mediated communication (CMC), where a computer communicates to a learner, students in dialogue-based CALL interact with a computer. Research on dialogue-based CALL is based on the assumption that "meaningful practice of a target language, as it occurs in conversations, leads to improvement in the learner's proficiency in that language, and that, even if a native speaker remains the ideal interlocutor, a computer can provide opportunities for such practice," (Bibauw, Francois, & Desmet, 2019).

Smart speakers have built-in commands that may be of particular use to language learners. Amazon Echo Dot, for instance, can be used as a dictionary by asking, "Alexa, what is the definition of...?" a selected word and the device will (try to) respond, or by asking, "Alexa, how do you spell...?" By asking "Alexa, what is a synonym for..." the word of your choice, the Echo may be utilized as a thesaurus or even a translator. Additional language learning skills are also available. Flashcard-style services are the most frequent, and they usually link to well-known sites such as "Quizlet" or "Chegg." Additionally, an Echo device can play audio files for listening comprehension or music for relaxation or quiet study time (Davie & Hilber, 2018).

Preliminary studies have been carried out on the use of smart speakers to enhance L2 learning, showing they can be used as a CMC tool and can be a valuable tool to help advance the integration, socialization, and personalization of the learning process in the classroom. For example, Moussalli and Cardoso (2016) conducted a study with four L2 English students to see if Alexa enhanced language learning outside of the school. The participants interacted with the virtual assistant for approximately 30 minutes, asking both pre-determined and learner-generated questions. The researchers discovered that students enjoyed interacting with the virtual assistant and saw it as a valuable tool for language learning. However, students found it was sometimes difficult for their English to be understood by the virtual assistant. In a follow-up study, Moussalli and Cardoso (2019) examined how students utilized Alexa and discovered they employed various tactics to overcome communication breakdowns, including repetition, rephrasing, and withdrawal. The authors also found the smart speaker had no trouble understanding accented speech, contradicting their earlier findings.

Dizon (2020) focused on ascertaining if Alexa might help enhance EFL listening comprehension and speaking skills. Results revealed that AI speakers helped students to improve their speaking but not listening skills. The results of the speaking tests showed that, while the experimental group made a slight improvement, the control group did worse on the posttest than on the pretest. The author feels improvement in L2 speaking underlines the potential of AI speakers to enhance foreign language development and confirms prior findings of the benefits of dialogue-based CALL for language learners (Bibauw *et al*., 2019). This interaction is especially crucial when students learn a foreign language, where they are likely to have few speaking opportunities outside of the classroom.

Application to Smart CALL

Case Study 1

In this section, we present three case studies that evaluate the use of AI smart speakers as a tool to help improve the English skills of native Japanese students by enhancing the socialization and personalization of their learning. The primary purpose of the first case was to ascertain the effectiveness of a training program that incorporated the AI smart speakers Google Home Mini and Amazon Alexa to improve the English proficiency of native Japanese undergraduate students. It also integrates 21st-century learning skills for developing international cultural awareness as part of a flipped learning (FL) environment. Pretest and posttest TOEIC scores and post-training survey results were used to evaluate the overall effectiveness of the training program.

Two research questions were targeted:

a. Could the participants improve their English proficiency and understanding of 21st-century skills after exposure to the AI/BL/FL activities?
b. Was the application of AI/mobile learning and Content and Language Integrated Learning (CLIL) helpful in improving the participants' English skills?

In 2008, Harvard researcher Tony Wagner (2016) identified the following "7 Survival Skills" necessary for the modern workplace:

a. Critical thinking and problem solving
b. Collaboration
c. Agility and adaptability

d. Initiative and entrepreneurialism
e. Effective oral and written communication
f. Accessing and analyzing information
g. Curiosity and imagination

In addition to these "7 Survival Skills," one more skill (the 8th C) should be added, which we will refer to as "Coexistence with AI." Consequently, there are 8C skills for 21st-century education. In this study, these 8C skills are integrated for developing EFL skills and intercultural awareness.

Method

Case study 1 was conducted over two semesters (April 2018 to January 2019). Twenty-four students participated in the study, all native Japanese and third-year economics majors at a private university in Tokyo. Participants were divided into eight groups where they carried out group-oriented research to improve their English proficiency in using AI speakers for nearly ten months. For example, they set up research questions, "How can we improve our English proficiency using an AI speaker?" At the end of the semester in January, they created and delivered 15-minute presentations about their research during a seminar trip in Tochigi, Japan.

Training procedure

Students received training to improve their English proficiency in a seminar by actively participating in flipped learning lessons for several years. TOEIC mean scores typically improved only 150 points, never achieving an increase of 200 points or more in TOEIC during the training period of ten months, which was part of our motivation to use an AI speaker to increase the comprehensible input of English.

The technologies utilized included Google Home Mini (Figure 6.1), Amazon Alexa (Figure 6.2), ATR CALL Brix, and the mSNS programs Facebook, Twitter, Line, and other language learning programs. TOEIC was used as a measure to determine if the students' English skills improved and help ascertain the overall effectiveness of the BL/FL program using AI speakers. TOEIC was administered as a pretest in April 2018 and a posttest in January 2019.

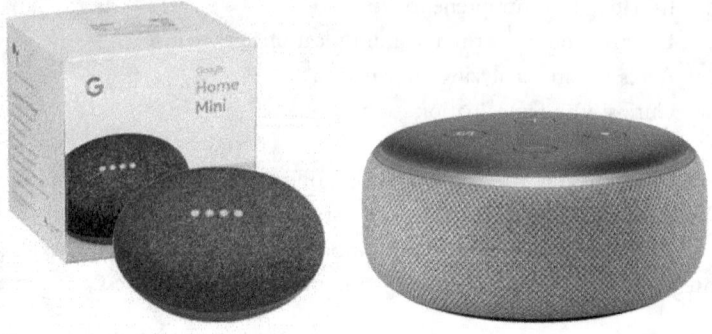

Figure 6.1 *Google Home Mini.*   **Figure 6.2** *Alexa Echo Dot.*

During training, participants were divided into eight subgroups, with half of four groups using Google Home Mini and the other half of four groups using Amazon Alexa. The AI speakers were integrated into the daily lives of the participants over the four months. A timer was regularly set while interacting with the AI speakers to practice English listening, speaking, pronunciation, and vocabulary skills using various software programs. Some groups used Google Home Mini daily to improve their English listening and speaking skills using the following software applications: "Best Teacher," "Travel English," "Let's play around with English," and BBC/CNN news, "Kikutan," "English Quiz" by Arc, "Liberty English," and "Kindle."

While studying with the smart speakers, participants recorded short movie clips of their learning experiences which were uploaded to Facebook. Participants also kept written diaries with their observations about the contents and duration of their studies, periodically recording their thoughts using a smartphone. At the end of the training period, participants of all eight subgroups delivered presentations of their impressions of the BL/FL-lesson training using the AI speakers, with a majority indicating the activity had a positive effect on their learning experiences.

Including the above AI training procedure, the following tasks were incorporated in training:

1) Practiced English using the AI speakers Google Home Mini and Amazon Alexa.

2) Watched online TED Talks using their mobile devices; wrote 300-word summaries, created PowerPoint presentations, and discussed their summaries with a group of native English speakers four times.
3) Studied worldviews after viewing online lectures by several Oxford University scholars, which focused on ontological and epistemological issues, delivered PPT presentations, and created digital stories with their iPads. They presented their summaries with English native speakers and further discussed comparative worldviews between East and West.
4) Used ATR CALL Brix to practice TOEIC and measure their improvements of English proficiency. (ATR CALL Brix is a unique program developed by Uchida Yoko company for learning English grammar, listening, reading, and writing.)
5) Studied the theory behind 21st-century skills and, with iPads, delivered PowerPoint presentations summarizing the contents.
6) Interacted with English native speakers who assessed their presentations and discussed worldviews and cultural issues – the native speakers included eight university students from the US.
7) Flipped lessons were put into practice focusing on the presentations and discussions in the class after they received comprehensible input about the assigned tasks every week.
8) Students assessed their presentations based upon six items using the computer evaluation "PeerEval" (Figure 6.3). Using this system, students could better understand their presentation strengths and weaknesses. After their presentations, they could examine the average score of each category as assessed by the evaluators (see Figure 6.4).

Results of Pretest/Posttest TOEIC

As shown in Figure 6.5, students improved both their listening and reading scores. Their listening mean scores increased from 185 (SD=55) to 313 (SD=76), and their reading mean scores also increased from 237 (SD=74) to 304 (SD=57). Pretest and posttest total TOEIC results of Case Study 1 (n=24) during the ten-month training period (April 2018 to January 2019) increased from a mean score of 422 (SD=115) or equivalent to AI CEFR level to 617 (SD=114) or equal to B1 CEFR level. The mean score of 195 points improved from pretest to posttest. The pre-/post-test TOEIC results were analyzed using a series of t-tests, indicating the differences were statistically significant ($p < .01$).

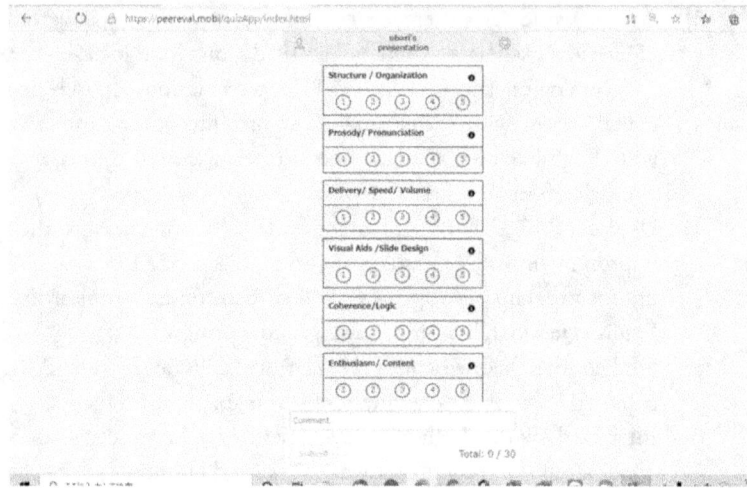

Figure 6.3 *PeerEval.*

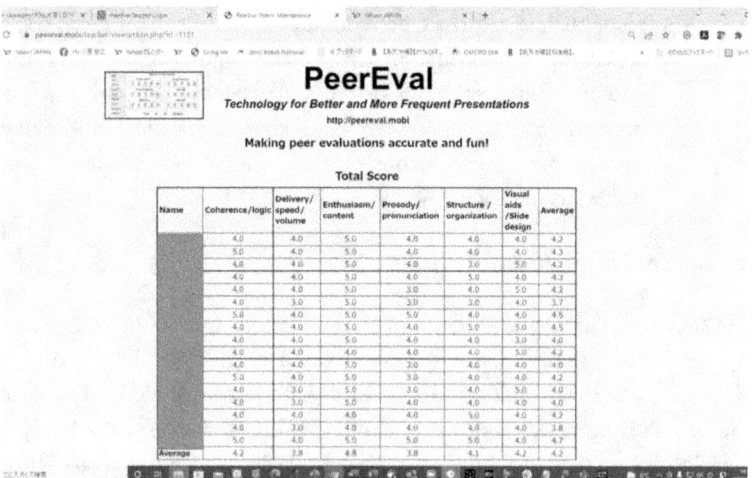

Figure 6.4 *Assessment of PeerEval.*

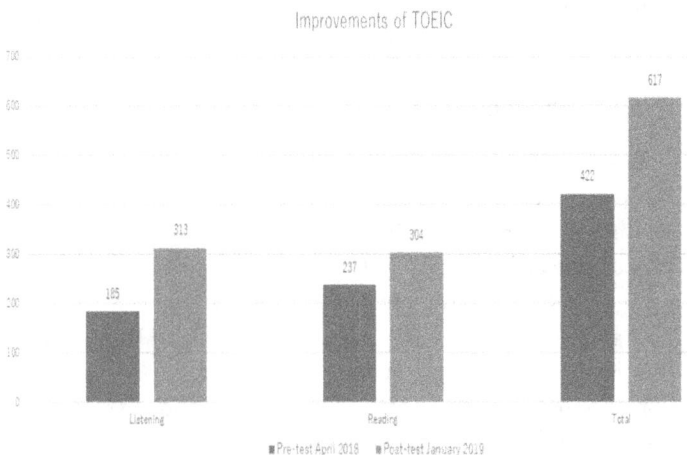

Figure 6.5 *Pretest vs. posttest TOEIC scores.*

Post-training questionnaire

A post-training survey was administered to 24 students to ascertain their overall impressions of the program. Responses to a few survey questions are summarized as follows:

(Q1) The online lectures were beneficial in improving my English proficiency: 88% agreed (n=24).
(Q2) SNS (Facebook, Line, Twitter) helped me learn English: 92% agreed (n=24).
(Q3) This program helped me learn 21st-century skills: 90% agreed (n=24).
(Q4) Campus Crusade for Christ (CCC) members helped change my worldviews through face-to-face discussions: 88% agreed (n=24).
(Q5) Collaborative work helped improve my learning and English proficiency: 94% agreed. (n=24)
(Q6) AI speaker helped improve my English skills: 76% agreed (n=24).
(Q7) AI speaker helped improve my listening skills: 87% agreed (n=24).
(Q8) AI speaker helped improve my speaking skills: 57% agreed (n=24).
(Q9) AI speaker helped improve my reading skills: 13% agreed (n=24).
(Q10) AI speaker helped improve my writing skills: 4.3% agreed (n=24).

(Q11) Presentation practice with PowerPoint helped improve my English proficiency: 100% agreed (n=24).

Post-training comments

(S1) I could set up the AI speaker to a particular time to make studying part of my daily routine by listening to the news. Alexa has practical applications for learning English.

(S2) AI speaker helped improve my English listening comprehension and speaking skills. Studying was much easier, and I was more motivated to learn English. I was increasingly exposed to listening to English, which was the significant advantage of using an AI speaker.

(S3) AI speaker has several advantages – more opportunities to listen to authentic English and practice more English speaking. We feel as if we are having a conversation with a native speaker of English.

(S4) AI speaker has two advantages – First, it is easy to use with only one's voice to study English. Second, it helps to improve my English-speaking ability. I could be more actively engaged in learning English with the AI speaker. I felt I could improve my English skills over a shorter period.

(S5) I did not have to sit at my desk to study English. I could easily engage in learning English with Alexa, which has many applications for learning English.

(S6) Hurdles to learning English decreased, which made learning a part of my daily routine. I could practice English loudly without hesitation.

(S7) AI speaker could create a virtual environment where I felt I was speaking with a native speaker of English. However, it did not help to improve my reading and writing skills. The study is where I usually sit at the desk. However, after I used the AI speaker, my studying image changed to make me feel the joy of learning.

(S8) I felt it would be very advantageous for early childhood English education due to its many applications. We could acquire news information without using a smartphone by the AI speaker. An AI speaker could attract children by motivating them to learn with great pleasure, not just sitting at a desk.

Discussion

The participants used the smart speakers Google Home Mini, Amazon Alexa, and other language programs during training. TOEIC was used as a measure to determine if the students' English skills improved and to help ascertain the overall effectiveness of the BL/FL program. The mean TOEIC scores significantly improved over ten months. The total mean score of TOEIC improved 195 points from 422 (SD=115) to 617 (SD=114). The fact that the students made more progress in listening than reading comprehension in TOEIC could be due to using the AI speaker to some extent.

Survey results revealed 76% agreed the AI speaker helped improve their English, mainly listening skills. On the other hand, only 13% agreed that the AI speaker enhanced reading skills, although the mean reading score of TOEIC improved less than the mean listening score. Only 4.3% agreed that the AI speaker enhanced writing, although we could not get the results of the writing test score this time. The use of an AI speaker could be helpful in learning listening from the questionnaire and TOEIC listening test results.

In addition, flipped lessons were put into practice focusing on the presentations and discussions in the classroom after students gained sufficient comprehensible input about the assigned tasks each week. As a result, their listening, speaking, and writing skills, to some extent, were reinforced. The students studied worldviews and held discussions with CCC (Campus Crusade for Christ) members, which changed their worldviews, as 88% agreed that the interactions with CCC members influenced their worldviews through face-to-face interactions.

Learning 21st century skills was integrated into training, and 90% of students agreed it helped broaden their skills. Various digital technologies were used to understand different topics. The distinction between the classroom and outside-class activities was drawn. Each student could gain as much comprehensible input outside of the class with an AI speaker and could engage more in interaction and discussions with critical and creative thinking as they could inside the classroom. However, it was a challenge to carry out this research by focusing only on using AI smart speakers to improve students' English skills due to the integration of various technologies with many learning strategies. Most important in learning English is face-to-face interaction and how much comprehensible input we can gain from multiple learning sources, whether analog or digital.

Summary

An assessment of pretest and posttest TOEIC scores revealed a combination of the AI/BL/FL activities utilizing AI smart speakers positively affected the students' English language learning. Overall, the students' listening and oral communication skills improved, which may have been due to the integration of the language learning activities, which focused on a social constructivist approach while utilizing the AI smart speakers Alexa and Home Mini. Additionally, the post-course survey revealed both groups were satisfied with the online course materials and motivated by the AI/BL/FL environment incorporating 21st-century skills. Students cited improved recognition of ambiguities within cross-cultural contexts and improved global communication skills. The students' oral summaries were also enhanced through interaction with the AI smart speakers and native English speakers. As a whole, these results would seem to indicate the integration of AI smart speakers into the BL/FL training program played a role in improving the students' overall language proficiency and expanding their worldviews.

Case Studies 2 and 3

Recently, Trilling and Fadel (2009) emphasized the importance of 21st-century skills, including the 3Rs and 7Cs, as being particularly important (see Figures 6.6 and 6.7). But now, an 8th C (coexistence with AI) should be added to coexist with AI (Kivunja, 2015; Wagner, 2016). Kurzweil (2005) predicted that AI would advance exponentially and approach the singularity in 2045. In the article "The Future Employment," it is mentioned that approximately 48 percent of present jobs will be replaced by AI-related jobs (Frey & Osborne, 2013). Harari (2018) comments that "humankind is likely to be divided into two main camps-those in favor of giving AI significant authority, and those opposed to it." Harari also predicted people would be divided into two camps, one using AI and the other used by AI. Therefore, the 8Cs will play an essential role in the pedagogy of English education. Based on this concept, this chapter was written to promote global education.

Figure 6.6 *21ˢᵗ century skills: 3Rs and 7Cs.*

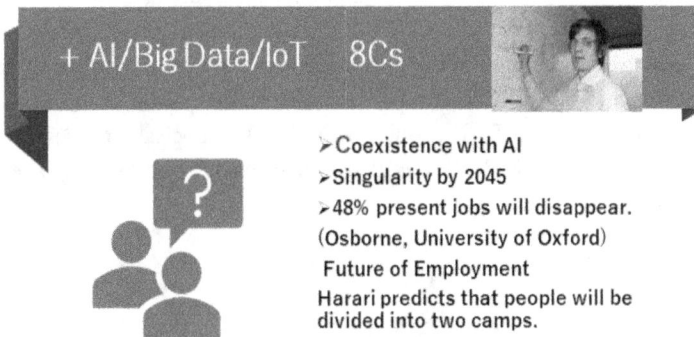

Figure 6.7 *Coexistence with AI.*

Method

To replicate the first case study, which revealed the benefits of smart speakers in L2 learning, two additional case studies were carried out. The second case study was conducted over two semesters (April 2019 to January 2020). Fifty-nine undergraduates participated, all native speakers of

Japanese. Participants were divided into two groups: The experimental group (n=30) used a smart speaker during the training period, while the control group (n=29) did not use a smart speaker. Case Study 3 included a separate group of Japanese participants (n=23). As in Case Study 1, TOEIC was used as a measure in the additional case studies to determine if the students' English skills improved and to also help ascertain the overall effectiveness of the BL/FL program. TOEIC was administered to both groups as a pretest in April 2019 and a posttest in January 2020 to determine any differences in improvement.

Training procedure

The technologies utilized in training included Amazon Alexa and Google Home Mini (Figure 6.8), ATR CALL Brix, and the mSNS programs Facebook, Twitter, and Line. During training, the experimental group participants used Amazon Alexa at home with numerous applications and filmed and kept diaries about their studies. The AI speakers were integrated into their daily lives over the ten-month training period. A timer was set while interacting with the AI speakers to practice English listening, speaking, and vocabulary skills using various software programs. The control group used ATR CALL Brix online learning materials at home, focusing on listening, reading, and vocabulary learning. Therefore, the main difference between both groups was whether participants had used an AI speaker or ATR CALL Brix online materials. Pedagogical activities for both groups were nearly identical in that they studied World Heritage sites and worldviews.

Figure 6.8 *Amazon Alexa and Google Home mini.*

In Case Studies 1 and 2, we did not use a speaking test. But participants of Case Study 3 were administered the pre-TOEIC and OPIc speaking tests in April 2019 and post-TOEIC and OPIc speaking tests in January 2020. Participants of Case Study 3 were divided into six subgroups, with half using Google Home Mini and half using Amazon Alexa. Half of the participants used Google Home Mini daily to improve their English listening and speaking skills using the following software applications: "Best Teacher," "Travel English," "Let's play around with English," and BBC/CNN news. The other half of participants used Home Mini daily to improve their listening and speaking skills using the following programs: Kikutan, English Quiz by Arc, Liberty English, and Kindle. While studying with the AI speakers, participants recorded short movie clips of their learning experiences which were uploaded to Facebook, just like Case Study 1. Participants also kept written diaries with their observations about the contents and duration of their studies.

Including the above AI training procedure, the following additional tasks were incorporated during training in Case Study 3:

1) Watched online TED Talks using their mobile devices; Wrote 300-word summaries, created PowerPoint presentations, and discussed their summaries with English native speakers four separate times.
2) Studied worldviews after viewing online lectures by Oxford University scholars, which focused on ontological and epistemological issues, delivered PPT presentations, and created digital stories with their iPads.
3) Listened to the CQ (Cross-cultural Quotient) from Prof. Weakley of Western Kentucky University (Figure 6.9) and interacted with English native speakers who assessed their presentations and discussed worldviews and cultural issues—the native speakers included eight university students from the United States.

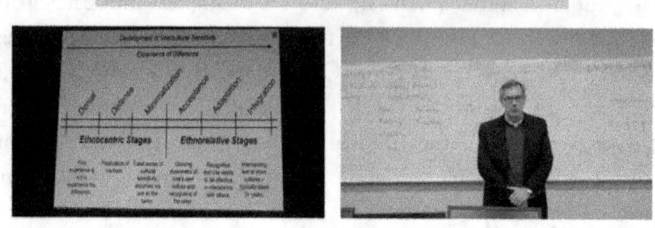

Figure 6.9 *Visiting academic, Professor Weakley.*

Results of TOEIC and OPIc Speaking Test

Mean TOEIC scores of the experimental group improved from 407 (SD=113) to 604 (SD=92), increasing 197 points. Mean TOEIC scores of the control group improved from 447 (SD=93) to 598 (SD=147), an increase of 147 points.

The mean TOEIC scores in Case Study 3 improved from 461 (SD=136) to 681 (SD=141), an increase of 229 points, and the mean OPIc speaking test scores improved from 3.9 (SD=0.9) to 4.7 (SD=1.25). These results suggest that the integration of AI smart speakers, social media, and 21st-century skills may be an effective way to improve the English language proficiency of adult ELT learners. The pre-/post-test results in both case studies were analyzed using a series of t-tests, indicating the differences in TOEIC scores between the experimental and control groups were statistically significant ($p < .01$).

Post-training survey (Case Study 3)

A post-training survey was administered at the end of their respective AI/BL/FL training to ascertain their overall impressions of the program. Responses to a few questions are summarized below:

(Q1) AI speaker helped improve my English skills: 81% agreed (n=23).
(Q2) AI speaker helped improve my listening skills: 87% agreed (n=23).
(Q3) AI speaker helped improve my speaking skills: 65% agreed (n=23).

(Q4) AI speaker helped improve my reading skills: 32% agreed (n=23).
(Q5) AI speaker helped improve my writing skills: 26% agreed (n=23).

Conclusion

In the three case studies presented, the mean TOEIC scores significantly improved over two semesters. The results of Case Study 2 indicated the experimental group using AI speakers as part of their training performed better on TOEIC in the posttest than the control group who did not use AI speakers. The results of Case Study 3 also revealed that the integration of AI speakers and flipped learning helped the experimental participants improve their TOEIC scores by 229 points. We carried out a replication study and proved that Case Study 1 and Case Study 3 had similar results, with participants improving their TOEIC score with a mean of approximately 200 points.

The follow-up survey gauged student attitudes toward the effectiveness of smart speakers in improving English skills. Results in Case Study 3 showed 87% agreed the AI speaker improved their English, mainly listening skills. 65% percent of students agreed the AI speaker helped enhance their speaking skills, as the students' mean OPIc speaking test scores increased from 3.9 (SD: 0.9) to 4.7 (SD: 1.25)/total score 8. On the other hand, only 32% agreed the AI speaker helped improve reading skills, and only 26.3% felt it improved writing skills.

For a comparison, in 2019, a separate group of first-year undergraduates majoring in economics were enrolled in three required English courses (Reading, Writing and Communication, and Fundamental English). They took TOEIC as a pretest (mean score: 455/SD: 42.4) in March 2019 and posttest (mean score: 448/SD:50.4) in December 2019, which revealed a nonsignificant decrease in improvement in TOEIC scores. L2 pedagogically could thus be greatly enhanced by including AI smart speakers.

The participants thought that using a smart speaker was a fun, easy-to-use, and practical approach to studying English and felt it improved their listening, speaking, and vocabulary skills. Having their commands understood by the AI smart speaker instilled confidence, and they liked being exposed to authentic native pronunciation by listening to the news. Shortcomings included being misunderstood by the smart speaker due to a poor accent. The lack of human element increased boredom for some, which may explain why a number of the subjects gave up on using their smart speaker on a daily basis.

These results would appear to support Dizon and Tang (2020), who found that Japanese students generally had positive views of the virtual assistant Alexa despite a few drawbacks, such as comprehension-related and technological challenges. However, despite their excellent impressions of Alexa, actual use revealed many were not interested in using the virtual assistant for English learning on a long-term basis. Another finding showed that students tended to give up when communication broke down rather than retrying or repeating the command, which is essential given the study's autonomous and natural setting. The authors concluded more training and support could have increased chances for modified output in these circumstances. However, these results contrast with a study by Underwood (2017) in which primary school students used personal assistants for nine months. It was found that even when a smart speaker couldn't comprehend a command, students didn't give up; instead, they rephrased their responses so that they might be understood.

One of the more apparent advantages of smart speakers for language learning appears to be improved learner autonomy, enabling additional possibilities for meaningful interaction in the target language and allowing for listening and speaking practice in a less stressful environment (Wallace, 2015). In particular, AI speakers appear to be beneficial in developing speaking skills, notably pronunciation (e.g., Dizon, 2020; Obari *et al.*, 2020). AI speakers allow students to obtain valuable listening and speaking practice outside the classroom, resulting in greater learner autonomy (Dizon & Tang, 2020). The results of our three case studies corroborate this claim. Although engagement with a human speaker is preferable, some students may be uncomfortable speaking in the target language to others or have limited opportunity to converse with another L2 speaker outside of formal settings. As a result, a smart speaker could be an excellent language tool for self-learning.

Although prior research shows virtual assistants have a high rate of L2 speech comprehension (e.g., Moussalli & Cardoso, 2019), some studies reveal weaknesses, casting some doubt on their ability to interpret languages (e.g., Dizon, 2017; Moussalli & Cardoso, 2016; Underwood, 2017). These studies have shown that students have trouble understanding and being understood by Alexa, which is not surprising considering that virtual assistants were initially designed for native speakers. However, even for adults with clear pronunciation, the voice activation interface can be tricky (Metz, 2017). Selak (2017) emphasizes the importance of controlling expectations when introducing the Echo to students—the device will not be able to understand and respond to all questions, and students should not expect it to. But there is the hope that with improved speech recognition, this problem will eventually be naturally corrected.

Because these devices must always be in listening mode to reply to users, voice assistants and smart speakers raise security and privacy problems (Charleton, 2018). A third of smart speaker owners are worried about handing their personal and financial information to a voice-activated gadget (Wharton, 2018). Smart speakers may pose a real threat to privacy because the personal assistant listens in on what is spoken in the house. However, despite the risk of losing privacy, two-thirds of owners say they would not abandon their devices, and over 40% of owners consider their smart speakers a necessary tool in their daily lives (Charlton, 2018). Nonetheless, smart speaker companies should adequately address privacy and security concerns for the devices to be used in the classroom.

The few studies carried out on the use of AI speakers to enhance L2 learning have been mainly limited to small-scale investigations. Although research on the application of smart speakers for L2 learning is still in its infancy, further studies with more subjects and varied L2 learning contexts would be helpful. Another area of inquiry might focus on learner and teacher training in utilizing smart speakers more effectively.

Acknowledgments

Soken Grant supported this work (2018~2021), JSPS KAKENHI, Grant in Aid for Scientific Research (C), 2019-2022. Grant Number: 19K00798.

References

Bekmyrza, K. (2019). Using chatbot to increase students' engagement in education process at high school. Retrieved from https://www.internauka.org/archive2/vestnik/11(61_2).pdf

Bibauw, S., François, T., & Desmet, P. (2019). Discussing with a computer to practice a foreign language: Research synthesis and conceptual framework of dialogue-based CALL. *Computer Assisted Language Learning, 32*(8), 827–877.

Bunyard, S. (2019). *Assistance from Alexa: The social and material benefits of the Internet of Things.* Retrieved from https://scholarcommons. scu.edu/cgi/viewcontent.cgi?article=1044&context=engl_176

Canalys. (2018). *Media alert: Smart speaker installed base to hit 100 million by end of 2018.* Retrieved from https://www.canalys.com/static/press_release/2018/090718%20Media%20alert%20Smart%20speaker%20installed%20base%20to%20hit%20100%20million%20by%20end%20of%202018.pdf

Charlton, A. (2018). Smart speaker adoption rate outpaces smartphones and tablets. *GearBrain.* Retrieved from https://www.gearbrain.com/smart-speaker-sales-in-us-2525669732.html.

Davie, N., & Hilber, T. (2018). *Opportunities and challenges of using Amazon Echo in education.* International Association for Development of the Information Society.

Dizon, G. (2017). Using intelligent personal assistants for second language learning: A case study of Alexa. *TESOL Journal*, 8(4), 811–830.

Dillon, T. (2018). Creating an Alexa-enabled textbook exercise: An easy approach to custom automatic speech recognition application. *KOTESOL Proceedings 2018*, 259.

Dizon, G. (2020). Evaluating intelligent personal assistants for L2 listening and speaking development. *Language Learning & Technology*, 24(1), 16–26.

Dizon, G., & Tang, D. (2020). Intelligent personal assistants for autonomous second language learning: An investigation of Alexa. *The JALT CALL Journal*, 16(2), 107–120. https://doi.org/10.29140/jaltcall.v16n2.273

Dodigovic, M. (2007). Artificial intelligence and second language learning: An efficient approach to error remediation. *Language Awareness*, 16(2), 99–113.

Frey, C.B., & Osborne, M. (2013). *The future of employment: How susceptible are jobs to computerisation?* Retrieved from https://www.oxfordmartin.ox.ac.uk/publications/the-future-of-employment/

Harari, Y.N. (2018). *21 lessons for the 21st century.* New York: Random House.

Jahan, H. (2017). Reshaping learning through artificial intelligence. *International Educational Applied Scientific Research Journal* 2(10), 8–10.

Juniper Research. (2017). *Amazon Echo & Google Home to reside in over 50% of US households by 2022, as multi-assistant devices take off.*

Retrieved from https://www.juniperresearch.com/press/press-releases/amazon-echo-google-home-to-reside

Kepuska, V., & Bohouta, G. (2018, January). Next-generation of virtual personal assistants (Microsoft Cortana, Apple Siri, Amazon Alexa and Google Home). In *2018 IEEE 8th Annual Computing and Communication Workshop and Conference* (CCWC) (pp. 99–103). IEEE. https://doi.org/10.1109/ ccwc.2018.8301638

Kessler, G. (2018). Technology and the future of language teaching. *Foreign Language Annals, 51*(1), 205–218.

Kinsella, B. (2020). Google Assistant actions grew quickly in several languages in 2019, matched Alexa growth in English. *Voicebot.* Retrieved from https://voicebot.ai/2020/01/19/googleassistant-actions-grew-quickly-in-several-languages-in-2019-match-alexa-growth-inenglish/

Kivunja, C. (2015). Teaching students to learn and to work well with 21st century skills: Unpacking the career and life skills domain of the new learning paradigm. *International Journal of Higher Education, 4*(1), 1–11.

Kurzweil, R. (2005). *The singularity is near: When humans transcend biology.* New York: Loretta Barrett Books Inc.

Metz, R. (2017). *Growing up with Alexa.* Retrieved from https://www.technologyreview.com/2017/08/16/149722/growing-up-with-alexa/

Moussalli, S., & Cardoso, W. (2016). Are commercial "personal robots" ready for language learning? Focus on second language speech. In S. Papadima-Sophocleous, L. Bradley, & S. Thouësny (Eds.), *CALL communities and culture–short papers from EUROCALL,* (pp. 325–329). Research-publishing.net. http://dx.doi.org/10.14705/rpnet.2016.eurocall2016.583

Moussalli, S., & Cardoso, W. (2020). Intelligent personal assistants: can they understand and be understood by accented L2 learners? *Computer Assisted Language Learning, 33*(8), 865–890.

Obari, H., Lambacher, S., & Kikuchi, H. (2020, June). Utilizing AI smart speakers to improve the English skills of Japanese university students. Paper presented at the *JALT CALL 2021 Conference: Remote Teaching and Beyond*, Aomori, Japan.

Obari, H., & Lambacher, S. (2014). Impact of a blended environment with m-Learning on EFL skills. In S. Jager, L. Bradley, E. J. Meima & S. Thouësny (Eds.), *CALL design: Principles and practice - proceedings of the 2014 EUROCALL Conference, Groningen, The Netherlands* (pp.

267-272). Research-publishing.net. https://doi.org/10.14705/rpnet.2014.000229

Popenici, S. A., & Kerr, S. (2017). Exploring the impact of artificial intelligence on teaching and learning in higher education. *Research and Practice in Technology Enhanced Learning, 12*(1), 22.

Richter, F. (2020). Smart speaker adoption continues to rise. Retrieved from https://www.statista.com/chart/16597/smart-speaker-ownership-in-the-united-states/

Russell, S. J. & Norvig, P. (2009). *Artificial intelligence: A modern approach* (3rd ed.). Upper Saddle River, NJ: Prentice Hall.

Selak, B. (2017). Amazon Alexa in the classroom. Retrieved from https://www.coolcatteacher.com/amazon-alexa-classroom/

Schwartz, E.H. (2019). 20 Alexa skills you should try. Voicebot. Retrieved from https://voicebot.ai/2019/12/25/20-alexa-skills-you-should-try/

Terzopoulos, G., & Satratzemi, M. (2019, September). Voice assistants and artificial intelligence in education. In *Proceedings of the 9th Balkan Conference on Informatics* (pp. 1-6).

Terzopoulos, G., & Satratzemi, M. (2020). Voice assistants and smart speakers in everyday life and in education. *Informatics in Education, 19*(3), 473-490.

Trilling, B., & Fadel, C. (2009). *21st-century skills: Learning for life in our times.* Hoboken, NJ: John Wiley & Sons.

Trivedi, N. (2018, October). ProblemPal: Generating autonomous practice content in real-time with voice commands and Amazon Alexa. In *E-Learn: World Conference on E-Learning in Corporate, Government, Healthcare, and Higher Education* (pp. 80-82). Waynesville, NC: Association for the Advancement of Computing in Education (AACE).

Tsinonis, T. (2018). How to use ICT in the classroom effectively: The technological blend. In A. Visvizi, M.D. Lytras, & L. Daniela (Eds.), *The future of innovation and technology in education: Policies and practices for teaching and learning excellence* (pp. 111-125). Emerald Publishing Limited.

Turing, A.M. (1950). Computing machinery and intelligence. *Mind, 49*, 433-460.

Underwood, J. (2017). Exploring AI language assistants with primary EFL students Research-publishing.net. In *EUROCALL 2017 Conference (Southampton, United Kingdom)*.

Wagner, T. (2014). *The global achievement gap.* New York: Basic Books.

Wagner, T. (2016). *7 Survival skills*. Retrieved from https://www.linkedin.com/pulse/7-survival-skills-tony-wagner-summarized-tweets-jim-vanides/

Wallace, L. (2015). Reflexive photography, attitudes, behavior, and CALL: ITAs improving spoken English intelligibility. *CALICO Journal, 32*(3), 449–479.

Wharton, S. (2018). Many consumers still concerned about smart-home devices. eMarketer. Retrieved from https://www.emarketer.com/content/tbd

Wooldridge, M. (2009). *An introduction to multiagent systems*. Hoboken, NJ: John Wiley & Sons.

7
Socialization in telecollaboration: The smart use of WhatsApp to develop social presence in the HI-UB project

Olivia Espejel
Pilar Concheiro
Joan-Tomàs Pujolà

Introduction

This mixed methods study focuses on the identification and analysis of social presence (Garrison, 2009) in the interaction established during the development of a language learning task based on the "smart" use of WhatsApp. This digital task is the second one of the HI-UB telecollaboration project amongst learners of Spanish from the University of Iceland (HI) and pre-service teachers from the University of Barcelona (UB). The task aims for the HI students to practise the language and for the UB pre-service teachers to create a climate of confidence, to maintain social relations trying to consolidate a sense of belonging to a language learning community and to explore mobile instant messaging (MIM) as a pedagogical tool.

Literature Review

The HI-UB telecollaboration project offers language learners the opportunity to engage in authentic language practice with native speakers and also offers pre-service teachers a unique opportunity to experience and reflect on the teacher's role in digital learning contexts and to develop teachers' telecollaborative competences (O'Dowd, 2015; Vinagre, 2016). This project also aims to train participants' digital communicative competence and develop intercultural skills through collaborative digital tasks. It is precisely the collaborative feature that helps to develop the sense of belonging to a community of learning, and therefore, fostering opportunities for meaningful interaction and socialization of participants who are physically and culturally apart is vital for task success (Albá Duran *et al.*, 2020).

The Community of Inquiry (CoI) (Garrison, Anderson, & Archer, 2000) is a suitable framework on which to base our telecollaboration objectives and as a starting point of our analysis since this model emphasizes the relevance of the social aspect of learning. The CoI framework includes three presences, Cognitive, Teaching and Social, as key elements in the configuration of an online learning community. Cognitive presence accounts for the construction of meaning through sustained reflection and discourse. Teaching presence is related to the design and facilitation of the other two presences (Rourke, Anderson, Garrison, & Archer, 2001). Social presence (henceforth SP) is defined as "the ability of participants to identify with the community (e.g., course of study), communicate purposefully in a trusting environment, and develop interpersonal relationships by way of projecting their individual personalities" (Garrison, 2009, p. 352), thus, being this last presence essential for group cohesion and key to the task under the study.

Rourke *et al.* (1999) established three categories of SP which are found in the interaction of a learning community:

- Affective: expression of emotions, use of humour, self-disclosure
- Interactive: ability to manage conversational threads according to the channel features
- Cohesive: linguistic indicators of group cohesion like vocatives, inclusive pronouns, etc.

The indicators of these SP categories help us identify which are more relevant to achieve more social and interpersonal interactions within a learning community.

Within digital communication contexts, SP is also related to digital propinquity, also referred to as electronic propinquity (Korzenny, 1978) or virtual propinquity (Perry & Ricca, 2006), which implies developing a sense of proximity, nearness, and presence in any digital communication environment. In addition, the notion of rapport management (Spencer-Oatey, 2008) is a relevant issue to understand how SP is maintained as it focuses on building social relationships in interaction beyond the linguistic strategies used by interlocutors. Spencer-Oatey (2008) identifies three factors that influence interpersonal rapport: face sensitivities (the recognition of personal qualities and identity), sociality rights and obligations (what people judge as appropriate in a given context), and interactional goals (whether the interaction is transactional or oriented to social relation).

The specific features of MIM are prone to developing different degrees of SP that can help build the necessary digital propinquity for a relaxed atmosphere for language practice and maintain harmonious social relations. SP can be shown in different ways that allow participants to speak openly about their lives, preferences and opinions, to use humour, and to show empathy and nearness: sharing pictures, using emojis or GIFs, engaging in multimedia communication or providing internet links, among others. The discourse combinations of visual aids that can be used on WhatsApp such as photos, videos and animated GIFs together with voice-recorded files provide an enriched multimodal discourse that should be analysed from an internet pragmatics perspective (Yus, 2019) to interpret the personal and social implications of the messages. These multimodal elements go beyond the learning of a particular language as GIFs, memes, stickers, emojis among others have entered the realm of global intercultural communication. Herring and Dainas (2017) refer to these graphical communication devices as "graphicons" which function as propositions within messages or as stand-alone turns in conversational exchanges. For instance, the use of emojis, adding emotions, irony or jokes, has to be accounted for to help language learners be effective within this type of digital communication. Moreover, emojis are also clear indicators of SP in MIM and can lead to increased social connectedness and create closer interpersonal social relationships (Hseih & Tseng, 2017; Riordan, 2017). Therefore, how they are used can influence the type of social interaction that one wants to establish with their MIM interlocutors.

The benefits of MIM for language learning have been studied to develop students' communicative skills such as speaking (Andujar & Cruz, 2017), reading (Gutiérrez-Colón *et al*., 2013) writing (Andujar, 2016; Martínez Parejo, 2016) listening (Fauzi & Angkasawati, 2019), and also language systems such as vocabulary (Bensalem, 2018). Research has also focused on the use of WhatsApp for language learning beyond the in-class time (Tragant *et al*., 2021) to implement dynamic assessment on vocabulary and grammar (Andujar, 2020), to increase students' motivation (Alamer & Al

Khateeb, 2021) or to explore pragmatic competence in a cross-cultural project (García-Gómez, 2020). Much remains to be learned about the affordance of MIM for language teacher education and as a means to develop a language learning community within a telecollaboration project.

When designing any telecollaboration learning experiences teachers need to ensure that SP does emerge during collaborative tasks through a careful design of the educational experience. Furthermore, SP in telecollaboration has been found to foster and support the Teaching and Cognitive presences (Espejel, 2017) which enables meaningful social interactions amongst language learners. The WhatsApp task analysed in this study tries precisely to foster elements of SP that can ensure student engagement in a telecollaboration project, in which the distance, either physical and cultural, should be shortened or overcome in a digital environment.

Research Questions / Objective

The main objective of this study consists of analysing the social presence in the interactions that took place on WhatsApp during task 2 of the HI-UB telecollaboration project. To achieve this general objective, we seek to answer the following questions:

- What kind of activities do the pre-service teachers propose their partners to carry out via WhatsApp?
- How is social presence developed in the WhatsApp interactions through these activities?
- How do participants make the most of the affordances of WhatsApp in the learning activities to achieve the telecollabo- ration goals of teaching and learning a foreign language while developing an online learning community?

Methodology

Context

In the 2019–2020 edition of the HI-UB telecollaboration project 15 students (12 females, three males) who enrolled in a Spanish conversation course from the University of Iceland took part in this study; 12 of them were Icelandic, two Erasmus students, one from Italy and the other one from France, and one student came from the USA. The group was quite heterogeneous regarding their educational background, as this is an elective subject which students from different degrees at HI can enrol. The HI students' age ranged from 21 to 69. They had a B1 level according to the Common European Framework of Reference for Languages (European Council, 2001), and there was a Spanish heritage speaker among those with an Icelandic nationality. By contrast, the pre-service teachers from the UB were 24 in total (15 females, nine males): 18 were Spanish, one was from Morocco, one Colombian, one Canadian, one from Serbia and one from the USA. They were between 20 and 40 years old. Although most of them were native speakers of Spanish, three of them with a different L1 had a C2 level in Spanish. The telecollaboration project is the core activity for the assessment of the subject "ICT for language teachers" in the master's degree "Training of Teachers of Spanish as a Foreign Language."

In the first task of the HI-UB telecollaboration project, participants from both universities had provided a video using Flipgrid to introduce themselves and a subsequent video conference meeting to get to know each other (Concheiro, Espejel, & Pujolà, 2021). The second task, that was carried out using WhatsApp, lasted one week and allowed them to keep knowing each other, to lower possible negative emotions that could have arisen during the first video conference meeting and to interact in a different digital communication channel. For this task, the pre-service teachers at the UB were in charge of planning the learning activities which helped them to explore all the possibilities that this MIM app could offer as a didactic tool to foster interaction and language learning. The pre-service teachers had to devise a minimum of three micro tasks using WhatsApp, taking into account their HI partners' needs and interests to help them develop their digital communicative competence in Spanish. Teacher trainers at the UB encouraged them to take advantage of the multimodal affordances of the app to serve their pedagogical aims. To organise the WhatsApp groups, participants were divided into nine groups of three participants and three groups of four.

Data collection and analysis

Data collection took place after the task and pre-service teachers firstly had to download the WhatsApp conversations in txt format. As the multimodal elements such as audios, videos, GIFs or photos had to be downloaded separately, they were sent to researchers in separate files. To prepare all the data for the analysis, a description of the multimodal elements was added to the texts of the interactions. Moreover, for ethical reasons, all personal information such as phone numbers was erased and names were reduced to initials (name and university). Finally, the activities that were suggested by the pre-service during Task 2 were classified according to three general teaching objectives (see Table 7.1). After the classification of the activities a content analysis was applied to identify the categories of social presence based on an adaptation of the SP indicators by Rourke *et al.* (2001) (see Table 7.2) and each intervention was tagged using ATLAS.ti. The tagging process was conducted by the three researchers independently and they then compared the results to reach an agreement to assure a higher reliability of the coding process.

All the participants in the HI-UB telecollaboration project were also asked to write a reflection expressing their opinions and feelings about what they learnt and how they felt while carrying out this task using WhatsApp. Whereas students from HI emailed their reflections to their teacher, the UB participants wrote their reflections in their own e-portfolio about the activities they planned and how their HI partners reacted to them. They were specifically asked to describe the pedagogical use of the app they deployed: what kind of multimodal elements they used, which of these they fostered, what strategies they used to trigger interaction, and how they corrected their partners. The data from the participants' reflections were tagged to identify instances where they reflected how they had handled SP in the task.

Results

The types of activities that the pre-service teachers proposed their partners to undertake in Task 2 via WhatsApp are classified according to the following three general learning objectives: linguistic, sociolinguistic and conversational, the latter being divided into two subcategories of open and present topics. Table 7.1 shows the classification of the 40 activities found in the data with the examples for each category.

Table 7.1 *Types of activities on Task 2 via WhatsApp.*

Type	Objectives	Examples
Linguistic (n=13)	Eliciting vocabulary, specific language structures or practicing pronunciation.	Writing sentences in Spanish from a series of emojis. Recording audios saying tongue twisters. Self-correcting mistakes.
Sociocultural (n=4)	Based on film knowledge, traditional riddles or proverbs	Solving popular riddles. Guessing film titles from a series of emojis. Guessing sayings and proverbs from a series of emojis.
Conversational: open topics (n=7)	Conversations that revolve around personal interests but do not focus on the time that conversation is taking place	Selecting a place where they would like to travel and explaining why. Sharing funny or cute pictures. Recommending a series, a book and a song to participants.
Conversational: present topics (n=16)	Typical conversations of instant messaging that focus on what's going on at that present moment	Recording an audio about how their weekend is going. Explaining how their day is going on. Sharing pictures of their weekend.

The most frequent activities are conversational with an emphasis on topics that are relevant at the moment of the interaction, such as sharing pictures of the weekend or finding out what plans they had for that day. This conversational type is the most common in a MIM channel in which interlocutors talk about topics that are meaningful for them at the moment of the interaction. These interactions help participants to deal with meaningful personal topics providing opportunities for self-disclosure, for developing digital propinquity, and thus building a more cohesive learning community. The second most frequent activities refer to linguistic aspects of learning Spanish, which may seem logical as pre-service teachers try to help their partners learn the language by suggesting activities that help practising specific language structures or reflect on metalinguistic knowledge. The sociolinguistic type and the open topic conversations occurred to a lesser extent. Both groups of conversational activities logically tend to provide longer interactions compared to the linguistic and sociocultural ones. In general, all the activities prompt participants to take action in an informal and relaxing manner.

Regarding the instances of social presence in the WhatsApp interactions, this study identified three types of categories. Table 7.2 includes some examples of the SP categories adapted from Rourke *et al.* (2001) identified in our data.

Table 7.2 *Examples of SP categories on the WhatsApp task.*

Category	Indicators	Examples
Affective	Expression of emotions, use of humour, self-disclosure.	**G1_2 (1)** R (UB): [Photo of Z (UB) and R (UB) in the street hugging and smiling to camera] **G4_1 (1)** T(HI): Este finde yo estaba en Reykjavík, visitando mis amigas 😊 **G5_1 (2)** D (HI) <Audio: Pues hoy no he sacado ninguna foto porque tenía que estudiar. Me desperté a las ocho y media, desayuné, me duché y empecé estudiar porque tenía el examen de historia japonese a las tres de la tarde hoy. Y luego me volví a casa y ahora estoy haciendo esta presentación. Es un tema libre y elegí de hablar sobre Koby Briant porque era mi jugador preferido por eso me gustaría hacer algo sobre él porque se murió la semana pasada y por eso de verdad estoy un poco triste pero creo que va a ser una cosa bonita por el jueves esto.>
Interactive	Ability to manage conversational threads: asking questions, opening new threads, turn taking and indicators such as greetings and goodbyes.	**G1_1 (1)** I (UB) ¡Me parece genial! ¿Quieres empezar tú, A (UB)? **G5_1 (1)** N (UB) : Buen día, D
Cohesive	Politeness, appreciation and indicators of group cohesion.	**G4_1 (1)** D (UB): 😊 😊 😊 😊 muy bien T!! D (UB): Qué rápida! Luego te decimos algo más, pero está superbien!!! 😊 **G1_1 (2)** M (HI): Hahah muy bueno actividad!

Multimodality in WhatsApp interactions is also a common feature in MIM communication and manifested in diverse formats: audio, video, images, GIFs, etc. The role of multimodal elements in our data is very relevant as they strengthen SP in different ways. For example, emojis are a novel way to communicate messages beyond emotions with different pragmatic functions (Catamutto & Vela Delfa, 2019; Sampietro, 2019) and are used in a wide range of ways to develop SP as can be observed in the examples provided in Table 7.3.

Table 7.3 *Use of emojis that show SP.*

Category	Indicator	Example
Affective	Humour	G4_1 (2) AM (UB): Jajajajajajaja una imagen vale más que mil palabras 😊
	Emotions	G3_1(2) J (HI) 😊 😊 😊 J (HI): Me Gusta el trailer! Yo quiero ver pronto
	Empathy	G4_1 (2) A (UB): Totalmente, así me siento yo cada mañana de lunes a viernes 😊
	Playful use of language	G6_1 (2) H (UB): Tengo escamas no soy 🐟 tengo 🐾 no soy 🐕 ..
Interactive	Greetings and goodbyes	G6_1 (2) H (UB): Buenos días 😊
		G3_1 (3) J (HI): Buenas noches 🌙 😊 😊
	Turn-taking	G1_1 (1) A (UB): Sí empiezo yo 😊
Cohesive	Courtesy	G1_2 (3) C (HI) Gracias ❤ 😊
		G5_1 (3) M (UB): No te preocupes 😊
	Appreciation	G3_1 (5) N (UB): 😊 😊 😊 😊 muy bien!!

All participants in the project used a large number of emojis in their WhatsApp conversations, which is quite common in MIM interactions. They appear in different formats as a stand-alone messages or accompanied by other emojis (😊 😊) to form complete semantic syntagms and, in other cases, they are repeated (😊 😊 😊 😊) for emphasis purposes. They are also used before or after text (😊 😊 😊 😊 very well !! / Yes I will start) with different pragmatic functions and communicative effects. As

Table 7.3 shows, their use reflects instances of SP belonging to the three categories under study: affective, interactive, and cohesive, and sometimes their use can be classified into more than one category.

GIFs are also present, but to a lesser extent than emojis, and are used in our data to react to a previous intervention or as a substitute for an answer. In an activity to guess the plot of a mystery story, a language learner uses a GIF with a phatic function (showing SpongeBob and Patrick Star thinking), so their partners can quickly realise that she is in the process of solving it. In another instance of the activity, another GIF is used as a substitute for a written message. Instead of providing the written answer of the task, the GIF illustrates the hypothesis that solves the mystery of the story, adding a humorous touch to her reply.

Another relevant multimodal component is the use of audios and videos. In some activities pre-service teachers asked learners to record specific audios and videos about themselves and their personal lives and routines. These multimedia resources provide, on the one hand, oral practice and on the other, a great amount of personal information with elements of non-verbal communication such as intonation patterns, hesitations, giggles, etc. which in turn reinforce a sense of propinquity and interpersonal rapport.

Photos also reinforce textual communication in MIM. This is not an exception in our data in which a photo is the core of the activity and acts as the main trigger for the conversation. This is the case in group G4_1 when sharing a cute picture of a cat triggers the conversation about their own pets. Also, in the same group the sharing of a picture of their favourite place in town ends in an exchange of advice for a future trip to the partner's town. Another instance in which photos are powerful communicative resources in MIM is when in group G2_1 an HI student tells that her favourite film is "La vita è bella" and her UB partner answers some interventions later with a picture of a famous scene of the film, showing appreciation and interest. That image also has a phatic function as it reminds the interlocutor that the conversational thread is still open despite the fact that other threads have been started.

In regard to SP categories identified in the analysis, Table 7.4 illustrates the instances of SP categories for each group of participants. The cohesive category is the more salient of the UB interactions, as pre-service teachers usually encouraged and praised their partners during or after an activity, followed closely by the affective category. UB pre-service teachers had to lead and manage the learning activities and engage their HI partners so they needed to resort to different ways of expressing SP to achieve these goals. Similarly, the affective category is the main SP used by HI participants in their interventions as a way to support their personal information they were asked to provide. In general, the frequency of instances in Table 7.4 shows the friendly environment that was created with lots of affective and cohesive instances for each group that contribute to consolidate a sense of belonging to the telecollaboration learning community.

Table 7.4 *Instances of SP categories in the interventions.*

Categories	HI (n=15)	UB (n=24)
Affective	89	118
Interactive	19	57
Cohesive	52	124

When analysing the categories of SP according to the type of activity proposed (see Table 7.5), some relevant differences are revealed regarding the frequency of categories.

Both types of conversational activities trigger more instances of affective SP than other categories since these activities lead to longer interactions and increase the opportunities for self-disclosure and affection. Whereas with activities that focus on linguistic and sociocultural objectives, the cohesive SP is more frequent because the interaction in these activities includes the positive feedback provided by UB pre-service teachers as indicators of group cohesion.

When analysing the interventions in more detail to find out how participants develop a language learning community, the SP is key to fostering different opportunities of interaction. Similar activities such as in Examples 1 and 2 have very different outcomes in each group. A highly recurring type of activity classified as conversational asks students to show photos and talk about them. This MIM activity potentially gives rise to a lot of affective social presence, but sometimes pre-service teachers do not take full advantage of this conversational activity to build interpersonal rapport.

Table 7.5 *Instances of SP categories by activity types.*

Categories	Conversational present topics	Conversational open topics	Linguistic	Sociocultural
Affective	114	50	31	12
Cohesive	78	29	45	24
Interactive	42	15	14	5

Example 1 *Group 6.1. Activity 1. Extract 14:07-15:36.*

#	Time	SP Category[a]	Participant	Interventions
1	14:07	int	H (UB)	Holà I (HI) 😊
2	14:37	coh	H (UB)	H (UB): Este es el grupo en el que vamos a trabajar juntos: tú, E (UB) y yo
3	14:56	coh	I (HI)	Muy bien 😊
4	15:03	coh	H (UB)	Qué tal va el día?
5	15:04	afe	I (HI)	Bien, acabo de llegar a Hveragerði (el pueblo donde vivo) y estoy esperando a que mis hijos terminen el cole
6	15:06	afe	E (UB)	Qué tal el tiempo por ahí?
7	15:07	afe	I (HI)	Lleva lloviendo desde ayer y queda poca nieve, pero mucho hielo 😬
8	15:07	-	I (HI)	Ahora hace 6 grados
9	15:07	afe	I (HI)	<foto de un aparcamiento con un poco de nieve en el asfalto y niebla al fondo>
10	15:08	afe	H (UB)	Aquí hace buen tiempo 😀
11	15:08	afe	H (UB)	<foto del cielo azul entre edificios>
12	15:09	afe	E (UB)	Cuidado con el hielo, que como te resbales te puedes dar un buen tortazo! Aunque seguro que vosotros ya estáis acostumbrados por allí 😊
13	15:09	afe	I (HI)	Hay tanta neblina aquí, que no se ven ni las nubes 😬
14	15:09	coh	I (HI)	Me da envidia tu foto 😊
15	15:36	coh	H (UB)	Y la tuya también 😊 da ganas de hacer el Tubing o el Snowboard 🎿

Note. [a]Coding: Affective (afe), Cohesive (coh), Interactive (int).

Example 1 shows missing opportunities for group cohesion and for showing propinquity. In this example, a pre-service teacher opens the conversation in intervention 1, with a greeting and a polite question about how the day is going. After the greetings, in intervention 6, E (UB) asks about the weather in Iceland, opening a new conversational thread. There is some affectivity in the use of humour in intervention 12 when E (UB) talks about slipping on ice, however this comment goes unnoticed or, at least, gets no reaction. Furthermore, the personal information given by the HI participant in intervention 5 does not give rise to a further inquiry about HI participant's life through questions such as, "What is your town like? Is the school far from your home?" among other possible questions. Finally, we see that the cohesive dimension related to politeness is very present in interventions 4 *(how is your day?)*, 14 *(I envy your picture)* and 15 *(I envy yours)*. Although they include all the polite indicators of SP appropriate for a MIM interaction, there is a lack of more affective moves that affects negatively the development of digital propinquity and interpersonal rapport in this conversation.

In contrast, the conversation in Example 2 in group 4_1 has a similar structure, but develops quite differently.

Example 2 *G4.1. Activity 1. Extract 13:47- FD14:08.*

#	Time	SP Category[a]	Participant	Intervention
1	13:47	(int) (afe)	A (UB)	Por cierto, chicas, ¿cómo fue vuestro fin de semana? Aquí en Barcelona hizo un tiempo de lujo, ¡soleado y más de 20º! Yo aproveché para ir a la playa 😎
2	13:49	(afe)	A (UB)	<adjunto:foto calle, palmeras, cielo azul>
3	13:49		A (UB)	<adjunto: foto playa>
4	13:49		A (UB)	<adjunto: foto cielo despejado>
5	13:50	(afe)	A (UB)	El agua está aún demasiado fría para bañarse, pero había algún valiente que se atrevió a bañarse 😊
6	13:50	(int)	A (UB)	¿Vosotras qué hicisteis?
7	15:03	(coh)	M (HI)	Es hermoso! Estoy celosa
8	15:04	(afe)	M (HI)	En cuanto a mí, festejé (aquí es una foto de mi amigo habiendo festejado demasiado)
9	15:04	(afe)	M (HI)	<foto de un chico en la nieve con los brazos en el aire en posición de alegría>
10	15:05		M (HI)	Y el tiempo también fue agradable en Islandia, entonces salí a caminar
11	15:05	(afe)	M (HI)	<adjunto: foto vistas nevadas de cascada semicongelada>
12	17:58	(int) (afe)	A (UB)	Se nota jaja

13	17:59	(coh)	A (UB)	Wow, ¡qué pasada!
14	17:59	(coh) (int)	A (UB)	Es muy bonito. ¿Ese sitio está cerca de donde vives?
15	18:43	(coh)	AM (UB)	😊
16	18:49	(coh) (afe)	AM (UB)	Qué maravilla! Es precioso!! Por donde yo vivo apenas se ve nieve, aunque depende de la zona 😊
17	18:53	(afe)	M (HI)	Tengo que tener el bus durante 30 minutos !
18	18:53	(afe)	M (HI)	Aquí no hay un día sin nieve 😊
19	18:55	(coh) (afe)	T (HI)	Aaa Alberto es difícil ver tus fotos 😊 ¡Estoy muy celosa jeje!
20	18:57	(afe)	T (HI)	Este finde yo estaba en Reykjavík, visitando mis amigas 😊
21	19:15	(afe) (int)	AM (UB)	<adjunto: GIF Jack Nicholson congelado>
22	19:16	(coh) (int)	AM (UB)	Qué bien!! Y qué sueles hacer por Reikiavik? 👀
23	19:17	(afe)	AM (UB)	<adjunto: foto A.M tomando un cóctel en un bar>
24	19:20	(coh)(int)	A (UB)	Bastante cerca entonces. Qué suerte tienes 😊
25	19:23	(int)	A (UB)	La verdad es que se estaba de miedo, ¡ojalá hiciese siempre ese tiempo!
26	09:17	(afe)	T (HI)	La razón principal por la que voy allí es para visitar mis amigas. También tuve que asistir clases en la escuela y hacer algunas compras 😊 😊
27	09:20	(afe)	T (HI)	No hay tanta nieve en Reikiavik como en Akureyri donde vivo yo 😊 😊
28	09:20	(afe)	T (HI)	<adjunto: foto de calle nevada y oscura. Se adivina la silueta de un coche bajo la nieve.>
29	09:21	(afe)	T (HI)	<adjunto: foto de nieve y un agujero por el que se distingue el exterior>
30	12:44	(coh) (afe)	AM (UB)	Ay, dios mío! Tu coche está todo cubierto de nieve! 😱 😱 😱 Qué faena
31	14:07	(coh)	A (UB)	😱 😱 😱
32	14:08	(coh)	A (UB)	Imagino que no fue fácil arrancar el coche ese día, ¡madre mía!

Note. [a]Coding: Affective (afe), Cohesive (coh), Interactive (int).

In this example, the photo sharing implies more personal information than the instances in Example 1. There is also humour included in interventions 8 and 9, where the HI participant shows a picture of a friend "celebrating too much," implying that he had a few drinks. This humorous intervention gets a reply in intervention 12 (with a *ja, ja*, the Spanish onomatopoeia for laughter). In addition, the UB participants take the opportunity to inquire about personal issues such as in intervention 22 *(What do you usually do in Reykjavík?)*. Finally, although the cohesive dimension is present in interventions 30 *(Oh, my God! Your car is covered in snow! That sucks!)*, 31 *(emojis that mean to be shocked)* and 32 *(I guess it wasn't easy starting the car that day, oh my!)*, these examples are related more to empathy than to politeness. These varied interventions, which participants take advantage of, demonstrate a greater development of digital propinquity and engagement in the task as they use different approaches to foster affective SP.

The qualitative analysis of the reflective texts also reveals the participants' perception of SP in the MIM task and its usefulness for a pedagogical use to practise language. During the task in group 4_2, after carrying out a couple of conversational activities, pre-service teachers come up with a linguistic activity that consists of asking the HI participant to try to correct her mistakes in the previous activities. Although this self-correction activity could be a way to make her feel uneasy, in her reflexion, F (HI) said:

> *In this task I wasn't as nervous as in the first one.*

This is likely due to the fact that a) the MIM channel is less demanding than a video conference meeting and perceived as more informal and less intimidating, b) she has talked to her partners previously and thus, developed some trust, or c) the first two conversational activities with her UB partners on WhatsApp helped her to feel comfortable. She also mentioned:

> *I really liked the opportunity to correct my own mistakes because I think it is one of the best ways to learn.*

Having that opportunity to self-correct proves useful for her as she had the chance for metalinguistic reflection which she considers as part of the learning objective of the Whatsapp task.

Moreover, D (HI) in group 5.1 reflects on the characteristics of the MIM activities and how they fit both the language learner's needs and the communication channel. He comments that UB partners focused on one of his main learning objectives, and also highlights how the conversation flows naturally and that the friendly atmosphere helped him feel relaxed and safe:

> *We carried out the second task **entirely** on WhatsApp, **focusing on one of my main objectives:** to practice conversation (oral and/or written) on topics that concern everyday life, in order to improve my*

> *vocabulary with colloquial expressions that I will include later in the course of reflection. It's very interesting to see how **everything is developing in a simple and natural way, as if it were just chatting with friends or acquaintances**. This **avoids pressure or fear of making mistakes, as you don't feel judged directly.** I therefore have the opportunity to "carry out" the task without particular anxiety and, subsequently, **to review and think about the work done and any mistakes made.***

This view is matched with N (UB)'s reflection that describes how he and his UB partner chose activities that fit naturally on WhatsApp, taking into account their HI partners' needs analysed in the first task of the project:

> ***The objectives of the activities carried out were formulated in line with the needs and preferences indicated by D (HI) during the first video conference.** He explained to us that he would be interested in improving his oral and written skills and that, furthermore, he sees this project as an ideal opportunity to expand his repertoire of set phrases and colloquialisms. Hence, M (UB) and I decided to set the main objective of **promoting oral and written communication on everyday topics using informal and colloquial language.***

The third participant in this group, M (UB) also comments that he and his UB partner specifically chose "natural conversations on WhatsApp":

> *Here comes the first challenge: What activities do one design that can be meaningful and at the same time, harmonize with the characteristics of WhatsApp? Should we propose typical language activities or create something that tunes better with WhatsApp? Since we wanted him to talk about his routines, we decided to **stick to common use of WhatsApp conversations and be more informal.***

The use of multimodal elements on WhatsApp and the generation of digital propinquity is highlighted by participant D (UB), from group 5_2. She states that they use emojis to express emotions and get closer to one another:

> We and T (HI) have taken advantage of the emoticons to **create a feeling of closeness and express emotions,** for example she has not hesitated to add the emoticon of a face sweating before a linguistic structure that was difficult for her or to say thank you using emojis like smiling faces or even hearts. **Emojis have allowed us to provide feedback in an effusive way** through emojis like the applause one, the hand with the thumb up, and many smiley faces as well. **The experience has been very interesting and smooth!**

And T (HI), her partner from Iceland, says that she liked working with emojis in the activities that had been specifically prepared for her:

> **They proposed activities specially designed for me.** They asked me what I had done last weekend and we used the audio feature for that. They also sent me some emoticons and asked me to tell them a story using them as a prompt. It was a bit difficult, but **I liked the activity.**

Furthermore, in regards to the multimodal communication elements, the reflection of C (HI) from group G1_2 makes it clear the importance of these elements to generate a fun, safe environment and, in addition, to select the more appropriate GIF involved a cognitive effort as described in the following example.

> R (UB) commented on my GIFs with an emoji which I understood as a sign of her liking them. **Finding the right GIFs is also a lot of fun.** My group partners don't use GIFs but they use emojis a lot.

> There is something else that I found interesting and this is that Z (UB) managed to record a drum roll sound before providing the answer to the mystery story. **That was super cool.**

These reflections on the task illustrate that SP is perceived as an essential part of the successful interaction using WhatsApp and key to achieving a cohesive language learning community and demonstrating the smart use of this MIM.

Application to Smart CALL

This study of the use of WhatsApp in a telecollaboration project reveals the importance of using technology in a meaningful way that takes advantage of the MIM features to develop participants' digital communicative competence and build the necessary SP to create an entrusting language learning community. In our context, WhatsApp is both the medium and the resource for language practice and for the professional development in CALL teacher training. In addition, it has proved to be an excellent tool to develop digital propinquity among each group of participants. The use of technology in itself does not provide any smart CALL. In fact, it is the meaningful pedagogical aim of the task that makes it smart.

In the design process of any telecollaboration project, it is essential to plan consciously how to foster SP to facilitate collaborative work. SP should function as a cohesive way to develop a safe learning environment and to create the right climate to provide a meaningful educational experience. One of the common objectives of both groups of participants in the second task of the HI-UB telecollaboration project was precisely to achieve that cohesion so all participants could feel relaxed and responsible in the respective roles they were assuming in the project. This behavioural expectation associated with roles influence their interpersonal rapport (Spencer-Oatey, 2008) and directly affects the group cohesion that is key for the success of the development of the telecollaboration project.

The WhatsApp task in our data sample seems to achieve its pedagogical objectives since the SP is perceived in all the types of activities proposed by the pre-service teachers and, all SP indicators for all three categories are present in the interaction of both groups of participants. Furthermore, in their reflections participants describe how the conversations have occurred naturally in a friendly and relaxed learning climate. It is precisely this relaxed climate that has a positive impact on the learning process of the target language which HI students explicitly refer to in their reflections.

UB pre-service teachers have proposed activities that foster higher instances of SP taking advantage of the affordances of WhatsApp. In fact, the type of activities that have been carried out the most times are conversational activities and the most frequent within this group are those that favour and promote a feeling of naturalness within the MIM conversations that go beyond the formal interactions outside the classroom. This WhatsApp task is part of a telecollaboration project within a formal course and as in Tragant *et al.*'s context (2021) the task blurs the boundaries between the formal and the informal learning, which provides extra language practice that should be constantly encouraged by using instances of SP.

Regarding our data, SP appears to be a key factor for developing interactive tasks in a digital environment (as seen in Example 2 above) and determines the level of student engagement: the more engaged students are in a task, the more they show SP in their interactions, and the other way round. In fact, they feed back to each other. MIM interactions which foster SP allow for more meaningful practice with a personal component. Indeed, the intrinsic multimodal elements that can be used on WhatsApp play a relevant role when it comes to expressing SP. The graphicons of emojis, GIFs, videos, photos and audios were used by both groups of participants to support their SP in the three described categories: affective, interactive and cohesive. Specifically, the elements that have been used the most and with the greatest variation in terms of their pragmatic value are emojis. In that matter, Sampietro (2019) points out that emojis are closely related to politeness and social rapport which are common CMC features in Spanish. Unlike García-Gómez (2020), in our data no evidence of *hostile interactions* can be found, neither pragmatic failures that lead to misunderstandings between native and no native speakers, nor critical incidents regarding differing cultures-of-use (Fuchs, 2019; Thorne 2003). Therefore, WhatsApp can be considered in our telecollaboration context as an appropriate digital tool to develop communicative competence in general and digital pragmatic competence in particular.

Out of the three categories of SP, the affective one is particularly interesting with regard to the development of the objectives of the task. As seen in example 2, empathy is key to engaging interlocutors and providing greater opportunities for group cohesion and hence, for more language practice. Empathy is understood here as "an affective response to the apprehension or comprehension of another person's emotional state, eliciting feelings similar to those of the other person, essentially matching their state" (Bockarova, 2016). In consequence, being empathic in the interaction works effectively as a factor to increase engagement, reciprocity, interpersonal rapport and closeness.

Both groups of participants achieve their learning goals through activities that involve close collaboration. In particular, the work carried out by pre-service teachers while planning and managing the activities on

WhatsApp was complex since they had to assume different roles: as teachers, as native or highly competent language models through their interactions, as expert users of MIM technology since they were encouraged to take advantage of the communicative and pedagogical potential of WhatsApp, and as partners in a telecollaboration project. Therefore, the management of this second task by pre-service teachers required the smart implementation of multiple skills helping them to put into practice multiple teaching competencies for their professional development. With this WhatsApp task pre-service teachers are engaged in experiential learning (Vinagre, 2017) which facilitates an understanding of what telecollaboration for language teaching and learning entails.

In parallel, HI students benefit from the opportunity to focus on those aspects of second language learning that they find most interesting or challenging by means of interacting with native or highly competent speakers. The high amount of SP in the conversations, the informal style characteristic of the MIM environment and the personalization of the activities result in high levels of satisfaction that are manifested in the reflections of the HI participants. Whereas most activities are conversational and pre-service teachers tend to provide implicit feedback to their partners, a teaching strategy closely related to SP, there are also a significant number of linguistic activities. From those types of activities, the third activity in group 4_2 as detailed above, develops a smart pedagogical approach in which the learner is the centre of the learning process. Contrary to the approach reported in Andujar's study (2020), in which corrective feedback was provided by the teacher, the pre-service teacher in this case offers the learner the chance to correct herself, prompting to develop a metacognitive self-reflection. This activity proves particularly interesting because it coincides with HI participant's beliefs on corrective feedback and also fosters learner autonomy.

Although in this study we have focused on the importance of SP in MIM interactions, the other two aspects of smart CALL delineated in this book are intrinsically linked. The WhatsApp task also focuses on personalization as UB pre-service teachers are the ones who have to decide the more meaningful activities for their HI partners. The more meaningful the learning activity, the more likelihood of task success since meaningfulness is going to influence their partners' engagement in the activities. The suggested activities by pre-service teachers in all cases have taken into account their HI partners' interests in relation to the topics introduced and the level of the language they should focus on to make the activities attainable. Regarding contextualisation, the WhatsApp task has also prompted pre-service teachers to be aware of the limitations and affordances of the sociocultural, educational, and geotemporal context (Colpaert, 2021) in which the task is taking place. In their reflections, pre-service teachers report identified tensions and challenges they encountered when they had to face how to deal with digital communication when you have never met a student in person, how to deal with a different educational culture, how to engage learners so they feel at ease practising the language in an online environment and how learners could respond emotionally to their suggested learning activities.

The results of this mixed methods study must be interpreted with caution and a number of limitations should be borne in mind such as the small sample size and the specific cultural background of the participants. Showing closeness and social rapport in virtual exchange CMC are culturally dependent. Therefore, future research, if replicating the study, should consider whether it provides similar results when applying the same type of tasks with participants of different cultural backgrounds from this study.

Conclusion

This small-scale study reveals that the participants of the HI-UB telecollaboration project carried out a "smart" use of WhatsApp to develop the necessary SP for the task to be successful. This pedagogical aim is achieved through a careful design of the task in which participants have the chance to exploit the affordances of MIM for educational purposes. The success of the task is also a consequence of the participants' effort to take advantage of the learning opportunities that the project offers. Moreover, the results of the analysis of SP in the WhatsApp interactions shed light on the importance of the affective category to develop group cohesion and social rapport in a telecollaboration project. The experiential learning that pre-service teachers have gone through has helped them to reflect on the smart use of a MIM and to understand the importance of SP in technology-enhanced language learning and teaching.

References

Albá Duran, J., Oggel, G., Espejel, O., & Pujolà, J.T. (2020). Factores de éxito de un proyecto de telecolaboración en el contexto de enseñanza y aprendizaje de segundas lenguas. *Culture Crossroads, 15,* 31–60. http://www.culturecrossroads.lv/pdf/281/en

Alamer. A., & Al Khateeb, A. (2021). Effects of using the WhatsApp application on language learners motivation: a controlled investigation using structural equation modelling. *Computer Assisted Language Learning.* Advance online publication. https://doi.org/10.1080/09588 221.2021.1903042

Andujar, A. (2016). Benefits of mobile instant messaging to develop ESL writing. *System, 62,* 63–76. https://doi.org/10.1016/j.system.2016. 07.004

Andujar A., & Cruz-Martínez, M. (2017). Mobile instant messaging: Whatsapp and its potential to develop oral skills. *Comunicar, 50,* 43–52. https://doi.org/10.3916/C50-2017-04

Andujar, A. (2020). Mobile-mediated dynamic assessment: A new perspective for second language development. ReCALL, *32*(2), 178–194. https://doi.org/10.1017/S0958344019000247

Bensalem, E. (2018). The impact of Whatsapp on EFL students' vocabulary learning. *Arab World English Journal, 9*(1). https://dx.doi.org/10.24093/awej/vol9no1.2

Cantamutto, L., & Vela Delfa, C. (2019). Emojis frecuentes en las interacciones por Whatsapp [Frequent emojis in WhatsApp interactions]. *Círculo de Lingüística Aplicada a la Comunicación, 77,* 171–186. https://doi.org/10.5209/CLAC.63282

Colpaert, J. (2021, July 9). The role of open data and corpora in the contextualization of the language learning and teaching process. [Keynote presentation] TeLLT & CoLLT 2021 conference, Hong Kong. Retrieved from https://www.eduhk.hk/lml/telltcollt 2021/

Concheiro, P., Espejel, O. & Pujolà, J.T. (2021). Flipgrid, a video app for virtual exchange, propinquity, and language learning. *Perspectiva, 39*(1), 1–17. https://doi.org/10.5007/2175-795X.2021.e70066

Council of Europe. (2001). Common European framework of reference for languages: Learning, teaching, assessment. Press Syndicate of the University of Cambridge. Retrieved from https://rm.coe.int/16802fc1bf

Espejel, O. (2017) Las presencias social, docente y cognitiva en la comunicación mediada por computadora en un proyecto de telecolaboración interuniversitario en el ámbito de español lengua extranjera [The social, teaching and cognitive presence in CMC in an interuniversity telecollaboration project in the context of Spanish as Foreign Language] [Doctoral dissertation, Universitat de Barcelona]. TDX. Retrieved from https://www.tdx.cat/handle/10803/482210#page=9

Fauzi, I., & Angkasawati, P. (2019). The use of listening logs through WhatsApp in improving listening comprehension of EFL students. *Journal of Applied Linguistics and Literature, 4*(1), 13–26. https://doi.org/10.33369/joall.v4i1.6773

Fuchs, C. (2019). Critical incidents and cultures-of-use in a Hong Kong–Germany telecollaboration. *Language Learning & Technology, 23*(3), 74–97. http://hdl.handle.net/10125/44697

García-Gómez, A. (2020). Learning through WhatsApp: Students' beliefs, L2 pragmatic development and interpersonal relationships. *Computer Assisted Language Learning*. Advance online publication. https://doi.org/10.1080/09588221.2020.1799822

Garrison, D.R. (2009). Communities of Inquiry in Online Learning. In P. Rogers, G. Berg, J. Boettcher, C. Howard, L. Justice, & K. Schenk (Eds.), *Encyclopedia of Distance Learning, Second Edition* (pp. 352–355). IGI Global. https://doi.org/10.4018/978-1-60566-198-8.ch052

Garrison, D.R., Anderson, T., & Archer, W. (2000). Critical inquiry in a text-based environment: Computer conferencing in higher education model. *The Internet and Higher Education, 2*(2-3), 87–105. https://doi.org/10.1016/S1096-7516(00)00016-6

Gutiérrez-Colón, M., Gimeno, A., Appel, C., & Hopkins, J. (2016). Improving Learners' Reading Skills Through Instant Short Messages: A Sample Study Using WhatsApp. In A. Gimeno, M. Levy, F. Blin, & D. Barr (Eds.), *WorldCALL: Sustainability and computer-assisted language learning (Advances in digital language learning and teaching* (pp. 266–281). http://dx.doi.org/10.5040/9781474248327.0027

Herring, S.C., & Dainas, A.R. (2017). "Nice picture comment!" Graphicons in Facebook comment threads. In *Proceedings of the Fiftieth Hawai'i InternationalConference on System Sciences (HICSS-50)*. IEEE.

Retrieved from http://ella.slis.indiana.edu/~herring/hicss.graphicons.pdf

Hseih, S.A., & Tseng, T.H. (2017). Playfulness in mobile instant messaging: Examining the influence of emoticons and text messaging on social interaction. *Computers in Human Behavior, 69*, 405-414. https://doi.org/10.1016/j.chb.2016.12.052

Kozernny, F. (1978). A theory of electronic propinquity: Mediated communication in organizations. *Communication Research, 5*(1), 3-24. https://doi.org/10.1177/009365027800500101

Martínez Parejo, R. (2016). Desarrollo de la competencia escrita en la enseñanza de lenguas extranjeras a través del uso de dispositivos móviles. [The development of written competence in teaching foreign languages through the use of mobile devices]. *Revista Complutense de Educación, 27*(2), 779-803. https://doi.org/10.5209/rev_RCED.2016.v27.n2.48317

O'Dowd, R. (2015). The competences of the telecollaborative teacher. *The Language Learning Journal, 43*(2), 194-207. https://doi.org/10.1080/09571736.2013.853374

Perry, W.M., & Ricca, A.V. (2006). Instant messaging: Virtual propinquity for health promotion networking. *Global Health Promotion 13*(3), 211-212. https://doi.org/10.1177/175797590601300309

Riordan, M.S. (2017). Emojis as tools for emotion work: Communicating affect in text messages. *Journal of Language and Social Psychology, 36*(5), 549-567. https://doi.org/10.1177/0261927X17704238

Rourke, L., Anderson, T., Garrison, D.R., & Archer, W. (2001). Assessing social presence in asynchronous, text-based computer conferencing. *Journal of Distance Education, 14*(3), 51-70. Available from https://www.learntechlib.org/p/92000/

Sampietro, A. (2019). Emoji and rapport management in Spanish WhatsApp chats. *Journal of Pragmatics, 143*, 109-120. https://doi.org/10.1016/j.pragma.2019.02.009

Spencer-Oatey, H. (2008). Face, (Im)Politeness and rapport. In H. Spencer-Oatey (Ed.), *Culturally speaking: Managing rapport through talk across cultures* (2nd ed.) (pp. 11-47). London: Continuum International Publishing Group.

Thorne, S.L. (2003). Artifacts and cultures-of-use in intercultural communication. *Language Learning & Technology, 7*(2), 38-67. http://dx.doi.org/10125/25200

Tragant, E., Pinyana, A. Mackay, J., & Andria, M. (2021). Extending language learning beyond the EFL classroom through WhatsApp. *Computer Assisted Language Learning*. Advance online publication. https://doi.org/10.1080/09588221.2020.1854310

Vinagre, M. (2016). Developing teachers' telecollaborative competences in online experiential learning. *System 64*, 34–45. http://dx.doi.org/10.1016/j.system.2016.12.002

Yus, F. (2019). An outline of some future research issues for internet pragmatics. *Internet Pragmatics, 2*(1), 1–33. https://doi.org/10.1075/ip.00018.yus

8

Socialization in language learning: Topic modeling and bibliometric analysis

Xieling Chen
Di Zou
Haoran Xie
Gary Cheng

Introduction

With the advent of Web 2.0, interactive semiotic spaces supported by various social web tools promote the view of language as a social practice that characterizes different communities (Álvarez Valencia, 2016). Social media are "a group of Internet-based applications that build on the ideological and technological foundations of Web 2.0" (Kaplan & Haenlein, 2010, p. 61). They allow user-generated content to be created and exchanged. Characterized by promoting collaboration and interaction and linking cognitive and social processes, social media tools can engage learners in meaningful social interaction (Kimmerle *et al.*, 2015; Reinhardt, 2019). During the interaction, learners have rich opportunities to develop new literacies, experiment with translingual identities, and negotiate meanings to develop communicative competence, pragmatic competence, and knowledge of values, identities, and ideologies (Jin, 2018; Yeh & Swinehart, 2020). This is especially important in second language acquisition (SLA), where learners need frequent, authentic social interaction for language practice and usage (Lucas *et al.*, 2008).

Recognizing these benefits, educators are interested in integrating various social media tools into second language classrooms to promote learners' communication and collaboration and the sharing of learning materials. Affordances of social media's use in SLA include allowing authentic interaction and communication, promoting collaborative learning, reducing learning anxiety, providing immediate and personalized feedback, and improving learners' motivation and learning autonomy (Henry *et al.*, 2018; Yen *et al.*, 2015; Hattem, 2014; Junior, 2020). As a result, there is a growing interest in exploring learners' participation and language development facilitated by social media use. This study identifies research status, trends, and topics concerning socialization in language learning using a topic-based bibliometric methodology. Relevant literature on socialization in language learning from the Web of Science database was analyzed to understand where the research field has been and where it is going. We particularly focused on research questions such as "what technologies have been adopted to facilitate socialization in language learning?" and "what research topics have been investigated?" Because traditional manual coding and systematic reviews are prone to error and coding inconsistency when evaluating limited literature data, we integrated rigorous machine learning algorithms and statistical tests by using a topic-based bibliometric methodology. Such a methodology is smarter because it allows time-honored bibliometrics to mine large volumes of literature data. This research focuses on diverse aspects of socialization in language learning facilitated by social media use. These aspects include the top contributors (e.g., journals, subjects, countries/regions, and institutions), research topics and the dynamics of interest in topics. Results derived from our smart analysis provide insights into effective ways to advance smart computer-assisted language learning from a socialization perspective through scientific collaborations and the effective adoption of innovative technologies and analytical techniques.

Literature Review

Motivated by the "social turn" in SLA (Block, 2003, p. 3), several diverse socially driven theories or frameworks have emerged, including sociocultural theory, situated learning, and language socialization. Within these theories or frameworks, language development is a social phenomenon where social contexts are essential for understanding a second language

(Malerba Candilio, 2015). Language socialization includes "socialization through the use of language and socialization to use language" (Schieffelin & Ochs, 1986, p. 163). Social interaction mediates "the development of communicative competence and knowledge of values, practices, identities, ideologies and stances of the community" (Duff & Talmy, 2011, p. 98).

Since meaningful social interaction is necessary for SLA, language educators have attempted to incorporate various communicative practices into their classrooms (Reinhardt, 2019). According to Blake (1998), "technology can play an important role in fostering second language acquisition by electronically increasing learners' contact with a wide array of authentic materials" (p. 210). Online communities have become prevalent in SLA with their collaborative socializing and interactive nature (e.g., Warner & Chen, 2017; Ros et al., 2010; Anwaruddin, 2018; Fornara & Lomicka, 2019). Such a prevalence is mainly due to their capabilities to link cognitive and social processes and offer insights into how language is acquired via collaborative interaction (Malerba Candilio, 2015). Social media tools (e.g., blogs, instant messages, and social networking sites (SNSs) involve "a group of Internet-based applications that build on the ideological and technological foundations of Web 2.0" (p. 61). SNSs are social environments that allow SLA learners to exchange self-created content (Razak et al., 2013).

The affordances of social media in SLA are increasingly recognized (e.g., Sun, 2009; Arndt & Woore, 2018; Mompean, 2010; Miyazoe & Anderson, 2010; Jerónimo & Martin, 2021). Social media tools allow learners to share individual life experiences and work collaboratively in constructivist learning environments (Ou-Yang & Wu, 2017). They also encourage learners to build personal identities in social communities (Qian et al., 2018). Facebook's social nature benefits instructors and learners by promoting interactions among learners and between instructors and learners (Börekci & Aydin, 2020; Aydin, 2014). Thus, various social media tools are increasingly being combined into curriculums to support SLA in synchronous and/or asynchronous environments (Yilmaz & Keser, 2016). As a result, many studies in language education are available.

Previous studies have reviewed social media use in education. For instance, to explore "the role of social media in the higher education classroom (real and virtual)" (p. 60), Tess (2013) systematically reviewed relevant literature published until 2012. Their study indicated that while infrastructure supporting social media's utilization existed in many educational institutions, instructors were hesitant to adopt it as a pedagogical tool. Chugh and Ruhi (2018), who reviewed articles published between 2013 and 2016 focusing on Facebook's use in higher education, revealed increased use of Facebook. A recent review by Manca (2020) analyzed 46 studies in terms of pedagogical affordances and the benefits of social media tools for learning. They found that WhatsApp was well studied while limited studies about Instagram, Pinterest and Snapchat were available. Manca highlighted the need for larger samples of studies by extending the coverage to K-12 and other relevant contexts. Although these reviews have broadly advanced knowledge in the area, few studies have focused exclusively on social media use in language education. The present study fills this gap by summarizing extant literature concerning social media use for language education using rigorous machine learning algorithms and statistical tests, namely, a topic-based bibliometric methodology. Compared to traditional manual coding and systematic reviews, which are prone to error and coding inconsistencies when evaluating limited literature data, the topic-based bibliometric methodology is smarter. Although the bibliometric methodology has been popularly used in literature analysis in varied research areas, including CALL (e.g., Chen *et al.*, 2021; Goksu *et al.*, 2020; Jung, 2005; Lei & Liu, 2019). The integration of topic modeling allows time-honored bibliometrics to mine large volumes of literature. Thus, it enables a comprehensive understanding of the subject matter. This study focuses on top contributors (e.g., journals, subjects, countries/regions, and institutions), especially research topics and the dynamics of interest in topics. Findings from this methodology may help language educators see the potential for integrating social media into their classrooms. Accordingly, this study encapsulates research on social media's effective use for language education to date to uncover potential future research directions and pedagogical practices.

Methodology

Figure 8.1 illustrates the data search, screening, and analyses. We searched in the Web of Science (WoS) to collect the target literature using the following query:

(TS=(("social media" OR "social network*" OR "social software" OR "Twitter" OR "Facebook" OR "web 2.0" OR "Blog*" OR "YouTube" OR "WhatsApp" OR "Wikis" OR "Instagram" OR "Web log" OR "podcast*" OR "Webcast" OR "MySpace" OR "LinkedIn") AND ("literacy learning" or "language learning" or "second language"))) AND (Year of publication = till 2020) AND (Article type = journal articles)) AND (Language = English)

Our search generated 337 articles from which we isolated the following information: title, publication year, author(s) and institution(s), and abstract. We then manually screened for relevance based on the exclusion criteria presented in Figure 8.1. When screening the articles, we first looked at whether they were related to language learning. This step excluded 53 articles that were not directly related to language learning. We then checked whether articles included content about social media use for language learning; this step excluded another 74 articles without such details. We then assessed whether the remaining articles were based on original content, and this step excluded 67 reviews, survey studies, and position papers. This screening procedure left 143 relevant articles.

We then analyzed the 143 articles in terms of the following: annual distribution, journals, subject areas, contributors and research topics. For our analysis, we used descriptive statistics, bibliometric indicators, keyword frequency analysis, structural topic modeling (STM) (Roberts *et al.*, 2014), and the Mann-Kendall trend test. For topic modeling (Chen *et al.*, 2020; Chen *et al.*, 2021), we: 1) collected terms from titles, abstracts, and keywords, 2) assigned weights 0.4, 0.4, and 0.2 to terms from titles, keywords, and abstracts, 3) filtered terms by setting Term Frequency-Inverse Document Frequencies as 0.03, 4) selected topic models using exclusivity and semantic coherence criteria (see Figure 8.2 indicating the comparatively better performance of models with 14 and 16 topics), and 5) manually compared models with 14 and 16 topics based on representative articles and terms. The 16-topic model was selected. Two domain experts examined the statistical results to summarize topic labels.

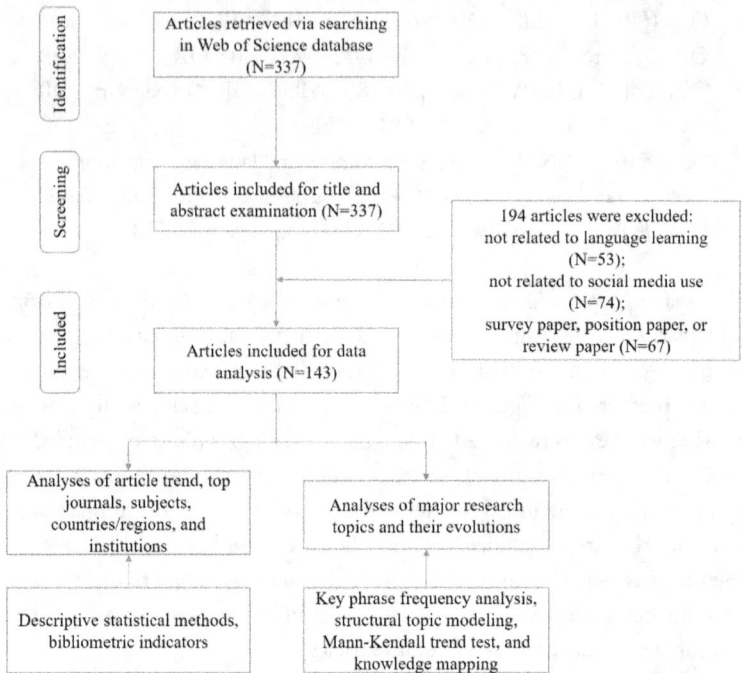

Figure 8.1 *Flowchart of data collection and analyses.*

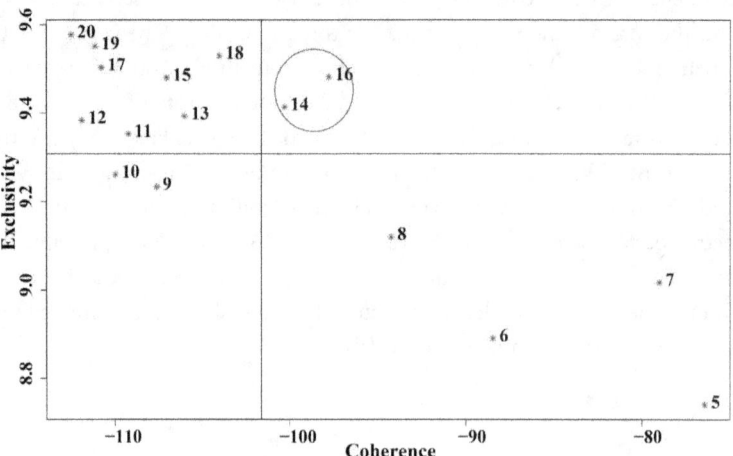

Figure 8.2 *Model selection.*

Results

Publication trends, top journals, subjects, and contributors

Figure 8.3 shows the annual trends, indicating three stages of development. From 2007 to 2013, the number of articles experienced a significant increasing trend. During 2013-2016, the frequency peaked at about 15-20. Subsequently, a slight decrease occurred, with the annual number hovering around 11.

The 143 articles were published in 42 journals. The top two journals (i.e., Language Learning & Technology and Computer Assisted Language Learning) (Figure 8.4) accounted for 32.17% of the 143 articles. Other important journals were ReCALL, Australasian Journal of Educational Technology, and System.

There were 17 WoS subject categories. The top three, ranked by article count (Figure 5), were Education & Educational Research, Linguistics, and Language & Linguistics. Several articles each also fell into Information Science, Psychology, and Computer Science.

There were 32 countries/regions and 159 institutions. Figure 8.6 presents the top 10 countries/regions with the most articles, among which the top three were the USA, Taiwan, and Spain. Figure 7 presents the top 12 institutions with the most articles. The top three were the City University of Hong Kong, the University of Hong Kong, and the National Kaohsiung University of Applied Sciences.

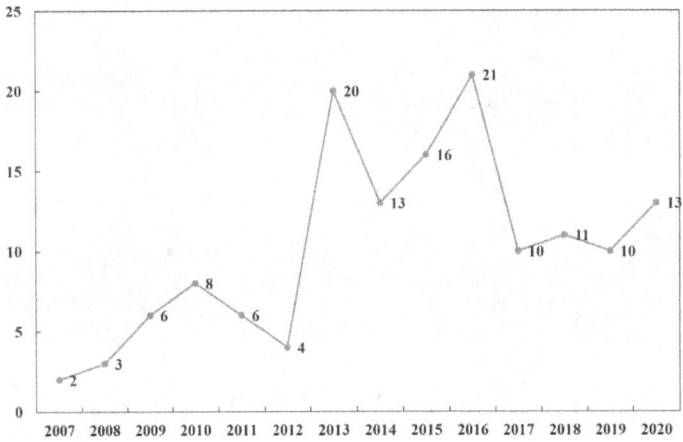

Figure 8.3 *Year-by-year analysis.*

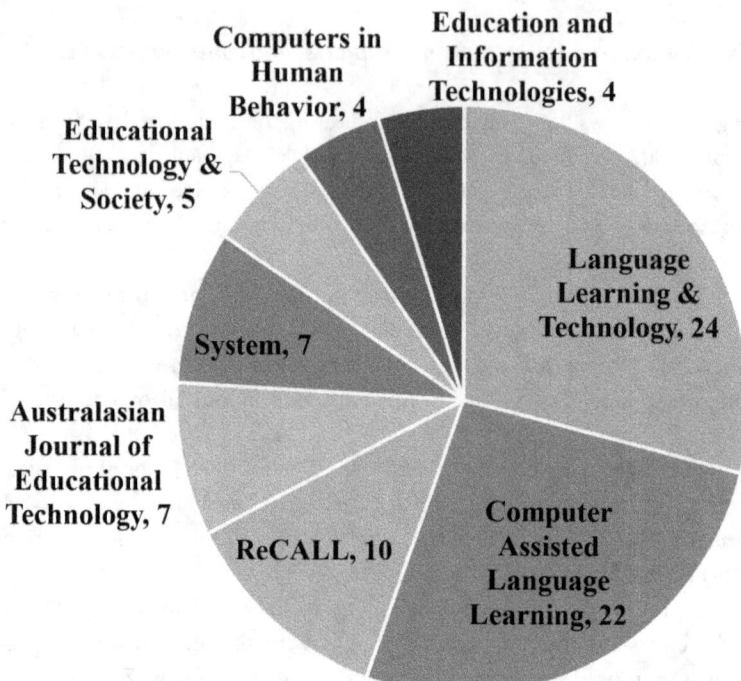

Figure 8.4 *Top journals.*

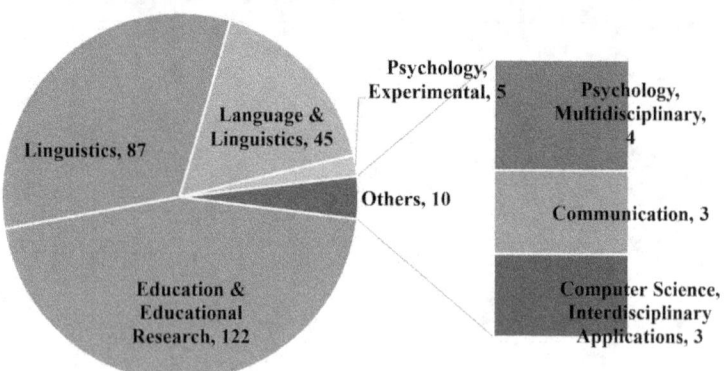

Figure 8.5 *Top subjects.*

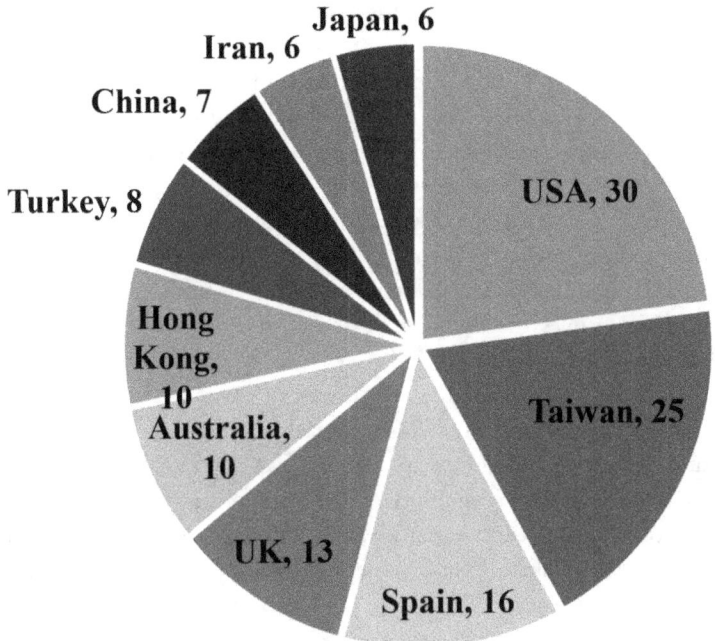

Figure 8.6 *Top countries/regions.*

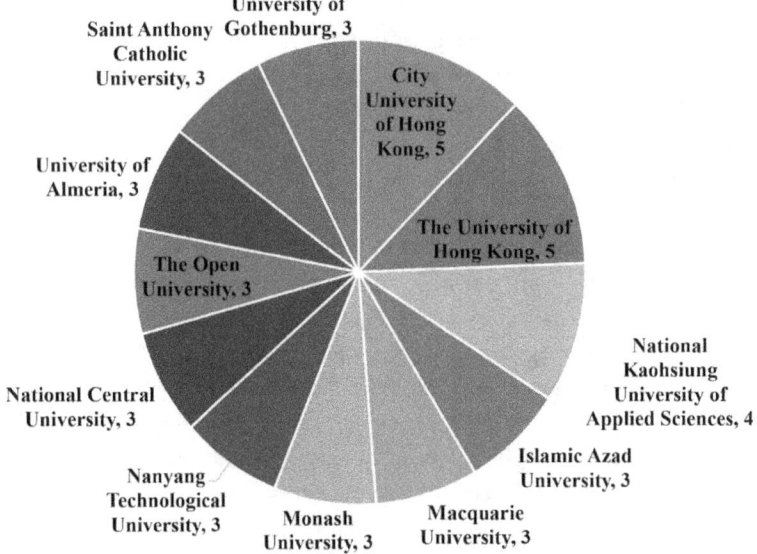

Figure 8.7 *Top institutions.*

Important terms and research topics

Figures 8.8 and 8.9 show the important terms during 2008-2015 and 2016-2020, respectively. Due to technological advances, the types and applications of technologies have increased. Figure 8.10 presents the STM results, and Figure 8.11 provides a year-by-year analysis of topic proportion. The two most popular topics were instant message-enhanced collaborative writing and podcasting for listening skills and pronunciation improvement. A trend test indicated that instant message-enhanced collaborative writing and seamless learning with social media received significantly increasing research interest.

These results indicate that diverse technologies such as computer-mediated communication (CMC), social media, wikis, audio-blogs, podcasts, multimedia, and telecollaboration were adopted throughout the years. Purposes for the applications of these technologies include facilitating socialized bilingual education to learn about the culture and acquiring primary language skills (e.g., listening, vocabulary, pronunciation, writing, and oral proficiency). There was an increasing prevalence of digital storytelling, voice blogging, digital games, and virtual worlds to facilitate socialized language learning among populations at various levels (e.g., high and elementary school students and pre-service teachers). Language was acquired or practiced through informal learning, online exchanges, and intercultural communication in authentic contexts. In terms of learning outcomes, social media tools commonly enhance language learners' motivation, literacy engagement, cultural adaptation, identity construction and social engagement.

Furthermore, analytical technologies such as social network analysis and learning analytics were increasingly adopted as time advanced, particularly in recent longitudinal studies. These analytical technologies have a common advantage in revealing the relations between diverse participants, variables, and factors involved during socialization in language learning.

Socialized language learning relates to self-regulated learning, situated learning, and task-based teaching. With a particular focus on personalized and smart language learning, learner cognition and affect embodied in interactions in meaningful ecologies and corrective feedback is increasingly concerned by language researchers and educators.

Figure 8.8 *Important terms during 2008–2015.*

Figure 8.9 *Important terms during 2016–2020.*

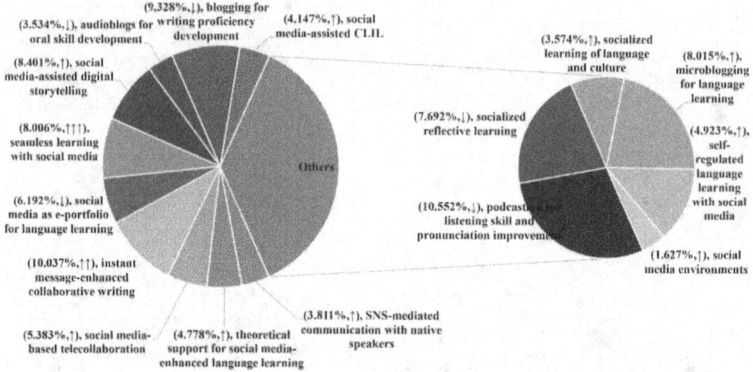

Figure 8.10 *Identified topics with suggested labels, topic proportions, and developmental trends.*

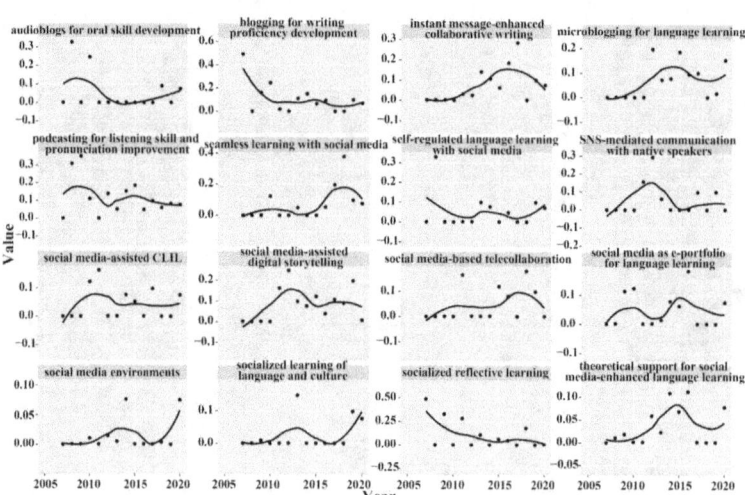

Figure 8.11 *Year-by-year analysis of the topic proportion.*

Application to Smart CALL

Implications from performance analysis

Our smart topic-based bibliometric analysis showed rapid growth of research outputs concerning socialization in language learning. This is in line with "the prospect of the evolution of computer-assisted language learning from a predominantly classroom-based entity into one that is free from time and space boundaries" (Stockwell, 2007, p. 365) brought by technological advances that permitted users to send and receive data (Stockwell, 2012). Socialization in language learning is increasingly becoming a research sub-field where disciplines such as linguistics, psychology, and computer science merge. This is consistent with Duff and Talmy's assertion (2011) that "language socialization has its theoretical roots in a variety of disciplines that are drawn on to different degrees by scholars doing second language or multilingual socialization research" (p. 97). This also aligns well with the idea of transdisciplinarity in CALL (Colpaert, 2018; Colpaert, 2004a) as "a new and effective way of language knowledge building [by] crossing boundaries between nations, disciplines and actors [with] a greater engagement between scientific and societal actors to develop more robust answers to complex societal challenges" (pp. 484-485) in language learning. Social media tools relate language learning to learners' daily lives to foster opportunities for target language use with other learners. By integrating language learning into everyday life, particularly in the form of "mediated communication" (Colpaert, 2004b), socialization appeared to enable second language learners to become "part of [the] social and cultural environment to engage in frequent and rich participation in second language life-worlds" (Wagner, 2015, p. 75).

Important technologies and issues during 2007-2012

Among the papers published in this period, the advent of podcasting was widely covered. With the expansion of broadband and wireless connectivity, podcasting has revolutionized access to media and education resources and become popular as a pedagogical instrument (Lee, 2009). Podcasting promotes flexibility and portability. It allows "on-demand deliverability" (Donnelly & Berge, 2006) and self-organization of learning (Chinnery, 2006). It enables time-shifting, multitasking, and dynamic and automatic audio/video file handling based on web syndication protocols

(Rosell-Aguilar, 2007). Due to podcasting's authentic content, language learning, as a discipline where audio recordings are typically integrated into learning activities, quickly became a beneficiary (Abdous et al., 2009; Stockwell, 2010). By "allowing students to easily and immediately access materials from a variety of sources and to engage with those materials where and when they please" (Beres, 2011, p. 94), podcasting draws learners into the target language's communicative world. It promotes contextualized language learning and immersion (Lord, 2008). When practicing speaking and language skills outside of class, learners can create their materials and immerse themselves in authentic listening to actively explore, observe, process, and interpret language (Rosell-Aguilar, 2007). By extending interactive communication beyond lecture experience (Abdous et al., 2012), podcasting augments learning motivation and engagement, promotes collaborative knowledge building, supports real learning, facilitates social presence and diminishes the sense of isolation.

Reflection or reflective learning was frequently mentioned in the literature during the period. This is because language structures are "reflective of and emergent from cultural, social, and ideological forms of knowledge that are learned in and through language" (Duff & Talmy, 2011, p. 95). According to Jordi (2011), reflection requires a learner to move beyond her framework of interpretation and socially constructed concepts to seek new perspectives. This is consistent with Wenger's social theory (1998) that learning has to occur in a context of social participation. In this sense, learning can occur first by socially partaking in community practices and then via individual meta-reflection. Another important concept in language socialization, learner autonomy, emphasizes the "reflective" capacity of learning or critical reflection (Hafner & Miller, 2011). According to Thorne (2003), online behaviors reflect contextually contingent "cultures of use". This fits well with experiential learning, which emphasizes learning through reflection on doing (Arnold & Paulus, 2010). Reflective practice is "the relationship between an individual's thoughts and action and the relationship between an individual and his or her membership in a larger collective called society" (Bartlett, 1990, p. 204). Colpaert (2006) suggested that CMC tools are promising for experiential learning. Communities of practice formed by SNSs are thus suitable platforms for the reflective practice among learners. According to language scholars and practitioners, social media tools facilitate personal identity development and learners' reflective learning processes, foster community unification, and promote learning performance through "individual knowledge construction and group knowledge sharing" (Liaw *et al.*, 2008, p. 951).

Important technologies and issues during 2013-2014

Alongside the increasing adoption of Web 2.0 in pedagogical practices for language education, during this period, there was a growing interest in wiki use to "enable users to create and edit subject-specific knowledge collaboratively within a shared and openly accessible digital space" (Wang, 2014, p. 383). Wikis provide meaningful interactions and authentic experiences with collaborative and interactive communication characteristics. Consistent with social-constructivist approaches, Wikis can promote online collaboration, facilitate interaction, share knowledge, exchange ideas, reflect on knowledge learned, and benefit learners in language skill development (Wang *et al.*, 2013). In wiki-based collaborative writing, scaffolding often occurs among learners when they work in groups. "[C]ollective scaffolding" in a social setting allows learners to achieve a better performance than when working alone, where the learners are both individually novices and collectively experts. This can guide learners to solve complex linguistic problems (Li, 2013).

Higher education is being revolutionized by increased computing power. These improvements include increases in wireless broadband access and advances in telecommunications and hardware technologies. In particular, significant drivers could be advances in mobile supercomputers that can perform real-time speech recognition and enhanced augmented reality that simultaneously provides high-bandwidth access to SNSs across formal and informal learning. Good examples of this are the ubiquity of learners' own devices and the employment of bringing your own technology programs across educational institutions (Song, 2014). These pedagogical innovations are a result of not only mobile proliferation but also concurrent socio-technological practices. Mobile learning is proven to enhance learning outcomes and develop higher-level learner autonomy in synchronous and asynchronous contexts (Ally & Tsinakos, 2014). Therefore, educators and curriculum designers gradually sought ways to promote sophisticated interactions in language learning via mobile social networks like WhatsApp and Line.

Blogs, which by nature are interactive, open, visual, asynchronous, and decentralized, are truly transformational technologies outperforming traditional CMC learning applications by enabling students to learn autonomously and collaboratively while simultaneously developing interactive connections with others (Zhang *et al.*, 2014). When blogs' pedagogical benefits, which enable learners to express emotions during learning and receive social or cognitive support from classrooms, were recognized, educators began integrating them into language classrooms (e.g., Lin *et al.*, 2014; Shen, 2013). With blogs as web publishing tools, learners search the Internet for appropriate words to express themselves and view the postings of others. Their worldviews are shaped in writing while interacting with and receiving feedback from real audiences and reflecting on their writing based on audience responses. Such practices enrich writing styles in terms of organization, paraphrasing and referencing, which assists interpretative and critical-thinking skill development and facilitates resource exchange and self-reflection (Vurdien, 2013).

Important technologies and issues during 2015-2016

In this period, an increasing number of social media tools, for instance, Facebook, blogs, chat, and Skype, were investigated (e.g., Jin, 2015; Özdemir, 2017; Terhune, 2016; Huang, 2015). Web 2.0 digital storytelling with interactive functions for crafting multimodal narratives was increasingly used in collaborative task/project-based learning in language classrooms allowing learners to discuss language problems and build collaborative target language knowledge. The increase in digital storytelling use based on social media tools was driven by the growing consensus about the benefits of student-produced materials. As these materials concentrate more on processing new lexical information, they can contribute to learners' comprehension enhancement and thus lead to higher retention (Liu & Chen, 2015). Consistent with the theory of social constructivism, interactions in digital storytelling activities contribute to higher mental function development. Similarly, Nishioka (2016) suggested that knowledge built via collaborative dialogue is "gradually internalized by the learner as individual knowledge and later used as a cognitive tool" (p. 41).

Assessment is intertwined closely with learning to pursue maximized opportunities to expand learners' Zone of Proximal Development (Tarighat & Khodabakhsh, 2016). There was increasing interest in e-portfolio assessment via SNSs in language learning, primarily written composition assessment. This popularity results from the rejection of traditional writing assessment methods where instructors use only one sample work to assess student writing. Alternative assessment using portfolios with a dual summative–formative role (Barrot, 2016) thus received increasing attention to promoting dynamic assessment, real-time feedback and online editing and drafting. In conjunction with advances in information and communication technologies, portfolio assessment shifts paper-based portfolios to e-Portfolios. E-Portfolio includes formative functions such as "showcasing and sharing learning artifacts, documenting reflective learning processes, connecting learning across various stages and enabling frequent feedback for improvements" (Yang *et al.*, 2016, p. 1276). It fits well with the new generation learning via e-mail, websites, and SNSs. This assessment mode allows more access to learners' work and triggers "peer feedback, collaborative learning, information exchange, and resource sharing" (Barrot, 2016, p. 288).

Negotiation of meaning contributes to promoting interaction essential for successful SLA and intercultural competence development (Jenkins, 2015). SNSs provide "real" social contexts where synchronous and asynchronous text, audio/video exchanges and conversations are accessible and promote learning by doing (Malerba Candilio, 2015). Learners can negotiate meaning in a target language and put their first and second language worlds into intercultural contact. Traditionally, to understand meaning negotiation and peer assistance on SNSs, researchers have to analyze learners' conversations in these spontaneous contexts mostly via manual dialogue coding. However, technological advances in automatic speech recognition show promise to not only facilitate students' practice and instructors' feedback for L2 conversations but also provide scaffoldings for students' dialogue interaction "by using, for example, an introductory video so that they know what to do in the dialog" (Van Doremalen *et al.*, 2016, p. 842). Negotiating meaning also occurs in form-focused instruction, "as a reaction to linguistic problems occurring incidentally during communicative activities." These activities commonly "incorporated more social, cultural, and sociocultural perspectives" (Nassaji, 2016, p. 36).

Language socialization is a popular concept in multilingual socialization and translanguaging research. In bilingual education, translanguaging, as a socio-educational process, allows learners to build and continuously alter their sociocultural identities and values using the linguistic signs for connections with audiences in community engagement (Creese & Blackledge, 2015). SNSs cover multilingual resource use shaped by "digital writtenness, access to the global mediascape...and orientation to networked audiences" (Androutsopoulos, 2015, p. 17). Multilingualism is thus highly valued in social media-mediated learning contexts; it allows learners to adopt identities as expert multilingual and engage in translingual practices by creatively expressing themselves using diverse language resources. Scholars increasingly recognized the importance of understanding language learners' translingual practices in online spaces beyond classrooms (Hafner et al., 2015).

Important technologies and issues during 2017-2018

There was increasing interest in audiobook use in language learning. Previously, although textual and video modalities were popular teaching tools, interactive audio for encouraging richer multimodal resource adoption was lacking. Building on multimodality theory and social semiotics focusing on social communication, interactive audiobooks can turn passive readers into the director[s] of a story by enabling learners to interact through sound (Marchetti & Valente, 2018).

Our review indicates increased use of social media to facilitate content and language integrated learning (CLIL). In CLIL, an additional language and a (content) subject are learned simultaneously. The prevalence of CLIL results from the demands for linguistic, communicative and intercultural competencies (Byram & Wagner, 2018). Social media tools are increasingly adopted to develop plurilingual and intercultural awareness. With the affordances of realistic situations for language development, these tools increase learners' motivation for learning languages by necessitating the use of the target tongue in real-life contexts.

Alongside the prevalence of flipped instruction in SLA is an increasing attempt to integrate social media tools into pre-class activities stimulating students to actively communicate and interact. A rich and ubiquitous learning environment constructed by online community-based flipped learning approaches allows instructors to interact more with learners on SNSs and develop better relationships with learners. Such an environment also enhances learners' critical thinking and collaborative relationships (Lin & Hwang, 2018). This combined strategy makes learners more responsible for their learning and promotes learner autonomy. This is consistent with the concept of the "active learner," "autonomous learning," and "collaboration" emphasized by language socialization (Malerba Candilio, 2015).

As language socialization promotes communicative and interactional competencies, interaction and communication are essential. In such communicative practices, explicit/implicit socialization via linguistic and social interactions are involved (Ochs & Schieffelin, 2017). This socialization is in line with communicative language teaching, which is characterized by the integration of authentic materials into learning activities, with "learner's personal experiences [used] as learning resources connect[ing] in-class and out-of-class language tasks" (Wong et al., 2017, p. 2). Communicative language teaching treats interaction as a language learning objective, where learners participate in and reflect on linguistic interactions in diverse contexts (Meier, 2017). Dynamic interactive behaviors (e.g., peer-to-peer interaction) and communication flow and patterns are thus important variables in communicative language teaching, especially with social media use. Examples include web-based collaborative writing (Yim & Warschauer, 2017), collaborative digital storytelling (Anderson et al., 2018), and telecollaboration for corrective feedback provision (Akiyama, 2017).

Important technologies and issues during 2019-2020

There is an increasing interest in self-regulation in social media-mediated language learning during this period, especially in collaborative learning contexts. This is consistent with the growth in the need to employ second languages in daily life to improve learners' skills in managing and self-regulating the learning process, resources, duties, and tasks necessary for achieving learning goals (Vattøy, 2020). Self-regulation is an important educational concept for explaining learners' language learning achievement. It consists of diverse variables like goal orientation, task-specific strategies, and metacognitive strategies. In computer-assisted collaborative learning, learners' regulatory behaviors contribute to effective and efficient collaboration. This is mainly due to a stronger sense of community (Hernández-Sellés et al., 2019). Consequently, scholars showed interest during this period in verifying the relationship between learners' self-regulation, mostly by using experimental designs. In these experimental studies, self-regulation is commonly treated as a multidimensional variable. It includes factors such as goal settings, task strategies, time management, help-seeking, and self-evaluation, and how learners value online collaborative learning (Su et al., 2019; Fouz-González, 2019).

An interesting trend during the period was the appearance of emotional valence in socio-emotional communication related to social media-mediated language learning research. In a networked society, as SNSs allow dynamic and flexible information to be shared through peer interaction, social media-mediated learning appeals to emotional, personal and affective aspects, with reflection resulting from emotional responses (Peeters, 2019). On the other hand, correctly identifying one's interlocutor's emotions is crucial in all types of human communication, including those on social media (Hautasaari *et al.*, 2019). However, this task is difficult in text-based CMC mediums due to unavailable nonverbal and vocal emotional cues (Coyle & Carmichael, 2019), and misunderstandings about a messages' emotional tones can happen due to inconsistencies in communicative norms (Hautasaari *et al.*, 2019). Nevertheless, the effective use of SNSs, multimodalities and modern technologies shows good potential for language instructors to interject emotions into online learning contexts to allow real-time emotional connections among learners outside of classrooms (Han, 2019).

Another noteworthy trend was the increasing number of longitudinal studies. Language learning is an enduring practice where learners constantly partake in learning and socialization activities and lifelong discursive practices to increase proficiency and communicate appropriately. In this sense, longitudinal perspectives are important for understanding learners' trajectories and ways of participating in social communities (Ishihara, & Takamiya, 2019). However, previously, such studies were limited. A notable longitudinal study by Liu *et al*. (2019) explored elementary learners' participation in a two-year digital storytelling activity facilitated by SNSs. Results suggested that the learners' oral proficiency and engagement in collaborative learning activities improved due to community features.

In addition to online games, podcasts and digital storytelling based on social media, there was a growth in the use of student-generated Quizlet flashcards that positively impacted SLA, particularly for vocabulary acquisition. The use of flashcards is in line with the increasing emphasis on learners' creation of their learning materials. They must focus on language and new lexical information processing. This contrasts with the long-existing tradition of teacher-created materials (Setiawan & Wiedarti, 2020). Previously, the advantages of accessible Quizlet flashcards for vocabulary learning were well noted in the literature and pedagogical practice. However, research was scarce on student-created podcasts' effects.

Bueno-Alastuey and Nemeth's study (2020) filled this gap by showing the positive effects of student-created Quizlet flashcards for vocabulary acquisition and personal practice outside classrooms.

Conclusion

Based on the results, there is a need for more investigations covering several aspects. Most studies investigating social media use for language education have adopted analytical methods based on manual coding or basic statistical methodologies such as factor analysis and regression analysis. However, advances in artificial intelligence are insufficiently exploited. These include deep learning and learning analytics that effectively encourage personalized learning, precision education and advanced statistical methodologies such as structural equation modeling. Accordingly, we recommend that language researchers and educators stay abreast of the latest technological trends and their potential to facilitate socialization in language learning. For example, as language socialization appeals to emotional, personal and affective aspects (Burdelski, 2019), the analysis of emotions and emotional variance can reveal how learners experience social media-mediated language learning. This can be done by using sentiment analysis and affective computing technologies. Another example is to use deep learning and machine learning algorithms together with dialogue analysis, especially for large datasets. By taking advantage of machine learning's computational power when involving big data, the efficiency of dialogue analysis can be facilitated by quickly and automatically coding dialogue content into variables of researchers' interests. Another line of research is learning analytics for promoting personalization in social media-mediated language learning. For example, learning dashboards can be integrated to visualize learners' online behaviors, based on which, instructors can provide personalized recommendations about learning strategies and resources to trigger effective interventions. Additionally, structural equation modeling is suitable to understand under what conditions interactions strengthen relationships between language learners. This advanced statistical technique is more powerful than regression analyses in measuring and analyzing the relationships of observed and latent variables. In particular, a combination of structural equation modeling with visualization techniques such as social network analysis can contribute to more detailed insights into smart and meaningful interactions among learners and between learners and instructors in SNSs (Kárpáti, 2009).

Pedagogically, language teaching instructors should explore ways to develop effective teaching strategies to guide learners to fully take advantage of social media's socialization functionality. Social media tools allow learners to acquire language and practice conveniently (Kent *et al.*, 2016). They also allow learners to decide what and how to learn. However, challenges can arise when learners have no idea how to handle their learning tasks or use social media appropriately. Additionally, too much liberty and freedom might bring undesirable results (Truong, 2016). Thus, instructors need to monitor learners' learning processes on social media and provide scaffolding when necessary while also considering individual preferences and learning styles. Another challenge is the inconsistencies between the openness and diversity of create-to-learn paradigms brought by SNSs and the structured learning formats in educational institutions (Mao, 2014). Thus, instructors should cautiously frame learning activities on SNSs and explicitly link learners' creativity to the syllabus's core content and learning goals.

A final suggestion concerns promoting discipline collaboration. Given that language socialization is an interdisciplinary area with theoretical roots across disciplines, collaboration between scholars from relevant areas should be strengthened to ensure that technological and pedagogical novelties meet the demands and challenges socialization faces in language education. Language learning is a long-term process (Liu *et al.*, 2019). In this sense, conducting longitudinal studies, which are presently relatively few, should be promoted to understand whether and how social media tools improve language learning and how learners participate in long-term activities.

References

Abdous, M. H., Camarena, M. M., & Facer, B. R. (2009). MALL technology: Use of academic podcasting in the foreign language classroom. *ReCALL*, *21*(1), 76–95. https://doi.org/10.1017/S0958344 009000020

Abdous, M. H., Facer, B. R., & Yen, C. J. (2012). Academic effectiveness of podcasting: A comparative study of integrated versus supplemental use of podcasting in second language classes. *Computers &*

Education, 58(1), 43–52. https://doi.org/10.1016/j.compedu.2011.08.021

Akiyama, Y. (2017). Learner beliefs and corrective feedback in telecollaboration: A longitudinal investigation. *System, 64*, 58-73. https://doi.org/10.1016/j.system.2016.12.007

Ally, M., & Tsinakos, A. (2014). *Increasing access through mobile learning.* Vancouver, BC: Commonwealth of Learning Press.

Álvarez Valencia, J. A. (2016). Language views on social networking sites for language learning: The case of Busuu. *Computer Assisted Language Learning, 29*(5), 853–867. https://doi.org/10.1080/09588221.2015.1069361

Anderson, J., Chung, Y. C., & Macleroy, V. (2018). Creative and critical approaches to language learning and digital technology: Findings from a multilingual digital storytelling project. *Language and Education, 32*(3), 195–211. https://doi.org/10.1080/09500782.2018.1430151

Androutsopoulos, J. (2015). Networked multilingualism: Some language practices on Facebook and their implications. *International Journal of Bilingualism, 19*(2), 185–205. https://doi.org/10.1177/1367006913489198

Anwaruddin, S. M. (2018). Teaching language, promoting social justice: A dialogic approach to using social media. *CALICO journal, 36*(1), 1–18. https://doi.org/10.1558/cj.35208

Arndt, H. L., & Woore, R. (2018). Vocabulary learning from watching YouTube videos and reading blog posts. *Language Learning & Technology, 22*(3), 124–142. https://doi.org/10125/44660

Arnold, N., & Paulus, T. (2010). Using a social networking site for experiential learning: Appropriating, lurking, modeling and community building. *The Internet and higher education, 13*(4), 188–196. https://doi.org/10.1016/j.iheduc.2010.04.002

Aydin, S. (2014). Foreign language learners' interactions with their teachers on Facebook. *System, 42*, 155–163. https://doi.org/10.1016/j.system.2013.12.001

Barrot, J. S. (2016). Using Facebook-based e-portfolio in ESL writing classrooms: impact and challenges. *Language, Culture and Curriculum, 29*(3), 286–301. https://doi.org/10.1080/07908318.2016.1143481

Bartlett, L. (1990). Teacher development through reflective teaching. In J.C. Richards & D. Nunan (Eds) *Second language teacher education* (pp. 202–214). Cambridge: Cambridge University Press.

Beres, D.L. (2011). Mobile-assisted language learning from the student perspective: Encouraging effective language learning strategies outside of the classroom. In *Academic podcasting and mobile assisted language learning: Applications and outcomes* (pp. 93–110). Hershey, PA: IGI Global.

Blake, R. J. (1998). The role of technology in second language learning. In H. Byrnes (Ed.) *Learning foreign and second languages: Perspectives in research and scholarship* (pp. 209–237). New York, NY: Modern Language Association.

Block, D. (2003). *The social turn in second language acquisition*. Washington, DC: Georgetown University Press.

Börekci, R., & Aydin, S. (2020). Foreign language teachers' interactions with their students on Facebook. *Computer Assisted Language Learning, 33*(3), 217–239. https://doi.org/10.1080/09588221.2018.1557691

Bueno-Alastuey, MC., & Nemeth, K. (2020). Quizlet and podcasts: Effects on vocabulary acquisition. *Computer Assisted Language Learning*, 1–30. https://doi.org/10.1080/09588221.2020.1802601

Burdelski, M. (2019). Emotion and affect in language socialization. In S.E. Pritzker, J. Fenigsen, & J.M. Wilce (Eds.), *The Routledge handbook of language and emotion* (pp. 28–46). New York: Routledge.

Byram, M., & Wagner, M. (2018). Making a difference: Language teaching for intercultural and international dialogue. *Foreign Language Annals, 51*(1), 140–151. https://doi.org/10.1111/flan.12319

Chen, X., Zou, D., Cheng, G., & Xie, H. (2020). Detecting latent topics and trends in educational technologies over four decades using structural topic modeling: A retrospective of all volumes of computer & education. *Computers & Education, 151*, 103855. https://doi.org/10.1016/j.compedu.2020.103855

Chen, X., Zou, D., Xie, H., & Su, F. (2021). Twenty-five years of computer-assisted language learning: A topic modeling analysis. *Language Learning & Technology, 25*(3), 151–185. http://hdl.handle.net/10125/73454

Chinnery, G. M. (2006). Emerging technologies. Going to the mall: Mobile assisted language learning. *Language Learning & Technology, 10*(1), 9–16. Retrieved from https://scholarspace.manoa.hawaii.edu/bitstream/10125/44040/1/10_01_emerging.pdf

Chugh, R., & Ruhi, U. (2018). Social media in higher education: A literature review of Facebook. *Education and Information Technologies, 23*(2), 605–616. https://doi.org/10.1007/s10639-017-9621-2

Colpaert, J. (2004a). Transdisciplinarity. *Computer Assisted Language Learning, 17*(5), 459–472. https://doi.org/10.1080/0958822042000319665

Colpaert, J. (2004b). From courseware to coursewear? *Computer Assisted Language Learning, 17*(3–4), 261–266. https://doi.org/10.1080/0958822042000319575

Colpaert, J. (2006). Toward an ontological approach in goal-oriented language courseware design and its implications for technology-independent content structuring. *Computer assisted language learning, 19*(2–3), 109–127. https://doi.org/10.1080/09588220600821461

Colpaert, J. (2018). Transdisciplinarity revisited. *Computer Assisted language Learning, 31*(5–6), 483–489. https://doi.org/10.1080/09588221.2018.1437111

Creese, A., & Blackledge, A. (2015). Translanguaging and identity in educational settings. *Annual Review of Applied Linguistics, 35,* 20–35. https://doi.org/10.1017/S0267190514000233

Coyle, M. A., & Carmichael, C. L. (2019). Perceived responsiveness in text messaging: The role of emoji use. *Computers in Human Behavior, 99,* 181–189. https://doi.org/10.1016/j.chb.2019.05.023

Donnelly, K. M., & Berge, Z. L. (2006). Podcasting: Co-opting MP3 players for education and training purposes. *Online Journal of Distance Learning Administration, 9*(3). Retrieved from https://www.learntechlib.org/p/193222/

Duff, P. A., & Talmy, S. (2011). Language socialization approaches to second language acquisition: Social, cultural, and linguistic development in additional languages. In D. Atkinson (Ed.), *Alternative approaches to second language acquisition* (pp. 107–128). New York: Routledge.

Fornara, F., & Lomicka, L. (2019). Using visual social media in language learning to investigate the role of social presence. *CALICO Journal, 36*(3), 184–203. https://doi.org/10.1558/cj.37205

Fouz-González, J. (2019). Podcast-based pronunciation training: Enhancing FL learners' perception and production of fossilised segmental features. *ReCALL, 31*(2), 150–169. https://doi.org/10.1017/S0958344018000174

Goksu, I., Ozkaya, E., & Gunduz, A. (2020). The content analysis and bibliometric mapping of CALL journal. *Computer Assisted Language Learning*. Advance online publication. https://doi.org/10.1080/09588221.2020.1857409

Hafner, C.A., Chik, A., & Jones, R. (2015). Digital literacies and language learning. *Language Learning & Technology*, *19*(3), 1–7. Retrieved from http://llt.msu.edu/issues/october2015/commentary.pdf

Hafner, C.A., & Miller, L. (2011). Fostering learner autonomy in English for science: A collaborative digital video project in a technological learning environment. *Language Learning & Technology*, *15*(3), 68–86. Retrieved from https://www.learntechlib.org/p/52231/

Han, Y. (2019). Memeing to Learning: Exploring meaning-making in a language-learning chat group. *Technology in Language Teaching & Learning*, *1*(2), 68–90. https://doi.org/10.29140/tltl.v1n2.191

Hattem, D. (2014). Microblogging activities: Language play and tool transformation. *Language Learning & Technology*, *18*(2), 151–174. Retrieved from http://llt.msu.edu/issues/june2014/hattem.pdf

Hautasaari, A., Yamashita, N., & Gao, G. (2019). How non-native English speakers perceive the emotional valence of messages in text-based computer-mediated communication. *Discourse Processes*, *56*(1), 24–40. https://doi.org/10.1080/0163853X.2017.1323184

Henry, M., Carroll, F., Cunliffe, D., & Kop, R. (2018). Learning a minority language through authentic conversation using an online social learning method. *Computer Assisted Language Learning*, *31*(4), 321–345. https://doi.org/10.1080/09588221.2017.1395348

Hernández-Sellés, N., Muñoz-Carril, P.C., & González-Sanmamed, M. (2019). Computer-supported collaborative learning: An analysis of the relationship between interaction, emotional support and online collaborative tools. *Computers & Education*, *138*, 1–12. https://doi.org/10.1016/j.compedu.2019.04.012

Huang, H. C. (2015). From web-based readers to voice bloggers: EFL learners' perspectives. *Computer Assisted Language Learning*, *28*(2), 145–170. https://doi.org/10.1080/09588221.2013.803983

Ishihara, N., & Takamiya, Y. (2019). Pragmatic development through blogs: A longitudinal study of telecollaboration and language socialization. In M. Khosrow-Pour (Ed.), *Computer-assisted language learning: Concepts, methodologies, tools, and applications* (pp. 829–854). Hershey, PA: IGI Global.

Jenkins, J. (2015). Repositioning English and multilingualism in English as a Lingua Franca. *Englishes in Practice*, *2*(3), 49–85. https://doi.org/10.1515/eip-2015-0003

Jerónimo, H., & Martin, A. (2021). Twitter as an online educational community in the Spanish literature classroom. *Foreign Language Annals*. *54*, 505–524. https://doi.org/10.1111/flan.12522

Jin, S. (2015). Using Facebook to promote Korean EFL learners' intercultural competence. *Language Learning & Technology*, *19*(3), 38–51. Retrieved from http://llt.msu.edu/issues/october2015/action2.pdf

Jin, L. (2018). Digital affordances on WeChat: Learning Chinese as a second language. *Computer Assisted Language Learning*, *31*(1–2), 27–52. https://doi.org/10.1080/09588221.2017.1376687

Jordi, R. (2011). Reframing the concept of reflection: Consciousness, experiential learning, and reflective learning practices. *Adult Education Quarterly*, *61*(2), 181–197. https://doi.org/10.1177/0741713610380439

Jung, U.O. (2005). CALL: Past, present and future—A bibliometric approach. *ReCALL*, *17*(1), 4–17. https://doi.org/10.1017/S0958344005000212

Junior, R.C.G. (2020). Instanarratives: Stories of foreign language learning on instagram. *System*, *94*, 102330. https://doi.org/10.1016/j.system.2020.102330

Kaplan, A.M., & Haenlein, M. (2010). Users of the world, unite! The challenges and opportunities of Social Media. *Business Horizons*, *53*(1), 59–68. https://doi.org/10.1016/j.bushor.2009.09.003

Kárpáti, A. (2009). Web 2 technologies for Net Native language learners: a "social CALL." *ReCALL*, *21*(2), 139–156. https://doi.org/10.1017/S0958344009000160

Kent, C., Laslo, E., & Rafaeli, S. (2016). Interactivity in online discussions and learning outcomes. *Computers & Education*, *97*, 116–128. https://doi.org/10.1016/j.compedu.2016.03.002

Kimmerle, J., Moskaliuk, J., Oeberst, A., & Cress, U. (2015). Learning and collective knowledge construction with social media: A process-oriented perspective. *Educational Psychologist*, *50*(2), 120–137. https://doi.org/10.1080/00461520.2015.1036273

Lee, L. (2009). Promoting intercultural exchanges with blogs and podcasting: A study of Spanish–American telecollaboration. *Computer*

Assisted Language Learning, 22(5), 425–443. https://doi.org/10.1080/09588220903345184

Lei, L., & Liu, D. (2019). The research trends and contributions of System's publications over the past four decades (1973–2017): A bibliometric analysis. *System, 80,* 1–13. https://doi.org/10.1016/j.system.2018.10.003

Li, M. (2013). Individual novices and collective experts: Collective scaffolding in wiki-based small group writing. *System, 41*(3), 752–769. https://doi.org/10.1016/j.system.2013.07.021

Liaw, S.-S., Chen, G.-D., & Huang, H.-M. (2008). Users' attitudes toward Web-based collaborative learning systems for knowledge management. *Computers & Education, 50*(3), 950–961. https://doi.org/10.1016/j.compedu.2006.09.007

Lin, C.-J., & Hwang, G.-J. (2018). A learning analytics approach to investigating factors affecting EFL students' oral performance in a flipped classroom. *Journal of Educational Technology & Society, 21*(2), 205–219. https://www.jstor.org/stable/26388398

Lin, M. H., Li, J. J., Hung, P. Y., & Huang, H. W. (2014). Blogging a journal: Changing students' writing skills and perceptions. *ELT Journal, 68*(4), 422–431. https://doi.org/10.1093/elt/ccu032

Liu, P. L., & Chen, C. J. (2015). Learning English through actions: a study of mobile-assisted language learning. *Interactive Learning Environments, 23*(2), 158–171. https://doi.org/10.1080/10494820.2014.959976

Liu, C.-C., Yang, C.-Y., & Chao, P.-Y. (2019). A longitudinal analysis of student participation in a digital collaborative storytelling activity. *Educational Technology Research and Development, 67*(4), 907–929. https://doi.org/10.1007/s11423-019-09666-3

Lord, G. (2008). Podcasting communities and second language pronunciation. *Foreign Language Annals, 41*(2), 364–379. https://doi.org/10.1111/j.1944-9720.2008.tb03297.x

Lucas, T., Villegas, A.M., & Freedson-Gonzalez, M. (2008). Linguistically responsive teacher education: Preparing classroom teachers to teach English language learners. *Journal of Teacher Education, 59*(4), 361–373. https://doi.org/10.1177/0022487108322110

Malerba Candilio, M.L. (2015). *Social networking in second language learning* (Doctoral dissertation, Universitat Oberta de Catalunya).

Manca, S. (2020). Snapping, pinning, liking or texting: Investigating social media in higher education beyond Facebook. *The Internet and Higher Education, 44,* 100707. https://doi.org/10.1016/j.iheduc.2019.100707

Mao, J. (2014). Social media for learning: A mixed methods study on high school students' technology affordances and perspectives. *Computers in Human Behavior, 33,* 213–223. https://doi.org/10.1016/j.chb.2014.01.002

Marchetti, E., & Valente, A. (2018). Interactivity and multimodality in language learning: the untapped potential of audiobooks. *Universal Access in the Information Society, 17*(2), 257–274. https://doi.org/10.1007/s10209-017-0549-5

Meier, G. S. (2017). The multilingual turn as a critical movement in education: Assumptions, challenges and a need for reflection. *Applied Linguistics Review, 8*(1), 131–161. https://doi.org/10.1515/applirev-2016-2010

Miyazoe, T., & Anderson, T. (2010). Learning outcomes and students' perceptions of online writing: Simultaneous implementation of a forum, blog, and wiki in an EFL blended learning setting. *System, 38*(2), 185–199. https://doi.org/10.1016/j.system.2010.03.006

Mompean, A. R. (2010). The development of meaningful interactions on a blog used for the learning of English as a Foreign Language. *ReCALL, 22*(3), 376–395. https://doi.org/10.1017/S0958344010000200

Nassaji, H. (2016). Research timeline: Form-focused instruction and second language acquisition. *Language Teaching, 49*(1), 35–62. https://doi.org/10.1017/S0261444815000403

Nishioka, H. (2016). Analyzing language development in a collaborative digital storytelling project: Sociocultural perspectives. *System, 62,* 39–52. https://doi.org/10.1016/j.system.2016.07.001

Ochs, E., & Schieffelin, B. (2017) Language socialization: An historical overview. In P.A. Duff & S. May (Eds.), *Encyclopedia of language and education*: *Language socialization* (3rd ed.) (pp. 3–16). New York: Springer.

Ou-Yang, F. C., & Wu, W.-C. V. (2017). Using mixed-modality vocabulary learning on mobile devices: Design and evaluation. *Journal of Educational Computing Research, 54*(8), 1043–1069. https://doi.org/10.1177/0735633116648170

Özdemir, E. (2017). Promoting EFL learners' intercultural communication effectiveness: a focus on Facebook. *Computer Assisted Language*

Learning, *30*(6), 510–528. https://doi.org/10.1080/09588221.2017.1325907

Peeters, W. (2019). The peer interaction process on Facebook: A social network analysis of learners' online conversations. *Education and Information Technologies, 24*(5), 3177–3204. https://doi.org/10.1007/s10639- 019-09914-2

Qian, K., Owen, N., & Bax, S. (2018). Researching mobile-assisted Chinese-character learning strategies among adult distance learners. *Innovation in Language Learning and Teaching, 12*(1), 56–71. https://doi.org/10.1080/17501229.2018.1418633

Razak, N. A., Saeed, M., & Ahmad, Z. (2013). Adopting social networking sites (SNSs) as interactive communities among English foreign language (EFL) Learners in Writing: Opportunities and Challenges. *English Language Teaching, 6*(11), 187–198. http://dx.doi.org/10.5539/elt.v6n11p187

Reinhardt, J. (2019). Social media in second and foreign language teaching and learning: Blogs, wikis, and social networking. *Language Teaching, 52*(1), 1–39. https://doi.org/10.1017/S0261444818000356

Roberts, M.E., Stewart, B.M., Tingley, D., Lucas, C., Leder-Luis, J., Gadarian, S.K., Albertson, B., & Rand, D.G. (2014). Structural topic models for open-ended survey responses. *American Journal of Political Science, 58*(4), 1064–1082. https://doi.org/10.1111/ajps.12103

Ros i Solé, C., Calic, J., & Neijmann, D. (2010). A social and self-reflective approach to MALL. *ReCALL, 22*(1), 39–52. https://doi.org/10.1017/S0958344009990188

Rosell-Aguilar, F. (2007). Top of the pods—In search of a podcasting "podagogy" for language learning. *Computer Assisted language learning, 20*(5), 471–492. https://doi.org/10.1080/09588220701746047

Schieffelin, B.B., & Ochs, E. (1986). Language socialization. *Annual Review of Anthropology, 15*(1), 163–191. https://doi.org/10.1146/annurev.an.15.100186.001115

Setiawan, M.R., & Wiedarti, P. (2020). The effectiveness of Quizlet application towards students' motivation in learning vocabulary. *Studies in English Language and Education, 7*(1), 83–95. https://doi.org/10.24815/siele.v7i1.15359

Shen, Q.Y. (2013). Use of blog to improve English writing in the Chinese tertiary EFL classrooms. *English Language Teaching, 6*(10), 51–56.

https://doi.org/10.5539/elt.v6n10p51

Song, Y. (2014). "Bring Your Own Device (BYOD)" for seamless science inquiry in a primary school. *Computers & Education, 74*, 50–60. https://doi.org/10.1016/j.compedu.2014.01.005

Stockwell, G. (2007). Vocabulary on the move: Investigating an intelligent mobile phone-based vocabulary tutor. *Computer Assisted Language Learning, 20*(4), 365–383. https://doi.org/10.1080/09588220701745817

Stockwell, G. (2010). Using mobile phones for vocabulary activities: Examining the effect of platform. *Language Learning & Technology, 14*(2), 95–110. http://dx.doi.org/10125/44216

Stockwell, G. (2012). Working with constraints in mobile learning: A response to Ballance. *Language Learning & Technology, 16*(3), 24–31. http://dx.doi.org/10125/44294

Su, Y., Li, Y., Liang, J.C., & Tsai, C.C. (2019). Moving literature circles into wiki-based environment: the role of online self-regulation in EFL learners' attitude toward collaborative learning. *Computer Assisted Language Learning, 32*(5–6), 556–586. https://doi.org/10.1080/09588221.2018.1527363

Sun, Y. C. (2009). Voice blog: An exploratory study of language learning. *Language Learning & Technology, 13*(2), 88–103. http://dx.doi.org/10125/44182

Tarighat, S., & Khodabakhsh, S. (2016). Mobile-assisted language assessment: Assessing speaking. *Computers in Human Behavior, 64*, 409–413. https://doi.org/10.1016/j.chb.2016.07.014

Terhune, N. M. (2016). Language learning going global: Linking teachers and learners via commercial Skype-based CMC. *Computer assisted language learning, 29*(6), 1071–1089. https://doi.org/10.1080/09588221.2015.1061020

Tess, P. A. (2013). The role of social media in higher education classes (real and virtual)–A literature review. *Computers in Human Behavior, 29*(5), A60–A68. https://doi.org/10.1016/j.chb.2012.12.032

Thorne, S. L. (2003). Artifacts and cultures-of-use in intercultural communication. *Language Learning & Technology, 7*(2), 38–67. http://dx.doi.org/ 10125/25200

Truong, H. M. (2016). Integrating learning styles and adaptive e-learning system: Current developments, problems and opportunities. *Computers in Human Behavior, 55*, 1185–1193. https://doi.org/10.1016/

j.chb.2015.02.014

Van Doremalen, J., Boves, L., Colpaert, J., Cucchiarini, C., & Strik, H. (2016). Evaluating automatic speech recognition-based language learning systems: A case study. *Computer Assisted Language Learning, 29*(4), 833–851. https://doi.org/10.1080/09588221.2016.1167090

Vattøy, K.D. (2020). Teachers' beliefs about feedback practice as related to student self-regulation, self-efficacy, and language skills in teaching English as a foreign language. *Studies in Educational Evaluation, 64*, 100828. https://doi.org/10.1016/j.stueduc.2019.100828

Vurdien, R. (2013). Enhancing writing skills through blogging in an advanced English as a Foreign Language class in Spain. *Computer Assisted Language Learning, 26*(2), 126–143. https://doi.org/10.1080/09588221.2011.639784

Wagner, J. (2015). Designing for language learning in the wild: Creating social infrastructures for second language learning. In *Usage-based perspectives on second language learning* (pp. 75–102). De Gruyter Mouton.

Wang, Y.C. (2014). Using wikis to facilitate interaction and collaboration among EFL learners: A social constructivist approach to language teaching. *System, 42,* 383–390. https://doi.org/10.1016/j.system.2014.01.007

Wang, J., Zou, B., Wang, D., & Xing, M. (2013). Students' perception of a wiki platform and the impact of wiki engagement on intercultural communication. *System, 41*(2), 245–256. https://doi.org/10.1016/j.system.2013.04.004

Warner, C., & Chen, H. I. (2017). Designing talk in social networks: What Facebook teaches about conversation. *Language Learning & Technology, 21*(2), 121–138. https://dx.doi.org/10125/44614

Wenger, E. (1998). Communities of practice: Learning as a social system. *Systems Thinker, 9*(5), 2–3. Retrieved from https://participativelearning.org/pluginfile.php/636/mod_resource/content/3/Learningasasocialsystem.pdf

Wong, L. H., Chai, C. S., & Aw, G. P. (2017). Seamless language learning: Second language learning with social media. *Comunicar: Media Education Research Journal, 25*(50), 9–20. https://doi.org/10.3916/C50-2017-01

Yang, M., Tai, M., & Lim, C. P. (2016). The role of e-portfolios in supporting productive learning. *British Journal of Educational Technology, 47*(6), 1276–1286. https://doi.org/10.1111/bjet.12316

Yeh, E., & Swinehart, N. (2020). Social media literacy in L2 environments: navigating anonymous user-generated content. *Computer Assisted Language Learning*. https://doi.org/10.1080/09588221.2020.1830805

Yen, Y.C., Hou, H.T., & Chang, K.E. (2015). Applying role-playing strategy to enhance learners' writing and speaking skills in EFL courses using Facebook and Skype as learning tools: A case study in Taiwan. *Computer Assisted Language Learning, 28*(5), 383–406. https://doi.org/10.1080/09588221.2013.839568

Yilmaz, F G.K., & Keser, H. (2016). The impact of reflective thinking activities in e-learning: A critical review of the empirical research. *Computers & Education, 95*, 163–173. https://doi.org/10.1016/j.compedu.2016.01.006

Yim, S., & Warschauer, M. (2017). Web-based collaborative writing in L2 contexts: Methodological insights from text mining. *Language Learning & Technology, 21*(1), 146–165. https://dx.doi.org/10125/44599

Zhang, H., Song, W., Shen, S., & Huang, R. (2014). The effects of blog-mediated peer feedback on learners' motivation, collaboration, and course satisfaction in a second language writing course. *Australasian Journal of Educational Technology, 30*(6), 670–685. https://doi.org/10.14742/ajet.860

9
L2 learners' strategies for using machine translation as a personalized writing assisting tool

Sangmin-Michelle Lee

Introduction

The rapid development of technology has been significantly changing education and society. Among the cutting-edge technologies, machine translation (MT) has gained much attention in many areas. In recent years, foreign language (FL) learning, in particular, has given a great amount of attention to MT. Due to its convenience, immediacy, cost-effectiveness and multilingualism, an increasing number of FL students are already using MT for diverse purposes, including vocabulary learning, reading and writing (Briggs, 2018; O'Neill, 2019). Previous studies have found a number of pedagogical benefits of using MT in FL classrooms. From a language learning perspective, MT promotes students' vocabulary learning (Fredholm, 2019), helps students correct their language errors, fosters linguistic awareness, and enables students to focus more on the writing content (Lee, 2020; Stapleton & Kin, 2019; Tsai, 2019). Therefore, students can communicate better and write more accurately and fluently with MT (Garcia & Pena, 2011; Shadiev *et al.*, 2019). From a cognitive and metacognitive perspective, MT reduces students' cognitive load by providing language resources and promotes students' metacognitive language learning skills (Briggs, 2018; Shadiev *et al.*, 2019). From an affective perspective, MT lowers students' language apprehension and anxiety (Bahri & Mahadi, 2016), increases their confidence (Niño, 2008), and creates a more comfortable FL learning environment (Niño, 2009).

FL writing is a particular domain, which requires diverse skills and strategies, in which MT can effectively mediate students' learning (Lee & Briggs, 2021). More specifically, students often face two cognitively overwhelming challenges, the content and the target language during FL writing (Lee, 2020). Between two difficulties at hand, linguistic difficulties often become a more urgent issue for most FL learners because linguistic accuracy directly affects the overall quality of writing (Min, 2006; Van Waes & Leijten, 2015). Hence, FL learners exert their cognitive resources mostly on language and neglect other important areas, which would result in a poorer quality of writing (Briggs, 2018). Moreover, although adequate feedback is important to improve FL writing, it is often limited in many FL writing classrooms for various reasons (Tsai, 2019). Under the current situation, MT can be an alternative to facilitate FL writing. Despite controversies over MT, students and researchers alike have found pedagogical benefits of using MT in the FL classroom, and more research in recent years has confirmed these benefits (Fredholm, 2019; Niño, 2020, O'Neill, 2019; Stapleton & Kin, 2019). Researchers have also argued that MT has surpassed intermediate level EFL students and serves as a smart FL facilitating tool (Lee & Briggs, 2021; Stapleton & Kin, 2019).

Accordingly, extensive research has been published on the use of MT in FL classrooms in recent years; however, the topics still narrowly focused on students' perceptions of MT and the effectiveness of using MT, and other issues have been under researched. As it is expected that MT will be more widely used by learners with diverse levels and characteristics in the near future (Godwin-Jones, 2019), more diverse topics and issues regarding MT should be investigated to benefit student learning. Particularly in FL writing, individual learners use diverse strategies and resources during writing and revising, which influence the quality of outcomes. Therefore, the present study explored MT as a smart tool to aid students' FL writing by investigating the EFL learners' strategies for utilizing MT during writing.

Literature Review

Despite the long history of MT, MT only recently became prevalent in our daily lives and in educational settings due to its historical inaccuracy (Lee & Briggs, 2021). Since Google introduced neural machine translation (NMT), MT accuracy significantly increased at both the lexical and grammatical levels; therefore, many errors in outputs that had been the major obstacle to its users were reduced. In fact, the predecessors of NMT, such as statistical MT, rule-based MT, and hybrid MT, committed large numbers of errors at various levels (e.g., lexical, grammatical, and discourse) with the most notorious errors being for literal translation and incomprehensible sentences (Koehn, 2020). These predecessors also produced awkward, unnatural, and out-of-context translations. However, although NMT still has tendencies to make errors, recent MT studies showed that MT significantly reduced different levels and types of errors, ranging from literal translation to punctuation and from lexico-grammatical errors to contextual errors (Ducar & Schocket, 2018; Stapleton & Kin, 2019). This became possible due to the distinctive mechanism of NMT that can select the most similar meaning to the source text from the corpus and represent it instead of using the one-on-one translation method used by its predecessors (Koehn, 2020; Poibeau, 2017). Goldwin-Jones (2019) also noted that MT would be faster, more accurate and efficient than humans in the near future.

As MT accuracy advances, its use and role in language learning have also changed. In the early stage of using MT in language classrooms (from 2000 to 2016), MT was utilized as a bad language model that required postediting; in this model, language learners acquired linguistic knowledge by correcting MT outputs. However, the most recent studies claimed that MT has already surpassed intermediate level EFL students and can serve as a smart FL facilitating tool (Lee, 2020; Tsai, 2019). As MT produces better quality and more accurate outputs than average EFL learners in terms of vocabulary and grammar, it can successfully respond to their queries, properly aid FL writing, and facilitate learning (Niño, 2020; Lee & Briggs, 2021). Accordingly, the role of MT has been shifted to the CALL model, and numerous studies have confirmed that MT is now used as a valuable pedagogical asset in FL writing. The best examples are Niño's past and recent studies on MT. In her earlier studies (Niño, 2008, 2009), students used MT as a bad model in a postediting task and found a number of serious types of errors. However, in her recent study (2020), the students found MT to be a quite accurate and useful language reference tool and actually benefited from it during diverse translation tasks. Considering that linguistic accuracy is related to the overall quality of FL writing (Min, 2006), MT greatly helps FL learners improve their writing by providing lexical and grammatical aids. Tsai (2019) and Lee and Briggs (2021) showed that lexico-grammatical and orthographic errors were significantly reduced in students' writing using MT; consequently, accuracy, fluency, and overall writing quality were enhanced. Using MT also helps students use more accurate and more advanced levels of vocabulary and increases lexical density (Fredholm, 2019). Because MT assists FL students' language needs, students' cognitive loads can be reduced, and students can focus more on content and discourse aspects (Briggs, 2018). When students utilize MT, they need to compare their texts with MT outputs and determine the option that is the better choice. This process increases students' metalinguistic awareness and reflection on language, cultivates critical thinking and problem solving skills, and ultimately contributes to language learning (Shadiev *et al*., 2018).

In addition, Lee (2021) argued that the improvement of MT accuracy has also changed students' perceptions, attitudes, and usage in FL education. However, as Lee stated in her meta-analysis, due to the rudimentary stage of using MT in this field, most MT studies were limited mostly to students' perceptions towards using MT and the effectiveness of MT in lexico-grammatical terms and have not addressed other important issues, such as learner variables and effective pedagogical designs for using MT. The literature on FL writing has revealed that learners employ diverse strategies during writing and revision, and these strategies directly affect FL writing quality (Min, 2006; Josefsson, 2011; Yoon, 2016). For instance, FL learners adopt different writing approaches (e.g., process-based and product-based) and use various revision strategies regarding types (e.g., surface or text and macro or micro), size (e.g., word, phrase, sentence, and paragraph), and function (e.g., grammatical, cosmetic, texture, and cohesive), which ultimately affects the outcome quality (Min, 2006).

More recently, a variety of language reference tools, or "cognitive tools," such as concordancing, serve as intellectual aids for language learners and provide them with means to solve their lexico-grammatical problems and increase their independence in FL writing (Yoon, 2016). Similarly, MT, as one smart cognitive tool, mediates FL writing and supports personalized learning (Lee & Briggs, 2021). While these tools have been widely available, not every learner benefits equally. Depending on learner variables, such as language proficiencies and strategies for using the tools, the results may differ. Concerning the relationship between learners' proficiency levels and the effectiveness of using MT, previous studies presented inconsistent results. Whereas Garcia and Pena (2011) and Niño (2009) claimed that MT benefited beginning-level learners, Tsai (2019) and Lee (2020) argued that MT is not appropriate for them. A more recent study by Niño (2020), also showed that advanced learners seemed to benefit more from using MT because they were capable of choosing better options between their sentences and MT outputs. In other studies, students exhibited different revision patterns and actions according to their language proficiency (Lee, 2020; Min, 2006). For instance, less proficient students focused more on local and language problems, while more proficient students focused more on global and content issues (Niño, 2008; Yoon, 2016). While students' strategies for using MT will be another important factor affecting writing outcomes, no previous study has investigated this issue (Lee, 2021). Therefore, the current research addressed the following questions:

1. What strategies (action, size, and language direction) did EFL students use while using MT during writing and revising? Were there any significant differences in using MT in writing and revising?
2. Did the students' strategies for using MT vary depending on their language proficiencies?

Methodology

The present study started with a cohort of 39 Korean college students from diverse majors at two four-year universities in Korea. The students wrote two-thirds to one page long essays on two topics: what makes learning interesting and future education. For each essay, they submitted two drafts: first and revised drafts. For the first task, they wrote the first draft (also used as a writing proficiency level test) on their own, and they were allowed to use any online resources, including MT (Google Translate), for revision. For the second task, they were allowed to use the online resources for both the first and revised drafts. After completing the first draft in the first writing task, seven students who scored 1 were removed because they could not complete the task. These students barely wrote a few sentences for the first draft and could not make a revision for the first task. Hence, 32 students participated in the current study. The writing and revision processes were recorded by using the internal screen capture tool embedded in Windows. The durations of the recording ranged from 23 minutes to 126 minutes (mean = 38 minutes).

The present study employed a mixed method to conduct more robust research. As a primary method, quantitative content analysis of the students' essays and screen recordings of their writing processes were employed. All four drafts for two tasks were scored based on the 6-point TOEFL essay rubric and compared, to investigate whether there were significant differences using a t-test. The screen recordings were open-coded until themes emerged, and extended from Min (2006) and Lee (2020). Themes were categorized into five areas: action, translation direction, size, adoption rate and typing option. Based on the categories, the screen recordings were analysed again (selective coding). Action refers to how students used MT, and it included five categories: translation, comparison, search, double-checking, and checking their final outcomes. Translation represents students translating phrases or sentences from Korean into English without writing their own phrases or sentences first. Search means searching for English words. Comparison represents students comparing their outcomes with MT outputs. Double-checking represents students checking the results of their search outcomes using other resources such as Google or Naver (the largest Korean portal site) using MT. Checking the final outcomes means that the students pasted their final drafts into MT to verify them and check the errors. Translation direction refers to the language direction from the source text to the target text (e.g., Korean into English or English into Korean). The size refers to the language unit that the students input in MT, such as words, phrases, sentences, and paragraphs. The adoption rate indicates how much the students accepted MT outputs in their writing. This was categorized into five categories: all (100%), most (80 – 90%), half, part (less than 50%), and none. Last, the typing option contains two categories: copy & paste and type.

In addition, the study considered the Hawthorne effect because of the screen recordings. The literature warns that when research participants are aware that they are under study, they may display behaviours different from their usual ones because they know they are being watched (Oswald *et al.*, 2014). The literature usually recommends two methods to avoid the Hawthorne effect: collecting data anonymously and not being judgemental about participants. Due to the nature of the research, the former was not possible. In line with the second method, the writing tasks were not included in the final grade in the current study so that the students would not worry about their behaviours during the recording sessions.

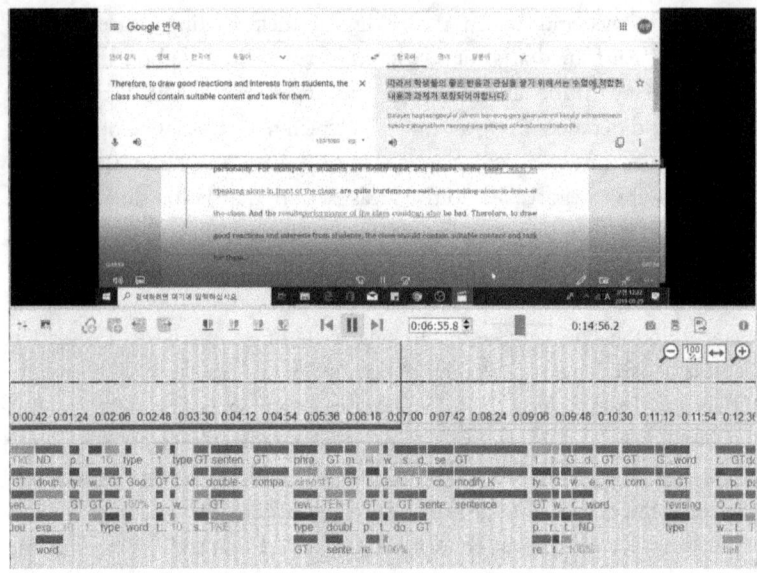

Figure 9.1 *Screen capture of the recording analysis.*

After completing writing tasks, twenty students out of 32 participants were interviewed. The students who were removed from the essay analysis (N = 7) were also included in the interviews because it was expected that the interviews with them would provide valuable insights into MT use by low-level proficiency students. The interviews were semistructured and asked the following questions: What were the strengths and weaknesses of MT? Tell me about your experiences using MT for the tasks. How did you use MT and what types of strategies did you use? MAXQDA was used to analyse the screen recordings (Figure 9.1) and the interviews, and SPSS 25 was employed for quantitative analysis. Two raters scored the students' essays and coded the recordings. The overall interrater reliability was 0.89.

Results

The mean score of the first draft was 4.25 and the mean scores of the remaining three drafts significantly increased. The t-tests (Table 9.1) and repeated measure ANOVA (F = 31.131, $p < .001$) confirmed that the difference was statistically significant. In terms of action, comparison was the most frequent action, followed by translating phrases or sentences, searching words, and double-checking results. Regarding translation direction, most students translated from Korean to English. The study also found that students employed some distinctive strategies. First, they modified source texts while using MT to obtain more accurate results (N = 35). As they used Korean more often as the source language, they often modified Korean texts. That is, they input Korean texts into MT, checked the MT English outputs, modified Korean texts (usually simplifying or paraphrasing them), and then checked the outputs again. Second, they switched languages in MT by using the switch source-target language function provided by Google Translate (N = 24). By doing so, they could verify more easily if the English translation matched their intended meaning. It should be noted that modification and language switch were overlapped with some categories in action (i.e. comparison), which also functioned as purposes of using MT. Finally, the screen recordings showed that the students utilized diverse resources to search and check their texts in addition to MT. They used Google Translate most frequently (49.8%), followed by an Internet dictionary (31.3%) and Google (10.8%). They also marginally used Naver, MS spelling check, Grammarly, and corpus websites. Most importantly, they utilized other resources to check the reliability of MT outputs or vice versa.

Table 9.1 *The means of the students' writing scores and t-test results.*

First task			Second task			
First	Revised		First		Revised	
M (SD)	M (SD)	t (sig)	M (SD)	t (sig)	M (SD)	t (sig)
4.25 (1.078)	4.82 (1.157)	23.835 (<.001)	4.87 (.959)	28.761 (<.001)	5.17 (1.083)	27.090 (<.001)

* t-tests were the results of a comparison with the first draft of the first task.

Regarding the size of the input into MT, sentences were the most frequently used unit, followed by phrases and words. The rate of adopting all, most, or some of the MT outputs was 39 percent. The rate of rejecting MT outputs entirely was 60 percent, which means that the students conferred with MT but did not actually use MT outputs in their drafts. Last, the results showed that most students typed the texts after checking MT (88%) outputs instead of copying and pasting them. The results were summarized in Table 9.2.

Table 9.2 *Strategies for using MT.*

Category	Strategy	Frequency (%)
Action	Translate	45 (13.7)
	Compare	131 (39.8)
	Search	50 (15.2)
	Double-check	79 (24.0)
	Check the final outcome	17 (5.2)
	Etc.	6 (1.8)
Translation direction	Korean -> English	253 (76.9)
	English -> Korean	76 (23.1)
Size	Word	61 (18.5)
	Phrase	93 (28.3)
	Sentence	130 (39.5)
	Paragraph	45 (13.7)
Adopting rate	All	81 (24.6)
	Most	30 (9.1)
	Half	3 (0.9)
	Part	19 (5.8)
	None	196 (59.6)
Typing option	Type	287 (87.2)
	Copy & paste	42 (12.8)

* N = 329 (cases)

Next, the present study compared the students' strategies during writing and revising. Overall, the students used MT more frequently when revising (N = 199) than during writing (N = 130), and the patterns appeared slightly different between them. Regarding action, comparison was the most frequently appearing category in both writing and revising; however, translation and double-checking were considerably higher in the revised versions (Figure 9.2). The frequency for search remained similar between them. The higher frequencies of using MT for search during revising showed that they kept adding new information to the revised versions.

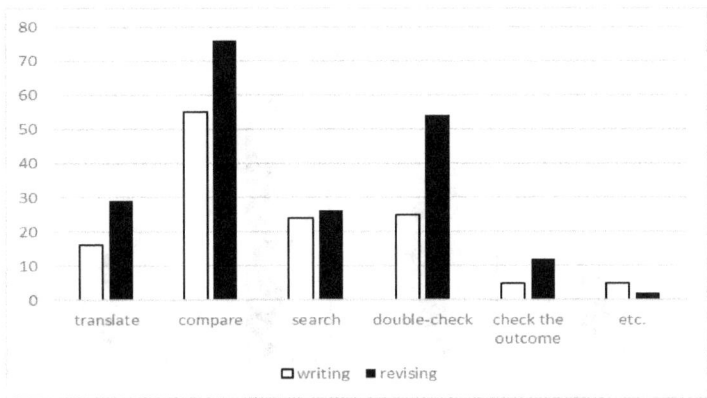

Figure 9.2 *Action performed when using MT.*

In terms of translation direction, the students translated from Korean to English in most cases in both writing and revising (Figure 9.3). Regarding the size, the overall ratings appeared the same between the versions, although different patterns (Figure 9.4). Not surprisingly, as the students checked their final outcomes more often during revising, they used MT more often for larger chunks, particularly paragraphs, during revising. The ratio of paragraphs was twice as high, and the ratio of sentences also increased in revising. Regarding the adoption rate of MT outputs, the rate of rejecting MT outputs was the highest, followed by adopting all outputs, and adopting half of the outputs was the lowest in both versions (Figure 9.5). The adoption rate of MT outputs (from part to all) increased from 53% in the first drafts to 63% in the revised drafts.

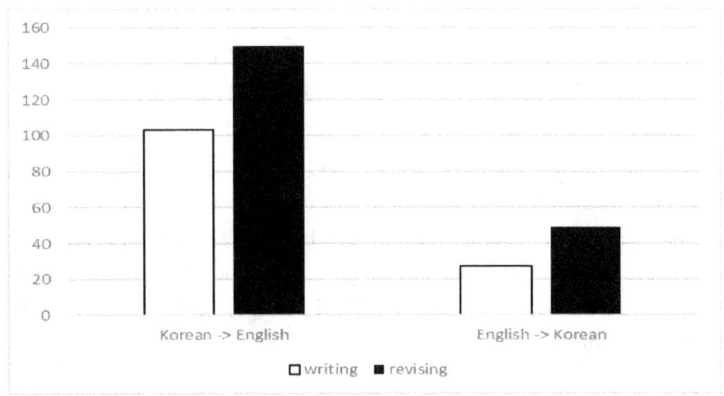

Figure 9.3 *Translation direction.*

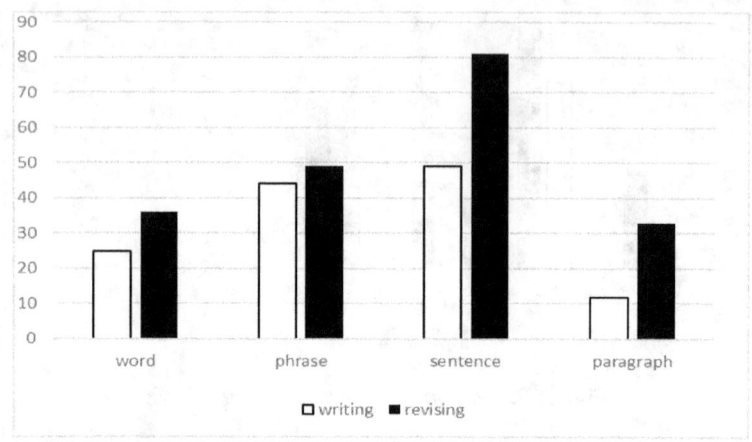

Figure 9.4 *Size of the input unit when using MT.*

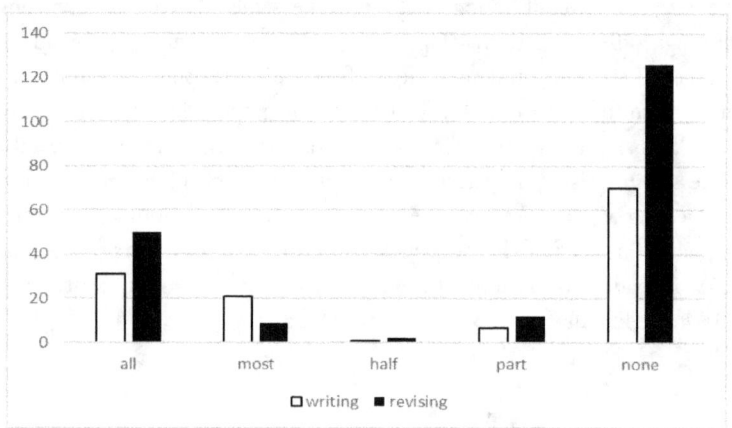

Figure 9.5 *Rate of adoption of MT outputs.*

Finally, the study examined using ANOVA whether students' English proficiencies would affect their behavioural patterns when using MT. However, there was no correlation found between the students' scores and other categories, except for translation in action ($p < .05$). This implied that the students with scores under 3 used MT for translation more often than the students with higher scores.

Interview results

Overall, the interview results were consistent with the recording analysis results. Overall, the students regarded MT as a useful, convenient, and effective personalized language reference tool that supported their FL writing and learning. Similar to the recording analysis results, the interview results showed that comparing their texts with MT outputs was the most frequently appearing action, as mentioned below:

> I think I can effectively use MT because I already have quite a good amount of knowledge about English. MT is a good complementary tool for my English writing. I usually use MT and a dictionary at the same time to obtain the best result, and this is greatly helpful to checking the reliability of MT results. I write my draft in English first, put the troublesome parts in MT, and compare the output with my text; if I am not still sure about the result, I check examples in a dictionary or Google, then finally determine the final outcome. Actually, this process can enhance not only the quality of my writing but also my English learning. (interview, JY)

Similar to the excerpt above, the majority of the interviewees responded that they usually wrote their own text first and then used MT to compare and select better expressions (N = 17). They also used MT frequently to search vocabulary and expressions. Concerning vocabulary, they mentioned that MT outperformed dictionaries "because it shows a word more appropriate for the specific context that I intend." When they sought a word in a dictionary, the dictionary usually suggested more than one word that was the English equivalent to the Korean word, and this further confused the students since the students did not know which option was correct for their purpose. In contrast, even when students needed to search only a single word, they could put the entire sentence or multiple sentences in MT, and this could allow students to obtain a better result. In addition, several students commented that MT presented more authentic and natural English expressions than their own text.

The students also said that MT helped them "communicate and express in English beyond my current capability," which had not been possible prior to using MT. Therefore, they could focus more on what they intended to write and express themselves better. Additionally, several students reported that using MT expanded their language repertoire in vocabulary, sentence structures, and expressions. One student said, "I tended to use the same sentence structures and limited expressions over the years, but since I started using MT, I came to be able to use more various structures, expressions and vocabulary." Another student mentioned that he learned the language "during the repeated process of checking MT outputs and comparing them with my texts and other resources." They listed convenience, speed, ease of use, and availability as advantages of using MT. The majority of the students, all but three students, said that MT was helpful and useful for both FL writing and learning English. However, those three students said that they did not feel that their English had actually improved due to using MT. One of the students was concerned that using MT negatively affected her writing. Because she knew that using a short and less complex sentence in the source language in MT could lead to better results in MT outputs, she said "short and simplified sentences intentionally in the first place to get better results" in the target language, which she worried "would become a habit and have a harmful effect on my writing style in a long term."

The students were also aware of other disadvantages of MT. The most frequently mentioned disadvantage was unnatural and inauthentic expressions. They explained that this was ascribed to the fact that MT was not yet fully capable of understanding the context and nuances of the Korean language. Particularly, they stated that MT outputs did not sometimes adequately translate the formality and politeness shown in the Korean language. The inability of MT to translate double-meaning words was also stated as a limitation. However, incomprehensible outputs and literal translations were not mentioned, and grammatical inaccuracy was mentioned by only a few students. Nonetheless, the students considered MT useful but still imperfect; therefore, they said that they should not adopt its outputs without reviewing them. Overall, the interviews clearly indicated that the students did not totally depend on MT. In contrast, they wrote their own texts first and used MT as a resource to improve their writing. A few students explicitly said that they should not become overdependent on MT, which would not help their English learning. The interview results were summarized in Table 3.

Table 9.3 *The interview results.*

Category	Themes	Frequency (%)
Positive	Convenience, ease of use, speed	14(70.0)
	Useful and helpful to English writing	13(65.0)
	Helping me find words and/or expressions	12(60.0)
	Assisting my writing/complementing my English	9(45.0)
	Individualized language learning tool	6(30.0)
	Helping me focus more on content	3(15.0)
Negative	Inauthenticity, lack of nuance	16(80.0)
	Inaccuracy	5(25.5)
	Overdependence	4(20.0)
	Not improving my English in the long term	3(15.0)
Strategy	Comparing with my own writing/final checking	12(60.0)
	Reviewing MT outputs	11(55.0)
	Double-checking MT outputs	9(45.0)
	Looking for words, (using as alternative to a dictionary)	8(40.0)
	Looking for expressions	8(40.0)
	Translating in different sizes	5(25.5)
	Using as a language learning tool	5(25.5)
	Simplifying/Modifying the input (Korean)	3(15.0)

N = 20 (persons)

As mentioned in the methods, the seven students who were removed from the essay and recording analyses were also interviewed to obtain some insights into low-level students' perceptions of using MT and their strategies for using it. In the interviews, they responded differently from the others. They were not convinced whether MT was helpful or harmful or how they should use MT for academic purposes. They said that MT definitely helped them write and communicate in English, but without it, they could not communicate in English at all; thus, they were concerned that they would rely too much on MT and could not improve their English. Out of these seven students, five of them said that they wrote in Korean first and translated the entire text into English using MT in the first drafts. The other two said that they used MT only for vocabulary because they thought that translating entire sentences or paragraphs would be unethical, although they often did so outside of academic settings to communicate in English. All of these students answered that they mostly used the outputs as suggested by MT without checking or modifying them. In summation, the interviews indicated that, depending on language proficiencies, the students perceived using MT differently and used it in different ways.

Application to Smart CALL

MT as a smart language facilitation tool

The present study showed that using MT helped FL students with both writing and revising. The t-tests confirmed that the students' scores increased when they used MT. This study particularly investigated their strategies of using MT in terms of size, action, translation direction, and the final adoption rate of MT outputs during writing and revising. The students in this study utilized diverse strategies regarding the use of MT. Prior MT studies expressed concerns that language learners may use MT indiscreetly and become overly dependent on MT, which would have a harmful effect on language learning (Kim, 2018). However, the current study showed that students critically and selectively used MT. The strategies that the students employed while using MT, such as search, double-check, and checking the final outcome in action and various adoption rates, revealed how the students used MT during writing. Based on their previous experience using MT, they were well aware of both the strengths and weaknesses of MT and used MT effectively to meet their needs during FL writing. More specifically, they utilized MT as a personalized smart language assisting tool, with which each individual student employed different strategies in action, size of translation, and adoption of MT outcomes depending on their language proficiency, previous experience with MT, and their perception toward MT accuracy.

In fact, they used MT as one of the resources available to them complementary to online dictionaries, Google, and other online resources. Compared with other resources, they viewed MT as a more convenient, effective, and smarter tool, mainly because it could identify the context of a query (word) and thus provide more adequate outputs. For instance, as mentioned in some interviews, this study showed that MT was more convenient to use to search for an English word than dictionaries due to its capability of translating larger chunks and identifying the context of the given word. As NMT translates texts based on large corpus data between the two languages under consideration instead of the one-on-one translation process, it can better understand the intended meaning and present more accurate outcomes (Ducar & Schocket, 2018; Koehn, 2020). For this reason, while earlier studies suggested using MT for smaller chunks to reduce errors and misrepresented translations (Jolley & Maimone, 2015; Pena & Garcia, 2011), recent MT studies recommend using MT for larger chunks (Ducar & Schocket, 2018; Lee, 2021). Similarly, the students in the present study used MT at the sentence level the most frequently. Furthermore, as Niño (2008) stated, lexical errors are comparatively easy to correct, even for lower-level students, compared to grammatical and discourse-level errors. Therefore, due to the enhanced accuracy of MT and the ease of acting upon the results, the students were able to fix lexical errors and use more adequate vocabulary in FL writing with MT.

Concerning grammar, the current study presented an intriguing finding. A number of MT studies emphasized that students were able to reduce grammatical errors with MT (Lee & Briggs, 2021; Stapleton & Kin, 2019; Tsai, 2019); Lee (2020) further categorized students' error changes in terms of purpose, such as mechanics, vocabulary, grammar, and expressions. However, the present study implied that the purposes for using MT could not be clearly delineated by examining students' writing outcomes or their action. When the students used MT at the word level, it was quite clear that they used it to search for a lexical item. On the other hand, when they used MT for larger chunks, such as sentences or paragraphs, the purpose seemed rather to be mixed. For instance, the students used MT to determine a certain expression, but if they also detected lexical or grammatical errors or found better alternatives, they made such changes regardless of their original purposes of using MT. In fact, in the screen recordings, it was not obvious that the students often used MT primarily for grammar checks; rather, for this purpose, they consulted with Grammarly or searched Google more frequently. Lee (2020) also mentioned that it was difficult to categorize the purposes of changes only by analysing students' writing outcomes because the analysis might not be the same as that for students' intentions. Similarly, although this study examined the students' writing processes beyond writing outcomes, it was difficult to clearly define students' purposes of using MT. In addition, there were no significant differences found in the students' use of MT between writing and revising except for a few minor areas. While students used MT at the paragraph level to verify their final outcomes during revising more often, they still searched words and translated sentences, eliciting new information during revising. As shown in Yoon (2016), in this study, the boundaries of writing stages were fluid, not clear cut, and the students mixed their use of MT for elicitation and verification during both writing stages.

The present study also showed that the students were not overly or solely dependent on MT. Most students wrote their own texts first prior to using MT, utilized diverse online resources to check the reliability of MT and did not merely accept the results. In fact, the students used a careful and complex process of examining the results using their linguistic knowledge and other resources in order to find a better solution. Not only the diverse strategies and resources that the students employed but also the adoption rate of MT outputs confirmed that they judiciously used MT. The rate of adopting MT outputs as-is was only 23.8% in writing and 25.1% in revising, and the rate of not accepting the MT results at all after consulting with MT reached 53.8% in writing and 63.3% in revising. The students compared their texts and MT outputs and combined parts to achieve better outcomes only in the small number of cases because this required more linguistic knowledge and cognitive efforts, thus being more challenging for them compared to adopting all or rejecting all. Additionally, the students rarely copied and pasted MT results, and most of them preferred typing the text after checking MT outputs. This result was another indication that the students did not merely copy MT outputs. The interview results also indicated that they effectively and strategically used MT for their needs, checked the reliability of MT outputs based on their linguistic knowledge and other resources, and were discreet in using MT.

Regarding the individual students' strategies, each student, not as a language proficiency group, showed their own idiosyncratic patterns when using MT. Although there were no statistically significant differences in strategies depending on the students' language proficiencies, the interviews revealed that according to their language proficiencies, students had different perceptions towards using MT and used different strategies. Whereas more proficient students regarded MT as a useful and effective language reference tool, the least proficient students did not know how to effectively use MT and did not use MT other than to translate sentences and search for words. As students' abilities, particularly their linguistic knowledge about the target language, play critical roles in utilizing feedback, their error corrections also differ according to their language proficiencies

(Josefsson, 2011; Yoon, 2016). According to Pae (2008), low-level students benefit from feedback less than high-level students because they lack the capability to select better options in their writing. MT studies also showed that more proficient students benefited more from MT in FL writing (Fredholm, 2019; Lee & Briggs, 2021). Similarly, in this study, using MT seemed to be too challenging and even disruptive for low-level students.

In addition to their lack of linguistic knowledge, a lack of confidence also negatively affected the low-level students' use of MT. In the interviews, due to their lack of knowledge and confidence, low-level students adopted the results as-is without reviewing them or crosschecking their reliability. This, in turn, put these students in the ethical dilemma that their writing was not their own creation but was the creation of MT and deterred them from using MT for educational purposes. Another possibility was that because of the Hawthorne effect, low-level students might have become more reluctant to use MT in this study. In other words, they might use MT more frequently and freely under other circumstances, but because of the screen recording, they might not want to show their ordinary MT behaviours. Nonetheless, as low-level students did not know whether MT outputs were better or correct, it would be difficult for them to learn the language from MT. In contrast, more proficient students perceived MT as a smart CALL tool, and their confidence allowed them to utilize it more effectively and manipulatively. Because more proficient students knew that translating longer texts generated more accurate outputs, they often translated sentences. Because they carefully reviewed outputs before using them, they perceived using MT at the sentence level as ethically acceptable.

There are several issues to consider. First, the long-term effect of ML is unclear. As several students in the current study reported, students may be able to learn language from MT in the long term. Or, as shown in Fredholm's study (2019), when support (MT) is withdrawn, students may not be able to achieve the same level of quality in language tasks. In other words, MT may have only an immediate effect on FL writing and may not have a longer effect on language learning. This issue requires further research. Second, this study showed that although the individual students' strategies varied, there were no significant relationships found between their language levels and strategies of using MT, except for translation. This implies that regardless of different language proficiencies and individual differences in strategies, each student developed idiosyncratic strategies optimized for their needs and goals over time. However, it should also be noted that this result was only possible for the students with scores over 3. Furthermore, this study showed that students' linguistic knowledge played a key role when making the final decision to select and accept MT outputs. This means that more proficient students can benefit more from MT and improve their writing more.

Therefore, to further benefit student learning, proper guidance and explicit instructions on using MT are required. This will be especially important for low-level students. Without the instructor's guide and intervention, low-level students would not be able to benefit from MT on their own. The availability of the tool does not guarantee that everyone can benefit from it. As high-level students can benefit more from MT, using MT in educational settings may further increase the gap between high-level and low-level students. As MT accuracy continues to increase, the pedagogical model should also change. Unlike early years when MT was a bad model, the current MT accuracy is already capable of catering to EFL learners in mechanics, vocabulary, grammar, expressions and cosmetics. As lexico-grammatical accuracy and appropriateness are required for good quality writing (Van Waes & Leijten, 2015), FL students devote much time to the surface-level features of writing without using sufficient resources for other features (Briggs, 2018; Tsai, 2019). With MT, FL students can address the surface-level problems and address other issues in writing. This will also greatly help them become more independent and confident FL writers. Additionally, instructors' perceptions of and classroom policies towards using MT, such as banning or restricting MT, may influence students' use of MT. Rather than merely banning MT, instructors need to provide students with adequate instructional design, guidance, and models to use MT (O'Neill, 2019). Writing workshops and explicit explanations of error correction prior to or after using MT will be beneficial to all levels of students.

Conclusion

MT has become omnipresent in FL students' learning and their daily lives (Niño, 2020). As MT accuracy has increased, MT constitutes a valuable asset for FL learning. Regarding FL writing, MT helps students reduce lexico-grammatical errors, express their ideas beyond their current level of English, and focus more on content. Previous studies were also concerned that students would merely adopt or copy MT outputs without examining them; as a consequence, MT may have a harmful effect on FL learning in the long term (Kim, 2018). However, the students in the present study showed that they used MT strategically, critically, and effectively to meet their needs. They used MT for diverse purposes during FL writing. Searching for words and translating phrases and sentences helped them verbalize their ideas and communicate more fluently in FL writing. Other purposes, such as comparing and checking outcomes, further provide linguistic support to students, which could raise their linguistic and metalinguistic awareness, polish their writing, and allow them to learn more about the target language (Lee, 2020; Yoon, 2016). The study, however, also indicated that beginning-level students were incapable of effectively using MT and that MT may even undermine their language learning by making them overly dependent on MT. Thus, when using MT, language instructors should consider diverse factors, such as students' prior knowledge about the target language, confidence, and motivation towards language learning.

The current study includes several limitations. First, although the current study did not include the students' scores in the final assessment and made them nonjudgmental, the Hawthorne effect might not be completely eliminated, and the students might have acted differently from their ordinary behaviours. Second, because the low-level students were removed from the research, most of the participants in this study were over the intermediate level, and the study could not fully investigate the low-level students' strategies of using MT. Last, as a quasi-experimental study, the study did not examine the long-term effect of using MT in language learning. A longitudinal study will be fruitful to investigate the long-term effects of MT. Future studies will also be required to explore the development process of students' strategies for using MT over a longer period and develop diverse approaches to integrate MT into language classrooms. Ignoring or banning MT in FL classrooms cannot benefit language learning (Briggs, 2018); therefore, language instructors should seek effective methods to cultivate students' meaningful use of MT.

References

Bahri, H., & Mahadi, T. (2016). Google Translate as a supplementary tool for learning Malay: A case study at Universiti Sains Malaysia. *Advances in Language and Literary Studies, 7*(3), 161–167. http://doi.org/10.7575/aiac.alls.v.7n.3p.161

Briggs, N. (2018). Neural machine translation tools in the language learning classroom: Students' use, perceptions, and analyses. *The JALT CALL Journal, 14*(1), 2–24. https://doi.org/10.29140/jaltcall.v14n1.221

Fredholm, K. (2019). Effects of Google Translate on lexical diversity: Vocabulary development among learners of Spanish as a foreign language. Revista Nebrija de Linguistica Aplicada a la Ensenanza de Las Lenguas, 13(26), 98–117. https://doi.org/10.26378/rnlael1326300

Garcia, I., & Pena, M. (2011). Machine translation-assisted language learning: Writing for beginners. *Computer Assisted Language Learning, 24*(5), 471–487. https://doi.org/10.1080/09588221.2011.582687

Godwin-Jones, R. (2019). In a word of SMART technology, why learn another language? *Educational Technology & Society, 22*(2), 4–13. Retrieved from https://www.jstor.org/stable/10.2307/26819613?seq=1&cid=pdfreference#references_tab_contents

Jolley, J. R., & Maimone, L. (2015). Free online machine translation: Use and perceptions by Spanish students and instructors. In A. Moeller (Ed.) *Learn language, explore cultures transform lives.* (pp. 181–200). Richmond, VA: Robert M. Terry.

Josefsson, E. (2011). Contemporary approaches to translation in the classroom: A study of students' attitudes and strategies. Retrieved from http://du.diva-portal.org/smash/get/diva2:519125/FULLTEXT01.pdf

Kim, N. (2018). A critical review of the impact of the fourth industrial revolution on the development of the basic communicative competence of Korean EFL learners. *Multimedia-Assisted Language Learning, 21*(3), 115–148. http://doi.org/10.15702/mall.2018.21.3.115

Koehn, P. (2020). *Neural machine translation.* Cambridge: Cambridge University Press.

Min, H. (2006). The effects of trained peer review on EFL students' revision types and writing quality. *Journal of Second Language Writing, 15*(2), 118–141. https://doi.org/10.1016/j.jslw.2006.01.003

Niño, A. (2008). Evaluating the use of machine translation post-editing in the foreign language class. *Computer Assisted Language Learning, 21*(1), 29–49. https://doi.org/10.1080/09588220701865482

Niño, A. (2009). Machine translation in foreign language learning: Language learners' and tutors' perceptions of its advantages and disadvantages. *ReCALL, 21*(2), 241–258. https://doi.org/10.1017/S0958344009000172

Niño, A. (2020). Exploring the use of online machine translation for independent language learning. *Research in Learning Technology, 28*. https://doi.org/10.25304/rlt.v28.2402

Lee, S-M. (2020). The impact of using machine translation on EFL students' writing. *Computer Assisted Language Learning, 33*(3), 157–175. https://doi.org/10.1080/09588221.2018.1553186

Lee, S-M. (2021). The effectiveness of machine translation in foreign language education: A systematic review and meta-analysis. *Computer Assisted Language Learning*. https://doi.org/10.1080/09588221.2021.1901745

Lee, S-M., & Briggs, N. (2021). Effects of using machine translation to mediate the revision process of Korean university students' academic writing. *ReCALL, 33*(1), 18-33. https://doi.org/10.1017/S0958344020000191

O'Neill, E. (2019). Training students to use online translators and dictionaries: The impact on second language writing scores. *International Journal of Research Studies in Language Learning, 8*(2), 47–65. https://doi.org/10.5861/ijrsll.2019.4002

Oswald, D., Sherratt, F., & Smith, S. (2010). Handling the Hawthorne effect: The challenges surrounding a participant observer. *Review of Social Studies, 1*(1), 53 – 73.

Pae, T.-I. (2008) A structural model for Korean EFL students' writing performance. *English Teaching, 63*(2), 121–137. https://doi.org/10.15858/engtea.63.2.200806.121

Poibeau, T. (2017). *Machine translation*. Boston, MA: MIT Press.

Shadiev, R., Sun, A., & Huang, Y.-M. (2019). A study of the facilitation of cross-cultural understanding and intercultural sensitivity using speech-enabled language translation technology. *British Journal of Educational Technology, 50*(3), 1415–1433. https://doi.org/10.1111/bjet.12648

Stapleton, P., & Kin, B. (2019). Assessing the accuracy and teachers' impressions of Google Translate: A study of primary L2 writers in Hong Kong. *English for Specific Purposes, 56*, 18–34. https://doi.org/10.1016/j.esp.2019.07.001

Tsai, S.-C. (2019). Using Google translate in EFL drafts: A preliminary investigation. *Computer Assisted Language Learning, 32*(5-6), 510–526. https://doi.org/10.1080/09588221.2018.1527361

Van Waes, L., & Leijten, M. (2015). Fluency in writing: A multidimensional perspective on writing fluency applied to L1 and L2. *Computers & Composition, 38*, 79–95. https://doi.org/10.1016/j.compcom.2015.09.012

Yoon, C. (2016). Concordancers and dictionaries as problem-solving tools for ESL academic writing. *Language Learning & Technology, 20*(1), 209–229. https://doi.org/10125/44453

10
Exploring the processes and products of collaborative multimodal writing in a French as a foreign language class

Miriam Akoto
Mimi Li

Introduction

This chapter reports on an empirical study on collaborative multimodal writing (CMW) which has recently attracted researchers' and instructors' attention following the social turn (Trimbur, 1994) and visual turn (Li & Storch, 2017; Purdy, 2014) in writing studies. CMW is a pedagogical practice in which students in pairs/small groups draw on digital technologies and co-construct multimodal writing products, which incorporate multiple semiotic resources (including but not limited to written texts, images, sound, movement, video, and/or hypertext) to address new audience through new genres. This instructional practice is grounded in two complementary theoretical frameworks—Vygotsky's (1978) sociocultural theory which undergirds collaborative writing and Kress and his colleagues' concept of multimodality (Kress, 2003; Kress & Jewitt, 2003; Kress & Van Leeuwen, 2001) which provides theoretical support for multimodal writing. Writing from a sociocultural perspective is reflected by substantive interaction between multiple writers and shared decision-making responsibility over the produced text (Ede & Lundsford, 1990; Storch, 2011, 2013). Meanwhile, writing from the multimodality standpoint means that written language is no longer considered to be the only starting point of the meaning making process (Jewitt, 2009) and writers draw from an arsenal of socially shaped semiotic resources (or modes) for meaning-making (Kress, 2003, 2010).

A plethora of empirical evidence indicates that collaborative writing (CW) not only fosters language negotiation and mutual scaffolding (DiCamilla & Anton, 1997; Li & Zhu, 2013; Storch, 2019; Swain & Lapkin, 1998), but also improves writing development (Bikowski & Vithanage, 2016; Strobl, 2014) and prepares students for future collaborative work in the professional world (Storch, 2005). Meanwhile, multimodal writing (MW) heightens students' awareness of the metafunctions of semiotic modes (Nelson & Hull, 2008; Shin & Cimasko, 2008; Shin et al., 2020), improves their multiliteracy skills, motivation and autonomy (Hafner, 2014, 2015; Jiang & Luk, 2016; Yi & Angay-Crowder, 2016), contributes to their linguistic and writing repertoires (Oskoz and Elola, 2016; Vandommele et al., 2017), and affords multiple opportunities for self-expression and identity development (Belcher, 2017; Jiang et al., 2020).

Despite flourishing research on CW and MW in L2 contexts, little research has explored CMW using digital technologies (Smith, 2019). A collaborative approach towards digital multimodal texts is likely to foster the development of learners' collaborative skills and L2 digital literacy skills, both considered indispensable for learners to complete authentic tasks in the digital world (Li & Zhang, 2021). Therefore, our study aimed to examine how French FL learners in a university Elementary French class jointly produce MW via Google Docs, focusing on both writing processes and products. To echo the themes of this book (e.g., *contextualization* and *socialization*), this chapter also discusses how technologies are adopted and writing tasks are devised to meet learners' needs in the specific context; how technologies and learning environments afford meaningful interaction, particularly interaction amongst learners. This chapter consists of two main parts. In the first part, we review the relevant literature, present the methodological approach and then report the overview of the study results. In the second part, we discuss how our study addresses the "smartness"-related themes of the book.

Literature Review

A considerable number of empirical studies on computer-mediated CW in L2 classrooms has been devoted to understanding the nature of students' online interactions/writing processes. Most of these studies have examined students' recursive writing and revision process (e.g., Abrams, 2016; Elola &

Oskoz, 2010; Kessler, 2009; Li & Zhu, 2013; Mak & Coniam, 2008). For instance, Mak and Coniam (2008) were among the first to explore writing change functions such as adding ideas, expanding ideas, reorganizing ideas and correcting errors in wiki-based writing within the ESL context. Other studies (e.g., Abrams, 2016; Elola & Oskoz, 2010) went a step further to identify specific types of revision behaviors within areas like content, stylistics, structure, and grammar. Moreover, another subset of studies (e.g., Alghasab & Handley, 2017; Li & Kim, 2016) has examined the nature of peer talk gathered through students' discussion posts in conjunction with the revision behaviors. For example, Li (2013) reported that students' online interactions focused on five key areas, namely content discussion, social talk, task management, technical communication, and language negotiation. Building on this work, Li and Kim (2016) later analyzed online interactions from the perspectives of language functions, writing change functions, and scaffolding strategies, and found students' dynamic interactions across tasks.

Another important area is concerned with assessing the qualities of students' CW products. Previous studies (e.g., Elola & Oskoz, 2010; Kuteeva, 2011; Mak & Coniam, 2008; Storch, 2005) have examined the textual quality of CW on wikis and Google Docs in terms of complexity, accuracy and fluency (CAF) (see review in Li, 2018). For instance, Mak and Coniam's (2008) study evaluated the wiki quality by tracking textual changes in the amount and the types of writing such as word count, t-unit, and purpose of revision. Other studies examined accuracy as an indicator of textual quality. While Arnold *et al.* (2009) and Lee (2010) observed increased grammatical accuracy, Kessler *et al.* (2012) and Ducate *et al.* (2011) claimed that students paid little attention to grammatical structures and were more concerned with overall meaning. Going beyond the CAF frameworks, Li and Zhu (2017) analyzed coherence and rhetorical structure of small groups' wiki writing.

Compared with CW, digital MW is a relatively younger field that has seen a significant spurt in published scholarship over the past years. Previous studies (e.g., Cimasko & Shin, 2017; Smith *et al.*, 2017; Yang, 2012) have closely examined the MW processes by investigating students' orchestration of multiple semiotic modes to create multimodal texts. For example, Smith *et al.*'s (2017) study used screen-recorded data to explore high school AP English students' multimodal composing processes across three multimodal projects. Likewise, Cimasko and Shin (2017) focused on the process by which one ESL student remediated a traditional academic text (i.e., argumentative essay) into a digital multimodal video. Other important composing processes that have also been studied included remix practices such as chunking, layering, blending (e.g., Hafner, 2014, 2015; Hafner & Miller, 2011) and synesthesia, transformation and transduction (e.g., Kress, 2003; Nelson, 2006; Oskoz & Elola, 2016). A few recent studies (e.g., Gánem-Gutiérrez & Gilmore, 2018; Lim, 2020) employed eye-tracking and screen-recording technologies to explore the processes of utilizing different semiotic resources and the amount of time students spent on each phase. Regarding the multimodal products, researchers analyzed the writing qualities by either using the CAF framework (Vandommele et al., 2017) or referring to multiple-traits grading rubrics (Hung et al., 2012; Hafner & Ho, 2020).

Although previous research has reported multiple benefits of online CW and MW, little research has explored the complex nature of students' interactions while collaboratively working on MW projects. Moreover, much of the studies on CW and MW were conducted in ESL/EFL contexts, but not in the French FL context. Therefore, this study aims to bridge the gap. To echo the themes of contextualization and socialization, we explore how technological tools (e.g., Google Docs) and learning environments (i.e., CMW tasks) can be adopted/adapted to suit the specific needs of elementary-level French FL learners at the tertiary level in the US, and how learners interact in the collaborative CALL project.

Our study was guided by the following research questions:

RQ1. What multimodal composing processes do the French FL learners engage in to jointly complete the writing task via Google Docs?
RQ2. What are the qualities of the French FL learners' CMW products?

Methodology

The study reported in this chapter is part of a larger research project in which we adopted a multiple-case study approach (Stake, 2006; Yin, 2009) to explore the process by which French FL learners collaboratively work to complete MW projects, the quality of the finished products and their perceptions on the integration of CMW. According to Yin (2009), "the evidence from multiple-cases is often considered more compelling" and "regarded as being more robust" than single-case research designs (p. 53). Also, the multi-faceted nature of our study lends itself well to a multiple-case study design as it allows us to not only explore the different dimensions of CMW but also compare and contrast results between cases within a bounded system.

Participants

This study was conducted with seven students enrolled in an Elementary French course at a southern public university in the U.S. The demographic information of the participants is shown in Table 10.1. Most of them were freshman students and some had previously taken Advanced Placement French courses in high school. Almost all were comfortable with using technology with the exception of Alejandro who gave a neutral answer in the pre-task questionnaire. As to the group formation, students were allowed to choose their own partner(s). The instructor (the first author) encouraged students to pair off with different minors in the hope of creating a more favorable environment for a meaningful collaborative experience (Storch, 2013).

Table 10.1 *Participants' profiles.*

	Name [1]	Age	Gender	Major
Group 1	Britney	20	Female	Theatre
	Eva	20	Female	Art
Group 2	Joshua	21	Male	Music
	Christine	20	Female	English
	Brian	20	Male	History/Political Science
Group 3	Alejandro	23	Male	Music
	Mary-Ann	21	Female	Music/Theatre

[1] Pseudonyms are used. Information was retrieved from the pre-task questionnaire surveys.

Task description and instructional procedures

The multimodal task was designed based on the multiliteracies framework (Cope & Kalantzis, 2015; New London Group, 1996) and genre-based writing pedagogy (Hyland, 2007). The task was tied to the course content which centered around the themes of family, food and travel/vacation. In each chapter, students were exposed to a variety of textual genres such as blog postings, personal ads, TV commercials, and videos on YouTube.

They participated in instructional activities that required them to interpret, collaborate, problem-solve, and reflect on the texts used. After they learned the chapter of travel/ vacation, students were invited to co-create and co-design a digital postcard describing their vacation activities via Google Docs. Google Docs was purposefully chosen as the collaborative platform for this study for two main reasons: (1) accessibility (i.e., students already have access to a free Gmail account through the university which allows them to use Google Docs); and (2) ease of collaboration (i.e., Google Docs allows multiple users to create and edit joint documents both synchronously and asynchronously). The students completed the CMW task over the course of six weeks. In Week 1, willing participants signed the informed consent forms and attended an instructor-led orientation workshop to get reacquainted with Google Docs. The workshop focused on familiarizing students with the use of certain features on Google Docs such as adding comments through the "Insert" tab, changing the page layout, inserting hyperlinks and adding images directly from Google images. Also, students were invited to review the grading rubric which aimed to guide their CW process and assess their joint multimodal texts. In Weeks 3 to 5, each pair/small group jointly wrote and co-designed their own digital postcards. Students were reminded to apply genre knowledge instructed by the instructor and to refer to three examples of postcards that were used as model texts. In Week 6, they shared their products with the rest of the class and received assessments/comments from their classmates. Each team then made the revisions outside of class based on the peer feedback and submitted their final products as part of the course requirements for the semester.

Data analysis

We adopted a qualitative approach to exploring how the pairs/small groups jointly worked to complete MW projects and the quality of their finished products. Data for this study were gathered from three different sources: (1) finished multimodal products; (2) archived Google Docs records; and (3) screen recordings collected using Camtasia.

Table 10.2 *Coding scheme for MW processes*

On-screen activity	Description & Examples
Internet search	Searching for information, explanation or inspiration in different stages, in different forms. e.g., reading informational websites, scrolling through images/clip arts, looking up words in an online dictionary or translation website, etc.
Content Production	Contributing new or additional information and/or removing existing information from the product. e.g., typing text, inserting hyperlinks
Written Text Edit	Adding or deleting parts of the written text (both in L1 and L2) and rephrasing or reorganizing sentences.
Visual & Spatial Edit	Adding or deleting visual elements (e.g., graphics, fonts, colors, memes, emojis, images/drawings, etc.) as well as spatial elements (e.g., positioning of texts, moving margins, spacing and fixing the general layout).
Resource Consultation	Accessing instructor provided resources (e.g., task prompt, examples, links to websites, etc.), e-textbook or course shell for information or clarification.

Analysis of the CMW process

The screen-recorded data helped us to understand two main components regarding students' MW processes: (1) the multiple semiotic resources that French learners used to complete the CMW task, and (2) the amount of time that they devoted to each process. We started the analysis process by importing all the screen recorded data into MAXQDA, a qualitative data analysis software, which allowed us to directly code the video files alongside the synced transcript from the audio recorded interactions. The first author analyzed students' on-screen activities by segmenting each participant's screen-recorded video into four episodes drawing on previous studies (Gánem-Gutiérrez & Gilmore, 2018; Lim, 2020) which also analyzed screen-recorded videos of students' on-screen writing behaviors. Each episode was defined as "a segment of the video that contained only one L2 writing process" (Gánem-Gutiérrez & Gilmore, 2018, p. 481). Each new episode was coded based on a writer's transition from one process to another. Based on the themes emerging from the data, the first author developed a coding scheme composed of five categories describing different types of on-screen activities, which was verified by the second author (see Table 10.2). Figure 10.1 shows a screenshot of the coded data of student's on-screen activities in MAXQDA. After completing the segmentation and coding process, we retrieved descriptive statistics about the amount of time that learners devoted to each process from MAXQDA, which were recorded in the Microsoft Excel. Then, we averaged all total times for each category and compared the total duration of time that each pair/small group spent on each process. As supplementary information, audio recorded data gathered via Camtasia revealed the group members' discussions during the CW task. Drawing on the audio transcripts, we identified three categories: content discussion, language negotiation, and task management, as displayed in Table 10.3. Furthermore, archived Google Docs history records retrieved all the changes that were made by each individual group member.

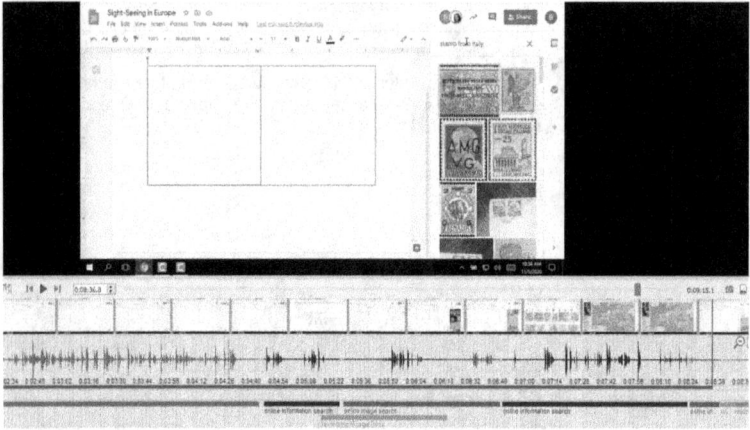

Figure 10.1 Screenshot of coding of on-screen activities via MAXQDA

Table 10.3 *Peer discussion categories*

Categories	Definitions
Content Discussion	Episodes where group members generated, discussed and reorganized ideas related to the content of the postcard.
Language Negotiation	Episodes where group members focused their attention explicitly on language use and deliberated over lexical, grammatical and mechanical choices.
Task Management	Episodes in which group members determined how to complete the task together and resolved issues such as time management, labor division, problem-solving, navigating and setting-up Google Docs, etc.

Analysis of the collaborative multimodal writing products

We examined the textual features of each small group's joint multimodal product based on two measures, that is, accuracy and fluency. Fluency was measured as the total number of words (Fernandez-Dobao, 2012; Storch, 2011) and accuracy was measured as the ratio of the number of errors to the number of total words (Storch, 2011). We did not include the measure of complexity due to the students' low L2 proficiency level. As to the errors, we analyzed three types drawing on Storch (2005): (1) syntactical errors (e.g., errors in word order, missing syntactic elements), (2) morphological errors (e.g., verb tense, subject-verb agreement, errors in use of articles and prepositions, errors in word forms), and (3) spelling errors. Although the CAF framework (Johnson, 2017; Zhang & Plonsky, 2020) is commonly used for traditional monomodal L2 writing, it does not take into account the design components inherent in MW. Consequently, researchers within the domain of MW (e.g., Kang & Kim, 2019; Lim, 2020; Yeh, 2018) have called for a broadened view of the assessment of product quality, emphasizing the importance of both linguistic and non-linguistic dimensions (e.g., visual, gestural, spatial and auditory designs) in line with the multimodality and multiliteracies frameworks. Therefore, we also drew on the multiple traits grading rubric and had the CMW products peer-assessed holistically. The rubric consisted of five categories: (1) content and organization, (2) language use, (3) multimodal design, (4) purpose and audience, and (5) originality and citation. The scores for each category was a number ranging from 1 to 5 (i.e., 5: excellent, 4: very good, 3: satisfactory, 2: fair, 1: poor). At the end of the semester, the instructor also graded the final products using the same grading rubric. Afterwards, we averaged all the scores assigned by the students and the instructor and compared the total scores that each small group received.

Results

Process

Our first research question asked about how students jointly completed the MW task. Specifically, we analyzed two main areas of students' MW processes: (1) the semiotic resources that they used, and (2) the amount of time that they devoted to each process. The screen-recorded data showed that the pairs/small groups drew on a variety of semiotic modes including written texts, images/drawings and hyperlinks to co-construct the digital multimodal projects. Table 10.4 displays an overview of students' use of semiotic modes.

Table 10.4 *Use of semiotic modes across the three cases.*

Semiotic mode	Group 1	Group 2	Group 3
Total written words	181	175	218
Images/drawings	5	5	4
Hyperlinks	2	3	0

To illustrate how the students utilized multiple semiotic resources, we present a sample writing product below.

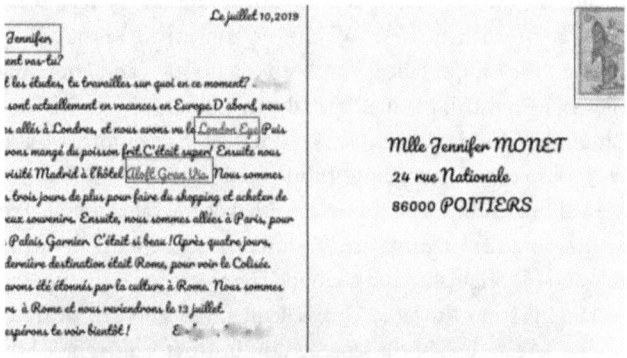

Figure 10.2 *Group 1's digital postcard entitled "Un voyage touristique en Europe" (Sight-seeing in Europe).*

Akoto & Lee 217

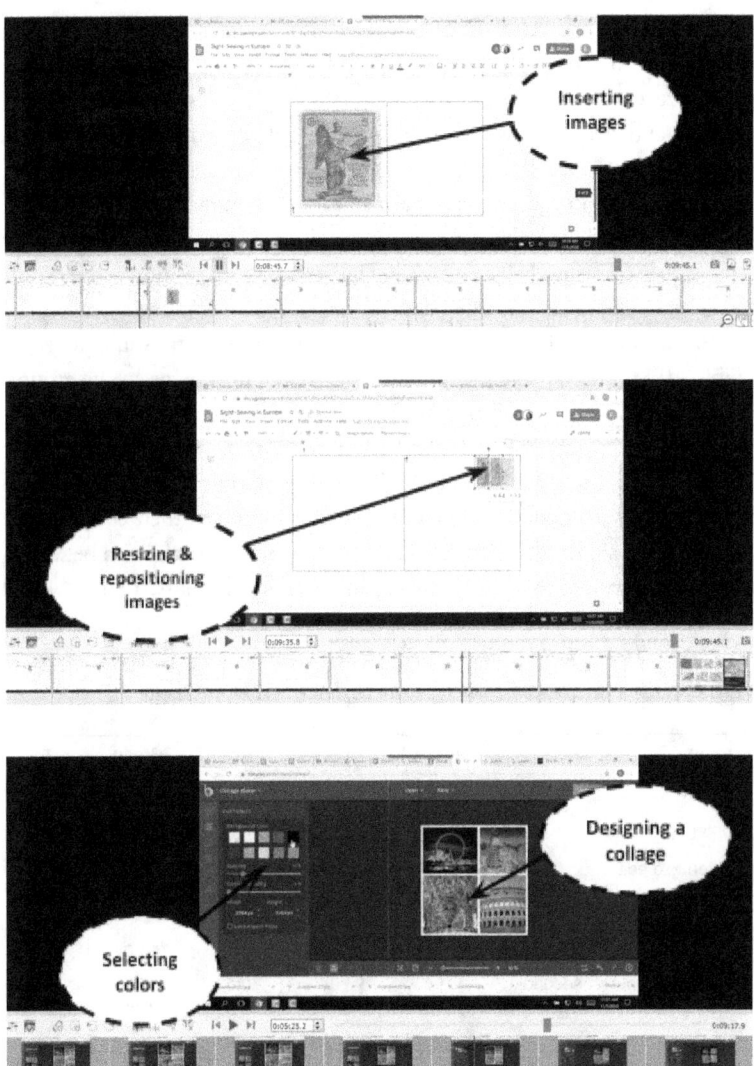

Figures 10.3-10.5 *Screenshots of sample semiotic modes used by Group 1.*

As shown in Figure 10.2, Britney and Eva co-created a postcard intended to be sent to a mutual friend in France named Jennifer Monet. They described the weather at their current vacation site, narrated their experiences thus far and their plans for the next destination. They also included a stamp, hyperlinks to the tourist attraction sites they visited and designed a collage of pictures as the cover of the postcard. While Groups 2 and 3 began their MW process by composing the written text, the members of Group 1, Britney and Eva, chose to start with the visual content of their postcard. They both searched the internet for images of their vacation destinations and saved these images to use as the inspirational foundation for their work. Next, they collaged different modes and used advanced image-editing techniques to bring their text to life. Figures 10.3 to 10.5 shows screenshots taken from the screen-recorded data of the group's MW process.

Additionally, the analysis of the screen-recorded data, summarized in Table 10.5, revealed some similarities and differences between the groups. For example, we observed that all the groups dedicated the largest amount of time searching the internet for information, explanation and/or inspiration ($M = 22.05$, $SD = 4.87$). However, while Group 1 spent the most amount of time (23.22) editing their written text, their counterparts in Group 3 paid least attention to it (13.38). A similar pattern can be seen in the time devoted to editing visual and spatial elements, that is, 16.12 (Group 1) versus 10.29 (Group 3).

Table 10.5 *Duration of time spent on different MW processes.*

Process	Group 1	Group 2	Group 3	Mean	SD
Internet search	20:22	27:57	18:35	22.05	4.87
Content production	18:21	19:27	14:32	17.27	2.61
Written text edit	23:22	20:17	13:38	18.92	5.04
Visual & spatial edit	16:12	13:48	10:29	13.30	2.92
Resource consultation	12:38	15:55	14:19	14.04	1.59
Total time (minutes: seconds)	90:15	96:04	70:53	85.57	13.36

While the screen-recorded data helped us to explore the kinds of semiotic resources that participants used and the duration of time they devoted to each composing process, the transcripts of the audio recorded data provided additional information on the discussions/interactions that they had while completing the task. We identified three categories of discussions, i.e., content discussion, language negotiation and task management. Table 6 below shows the frequency of each category of peer discussions.

Table 10.6. *Peer discussions across the three groups.*

Category	Group 1	Group 2	Group 3
Content Discussion	47	39	24
Language Negotiation	32	37	10
Task Management	27	25	50

As displayed in Table 10.6, Groups 1 and 2 participated in a considerable amount of discussion focusing on negotiating content with a total of 47 and 39 instances respectively. However, Group 2 focused more on resolving grammatical and syntactical problems in their written text and made the highest number of language negotiation (i.e., 37 instances). Group 3 on the other hand, paid less attention to language and were more preoccupied with task management and planning (i.e., 50 instances). The following illustrative excerpts for each of these interactions further highlight how group members scaffolded each other during the MW processes.

Excerpt 1: Content discussion (Group 1)

>**Britney:** [...] oh and you know how like in some postcards they have like cartoons of the luggage where like it's just got like stickers of places they've been or like, something like that for the cover of the postcard would be fun, right?
>**Eva:** yeah that would be nice but I was just thinking a collage for the cover
>**Britney:** oh yeah that's not a bad idea and maybe include pictures of like double decker buses or Buckingham Palace [...]
>**Eva:** uhhuh yeah that could work

In this excerpt, Britney initiated the group discussion by sharing an idea for the cover of the digital postcard and asking or eliciting her partner's opinion about it. Eva contributed to Britney's idea with her own vision for the cover to be a collage of pictures instead. Britney liked this collage idea better and added some more suggestions on how to bring it to life. There were several instances where this pair demonstrated mutual respect for each other's viewpoints and actively participated in the decision-making process.

Excerpt 2: Language negotiation (Group 2)

> **Christine:** uh Joshua I think that we have to move "beau" before the word not after
> **Joshua:** oh yeah because of BANGS ((laughing))
> **Christine:** yep ...
> **Brian:** oh yeah good catch! That reminds me we probably have to change "visiter "to the past right?
> **Christine:** uhuh and "visiter" goes with "avoir" in passé composé just fyi

Excerpt 2 above shows Christine, Joshua and Brian engaging in peer scaffolding as they determine the place of the adjective "beau." Christine reminds Joshua to change the placement of the adjective "beau" using the acronym BANGS (which stands for Beauty, Age, Newness, Gender, and Size) and move the adjective before the noun instead of after. The group members also discuss the tense of the verb used in one of the sentences and reach a resolution on the correct auxiliary verb to use in the past tense.

Excerpt 3: Task management (Group 3)

> **Mary-Ann:** [...] so do you think three activities is fine or should we add more?
> **Alejandro:** well I think the prompt says at least three so I guess we should just stick with that [...]
> **Mary-Ann:** yeah plus we'll also have to explain in detail exactly what we'll be doing there so I think we'd be better off with just three ((laughing))
> **Alejandro:** ((laughing)) yeah keep it simple
> **Mary-Ann:** cool so I can get started on writing up one or two so in the meantime maybe you should fix the address?

The discussion in Excerpt 3 shows Mary-Ann and Alejandro negotiating about the number of vacation activities to include in their postcard as well as dividing up the labor. Although this pair did not pay much attention to language negotiation, they were actively engaged in discussions revolving around task management.

Product

For our second research question regarding the qualities of students' finished products, we first discuss the textual qualities of the three multimodal texts based on two aspects: accuracy and fluency. We also show the scores of the three groups' final products.

In terms of textual features, we conducted an error analysis of the finished products focusing on three main categories: syntactic error, morphological error, and spelling error, and calculated the frequency of errors for each type. We also assessed writing accuracy by measuring the total number of errors divided by the total words. The results are displayed in Table 10.6.

Table 10.6 *Results of the error analysis of students' finished products.*

Error type	Group 1	Group 2	Group 3
Syntactic error	3	4	4
Morphological error	4	6	7
Spelling error	3	3	6
Total words	181	218	175
Distribution of errors (Total number of error/total word count)	5.52%	5.96%	9.71%

Although all three groups completed the task, there were some significant differences in the quality of the finished products. As shown in Table 10.6, Group 3's final product had the lowest word count (175 total word count) and the highest distribution of errors (9.71%) in comparison to that of Groups 1 and 2 who had 5.52% and 5.96% respectively. We found 4 instances of syntactic errors, 7 instances of morphological errors and 6 instances of spelling errors. For example, with regards to morphological errors, we found errors in the use of preposition and subject-verb agreement in the following sentences, "Nous sommes dans Hawaii! C'est beau ici et nous adore être sur cette île" (Nous sommes à Hawaii! C'est beau ici et nous adorons être sur cette île). For syntactic errors, we identified errors in word order such as "nous tellement adore" (nous adorons tellement) and "chaud temps" (temps chaud). A substantial number of spelling errors were also found such as "joures" (jours), "plungée" (plongée), "pliasir" (plaisir), and "magnificent" (magnifique). Group 2's final product, on the other hand, had the highest word count (218 total) compared to the other two products but it also had the second highest distribution of errors (5.96%). We found the least number of errors in Group 1's product with a total of 10 error instances, resulting the lowest error distribution (5.52%). Table 7 below also shows the average scores of each pair/group's digital multimodal postcard.

Table 10.7 *Overview of the three small groups' final product scores.*

Category (Total possible score)	Group 1	Group 2	Group 3
Content & Organization (5)	4.75	4.25	4
Language Use (5)	4.5	4.75	3.5
Multimodal Design (5)	4.75	4.5	4
Purpose & Audience (5)	4.5	4.25	4.25
Originality & Citation (5)	5	4.25	4.5
Total (25)	23.5	22	20.25

As Table 10.7 shows, Groups 1 and 2 produced relatively high quality products in comparison to Group 3. Group 1 obtained the highest total score, that is, 23.5 points out of 25 and specifically the highest scores in two categories, namely, 4.75 points in content and organization, and multimodal design. Group 2 also produced a good final product and received the second highest total score, that is, 22 points out of 25. This finding can be attributed to the substantial collective scaffolding that occurred within the two groups as reflected in peer discussions and jointly employing the multiple semiotic resources. Group 3 obtained the lowest total score (20.25 points out of 25), with the lowest score in language use (3.5 points). The poor quality in terms of language use was related to the group members' less engagement in the CMW task, reflected in less instances of peer discussion and less time spent on multiple writing phases (e.g., text edits, visual design, content production).

Application to Smart CALL

In this study, we contextualized the collaborative multimodal writing task in a tertiary-level French FL classroom and explored how French learners jointly utilized semiotic resources and negotiated the writing task to complete the collaborative multimodal writing project using Google Docs. Relating to the themes of this book (e.g., contextualization and socialization), in this section we discuss how the technological tool (i.e., Google Docs) and learning environments (i.e., collaborative multimodal writing tasks) were adapted to suit the specific needs of elementary level French FL learners at the tertiary level in this study. We also draw on sociocultural theory (Vygotsky, 1978) and its associated constructs (i.e., ZPD and collective scaffolding) to interpret the role of interactions amongst the French learners as they jointly produced MW via Google Docs. Our overall goal is to highlight the importance of *contextualization* and *socialization* in L2 writing pedagogy.

We are informed that knowledge is anchored by the context in which the learning activity occurs (Brown *et al.*, 1989). We perceive learning and knowing as context-specific social processes (Rogoff, 1990). In the L2 classrooms, instructors need to adopt the learning task and technology to cater to the needs and characteristics of L2 learners. In this French class in which our study was conducted, improving students' writing skills is one of the main course goals, and writing to learn is also a commonly adopted approach in the French program. Motivated by the benefits of L2 CW reported in previous studies (e.g., Li, 2018; Storch, 2013) and the learners' engagement in digital multimodal texts in real-life settings (e.g., Yi *et al.*, 2020), we implemented the collaborative multimodal writing project with French FL learners. Considering their familiarity with Google Docs, we used this technology as their CW platform. Also, all the learners shared their interest in traveling abroad in the future, so linking to the learning unit of "vacation," we devised the digital postcard creating task. Our study reinforced the role of Google Docs as a digital platform for CW reported in previous studies (e.g., Kessler *et al.* 2012; Strobl 2014; Yim *et al.*, 2017). Our results confirmed that Google Docs facilitates students' writing processes as it not only afforded opportunities for group members to co-write and co-edit the document synchronously but also promoted timely feedback and exchange of ideas. Of note, the screen-recorded data showed that group members/pairs devoted a substantial amount of time accessing the internet via direct Google search from within their Google Docs file to find information, explanation and/or inspiration at different stages of the co- construction process. After the students received well-structured training, the collaborative postcard creating task allowed them to fully engage in the learning of French language and the acquisition of the new writing genre, although the three groups showed different degrees of engagement and completed the final products with different levels of quality.

Moreover, our study reflected the students' learning through peer interaction during the CMW project. Sociocultural theory maintains that human development and learning come from social and cultural interaction, and language and interaction facilitate learning in the learners' Zone of Proximal Development (Vygotsky,1978). With peers' scaffolding, learners reach higher levels of performance than they might achieve by working alone (Donato, 2004; Ohta, 2000; Swain & Lapkin, 1998). In our study, the French learners were found to engage in discussing multiple aspects of writing, such as task management, content discussion, and language negotiation, as well as jointly involving with MW processes, including content production, visual modification, and resource consultation. Of note, the students were able to attend to linguistic problems and make adequate revisions based on the feedback provided by others, which may somewhat alleviate the concern that digital multimodal writing projects might come at the expense of linguistic development expressed in Qu (2017). However, as mentioned earlier, different degrees of engagement with the writing task were identified among the small groups, which led to different qualities of writing products. Our study thus supported the positive role of socialization and interaction in L2 learning and development.

Conclusion

To conclude, it is our hope that this study will spark the interest of L2/FL educators both in secondary and tertiary settings to implement collaborative multimodal writing tasks in their own classes. As the study illustrates, the successful integration of collaborative and multimodal writing is possible even for learners at the elementary level of proficiency. However, we would like to acknowledge some limitations of the study. Firstly, we only explored the implementation of one task type and diverse tasks would help us understand better the dynamics of student engagement and interaction. Secondly, this study focused on the students' writing processes as a group, and did not intend to distinguish each individual member's contribution within the groups. To obtain a richer understanding of the nature of online interactions, future research needs to explore distinctive patterns of interactions based on the equality and mutuality of individual members' participation within each small group. Future quantitative, experimental study designs could also examine the potential gains in writing development by comparing groups of learners engaging in collaborative multimodal tasks and those completing individual multimodal tasks. In that way could the role of collaboration for learning be further delved into. Moreover, what deserves further investigation is learners' perceptions of this type of new writing pedagogy and the perceived factors mediating their CMW processes. In short, CMW can potentially be an effective instructional task that is implemented in diverse L2 learning contexts.

References

Abrams, Z. (2016). Exploring collaboratively written L2 texts among first-year learners of German in Google Docs. *Computer Assisted Language Learning, 29*(8), 1259–1270. https://doi.org/10.1080/09588221.2016.1270968

Alghasab, M., & Handley, Z. (2017). Capturing (non-) collaboration in wiki-mediated collaborative writing activities: The need to examine discussion posts and editing acts in tandem. *Computer Assisted Language Learning, 30*(7), 664–691. https://doi.org/10.1080/09588221.2017.1341928

Arnold, N., Ducate, L., & Kost, C. (2012). Collaboration or cooperation? Analyzing group dynamics and revision process in wikis. *CALICO Journal, 29*(3), 431–448.

Belcher, D. (2017). On becoming facilitators of multimodal composing and digital design. *Journal of Second Language Writing, 38*, 80–85. https://doi.org/10.1016/j.jslw.2017.10.004

Bikowski, D., & Vithanage, R. (2016). Effects of web-based collaborative writing on individual L2 writing development. *Language Learning & Technology, 20*(1), 79–99.

Brown, J.S., Collins, A., & Duguid, P. (1989). Situated cognition and the culture of learning. *Educational Researcher, 18* (1), 32–42.

Burnett, R.E., Frazee, A., Hanggi, K., & Madden, A. (2014). A programmatic ecology of assessment: Using a common rubric to evaluate multimodal processes and artifacts. *Computers and Composition, 31*, 53–66. https://doi.org/10.1016/j.compcom.2013.12.005

Cimasko, T., & Shin, D. (2017). Multimodal resemiotization and authorial agency in an L2 writing classroom. *Written Communication, 34*(4), 387–413. https://doi:10.1177/0741088317727246

Cope, B., & Kalantzis, M. (2015). The things you do to know: An introduction to the pedagogy of multiliteracies. In B. Cope & M. Kalantzis (Eds.), *A pedagogy of multiliteracies: Learning by design* (pp. 1–36). Palgrave Macmillan UK. https://doi.org/10.1057/9781137539724_1

DiCamilla, F., & Anton, M. (1997). The function of repetition in the collaborative discourse of L2 learners. *The Canadian Modern Language Review, 53*, 609–633. https://doi.org/10.3138/cmlr.53.4.609

Dobao, A.F. (2012). Collaborative writing tasks in the L2 classroom: Comparing group, pair, and individual work. *Journal of Second Language Writing, 21*(1), 40–58. https://doi.org/10.1016/j.jslw.2011.12.002

Donato, R. (2004). Aspects of collaboration in pedagogical discourse. *Annual Review of Applied Linguistics, 24*, 284–302. https://doi.org/10.1017/S026719050400011X

Ducate, L., Anderson, L., & Moreno, N. (2011). Wading through the world of wikis: An analysis of three wiki projects. *Foreign Language Annals, 44*(3), 495–524. https://doi.org/10.1111/j.1944-9720.2011.01144.x

Dzekoe, R. (2017). Computer-based multimodal composing activities, self-revision, and L2 acquisition through writing. *Language Learning & Technology, 21*(2), 73–95.

Ede, L., & Lunsford, A. (1990). *Singular texts/plural authors*. Carbondale, IL: Southern Illinois University Press.

Elola, I., & Oskoz, A. (2010). Collaborative writing: Fostering foreign language and writing conventions development. *Language Learning & Technology, 14*, 51–71.

Gánem-Gutiérrez, G.A., & Gilmore, A. (2018). Tracking the real-time evolution of a writing event: second language writers at different proficiency levels. *Language Learning, 68*(2), 469–506. https://doi.org/10.1111/lang.12280

Hafner, C.A. (2014). Embedding digital literacies in English language teaching: Students' digital video projects as multimodal ensembles. *TESOL Quarterly, 48*(4), 655–685. https://doi.org/10.1002/tesq.138

Hafner, C. (2015). Remix culture and English language teaching: The expression of learner voice in digital multimodal compositions. *TESOL Quarterly, 49*(3), 486–509. https://doi.org/10.1002/tesq.238

Hafner, C.A., & Miller, L. (2011). Fostering learner autonomy in English for science: A collaborative digital video project in a technological learning environment. *Language Learning & Technology, 15*(3), 68–86.

Hung, H., Chiu, Y., & Yeh, H. (2013). Multimodal assessment of and for learning: A theory driven design rubric. *British Journal of Educational Technology, 44*, 400–409. https://doi.org/10.1111/j.1467-8535.2012.01337.x

Hyland, K. (2007). Genre pedagogy: Language, literacy and L2 writing instruction. *Journal of Second Language Writing, 16*(3), 148–164. https://doi.org/10.1016/j.jslw.2007.07.005

Jewitt, C. (Ed.). (2009). *The handbook of multimodal analysis*. London: Routledge.

Jiang, L. (2018). Digital multimodal composing and investment change in learners' writing in English as a foreign language. *Journal of Second Language Writing, 40*, 60–72. https://doi.org/10.1016/j.jslw.2018.03.002

Jiang, L., & Luk, J. (2016). Multimodal composing as a learning activity in English classrooms: Inquiring into the sources of its motivational capacity. *System, 59*, 1–11. https://doi.org/10.1016/j.system.2016.04.001

Jiang, L., Yu, S., & Zhao, Y. (2019). Teacher engagement with digital multimodal composing in a Chinese tertiary EFL curriculum. *Language Teaching Research*. https://doi.org/10.1177/1362168819864975

Jiang, L., Yu, S., & Zhao, Y. (2020). An EFL teacher's investment in digital multimodal composing. *ELT Journal, 74*(3), 297–306. https://doi.org/10.1093/elt/ccaa010

Kessler, G. (2009). Student-initiated attention to form in wiki-based collaborative writing. *Language Learning & Technology, 13*(1), 79–95.

Kessler, G., & Bikowski, D. (2010). Developing collaborative autonomous learning abilities in computer mediated language learning: Attention to meaning among students in wiki space. *Computer Assisted Language Learning, 23*(1), 41–58. https://doi.org/10.1080/09588220903467335

Kessler, G., Bikowski, D., & Boggs, J. (2012). Collaborative writing among second language learners in academic web-based projects. *Language Learning & Technology, 16*, 91–109.

Kuteeva, M. (2011). Wikis and academic writing: Changing the writer-reader relationship. *English for Specific Purposes, 30,* 44–57.

Kress, G., & Van Leeuwen, T. (2001). *Multimodal discourse: The modes and media of contemporary communication.* London: Edward Arnold.

Kress, G. (2003). *Literacy in the new media age.* London: Routledge.

Kress, G. (2010). *Multimodality: A social semiotic approach to contemporary communication.* Abingdon: Routledge.

Kress, G., & Jewitt, C. (2003). Introduction. In C. Jewitt & G. Kress (Eds.), *Multimodal literacy* (pp. 1-18). New York: Peter Lang.

Lee, L. (2010). Exploring wiki-mediated collaborative writing: A case study in an elementary Spanish course. *CALICO Journal, 27*(2), 260–276.https://dx.doi.org/10.11139/cj.27.2.260-276

Lee, S., Lo, Y., & Chin, T. (2021). Practicing multiliteracies to enhance EFL learners' meaning making process and language development: A multimodal Problem-based approach. *Computer Assisted Language Learning, 34*(1–2), 27–66. https://doi.org/10.1080/09588221.2019.1614959

Li, M. (2013). Individual novices and collective experts: Collective scaffolding in wiki-based small group writing. *System, 41*(3), 752–769. http://dx.doi.org/10.1016/j.system.2013.07.021

Li, M., & Akoto, M. (2021). Review of recent research on L2 digital multimodal composing. *International Journal of Computer-Assisted Language Learning and Teaching, 11*(3), 1–16. https://doi.org/10.4018/IJCALLT.2021070101

Li, M., & Storch, N. (2017). Second language writing in the age of CMC: Affordances, multimodality, and collaboration. *Journal of Second Language Writing, 36,* 1–5. https://doi.org/10.1016/j.jslw.2017.05.012

Li, M., & Kim, D. (2016). One wiki: Two groups: Dynamic interactions across ESL collaborative writing tasks. *Journal of Second Language Writing, 31,* 25-42. https://doi.org/10.1016/j.jslw.2016.01.002

Li, M., & Zhang, M. (2021). Collaborative writing in L2 classrooms: A research agenda. *Language Teaching.* Advance online publication. https://doi.org/10.1017/S0261444821000318

Li, M. & Zhu, W. (2013). Patterns of computer-mediated interaction in EFL collaborative writing groups using wikis. *Computer Assisted Language Learning, 26,* 61–82.

Li, M., & Zhu, W. (2017). Good or bad collaborative wiki writing: Exploring links between group interactions and writing products. *Journal of Second Language Writing, 35*, 38–53.

Lim, J.M. (2020). *Language in multimodal writing processes and performance: Developing multimodal writing tasks for L2 learners* (Unpublished doctoral dissertation). Michigan State University.

Mak, B., & Coniam, D. (2008). Using wikis to enhance and develop writing skills among secondary school students in Hong Kong. *System, 36*(3), 437–455.

Manchón, R.M. (2017). The potential impact of multimodal composition on language learning. *Journal of Second Language Writing, 38*, 94–95. https://www.doi.org/10.1016/j.jslw.2017.10.008

Nelson, M. (2006). Mode, meaning, and synaesthesia in multimedia L2 writing. *Language Learning & Technology, 10*(2), 56–76.

Nelson, M.E., & Hull, G.A. (2008). Self-presentation through multimedia: A Bakhtinian perspective on digital storytelling. In K. Lundby (Ed.), *Digital storytelling, mediatized stories: Self-representations in new media* (pp. 123–141). New York: Peter Lang.

New London Group. (1996). A pedagogy of multiliteracies: Designing social futures. *Harvard Educational Review, 66*(1), 60–93.

Ohta, A. S. (2000). Re-thinking interaction in SLA: Developmentally appropriate assistance in the zone of proximal development and the acquisition of L2 grammar. In J. P. Lantolf (Ed.), *Sociocultural theory and second language learning* (pp. 51–78). Oxford, UK: Oxford University Press.

Oskoz, A., & Elola, I. (2016a). Digital stories: An overview. *CALICO Journal, 33*(2), 157–173.

Oskoz, A., & Elola, I. (2016). Digital stories: Bringing multimodal texts to the Spanish writing classroom. *ReCALL, 28*(3), 326–342.

Purdy, J. (2014). What can design thinking offer writing studies? *College Composition and Communication, 65*(4), 612–641.

Qu, W. (2017). For L2 writers, it is always the problem of the language. *Journal of Second Language Writing, 38*, 92–93. https://doi.org/10.1016/j.jslw.2017.10.007

Rogoff, B. (1990). *Apprenticeship in thinking: Cognitive development in social context*. New York: Oxford University Press.

Sauro, S. (2017b). Online fan practices and CALL. *CALICO Journal, 34*(2), 131–146.

Shin, D.S., & Cimasko, T. (2008). Multimodal composition in a college ESL class: New tools, traditional norms. *Computers and Composition*, *25*(4), 376–395.

Shin, D.S., Cimasko, T., & Yi, Y. (2020). Development of metalanguage for multimodal composing: A case study of an L2 writer's design of multimedia texts. *Journal of Second Language Writing*, 47, 100714.

Smith, B., Pacheco, M., & de Almeida, C. (2017). Multimodal code-meshing: Bilingual adolescents' processes composing across modes and languages. *Journal of Second Language Writing*, 36, 6–22.

Smith, B.E. (2019). Collaborative multimodal composing: Tracing the unique partnerships of three pairs of adolescents composing across three digital projects. *Literacy*, *53*(1), 14–21.

Stake, R.E. (2006). *Multiple case study analysis*. New York: The Guilford Press.

Storch, N. (2009). The impact of studying in a second language (L2) medium university on the development of L2 writing. *Journal of Second Language Writing*, *18*(2), 103–118.

Storch, N. (2011). Collaborative writing in L2 contexts: Processes, outcomes, and future directions. *Annual Review of Applied Linguistics*, *31*, 275–288.

Storch, N. (2013). *Collaborative writing in L2 classrooms*. Bristol, UK: Multilingual Matters.

Strobl, C. (2014). Affordances of web 2.0 technologies for collaborative advanced writing in a foreign language. *CALICO Journal*, *31*(1), 1–18. https://doi.org/http://dx.doi.org/10.11139/cj.31.1

Swain, M., & Lapkin, S. (1998). Interaction and second language learning: Two adolescent French immersion students working together. *Modern Language Journal*, 82, 320–337. https://doi.org/10.2307/329959

Tardy, C. (2005). "It's like a story": Rhetorical knowledge development in advanced academic literacy. *Journal of English for Academic Purposes* 4(4), 325–338. https://doi.org/10.1016/j.jeap.2005.07.005

Trimbur, J. (1994). Taking the social turn: Teaching writing post-process. *College Composition and Communication*, 45, 108–118.

Vandommele, G., Van den Branden, K., Van Gorp, K., & De Maeyer, S. (2017). In-school and out-of-school multimodal writing as an L2 writing resource for beginner learners of Dutch. *Journal of Second Language Writing*, 36, 23–36. https://doi.org/10.1016/j.jslw.2017.05.010

Vygotsky, L.S. (1978). Mind in society: The development of higher psychological processes. Cambridge, MA: Harvard University Press.

Yang, Y.C., & Wu, W. (2012). Digital storytelling for enhancing student academic achievement, critical thinking, and learning motivation: A year-long experimental study. *Computers & Education, 59*, 339–352. https://doi.org/10.1016/j.compcom.2012.07.001

Yang, Y. F. (2012). Multimodal composing in digital storytelling. *Computers and Composition, 29*, 221–238.

Yeh, H.C. (2018). Exploring the perceived benefits of the process of multimodal video making in developing multiliteracies. *Language Learning & Technology, 22*(2), 28–37.

Yi, Y. & Angay-Crowder, T. (2016). Multimodal pedagogies for teacher education in TESOL. *TESOL Quarterly, 50*(4), 988–998. https://doi.org/10.1002/tesq.326

Yi, Y., Shin, D., & Cimasko, T. (2020). Special issue: Multimodal composing in multilingual learning and teaching contexts. *Journal of Second Language Writing, 47*, 100717–100716. https://doi.org/10.1016/j.jslw.2020.100717

Yi, Y., & Hirvela, A. (2010). Technology and "self-sponsored" writing: A case study of Korean-American adolescent. *Computers and Composition, 97*(2), 94–111.

Yin, R.K. (2009). *Case study research design and methods* (4th ed.). Thousand Oaks, CA: Sage Publications.

Yim, S., Wang, D., Olson, J., Vu, V., & Warschauer, M. (2017). Synchronous collaborative writing in the classroom: Undergraduates' collaboration practices and their impact on writing style, quality, and quantity. *Proceedings of the 20th ACM Conference on Computer-Supported Cooperative Work and Social Computing* (pp. 468-479). New York: ACM. https://doi.org/10.1145/2998181.2998356

Zhang, M., & Plonsky, L. (2020). Collaborative writing in face-to-face settings: A substantive and methodological review. *Journal of Second Language Writing, 49*, 100753. https://doi.org/10.1016/j.jslw.2020.100753

Zhang, M., Gibbons, J., & Li, M. (2021). Computer-mediated collaborative L2 writing: a systematic review. *Journal of Second Language Writing, 54*, 100854.

Zheng, B., Lawrence, J., Warschauer, M., & Lin, C.H. (2015). Middle school students' writing and feedback in a cloud-based classroom environment. *Technology, Knowledge and Learning, 20*(2), 201–229.

11
Case studies, multimodal OERs and online collaboration: Enhancing undergraduate learners' source-based expository writing skills in context

Jia Li

Introduction

Postsecondary students need effective skills in writing, especially source-based expository writing skills, to achieve academic success (Cumming *et al.*, 2016). Critical analysis and research-based writing predominates the types of assignments given to university and college students across disciplines. These expository writing assignments often require students to accurately read and interpret authors' core ideas, and objectively convey information in writing. Moreover, writing assignments in university often call on students to summarize and critique multiple readings, which in turn demonstrates their comprehension and integration of the subject area content (Bartolomeo-Maida, 2016; Brockman *et al.*, 2011; Maaka & Ward, 2000). Expository writing demands higher-level cognitive skills to present a position clearly with well-developed supporting theses and evidence (Beck, Llosa, & Fredrick, 2013; Perin *et al.*, 2017). This requires students to evaluate the alignment between the source content and their thesis statements, using proficient reading and writing skills to synthesize, paraphrase, and quote relevant information across texts. These writing skills have a significant impact not only on students' academic achievement, but also on effective communication skills in their respective disciplines, including career-ready professional writing skills—for example, business, technical reports, content development—required for their future professions.

However, research has shown that many first- and second-year undergraduate students, including (English) language learners, are inadequately prepared for the complexities of source-based expository writing (Gruenbaum, 2012; MacArthur & Philippakos, 2013). They often lack skills in organizing writing to convey major and supporting ideas, as well as having difficulties in reading comprehension, main idea recognition, and developing critical perspectives. Wang's (2009) study showed that only 55% of first-year university participants correctly identified the explicit main ideas of individual paragraphs, and only 11% correctly stated the main ideas of a multiple-paragraph expository text. Students need skills to evaluate, organize, and present ideas to establish their knowledge and objectivity (Schleppegrell, 2001). Thus, it is critical to develop effective instruction strategies to support these students, who often struggle with the combination of academic writing and reading skills at the onset of university.

Much research has addressed general reading and writing challenges, and acknowledged a close connection between these two language skills (Perin *et al.*, 2017), but instruction to improve students' reading and writing skills is often provided separately. Furthermore, fewer studies have been conducted on the development of integrated skills in the expository reading and writing that prevails in post-secondary education. In addition, though traditional lecture-based writing instruction has proven to be less ineffective (Nami, 2020) and "a paradigm shift" is needed for writing pedagogy (Baker, 2017), limited research is available that addresses both skills with innovative instruction through the use of digital technologies that appeal to university students, who can collaborate in learning by accessing online platforms in and out of class. Therefore, this article draws on relevant literature and my recent research projects with my team that developed and examined the impact of two interventions on enhancing the source-based writing skills of students in a Canadian university and community college. It focuses on two key aspects that are the subject of this present volume: *contextualization* and *socialization*; that is, a case-study pedagogical approach to providing contextualized writing instructions and curriculum content by developing and using multimodal open educational resources (OERs), and peer collaboration throughout the integrated reading-to-write process using a cloud-based platform.

Literature Review

Key terminologies

This chapter addresses contextualization and socialization as defined by Colpaert and Stockwell below, with the enriched operational concepts of both terms for the projects in light of relevant research evidence and literature.

> *Contextualization* is how technologies and learning environments can be adjusted to the specific context of the learner, and includes topics such as adaptation to the spatio-temporal location of the learner, adaptation to the cultural context of the learner, Open Data for relevant content, augmented reality (AR), and mobile language learning. *Socialization* is the way in which technologies and learning environments afford *meaningful interaction*, such as interaction amongst learners, interaction between the learner and the teacher, native speakers, content providers, or researchers, and telecollaboration. (Chapter 1, p. 4)

The case-study project using OERs that took place in asynchronous online classes also adopted the *contextualized teaching and learning* (CTL) approach. CTL, which is defined as "relating subject matter content to meaningful situations that are relevant to students' lives, offers one promising approach to helping students learn more effectively" by actively engaging them and promoting improved learning and skill development (Baker, Hope, & Karandjeff, 2009, p. 1). *Contextualization* is defined as "an instructional approach connecting foundational skills and college-level content" (p. 268) in Perin's (2011) literature review of 61 articles, which reports on research evidence that supports student learning through contextualization. She indicates that one of two distinct forms implemented in the classroom is *contextualized basic skills instruction*, which "involves the teaching of reading, writing, or mathematics skills ... against a backdrop of specific subject matter..." (p. 271). Considering the work noted above, the project's operational concept of *contextualization* is to use case studies with multimedia OERs to improve students' writing skills by providing them with instructional strategies and content that align with the current realities they face, i.e., the pandemic's impact and greenhouse gas emissions, plus their interest in accessing and acquiring information through digital media.

For the collaborative writing project using OneNote, our operational concept emphasizes *meaningful socialization*; that is, to nurture students' awareness and a classroom culture of meaningful and purposeful social interaction, and facilitate productive goal- and task-oriented socialization through designing well-structured reading-to-write activities and interesting content, along with instructor modeling and monitoring, clear instruction, and timely feedback (see Instructional design and content development section below for rationale and further explanations of socialization for learning).

Theoretical framework for reading-to-write instruction

The theoretical foundation underlying integrated reading and writing instruction and practices lies in a moderate to strong positive range of correlations between writing and a subset of reading skills, including reading comprehension, spelling, and vocabulary knowledge, as reported in the first language (L1) and English as a foreign language (EFL) research context. Schoonen's (2018) study with Grade 8, 9, and 10 students in the Netherlands found strong positive correlations between their reading and writing skills in EFL and in L1, Dutch. Students' vocabulary and spelling (orthographic) knowledge also demonstrated moderate to strong positive correlations with their reading ability and writing performance in both L1 and EFL.

The intricate relationships between reading skills and different genres of writing skills are explored. Perin *et al.*'s (2017) study showed that the general reading skills of low-skilled community college students in the U.S. were correlated with their summary-writing skills, and their general writing skills were also correlated with persuasive writing. Most importantly, the students' exposure to instruction in reading and writing the same genre of text may lead to great learning outcomes. Allen *et al.*'s (2014) study with university students in the U.S. found a strong correlation between their reading comprehension and the writing of argumentative essays. Similarly, an earlier study by Parodi's (2007) found a strong correlation between Chilean 8th graders' reading comprehension and argumentative writing in Spanish; there was about 52% commonality—"a quite extensive intersecting area between comprehension and production" (p. 236) of students' argumentative text. Our recent results are in line with previous studies and discovered positive but smaller correlations between reading and writing skills, spelling, and vocabulary knowledge of community college students who had weaker language skills (Li & Mak, 2022). These findings provided insights into the needs of integrated literacy tasks to enhance students' academic writing skills while providing reading comprehension and vocabulary instruction at the same time, particularly for students with limited proficiency skills. It raises our awareness, when designing innovative reading-to-write interventions, to carefully evaluate instructional timing, strategies, and student populations with specific levels of language skill.

Contextualized writing instruction: Case studies with multimodal OERs

It has been observed that reading and writing instruction at university departs from students' real-life experience and rarely makes a connection with their skills or content knowledge (Balzotti & Hansen, 2019). This, to a certain degree, has intimidated many students from expressing their ideas through academic discourse, to the extent that they miss much-needed opportunities to improve their writing skills. Case studies, as an instructional method, are often used in disciplines such as business, law, and medicine to provide students with authentic learning contexts and academic skill training. Case-based pedagogy has also been successfully introduced in science education (Arellano *et al.*, 2000; Cliff & Curtin, 2000). Regardless of their source, case studies have been found to be significantly more effective than other instructional methods at improving students' understanding of science concepts. They also are positively correlated to students' increased perception of the learning gains associated with oral and written communication skills and their ability to recognize the relevance of their learning to real-life experience. A survey of 1,634 American teachers, including 63% from colleges and universities, showed a strong and growing trend in using case studies in teaching and learning science (Herreid *et al.*, 2011).

However, few studies reported using case studies for writing instruction; I located just two studies in the professional writing context. To help students develop writing skills in economic analysis, Palmimi's (1996) study used rhetorical cases to create a realistic communication situation. The results showed highly positive student feedback regarding case assignments as being the "most valuable," and students reported sustained benefit to their basic writing skills from case-study instruction that could be applied in their jobs after graduation. Moreover, it is a novel but promising approach to writing instruction with technology scaffolds; even the survey results with teachers suggested "distance learning is a ripe field for the use of cases" (Herreid et al., 2011, p. 80). I was able to locate one relevant study by Balzotti and Hansen (2019) that incorporated Alternate Reality Games to provide students with technical writing instruction using Microcore playable case studies (PCS). The project created an authentic and immersive simulation to teach students to apply persuasive writing skills in a workplace context. The students found the Microcore PCS, which presented a clear rhetorical context to consider in their written assignments, to be engaging. The PCS "allowed instructors to clearly articulate proper approaches to writing for the specific audience and characters in the PCS", and the discussions and feedback of students and the instructor about intended readership were supported "at a high level of specificity" (p. 417). Given that many instructors rely on outside sources for their cases, and much research has been conducted using and developing multimodal instruction and content to support postsecondary students' writing development, mostly in an English as a foreign language (EFL) context (Alvira, 2016; Chen & Su, 2011; Kumar & Sultana; 2016; Majelan, 2014; Suhartono, & Laraswati, 2016), there is great potential to develop case studies for academic writing instruction using multimedia OERs.

Technology-supported collaborative writing: Leveraging socialization

Research on technology integration with writing instruction has adopted a process-oriented approach to teaching students specific writing skills in stages and to facilitate a series of collaborative writing activities. Using online collaboration tools—for example, Wikis, blogs, and Google Docs—students were able to achieve better understanding, construct knowledge, and receive social support. Specifically, small group discussions to brainstorm ideas and receive peer feedback aid students in resolving errors they cannot master individually (Loretto, DeMartino, & Godley, 2016; Vorobel & Kim, 2017), and to make revisions focusing on ideas and organization that are critical to developing expository writing skills (Bradley & Thouesny, 2017; Chao & Lo, 2011; Zheng et al., 2015). Some studies also reported a dual effect of enhancing reading comprehension as well as writing quality (Shen, 2013; Yeh, 2014).

Effect on students' writing performance

The measurable effect of technology-supported collaborative writing on post-secondary students' writing performance has been examined extensively. Most research that focused specifically on writing, such as content, organization, and grammar, reported a positive trend of results. The findings indicated that students who collaborated in reading and writing summaries online performed significantly better in six out of eight performance indicators than those involved in face-to-face collaboration. These indicators included main ideas, integration of ideas, organization, style, objectivity, and holistic writing (style, use of language, objectivity, and succinctness) (Passig & Maidel-Kravetsky, 2016). Research with English language learners also showed promising outcomes. EFL university students in Taiwan who wrote individually while receiving peer feedback online for revision improved significantly from pre- to post-test scores, specifically in content and holistic writing (Tai, 2016).

Similarly, students in studies that examined the general academic writing performance of EFL collaborative writing using Google Docs performed significantly better than those who wrote collaboratively through face-to-face interaction (Suwantarathip & Wichadee, 2014), or wrote individually using Google Docs (Alsubaie & Ashuraidah, 2017). Undergraduate EFL students who had access to a feature—monitoring and comparing behavior, including one's own contributions with that of other group members during collaboration—performed significantly better on difficult tasks than students who did not have access. This suggests group awareness helps students stay on task and collaborate more effectively (Liu et al., 2018).

Research into technology-supported collaboration on writing tasks has varied in design as well as measured outcomes. Based on a large number of writing samples and pre- and post-test writing and reading scores from a statewide student assessment program, a study with middle school students in the U.S. found no significant effect on reading and writing skills using Google Docs to write, either collaborative or individually. However, students' pre- and post-test scores in reading and writing were found to be positively associated, and students had a positive attitude towards using Google Docs for editing and exchanging feedback. Other studies in online feedback using a weblog or wiki indicated a higher level of student engagement and more time on tasks compared with traditional group workshops involving paper drafts, independent writing with a word-processor, and peer reviews (Neumann & Hood, 2009; Novakovich & Long, 2013).

Learners' perspectives

Regardless of the widely varied research design in online collaborative writing, students have reported an overall positive experience in two key areas. First, students deemed that online collaboration improved the quality of their writing because each team member brought different skill sets and perspectives, and generated more ideas during writing and peer review (Elola & Oskoz, 2010). Second, students appreciated online social interactions and were highly motivated to learn in such environments, which they perceived as supportive and relaxed (Alsubaie & Ashuraidah, 2017; Hosseinpour *et al.*, 2019). Online tools often enabled the writing process to be visible and fluid, so the team could collaborate with confidence through different stages, that is, idea conception and negotiation, composition, review, feedback provision, revision, and finalization, including observing and comparing peer writing. This greatly reduced the stress caused by the onerous tasks of peer editing and revising in traditional settings (Chao & Lo, 2011; Ebadi & Rahimi, 2017; Rahimi & Fathi, 2021; Strobl, 2014; Yang, 2016).

Mixed student perspectives and learning outcomes in collaborative writing using technology support have also been reported. Even though some students considered online collaboration beneficial for developing ideas and exchanging feedback for writing, they expressed concern about control over the text and the pace of work, and they indicated a preference for individual over collaborative writing (Strobl, 2014). A few factors, for example, language proficiency levels, affected the extent of the benefit perceived and received. Students with lower proficiency were concerned whether they had the required skills to collaborate meaningfully, including organizing collaboration outside of class, and if their contributions to group work were being fairly evaluated by peers (Alsubaie & Ashuraidah, 2017; Ducate *et al.*, 2011). In addition, students' familiarity with technology had an impact on their learning experience. For example, when using the Edmodo mobile app in collaborative writing, higher users (those with more digital literacy skills) were more positive in describing their experience than lower users, who expressed more frustration and often preferred to write on their own (Hosseinpour *et al.*, 2019).

To summarize, with convenient access to collaborative technology tools that enable efficient, safe, and meaningful social interaction for sharing and constructing knowledge, students tended to be more engaged and committed to writing tasks. Specifically, they were motivated to participate in editing and peer review, investing more time in revising their work. They gained more awareness of the writing process and paid more attention to how a task was completed at different stages. This ultimately helped them to develop confidence as writers and gradually become more self-reliant in their learning. Well-designed and facilitated writing instruction with technological scaffolding has great potential to improve postsecondary students' learning of expository discourse through collaboratively undertaking a series of online reading and writing activities.

Instructional design and content development: Models and principles

It is clear from these findings that case studies and collaborative writing online can greatly benefit students' writing performance. However, many of the reported instructional designs have addressed general writing challenges apart from reading issues. Fewer have explicitly focused on developing integrated skills in reading and writing expository text, though a close relationship between these two language skills, which share many linguistic properties, is well acknowledged. Most importantly, I was unable to locate any intervention study using digital technology to address the interconnected nature and demands of advanced source-based writing and expository reading assignments in postsecondary contexts. Therefore, I worked with a professional editor, a college writing instructor, a business writing specialist, two colleagues and my graduate students to develop two projects.

One project aimed to develop case studies by leveraging multimodal OERs to provide students with contextualized instruction (Li *et al.*, in progress). Based on a philosophy of professional education, the case-study pedagogical approach, which focusses on knowledge in action (Boehrer, 1995), has often been used traditionally in the training of workplace-related skills in education and other disciplines. What was novel here was the project's application of technology scaffolding in the context of writing instruction. To improve students' source-based expository writing skills, the other project used a cloud-based collaboration tool to enhance students' task-oriented interaction opportunities and efficiently facilitate their collaborative reading and writing practices, which often are taught separately (see also Li & Mak, 2022; Li *et al.*, submitted). These two projects were aligned with the curriculum objectives of two one-term courses in a Canadian university and college: "Fundamentals of Professional Writing" and "College Communication I." Given the intensive timeframe of the one-term courses, our instructional designs for both projects focused on developing well-structured critical content and instruction. This was facilitated by certain technological features that enabled students to learn writing skills in a context relevant to their life experience and through the digital media-supported social interaction they prefer.

Several technological and pedagogical models and principles guided the projects' development. *First*, based on the Universal Design for Learning (UDL) framework, my team followed its strong "user-aware" and "customizable" approach to develop and use instructional strategies and multimodal OER content for case studies that could be accessed, understood, and used by diverse students "to the greatest possible extent," "in the most independent and natural manner possible," and "in the widest possible range of situations" (Centre for Excellence in Universal Design-CEUD, 2021). The UDL approach is not only in line with the principles of Equity, Diversity and Inclusion (EDI) to engage diverse learners, but also takes human-friendly features into consideration, e.g., simple, intuitive, and flexible use, perceptible information, tolerance for error, and low physical effort (CEUD, 2021). Thus, basic and user-friendly features in OneNote were used to teach students important source-based writing, for example, critical reading strategies, paraphrasing, summarizing, and thesis development (see figures 5-9). *Second*, taking social constructivist theory (Vygotsky, 1978) into consideration, the intervention was developed with cloud-based collaborative tools to give students easy access to instruction and curriculum material, and facilitate rich opportunities for group discussion in context to encourage knowledge building and negotiations that mimic argumentative writing (Guthrie & Klauda, 2014; Storch, 2005). Collaboration in many aspects of writing practice has proven to be effective in enhancing postsecondary students' expository writing skills (Chang & Windeatt, 2016; Li & Mak, 2018). Working with peers, students could collectively generate, merge, and refine ideas and resolve problems. The online collaboration tool made it easy for students to see other students' writing, provide immediate feedback, and revise their writing. *Third*, adopting the experience-based learning framework (Andresen *et al.*, 2000; Bohon *et al.*, 2017), my team applied an evidence-based case-study approach to develop instructional strategies and content, focusing on students' real-life experiences, that is, authentic learning contexts and interests in tune with their academic and professional aspirations. This not only could enhance undergraduate students' writing skills for school assignments, but also prepare for their transition from university studies to the workplace. *Fourth*, to create a vivid and interactive virtual learning community with versatile instructional features, our pedagogical approaches were further informed by social presence theory (Short, Williams, & Christie, 1976). This was achieved by leveraging virtual conferencing, social media, and mobile apps that are in line with modern youths' interest in new technologies and their means of socialization.

Additionally, our instructional design referenced two specific designing principles. *First*, based on the ideas of expert learning that emphasize self-regulatory and reflection strategies (Ertmer & Newby, 1996), the interventions were designed to enable students to control and manage tasks, navigate their reading-to-write activities at their own pace, and modify their own and collaborative strategies by observing others' learning behavior and work progress. This was also supported by enriched multimodal instructional materials available in the cloud that they could access anytime, anywhere. *Second*, we adapted the designs of Bradley *et al.* (2010) and Chao and Lo (2011) to segment the reading-to-write process into multiple smaller, focused, yet integrated task units, each one tackling a specific aspect of expository writing skills at a time. This enabled students to disentangle the complex and seemingly daunting expository writing tasks and help them identify their own strengths and weaknesses in areas for improvement.

Instructional designs of two writing projects

Both projects, designed to be process-oriented, took place in intact classes with culturally and linguistically diverse students registered in a university- and college-level writing course; each lasted for one 14-week semester. While one project with university students employed a case-study approach to *contextualize writing instruction* and develop multimodal curriculum content using OERs, the other with community college students focused on collaborative writing on a cloud-based platform through *meaningful socialization*. Approvals from the Research Ethics Review Boards were obtained in the university and college where we recruited participants for the research (see Li *et al.*, in progress; Li & Mak, 2022; Li *et al.*, submitted, for research details). Pseudonyms are used in screen captures in Figures 11.5 to 11.9. The discussion of students' learning experience and learning outcomes resulting from the projects is presented in the next section. These projects shared the goal of improving students' source-based expository writing skills with key elements highlighted below:

1. The purpose of academic writing is to enhance readers' understanding of a topic with credible information and convincing arguments.
2. Information, such as research findings and statistical data as evidence, is essential to support claims made for academic expository writing.
3. To be truthful to information and evaluate it in the given contexts is important.
4. Focused and structured arguments should be made to support the main thesis and sub-thesis statements with accurate and proper references to relevant literature in the APA style.
5. It is crucial to demonstrate clear, critical thinking through academic writing.

Project 1

This project involved 26 Canadian undergraduates in a class of 47 students across disciplines. These students were registered in the online "Fundamentals of Professional Writing" course, where the class met weekly in Adobe Connect synchronously and Canvas asynchronously. Mixed methods were applied to examine the student experience of learning writing through the use of OER-based case studies by administering a survey to all participants. Individual interviews with 12 students were conducted via Zoom and recorded. Applying a case-study approach, this project focused on developing innovative *contextualized* instructional strategies and multimodal content materials using OERs (see Figure 11.1 and Appendix A) to support students to develop an in-depth understanding of and practical skills in professional writing with real-world relevance, including academic writing. My team developed six case studies, responding to major professional writing types, including academic writing, creative/narrative writing, business writing, journalism, technical writing, and content writing. Here I focus on academic writing, which includes a few key aspects.

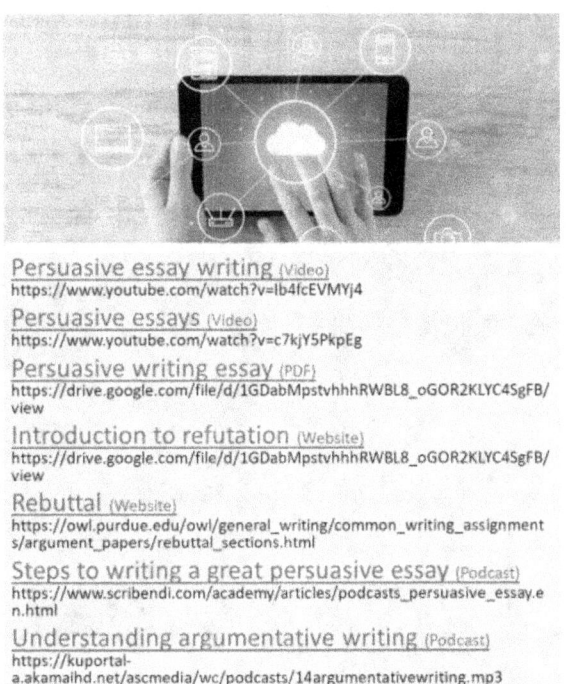

Figure 11.1 *Sample of multimodal content materials on persuasive essay using OERs.*

First, from a comparative perspective, we asked students to write a narrative story—the genre most innate to our communication nature—on a topic of their choice based on their personal experience. This was to help students identify the strengths and weaknesses in their general writing ability in a personal, individual context.

Second, students were involved in taking a stand or role-playing in current affairs, such as their perspectives on the impact of online instruction in higher education during and after the pandemic or debating a topic such as the proposal to raise the carbon tax rate (see Figure 11.2 and Appendix A).

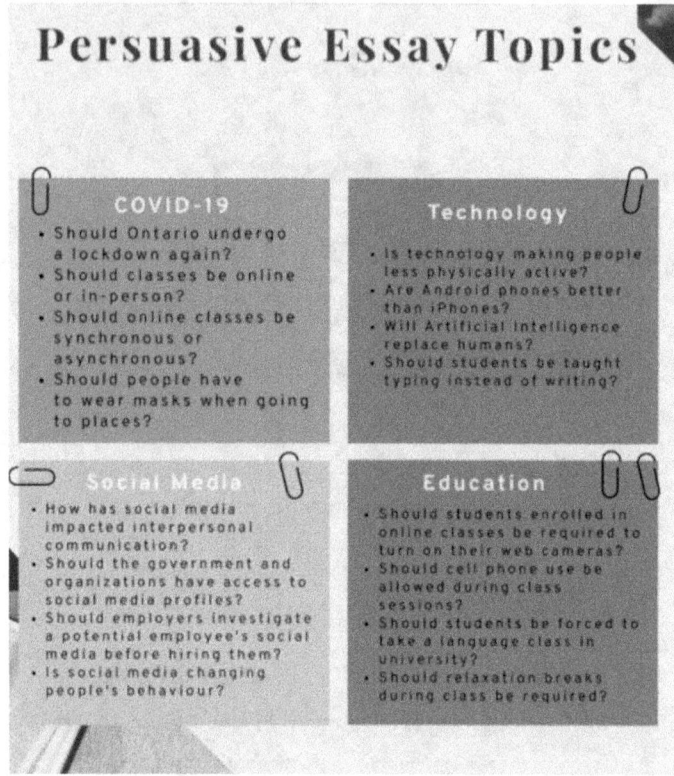

Figure 11.2 *Samples of persuasive topics.*

This was to develop students' argumentative and persuasive discourse skills from verbal to written through an array of reading-to-speak (in debate) and reading-to-write practices.

Third, a series of tutorials and group practices was organized to train key techniques for writing from sources (see Figure 11.3). These included incorporating paraphrased content with proper acknowledgement to source material, along with pragmatic research skills, such as searching literature online. *Finally*, we engaged students in virtual fireside chats with experienced writers like the former opinion page editor of the Toronto Star, Fred Edwards, talking about why, what, and how we write. This process, with its shared aspect of thinking aloud about techniques used in writing research to contextualize writing goals and analyze writing strategies, can enhance students' writing skills.

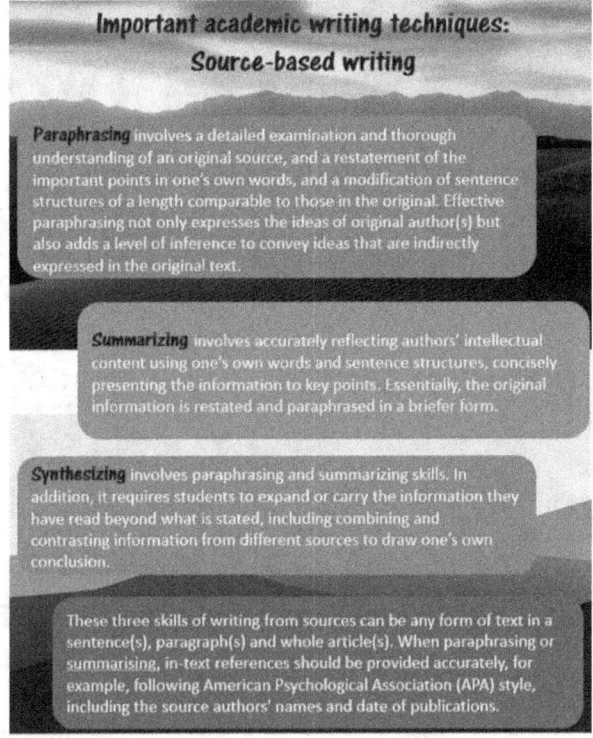

Figure 11.3 *Sample slide: Introducing specific source-based expository writing techniques.*

These student-hosted chats, along with an interview, encouraged students to ask writing experts critical questions about becoming a professional writer and some specific pieces they authored, which the students read prior to the chat (see Figure 11. 4).

Figure 11.4 *Sample of fireside chat[1].*

Project 2

Project 2 took place in a large community college with 69 students registered in four sections of College Communications I, a first-year academic English writing course. The course aimed to teach students to write clear, coherent arguments in response to readings. With an experimental study design, we examined students' writing performance between and within groups after the writing intervention. Additional data was also collected with 14 students through in-person audio-recorded individual interviews. For this project, the instructional design was centered on using OneNote, a cloud-based tool that is relevant to students' socialization experience today, to facilitate their cohesive collaboration throughout the reading-to-write process, the goal being to enhance their source-based writing skills. Students had a 3-hour face-to-face class meeting weekly, with one hour allocated to each unit of the 10-lesson intervention focusing on one element of source-based expository writing through online reading-to-write activities. Using the online tool, 2-3 student groups read assigned readings with support, wrote their responses, provided peer feedback, and edited each other's writing synchronously. Ultimately, they composed on the same page and combined each group member's contributions into one essay. Additionally, they could view other groups' work and learn beyond their immediate group. Their writing actions and output were monitored by their instructor, and feedback was provided in a timely manner for their drafts as well as the final version of writing assignments. Major integrated reading-to-write activities and helpful online tool features based on student feedback are described below.

First, we aimed to enhance students' reading skills by helping them recognize their reading behaviours against effective reading strategies. We asked students to discuss in groups and write about the strategies they thought would be effective and explain their reasons. This, in due course, helped students to express their ideas in writing as well. An essay was assigned to be read with built-in features, for example, easy access to the Internet and audio and video recording to support their interaction. These features could effectively facilitate students' discussions about their understanding of assigned readings, and brainstorming ideas could be used for their collaborative reading activities. For instance, a basic but important feature was embedded easy access to an online dictionary or thesaurus. By right clicking an unknown word in a passage, a "research" sidebar opened on the same screen where students could readily "look up" the word for its spellings, pronunciations, definitions, sample phrases, and synonyms (see Figure 11.5).

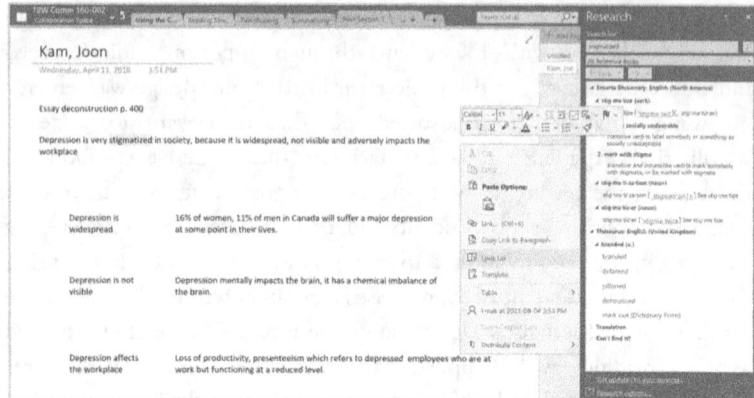

Figure 11.5 *Online dictionary or thesaurus assisting collaborative reading and writing tasks.*

Second, students worked together at different stages of the reading-to-write practice; for example, paraphrasing and summarizing. Figure 11.6 demonstrates a team of three students—Marich, Priti, and Yami—practicing paraphrasing based on an assigned, original passage in a turquoise font. The group composed the paraphrasing text in a black font and made multiple revisions synchronously. OneNote saves writing actions in real-time, thus the screen presents the students' final version with the instructor's encouraging note in the red sticker.

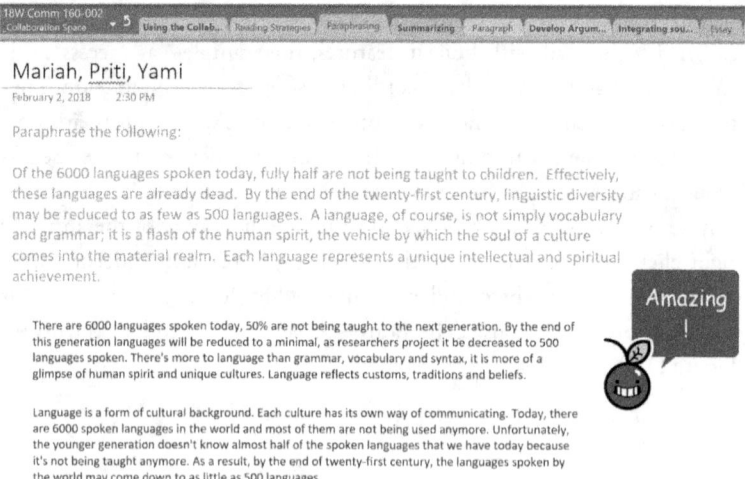

Figure 11.6 *Students collaborative reading-to-write activity: Paraphrasing.*

In Figure 11.7, two students—Karan and Gabby—practiced summarizing together from the phrase to paragraph level using strategies, for example, highlighting the ideas in the original text that they believed should be included in their summary.

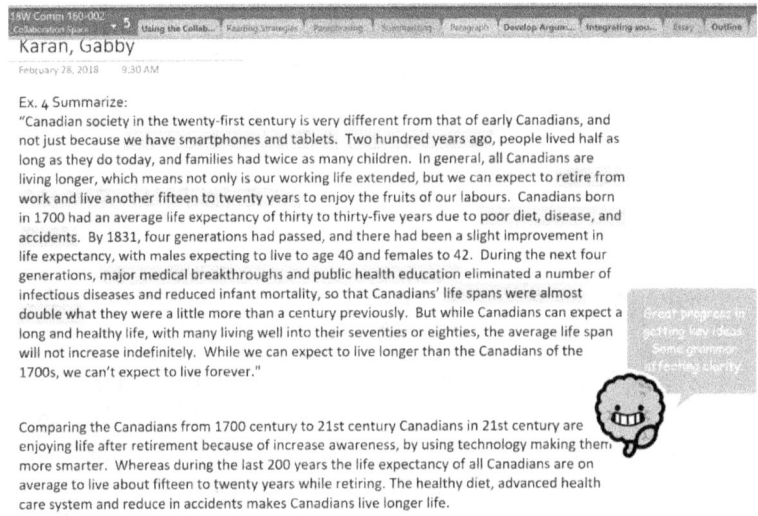

Figure 11.7 *Students collaborative reading-to-write activity: Summarizing.*

Third, we introduced expository writing to students in the online platform, asking them to read an essay together, discuss the argumentation techniques it used, and write a short paragraph responding to a question prompt. In this way, students learned to break down and evaluate the writer's argument. *Fourth*, students were asked to respond to a writing prompt by referencing evidence and others' ideas from an assigned essay to support their thesis statements. This is a critical skill in expository writing. *Finally*, with an assigned topic, they were required to present three arguments to support their position (main thesis) by providing specific, evidential, perspective-based supporting details. In Figure 11.8, the team of Wynne, Diego, and Changhao located an article in a book as a reference to support their argument (inside the frame on the left), and the instructor provided instant and detailed feedback on the right-side of the screen capture.

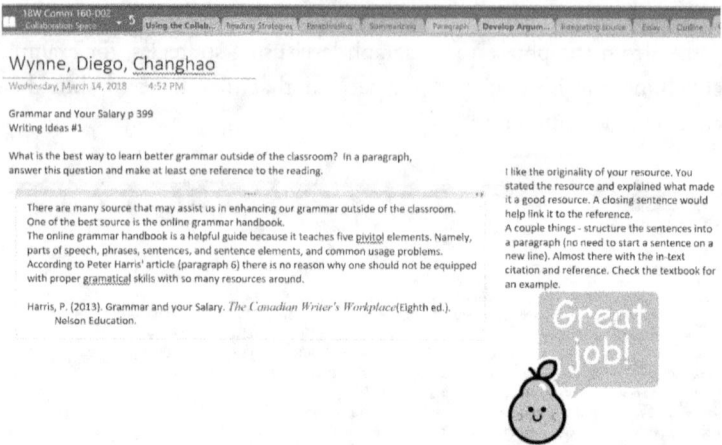

Figure 11.8 *Students working together integrating source to support an argument.*

In Figure 11.9, using a graphic organizer, Che, Taz, and SJ discussed the choice of three optional essay topics posted by the instructor, and developed an outline by organizing their ideas—thesis and sub-thesis—prior to their collaborative writing. The instructor's feedback is shown in a purple font in this screen capture. These activities, demonstrated in Figures 11.8–11.9, were often challenging, particularly if they occurred within a constrained time frame. With these online collaboration features, students were able to undertake such difficult tasks collectively and with increasing confidence.

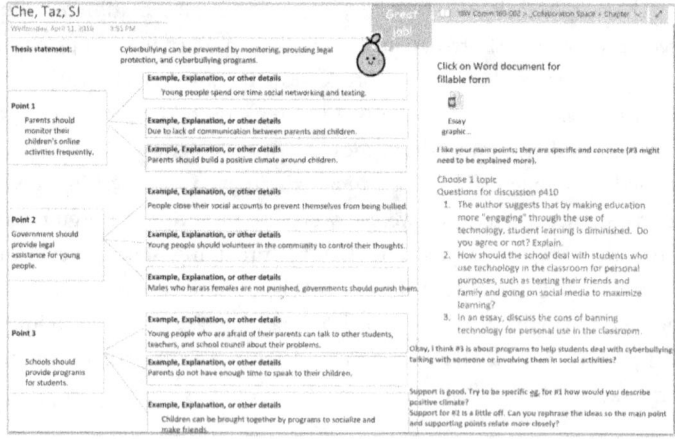

Figure 11.9 *Students collaborating in developing an outline for an essay.*

Application to Smart CALL

To examine the projects' effect on students' writing skills and collect their feedback, we conducted individual interviews and collected students' writing samples, in addition to administering self-developed and standardized tests for the collaborative writing project and surveys for the case-study project (see Li *et al.*, in progress; Li & Mak, 2002; Li *et al.*, submitted, for detailed data analysis and result reports). Descriptive statistics analysis of writing performance measures found that both higher- and lower-proficiency level student groups who received OneNote-supported intervention outperformed the respective control groups. Mean differences between pre- and post-test writing scores for higher-proficiency student treatment and control groups were 15.3 versus 14.2; for lower-proficiency treatment and control groups they were 14.2 versus 7.3. Most importantly, the results of one-way ANOVA and post-hoc tests comparing pre- and post-test writing scores of low-proficiency students showed that the treatment group had a significant improvement ($p = .01$) while the control group had no significant difference ($p = .70$).

Student interviews were transcribed verbatim, and thematic analysis was applied to the transcripts and their written feedback responding to open questions in the survey. Student feedback from both projects was positive overall. Many students indicated their interest in a longer engagement with the projects in an intact class setting or continuing to use the curriculum materials and the collaborative writing platform. Please see the student comments below:

> *"This should be a full course year-round... allows me to develop my writing skills for my other courses, but it was short lived. I wish I was able to continue with the course throughout the year to further develop those skills."* (Survey from Project 1 class)

> *"It was great for me because to be honest, I didn't think that I was the best at English before and I actually feel like I can write properly now...It really helped us work together to accomplish it."* (Interview transcript excerpts from Project 2 participants)

Given the focus of the volume, two relevant themes of results about contextualized instruction and meaningful socialization are discussed in the following section.

Contextualized instruction and learners' individual differences

Based on the students' feedback, *contextualized instruction* using creative writing and a case-study approach was engaging and effective in helping them learn academic writing. Comparing their writing assignments throughout the term, we observed a stronger trend of progressive improvement than that achieved by previous student cohorts without the experience of Project 1. *First*, having students write a personal narrative story and compare its differences from source-based expository writing enabled students to learn not only the strengths and weaknesses of their general writing skills but also the requirements of academic writing in a personalized context. A few students said: "I did not know that I can write." "I can actually enjoy writing, even writing for schoolwork, after your feedback pointing out the connections between my story and the papers other profs assigned." By referencing their personal stories for instruction, we got to know students individually and tailored the instruction in the context relevant to them. In turn, students demonstrated a stronger commitment to learning and writing practice, as shown in the following comments made in the survey from the Project 1 class:

> "The course itself gave me the opportunity to be a strong writer, which I haven't realized...including the improvements I was making and seeing how much growth it brought to me."

> "This is a great course. The course was taught well by the professor and her team. They are really interested in our success as better writers. I find this course also helps me to improve my writing for other courses."

Second, case studies enabled us to provide students with writing instruction in an enriched, authentic context, so they could make critical connections between their reading and writing skills and content knowledge by leveraging their exposure to public discourse and literature on current affairs. For example, the carbon tax and the pandemic's impact on higher education were two case studies for their final writing assignment. Students said they "had so much to say and write" about the case studies. This gave them "better ideas how to write an academic essay on the topic," one relevant to their experience, and with a clear awareness of "who is going to read it"—the assumed readership.

Third, our reading and writing measurements also indicated the significance of contextualized instruction, given that many factors, for example, access to reliable Internet and language proficiency, play a role in influencing students' learning outcomes and experience in online collaborative writing (see Li & Mak, 2022, for measurable outcomes using pre- and post-test scores in a factorial design). Students with lower reading skills made statistically significant improvements in writing performance after the collaborative writing online, while the control group who collaborated in writing face-to-face did not. However, there were no significant differences between the treatment and control student groups with higher reading skills. Thus, it is important to provide contextualized instruction, catering to students' characteristics and learning conditions, meeting their learning needs to optimize the effectiveness of writing interventions using technological means.

Designing content and features for meaningful socialization

Students perceived online collaborative reading-to-write practice as positive and engaging, which they largely attributed to its meaningful social interaction. With the enhanced capacity and convenience of technology, the instructional intervention enabled the inclusive participation of group members and mutually supportive interactions to facilitate learning, as noted in other studies (Li & Zhu, 2013). Students believed that one of its key benefits was the 10 lesson units of intervention content that we developed to focus on a systematic building of discrete writing skills in a comfortable social environment where they constructed and shared knowledge with peers in a progressive manner. Students were taught an element essential to developing expository writing skills in each class. The instructor broke down the complex writing task, modelled the target skill of the class, and continued with students' collaboration in practice, such as paraphrasing, summarizing, integrating sources, topic sentences, and idea organization.

Furthermore, students pointed out two beneficial design features of the intervention associated with social interaction: group tasks on integrated reading-to-write and real-time feedback (plus accessible information). Facilitating a relaxing environment using technology increased student motivation and perseverance. It encouraged even reticent students and students with weaker language skills to undertake difficult tasks with increasing confidence and actively participate as a contributing group member. In turn, most groups efficiently completed writing assignments, as revealed in previous results (Alsubaie & Ashuraidah, 2017; Guthrie & Klauda, 2014; Rahimi & Fathi, 2021). In addition, real-time feedback from peers and the instructor during collaborative writing proved to engage students effectively, as shown in three interview excerpts below:

"We enjoyed seeing others' writing and how we could easily leave a note and comment... It can make our writing better... I like the way that students can give and receive feedback. It gives a lot of insight and helps you improve in writing."

"I liked that while we were writing you were actually able to put your little input bubbles... on the screen... to help us correct it..."

"It's a lot better doing something and getting constructive criticism while you're doing it than doing an assignment, getting it back and it's wrong...It's nice that I'm able to be guided through it to see where I struggle and how to get there."

Our results affirm the findings reported in other studies, indicating that with the online tool making group work visible, the students appreciated the immediacy of peer and instructor feedback during rather than after the writing process (Bradley *et al.*, 2010; Elola & Oskoz, 2010). This is particularly important for students with lower skills who undertake reading-to-write tasks requiring complex cognitive skills.

Conclusion

To conclude, when writing instruction is well aligned with the interests of students who value constant connection, quick information access, and enriched multimodal content, it has great potential to provide effective support for their learning of academic writing skills across disciplines. Providing students with contextualised writing instruction through case studies, cloud-based collaborative writing platforms with well-structured content, and design features supporting meaningful socialization can effectively engage students and enhance their integrated language skills. This is one of the biggest challenges during their transition from high school to university studies (Fanetti, Bushrow, & DeWeese, 2010). The students in both projects seemed to be better prepared to resolve linguistic roadblocks effectively and focus on the higher-order skills required for complex idea processing, e.g., paraphrasing relevant information to help support arguments. They not only generated more ideas, as reported in previous studies (Chao & Lo, 2011; Strobl, 2014), but also distinguished between different types of ideas versus supporting evidence.

The present results helped us to develop an in-depth understanding on developing effective integrated reading-writing skill-building activities to nurture complex thinking through an instructional design combining collaborative technology. Furthermore, case studies developed with OERs demonstrated how to engage students in authentic writing scenarios to enhance their intrinsic motivation to write. This tackled the limitations of current university writing instruction, which often is isolated from relevant subject content. The rich multimodal content, involving expert writers, enabled students to learn the academic writing techniques that are required across disciplines and professions.

However, given the limitations of present projects, future writing interventions need improvement in certain aspects. *First*, real-time research is needed to identify feasible technology venues and access for all participating learners. Poor Internet connection was a major complaint reported by students in both projects; some students couldn't view OER videos used in case studies, and group work was often interrupted. This was consistent with previous findings indicating that connectivity and the compatibility between technology-based instructional features and required writing tasks have a great impact on students' learning experiences (Chao & Lo, 2011; Li & Zhu, 2013; Liu & Lan, 2016; Neumann & Hood, 2009). *Second*, interventions with a longer duration of 1-2 years would be effective in helping students' academic writing skills. Students expressed an interest in continuing with the projects; our results showed that, overall, the treatment groups' scores on writing performance improved more—but not statistically significantly more—than those of the control groups. *Third*, future writing instructional designs should take the needs of students with varied language proficiency levels into consideration in intact classes, providing students with more training using instructional features, particularly for lower proficiency level students. *Lastly*, instructor-assisted group formation by strategically organizing students with different strengths to collaborate in reading-to-write tasks will likely lead to a more rewarding learning experience and outcomes for diverse students.

Acknowledgments

The writing project with the case study approach using OERs, and a section of literature review in the article are funded by an Ontario Tech University's Teaching Innovation Fund and an Explore Grant of Social Sciences and Humanities Research Council (SSHRC), Canada.

The author would like to thank her graduate student assistants in the *Technology Assisted Language and Literacy Development Lab* for their assistance to the case study project, Novera Roihan, Amel Belmahdi and Amareen Brar.

Special thanks go to Lillian Mak for her work for the collaborative writing project, and Fred Edwards for his contribution to the case study project and editorial feedback on this manuscript.

References

Allen, L.K., Snow, E.L., Crossley, S.A., Jackson, G.T., & McNamara, D. (2014). Reading comprehension components and their relation to writing. *Annee Psychologique, 114*(4), 663–691.

Alvira, R. (2016). The impact of oral and written feedback on EFL writers with the use of screencasts. *PROFILE: Issues in Teachers' Professional Development, 18*(2), 79–92. http://dx.doi.org/10.15446/profile.v18n2.53397

Alsubaie, J., & Ashuraidah, A. (2017). Exploring writing individually and collaboratively using google docs in EFL contexts. *English Language Teaching, 10*(10), 10–30. https://doi.org/10.5539/elt.v10n10p10

Andresen, L., Boud, D., and Cohen, R. (2000). Experience-based learning. In Foley, G. (Ed.), *Understanding adult education and training* (2nd ed.). Sydney: Allen & Unwin.

Arellano, E.L., Barcenal, T.L., Bilbao, P.P., Castellano, M.A., Nichols, S., Tippins, D.J. (2001). Case-based pedagogy as a context for collaborative inquiry in the Philippines. *Journal of Research in Science Teaching, 38*(5) 502–528.

Baker, S. (2017). Students' writing 'in transition' from A-levels to university: How assessment drives students' understandings, practices and discourses. *Assessment & Evaluation in Higher Education, 42*(1), 18–36.

Baker, E.D., Hope, L., & Karandjeff, K. (2009). *Contextualized teaching & learning: A promising approach for basic skills instruction.* Research and Planning Group for California Community Colleges (RP Group). Retrieved from https://files.eric.ed.gov/fulltext/ED521932.pdf

Balzotti, J., & Hansen, D. (2019). Playable case studies: A new educational genre for technical writing instruction. *Technical Communication Quarterly, 28*(4), 407–421. https://doi.org/10.1080/10572252.2019.1613562

Bartolomeo-Maida, M. (2016). The use of learning journals to foster textbook reading in the community college psychology class. *College Student Journal, 50*(3), 440–453.

Beck, S.W., Llosa, L., & Fredrick, T. (2013). The challenges of writing exposition: Lessons from a study of ELL and non-ELL high school students. *Reading & Writing Quarterly, 29*, 358–380.

Boehrer, J. (1995). How to teach a case. Kennedy School of Government Case Programme (case No. C18-95-1285.0.). Retrieved from http://www.ksgcase.harvard.edu

Bohon, L.L., McKelvey, S., Rhodes, J.A., & Robnolt, V.J. (2017). Training for content teachers of English language learners: Using experiential learning to improve instruction. *Teacher Development, 21*(5), 609–634.

Bradley, L., & Thouesny, S. (2017). Students' collaborative peer reviewing in an online writing environment. *Themes in Science & Technology Education, 10*(2), 69–83.

Brockman, E., Taylor, M., Kreth, M., & Crawford, M.K. (2011). What do professors really say

Centre for Excellence in Universal Design. (2021). *The 7 principles of universal design.* Retrieved from http://universaldesign.ie/ what-is-universal-design/the-7-principles/the-7-principles.html

Chang, H., & Windeatt, S. (2016). Developing collaborative learning practices in an online language course. *Computer Assisted Language Learning, 29*(8), 1271–1286.

Chao, Y.J., & Lo, H. (2011). Students' perceptions of wiki-based collaborative writing for learners of English as a foreign language. *Interactive Learning Environments, 19*(4), 395–411.

Chen, Y.-S., & Su, S.-W. (2012). A genre-based approach to teaching EFL summary writing. *ELT Journal, 66*(2),184–192. http://dx.doi.org/10.1093/elt/ccr061

Cliff, W., & Curtin, L.N. (2000). The directed case method: Teaching concept and process in a content-rich course, Journal of *College Science Teaching, 30*(1), 64–66.

Cumming, A., Lai, C., & Cho, H. (2016). Students' writing from sources for academic purposes: A synthesis of recent research. *Journal of English for Academic Purposes, 23*, 47–58.

Ducate, L.C., Anderson, L.L., & Moreno, N. (2011). Wading through the world of wikis: An analysis of three wiki projects. *Foreign Language Annals, 44*(3), 495–524. https://doi.org/10.1111/j.1944-9720.2011.01144.x

Ebadi, S., & Rahimi, M. (2017). Exploring the impact of online peer-editing using Google Docs on EFL learners' academic writing skills: a mixed methods study. *Computer Assisted Language Learning, 30*(8), 787–815. https://doi.org/10.1080/09588221.2017.1363056

Elola, I., & Oskoz, A. (2010). Collaborative writing: Fostering foreign language and writing conventions development. *Language Learning & Technology, 14*(3), 51–71.

Ertmer, P.A., & Newby, T.J. (1996). The expert learner: strategic, self-regulated, and reflective. *Instructional Science, 24*(1), 1–24. https://doi.org/10.1007/BF00156001https://doi.org/10.1007/BF00156001

Fanetti, S., Bushrow, K., & DeWeese, D. (2010). Closing the gap between high school writing instruction and college writing expectations. *The English Journal, 99*(4), 77–83. Retrieved from http://www.jstor.org/stable/27807171

Gruenbaum, E.A. (2012). Common literacy struggles with college students: Using the reciprocal teaching technique. *Journal of College Reading and Learning, 42*(2), 110–116.

Guthrie, J.T., & Klauda, S. (2014). Effects of classroom Practices on reading comprehension, engagement, and motivations for adolescents. *Reading Research Quarterly, 49*(4), 387–416. https://doi.org/10.1002/rrq.81

Herreid, C.F., Schiller, N.A., Herreid, K.F., & Wright, C. (2011). In case you are interested: results of a survey of case study teachers. *Journal of College Science Teaching, 40*(4), 76–80.

Hosseinpour, N., Biria, R., & Rezvani, E. (2019). Promoting academic writing proficiency of iranian EFL learners through blended learning. *Turkish Online Journal of Distance Education, 20*(4), 99–116. Retrieved from https://dergipark.org.tr/en/pub/tojde/issue/49972/64052

Kumar, S.V., & Sultana, A.S. (2016). Integration of multimedia for teaching writing skills. *CALL-EJ, 17*(2), 57–86. Retirved from http://callej.org/journal/17-2/Kumar_Sultana2016.pdf

Li, J., & Mak, L. (2022). The effect of using an online collaboration tool on college students' learning of academic writing skills. *System, 105*(2022) https://doi.org/10.1016/j.system.2021.102712

Li, J., Mak, L., Hunter, B., & Cunningham, T. (submitted). Structured instructional design for integrated language skill development: College students' perspectives on collaborative reading-to-write activities on a cloud-based platform.

Li, J., Edwards, F., & Muirhead, B. (in progress). Action research: A case study approach to developing effective writing skills for professional purposes using role playing and multimodal content.

Li, J., Owen, M., Walchuk, K., & Mak, L. (in press). Helping students avoid plagiarism: A comprehensive approach to developing students' academic writing skills. *What Works? Research into Practice: A research-into-practice series*. The Literacy and Numeracy Secretariat and the Ontario Association of Deans of Education.

Li, M., & Zhu, W. (2013). Patterns of computer-mediated interaction in small writing groups using wikis. *Computer Assisted Language Learning, 26*(1), 61–82. https://doi.org/10.1080/09588221.2011.631142

Liu, M., Liu, L., & Liu, L. (2018). Group awareness increases student engagement in online collaborative writing. *The Internet and Higher Education, 38*, 1–8. https://doi.org/10.1016/j.iheduc.2018.04.001

Liu, S.H., & Lan, Y. J. (2016). Social constructivist approach to web-based EFL learning: Collaboration, motivation, and perception on the use of Google docs. *Educational Technology & Society, 19*(1), 171–186.

Loretto, A., DeMartino, S., & Godley, A. (2016). Secondary students' perceptions of peer review of writing. *Research in the Teaching of English, 51*(2), 134–161.

Maaka, M.J., & Ward, S.M. (2000). Content area reading in community college classrooms. *Community College Journal of Research and Practice, 24*(2), 107–125.

MacArthur, C.A., & Philippakos, Z.A. (2013). Self-regulated strategy instruction in developmental writing: A design research project. *Community College Review, 41*(2), 176–195.

Majelan, M.T. (2014). Enhancing content knowledge in essay writing class: a multimedia package for Iranian EFL learners. *Advances in Language and Literacy Students, 5*(2), 87–95.

Nami, F. (2020): Edmodo in semi-technical English courses: towards a more practical strategy for language learning/practice, *Computer Assisted Language Learning*. Advance online publication. https://doi.org/10.1080/09588221.2020.1819340

Neumann, D.L., & Hood, M. (2009). The effects of using a wiki on student engagement and learning of report writing skills in a university statistics course. *Australasian Journal of Educational Technology, 25*(3), 382–398. https://doi.org/10.14742/ajet.1141

Novakovich, J., & Long, E.C. (2013). Digital performance learning: Utilizing a course weblog for mediating communication. *Educational Technology & Society, 16*(4), 231–241.

Palmimi, D.J. (1996) Using rhetorical cases to teach writing skills and enhance economic learning. *The Journal of Economic Education, 27*(3), 205–216.

Parodi, G. (2007). Reading–writing connections: Discourse-oriented research. *Read Writ* 20, 225-250. https://doi-org.myaccess.library.utoronto.ca/10.1007/s11145-006-9029-7

Passig, D., & Maidel-Kravetsky, J. (2016). The impact of collaborative online reading on summarizing skills. *Education and Information Technologies, 21*(3), 531–543. https://doi.org/10.1007/s10639-014-9337-5

Perin, D. (2011). Facilitating student learning through contextualization: A review of the evidence. *Community College Review, 39*(3), 268–295. https://doi.org/10.1177/0091552111416227

Perin, D., & Hare, R. (2010). *A contextualized reading-writing intervention for community college students* (CCRC Brief No. 44). New York, NY: Community College Research Center, Teachers College, Columbia University.

Perin, D., Lauterbach, M., Raufman, J., & Kalamkarian, H.S. (2017). Text-based writing of low-skilled postsecondary students: relation to comprehension, self-efficacy and teacher judgments. *Reading and Writing, 30*(4), 887–915.

Rahimi, M., & Fathi, J. (2021). Exploring the impact of wiki-mediated collaborative writing on EFL students' writing performance, writing self-regulation, and writing self-efficacy: a mixed methods study. *Computer Assisted Language Learning*, 1–48. https://doi.org/10.1080/09588221.2021.1888753

Schleppegrell, M.J. (2001). Linguistic features of the language of schooling. *Linguistics and Education, 12*(4), 431–459.

Schoonen, R. (2018). Are reading and writing building on the same skills? The relationship between reading and writing in L1 and EFL. *Reading & Writing, 32*(3), 511–535. https://doi.org/10.1007/s11145-018-9874-1

Shen, F. (2013). Using group discussion with Taiwan's EFL college students: A comparison of comprehension instruction for book club, literature circles, and instructional conversations. *English Language Teaching, 6*(12), 58–78. https://doi.org/10.5539/elt.v6n12p58

Strobl, C. (2014). Affordances of web 2.0 technologies for collaborative advanced writing in a foreign language. *CALICO Journal, 31*(1), 1–18. https://doi.org/10.11139/cj.31.1.1-18

Storch, N. (2005). Collaborative writing: product, process, and students' reflections. *Journal of Second Language Writing, 14*(3), 153–173. https://doi.org/10.1016/j.jslw.2005.05.002

Short, J., Williams, E., & Christie, B. (1976). *The social psychology of telecommunications*. Hoboken, NJ: John Wiley & Sons, Ltd.

Suhartono, S., & Laraswati, I. (2016). The use of visual media in teaching writing. *Journal of English Teaching and Research, 1*(1), 37–43. https://doi.org/10.29407/jetar.v1i1.274

Suwantarathip, O., & Wichadee, S. (2014). The effects of collaborative writing activity using Google docs on students' writing abilities. *The Turkish Online Journal of Educational Technology, 13*(2), 148–156.

Tai, H. (2016). Effects of collaborative online learning on EFL learners' writing performance and self-efficacy. *English Language Teaching, 9*(5), 119–133. https://doi.org/10.5539/elt.v9n5p119

Vorobel, O., & Kim, D. (2017). Adolescent ELLs' collaborative writing practices in face-to-face and online contexts: From perceptions to action. *System, 65*, 78–89. https://doi.org/10.1016/j.system.2017.01.008

Vygotsky, L.S. (1978). *Mind in society: The development of higher psychological processes*. Cambridge, MA: Harvard University Press.

Wang, D. (2009). Factors affecting the comprehension of global and local main idea. *Journal of College Reading and Learning, 39*(2), 34–52.

Yang, Y. (2016). Transforming and constructing academic knowledge through online peer feedback in summary writing. *Computer Assisted Language Learning, 29*(4), 683–702. https://doi.org/10.1080/09588221.2015.1016440

Yeh, H.-C. (2014). Exploring how collaborative dialogues facilitate synchronous collaborative writing. *Language Learning & Technology, 18*(1), 23–37.

Zheng, B., Niiya, M., & Warschauer, M. (2015). Wikis and collaborative learning in higher education. *Technology, Pedagogy and Education, 24*(3), 357–374. https://doi.org/10.1080/1475939X.2014.948041

---

1. The fireplace image in Figure 11.4 is credited to Paloform. Retrieved from https://paloform.com/

Appendix A

Argumentative Writing

Definition
- Argumentative writing is a genre of writing that requires investigation of a topic, which includes collecting and evaluating evidence to help establish a position on a topic.
- You are responding to a question—perhaps a controversial one—using the work of others as evidence to support your point of view.

The Process
- **Choose a Topic** (see *Example Topics* below)
- **Finding Evidence**: Use scholarly literaure to support your argument, which can be found through search engines and databases, such as Google Scholar, Omni, Microsoft Academic, etc.
- **Pre-writing**: Read and take notes, brainstorm ideas, create an outline
- **Writing**: Arguments should be clearly presented, and accurately referenced and paraphrased
- **Revising & Formatting**: Spend abundant time editing, and format your paper using APA

Important Elements
- Write in third person; do not use "I, "we," "you"
- Use formal language (tip: write simply initially, then go back to advance the vocabulary)
- **Introduction**: include background information of topic and make a case as to why your topic is important (tip: use numerical/statistical data to back up claims where you can)
- **Body Paragraphs**: clear & specific thesis statement, followed by relevant arguments & evidence
- **Conclusion**: Summarize your writing and include impactful statements that are forward-looking

Helpful Videos
- Choosing a topic for an argumentative essay: https://www.youtube.com/watch?v=bxZ8wddtpnk
- Structuring an argument: https://www.youtube.com/watch?v=PvhQ-eNuJ8I
- Writing a thesis statement: https://www.youtube.com/watch?v=YBIimcHfyL4

Example Topics
- Should we undergo lockdown again?
- Should classes be online or in-person?
- Should online classes be synchronous or asynchronous?
- Will the development of artificial intelligence benefit or harm people?
- Should social media be integrated into the curriculum?

12

A first step to task design in computer-based L2 listening: Task characteristics elicitation

Monica S. Cárdenas-Claros
Kimberley Dassonvalle

Introduction

Research on CALL has witnessed a renewed interest in task design as evidenced by the number of peer-reviewed publications and conference presentations that link task design to technology (i.e., Colpaert & Gijsen, 2017; Chong & Reinders, 2020; Sun, 2020; TBLT Conference, 2019). This interest has also translated into a surge of studies addressing task design with a focus on output-based tasks such as L2 writing and L2 speaking (see meta-synthesis by Chong & Reinders, 2020). Notwithstanding, as in other areas of English Language Teaching research, task design in input-based –L2 listening, remains under-researched. While Vandergrift and Goh (2012) or Brown (2018) have provided some general indications on how to design tasks for listening comprehension, such guidelines do not necessarily transfer to computer-based L2 listening environments. In addressing this, some researchers (Cárdenas-Claros, 2011) have proposed general guidelines for designing help options in computer-based listening environments, or for video presentations (Otaif, 2021). However, no study has investigated task design for computer-based listening environments with holistic consideration for input, task, and support and guidance.

The study reported here is the first step of a multi-stage project that seeks to put forward a theoretically-and-empirically based framework for the design of tasks in computer-based L2 listening environments. Accordingly, it aims to identify characteristics of listening tasks in computer-based environments as reported by L2 listeners from Chile. Three reasons motivate this study. One at the contextual level and the others at the theoretical level. Contextually, in most English as a Foreign Language contexts (EFL) in South America and elsewhere listening is problematic (Cárdenas-Claros, 2022). After high-school students take 4 or up to 7 years of instruction in the foreign language, they are unable to comprehend spoken English as measured by standardized tests such as SIMCE (Chile), Saber Pro (Colombia), Exani II (Mexico) (Cárdenas-Claros, 2022). At the theoretical level, existing frameworks for task design in SLA (i.e., Ellis, 2009) and in technology-mediated TBLT environments (González-Lloret & Ortega, 2014) fail to cater for students' needs and wants. They have been constructed primarily using a top-down approach where experts rely on theories, but where the voice of the language learner is not necessarily taken into account (Colpaert *et al.*, 2019). Also, this piece of research would address recent calls to computer-based listening researchers to derive pedagogical insights and/or design guidelines drawn from empirical research (see Cross, 2017; Hubbard, 2017).

Following established Educational Engineering techniques (Colpaert, 2010), data derived from 68 entry-questionnaires and 21 focus group sessions where a cohort of 68 high-school students from public and semi-public schools explored, reflected, and shared their personal goals surrounding tasks characteristics in computer-based L2 listening environments. We use Colpaert (2010) conceptualization of personal goals defined as "an assumption in itself (about common traits of a group or subgroups), an abstraction of factors that appear to hinder or stimulate the learning process, an instantiation of a non-conscious volition" (p. 272). Transcriptions of these verbal interactions were analyzed, and emerging characteristics identified. Characteristics of computer-based listening tasks were grouped and presented across three main components: input; task structure; and levels of support and guidance. We open this chapter by first situating the constructs of our study, discussing task design frameworks and perspectives from SLA and CALL. We continue with descriptions of the study site, data collection, and analysis procedures. Lastly, we present results across the three themes, providing integrated data and discussing applications to smart CALL.

Literature Review

Second Language Listening

In this work, second language listening is understood as an active and complex process of meaning construction that results from the interaction of hearing, cognition, attention, and the nearly automatic and simultaneous processing of linguistic, psycho-linguistic, and pragmatic aspects (Rubin, 1994; Rost, 2005; Field, 2013). Here, we follow Field's (2013) model of listening processes that distinguishes lower-level processes and higher-level processes.

According to Field (2013), lower-level processes pass through input decoding, lexical search, and parsing. Input decoding is aided by phonological knowledge and describes the process of how the aural signal is understood and decoded as a phoneme. In input decoding, Field (2013) notes how connected speech considerably affects the form of a word, its sound, and how listeners compensate for variations in speaker accents, pitch range, and speech rates. Next, lexical search matches input words to the listener's lexicon assisted by lexical knowledge. According to Field (2013), one of the major problems for listeners is lexical segmentation, where "there are no regular between-word pauses in connected speech" (p. 100), the listener must assess where one word ends, and another begins. Finally, in parsing, Field (2013) clarifies that a group of words has to be held in the learners' minds long enough to recognize syntactical patterns. Varied exposure to a range of speakers and text types aids automatization of lower-level processes, allowing listeners to free up cognitive resources that can be later exploited in higher-level processes.

Associated with comprehension, higher-level processes go toward representations of meaning and discourse. Meaning representation starts from conscious or unconscious activation of schemata—that is, "a knowledge structure containing all that an individual knows about and associates with a particular concept" (p. 101)—and is the combination of contextual, schematic, and inferential information. Discourse representation, the highest level, deals with the micro and macro structures present in discourse and how listeners are able to identify them.

Computer-based Listening

Computer-based listening examines the use of digital applications that take advantage of the computer's ability to provide enhanced input (Cárdenas-Claros et al., 2021; Hubbard, 2017; Montero-Pérez, 2020). Hubbard (2017) and (Cárdenas-Claros, 2021) agree that using a computer, and by computer it refers to a tablet, desktop, mobile phone or notebook, to play an audio or video is not considered computer-based listening. Interaction and learner control are quintessentials of computer-based listening (see Cárdenas-Claros, 2021). Similar to interactive listening where L2 learners use different strategies for text comprehension and task completion (i.e., ask for clarification and repetition, check misunderstandings), in computer-based L2 listening, learners rely on textual support through transcripts, subtitles and/or captions to check understanding; use audio/video buttons to control the stream of aural input; access hyperlinks and glossaries to check word meanings and consult feedback to assess performance.

Cárdenas-Claros et al. (2021) noted that the development of L2 listening ability can be aided by interaction with help options in several ways. For instance, reading along from transcripts while listening to texts may help learners develop word segmentation skills as the transient nature of aural texts is compensated by the blank spaces that mark word boundaries when reading. Interaction with audio/video control bars allow listeners to cope with unfamiliar accents, speed of delivery, and presence of run-on words. Interaction with meaning technologies such as dictionaries, glossaries, and glossed words can help listeners understand word meanings and activate schemata to facilitate comprehension.

Task-based Language Learning

Task-based learning and teaching has been identified as the most advanced form of communicative language teaching. Viewed as the smallest unit of syllabus design and evaluation—and generally structured into pre-task, in-task, and post-task (Van den Braden, 2016; Ellis, 2003)—we understand task as "a holistic activity which engages language use in order to achieve some non-linguistic outcome while meeting a linguistic challenge, with the overall aim of promoting language learning through process or product or both" (Samuda & Bygate, 2008, p. 69).

Ellis (2003) further distinguishes between unfocused and focused tasks in his framework of Tasked-Based Language Teaching (TBLT). An unfocused task—designed to elicit general language—does not explicitly state linguistic rules or vocabulary needed to achieve task completion but expects learners to freely make use of their own linguistic resources. Conversely, focused tasks are designed to draw learners' attention to specific linguistic features and help them advance in second language proficiency. While there are alternatives (Samuda & Bygate, 2008; Nunan, 1989), this work focuses on the four-criteria framework put forward by Ellis (2003), which was an initial step to guide second language teachers in the design and assessment of tasks. Not surprisingly, this has been subject to continuous debate and has therefore been constantly refined. The most updated version is found in Ellis and Shintani (2013, p.135), stating that:

- The primary focus should be on "meaning"! (i.e., learners should be mainly concerned with encoding and decoding messages, not with focusing on linguistic form).
- There should be some kind of "gap" (i.e., a need to convey information, to express an opinion or to infer meaning).
- Learners should largely rely on their own resources (linguistic and non-linguistic) in order to complete the activity. That is, learners are not "taught" the language they will need to perform the task, although they may be able to "borrow" from the input the task provides to help them perform it.
- There is a clearly defined outcome other than the use of language (i.e., the language serves as the means for achieving the outcome, not as an end in its own right). Thus, when performing a task, learners are not primarily concerned with using language correctly but rather achieving the goal.

Mapping out Technology-mediated TBLT and Listening

Drawing on the distinction between focused and unfocused tasks previously examined, it may be apparent that an emphasis on lower-level processes development would yield easier to focused input-based tasks. An emphasis on higher-level processes would yield easier to more input-based unfocused tasks. However, Field (2013) notes that the different levels (lower and higher) do not act linearly but are rather recursive and complementary, making it challenging for task designers to operationalize and assess tasks. This may partially explain the scarcity of studies reporting the use of input-based tasks attending to primarily higher-level processes.

Of these, focus-on-form listening tasks have made their way into the literature. De la Fuente (2014), for instance, designed a study that explored the differential effects of medium of delivery of aural input during listening tasks on learners noticing and type of comprehension (top-down and bottom-up) of Spanish object pronouns during focus-on-form listening tasks. De la Fuente examined twenty-two college students enrolled in second year Spanish in a technology-enhanced classroom.

Learner-manipulated or mobile assisted language learning (MALL) and instructor-manipulated language learning (IMLL) were compared through a quasi-experimental design. Noticing in her study was operationalized using think-aloud protocols and post-test exposure comprehension assessment tasks. According to de la Fuente (2014), learners in the MALL group showed significantly higher levels of reported noticing, bottom-up comprehension, and top-down overall comprehension than learners in the IMLL group. Although these findings cannot be exclusively associated with the role of technology (mobile devices), they seem to suggest that direct manipulation of materials do help improve L2 listening comprehension. Notably, these findings were interpreted following primarily an SLA framework for interaction but did not use a framework for task design in computer-based listening environments.

Now, extending the work of Ellis (2009), Gonzalez-Lloret and Ortega (2014, p. 6) proposed a five-criteria framework in the context of technology-and-task integration. The stated criteria suggest that task should have:

1. A primary focus on meaning: learners should focus on the content, including semantic and pragmatic meaning, rather than on form.
2. Goal orientation: the task must have a communicative purpose and this should be triggered by learners' need to share information, solve a problem, or express an opinion.
3. Learner-centeredness: learners draw mainly on their own linguistic and nonlinguistic resources along with their digital skills.
4. Holism: tasks are authentic and representative of the real world, drawing on real-world processes of language use and integrating form and function.

5. Opportunities for reflective learning: learners have the chance not only to learn by doing, but also to consider the process as well as the outcome, encouraging cyclical and reflective learning.

Hubbard (2015) reflected on the use of Gonzalez-Lloret and Ortega's (2014) framework to discuss lessons learned from over a decade of teaching, development, research, and practice in an ESL course in advanced listening. According to Hubbard, the listening tasks in his course incorporated four of the five elements: primary focus on meaning, goal orientation, learner centeredness, and a particular emphasis on reflective learning. In his view, holism was more tenuous, as the course explicitly encouraged learners to engage their analytical faculties, but no guiding tools were provided to do so.

Alm (2015) also used Gonzalez-Lloret and Ortega's (2014) framework in a study involving listening-based tasks supported by technology. Alm (2015) ensured that input texts were not only authentic, but also that output-based tasks mimicked real life interactions. Accordingly, the learners of German in her study selected input texts from a list of ten iTune texts gathered by researchers consisting of news segments, soap operas, and documentaries. Students were then encouraged to keep a blog and a weekly reflection entry on what they had learned from the input text and how their impressions changed over time. Importantly, Alm (2015) reported that learners' preferences were catered to, they were not all assigned the same texts but rather chose from the list. Also, unlike multiple-choice comprehension tests, the type of task in her study "created natural listening and speaking situations and led to natural language use" (p. 43), a true goal of TBLT.

Task Design and Goal Elicitation

Task design remains idiosyncratic. Erlam (2015) and Alm (2015) agree that language teachers seem to be aware of TBLT and SLA criteria for task design, however, task design decisions are undeliberate: teachers imitate others, pick from lists of "best practices" or simply keep doing what seems to have worked well before in their classrooms. Colpaert *et al.* (2019) note that tasks are context-bound and should be understood as a piece of a puzzle that fits perfectly within the other components of the learning environment, hence, it is necessary to elicit the needs of the key stakeholders or final users to better task design. With this in mind, Colpaert and Spruyt

(2018) and Colpaert *et al.* (2019) suggest that tasks should be designed to create "acceptance" and "willingness" in the learners' mind. To achieve this, learners do not only need to be consulted about, but included in task design processes to increase the likelihood of task acceptance as basic needs such as usefulness, meaningfulness, and enjoyability are addressed. Meaningfulness is understood as the extent to which the proposed task results in something valuable for the learner; usefulness describes the extent to which the result of the proposed task will be valuable to others; and enjoyability is the realization of the two previous qualities.

Task Design for (Computer-based) L2 Listening

Very few publications deal with task design for (computer-based) listening. We structure this review from the perspective of input, task, and learner. Regarding input, researchers agree that, although the use of authentic materials is not a must in a TBLT approach, the input should "reflect what would be heard in the learner's daily life" (Brown, 2018, p. 3) or mirror real-life contexts (Park & Slater, 2014). Other authors describe input characteristics with regards to linguistic complexity (Brunfaut & Révész, 2015), emphasizing the need for rich and elaborate input (Park & Slater, 2014). Researchers have also referred to input considerations with regards to the amount and density (Brown, 2018) and the explicitness of information (Brunfaut & Révész, 2015) acknowledging that the less explicit the information is the more difficult to comprehend. Other suggestions deal with the genre (i.e., narrative, conversation, radio broadcast) and the students' interests (Brown, 2018; Vandergrift & Goh, 2012).

At the levels of task, guidelines for design suggest that tasks should be graded in terms of difficulty (Brown, 2018) and that task difficulty is determined to some extent by listeners' response characteristics (Vandergrift & Goh, 2012). That is, for instance, tasks that require ticking and selecting from options are less cognitively demanding than tasks in which learners are required to summarize or synthesize information (cf. Brunfaut & Révész, 2015, Duong *et al.*, 2021, Vandergrift & Goh, 2012). Also, with regards to assistance and support to help learners recover from breakdowns in understanding, Cárdenas-Claros & Gruba (2015) provided guidelines for the design of help options in computer-based listening and advocated for the design of help options that "are easy to use, promote learner control, support guidance, and stimulate learning" (p. 429). Otaif (2021) investigated interactivity in task design for computer-based listening when digital video is the mode of presentation. He reported that a 30-second span for listeners to view questions is ideal, that video input should be paused, and the task items should appear on the left side of the screen and listeners should view or hide subtitles on demand.

Authors have also suggested that listener familiarity and motivation toward topics is important (Brown, 2018). Vandergrift and Goh (2012) suggest that needs analysis should be taken into account for design purposes. Other authors suggest using participatory design tenets (Cárdenas-Claros & Gruba 2010; Otaif, 2021) to improve task completion and task performance. Although valuable, at times learners' voices get dimmed by the opinions of other stakeholders in participatory design sessions.

As seen in our review, most task design suggestions take a top-down perspective without much empirical support (i.e., Brown, 2018; Vandergrift & Goh, 2012). Others do not directly address task design but imply structure from research designs (i.e., Brunfaut & Révész, 2015) and, although other studies examine real-life to propose taxonomies in task design (i.e., Park & Slater, 2014), they primarily address language learners in tertiary education and learners are not consulted about task design. In our work, however, we second Colpaert's proposal to use an Educational Engineering approach to goal elicitation conducive to task design as willingness and task acceptance may increase. Accordingly, this study seeks to investigate characteristics of computer-based listening tasks as perceived by high schoolers. Stated as a research question, we investigate:

What characteristics should computer-based L2 listening tasks have according to the perception of high school learners of English in Chile?

Methodology

This qualitative case study is part of a larger study that seeks to put forward a theoretically and empirically based framework for task design in computer-based L2 listening environments. For this study, we isolate EFL listener goals to identify characteristics of computer-based listening tasks according to their perceptions. To comply with ethical requirements (Eckert, 2013), the study was approved by the University Human Research Ethics board. Both consent and assent forms were completed, and all participants volunteered to partake in the study.

Traditional ELT research elicits goals through needs analyses. Although they offer an overview of students' needs and wants, these usually take a top-down perspective, leaving experts to decide questions beforehand and rarely allowing for co-construction of meaning with participants (Gonzalez-Lloret & Ortega, 2014). They are also usually done individually, and then results are averaged. Hence, to truly understand listener goals, we echo Colpaert's (2010) that personal goals elicitation is an "intricate exercise" (p. 266) that requires learners to first reflect on factors that trigger or discourage the learning process and then reflect on what they would like to acquire. As we said, we use established techniques from the Educational Engineering approach.

Participants

The participants are 68 (29 male, 37 female, and 2 non-binary) high-school learners of English as a Foreign Language from Chile. On average, they have been studying English for 5.9 years, and, at the time of data collection, had 1.5 weekly hours of language instruction.

Table 11.1 *Demographics of participants.*

School				Participants		
Name	Type	Region of Chile	Age	# of participants	Average # of years studying English	# of classes per week
Sp_Peter	Public	VIII	14	12	5	1
Np_Paul	Public	I	13	9	6.1	2
Csp_Anton	Semi-private	V	14	10	7.8	1
Csp_Alexa	Semi-private	V	14	7	7.1	1
Csp_Gaby	Semi-private	VII	14	10	4.3	1
Nsp_Carl	Semi-private	III	14	11	6.5	1
Csp_Therese	Semi-private	V	14	9	4.8	3

Participants attended EFL classes from two public and five semi-private high-school institutions throughout the Chilean territory (regions I, III, V, VI and VIII). We worked with these schools because national test results (i.e. SIMCE, Aptis) consistently show that on average 12th graders in Chile score 48 out of 90 in aural comprehension tests, and even lower when students from public schools are compared to the ones from semi-private schools (for further information see Cárdenas-Claros, 2020). We worked with high-school students to broaden the horizons of computer-based L2 listening research which has been primarily conducted with participants from tertiary education; although relevant, such work rarely transfers to the settings that actually need informed interventions. Then, we asked teachers to select 9th graders articulate enough to discuss prior successful experiences with L2 listening and their expectations towards L2 listening tasks. No proficiency level was required. We worked with 9th graders as they came from a variety of middle schools, which better ensured a variety of experiences and goals.

Procedure

Given the 2020 health crisis, data from participating schools was collected online using Zoom (except from Csp_Therese). Data was gathered during four 90-minute sessions over a four-week period for each school. In the first session, students completed consent forms, assent forms, and selected and completed the entry questionnaire. Sessions two to four were focus groups (21 total). We made further adaptations to Colpaert's (2010) Educational Engineering techniques to elicit personal goals, so for each session, we designed focus group protocols that were shared in Google Drive for students to complete individually prior to opening the floor for discussion. This measure was necessary to allow time for reflection and to avoid that the participants would just follow the leaders' insights (Esterberg, 2002). In general, each focus group session was structured as follows:

- 10 minutes for welcoming and instructions.
- 15 minutes for individual written reflections.
- 50 minutes for group reflection.
- 15 minutes for wrap up and homework.

Participant's responses were video-recorded and students used pseudonyms at all times. Also, they were required to turn their camera off to protect their identities.

Instruments

The study developed four instruments: an entry questionnaire and three focus group protocols. The former gathered demographics and experience with both language learning and listening comprehension. The focus group protocols were constructed using listener goal elicitation prompts suggested by Colpaert (2010). Accordingly, the first focus group protocol prompted students with "When I think about my listening comprehension in English, I think about the following problems..."; the second, "When I think about these problems, I feel..."; and the third, "I feel... because... I wish my classes were..." Each protocol was piloted for both face-to-face and online data collection procedures, and changes were made as needed.

Data Analysis

A total of 25.19 hours of focus groups were transcribed for this study. We primarily used the data from focus groups 2 and 3, as these yielded the most information. To identify characteristics of computer-based listening tasks as perceived by the participants, we started with open coding. For this, six coders were asked to tag the data using self-explanatory codes. Discrepancies were solved with each coder as the authors of this chapter did the second round of analysis and grouped individual codes into macro-components. Then, the second author of the chapter revised the coding protocol and made changes as necessary. The first author served as second coder using the established protocol to 20% of the data. Intercoder reliability was calculated at .92

Results

Three macro-components resulted from analysis: *Input Task Characteristics*, *Task Structure*, and *Task Guidance and Support*. Clearly, the first two macro-components are paramount for the design of listening tasks, the third component predominantly addresses the design of computer-based listening tasks. The components are not presented in hierarchical order; indeed, analysis shows that they complement and, at times, overlap each other. Clusters are summarized in Tables 2 through 4, given by participant consensus from at least two different schools and found in the data four times. The first column in these tables sets out clusters; columns 2 to 8 report the number of occurrences per school; and the last column provides sample data. Complementarily, sample quotes describe sources. Thus, the quote Csp_Anton_FG_L30 is from a semi-private school (sp) located in central Chile (C) and corresponds to L30 from a focus group transcript (FG).

Input Task Characteristics

This describes the aural input features L2 listeners wish to be exposed to, including quality, length, variety, characteristics potential for learning, and levels of linguistic complexity. Additionally, it describes participant input preferences at the personal and group levels (Table 11.2).

Table 11.2 *Input task characteristics.*

	Nsp_Carl	Csp_Gaby	Csp_Alexa	Np_Paul	Csp_Anton	Sp_Peter	Csp_Therese	Sample quotes
Input components								
Quality	8	14	8	5	9	3	10	"It should be clear and concise, only focusing on audio content [voices], preferably without background noise and interruptions." Csp_Gaby_S3_Form_Olivia*
Length	12	18	13	11	7	6	1	"Between 1 and 3 minutes, because I think I would not be able to keep all the ideas in my head if it were longer. If it's too short, I might understand everything, but I wouldn't want it to be that short." Np_Paul_S3_FG_L149-L151
Varied input	7	0	1	0	1	0	0	"It should be varied, not just the typical dialogue 'hi, mi name is...' but audiobooks, short stories, or informative audios." Nsp_Carl_S3_Form_Camila
Potential for learning								
Everyday language	2	3	0	4	2	0	1	"It should have everyday vocabulary, not basic, but that will help us communicate with a foreign person." Np_Paul_S3_FG_L64
Repetition	10	16	11	9	7	11	2	"E: it seems that everyone agrees with repeating the audio 2 times. Does anybody need a third or a

								fourth time?" "S: I would say that two is the minimum, but if it is a 1:30 audio and most of it is just ideas that don't add anything or might distract us, I think that students might want another repetition, but three times top." Csp_Alexa_S3_FG_L257-258
Address proficiency level	1	0	0	0	4	0	0	"It should be easy to understand according to the level of the students." Csp_Anton_S3_FG_L2
Speaker characteristics	10	16	2	10	5	9	0	"E: That's an interesting idea, Alex, that the speakers should be adults, why is that? "A: mmm because sometimes with children's voices ... the audio gets distorted." Sp_Peter_S3_FG_L82
Input linguistic complexity								
Phonological complexity	7	13	7	14	17	1	7	"It should be more fluent and understandable and at the same time that speakers talk with a certain speed so that I can understand every word." Csp_Therese_S3_FG_L88
Lexical complexity	0	0	1	5	3	0	2	"It should have a variety of common expressions that native speakers of English use" Csp_Anton_S2_Form_Tamara
Speed of delivery	8	12	13	4	9	7	13	"I get confused when the people in the audio speak too fast. I would like them to talk slower to understand better." Csp_Therese_S2_FG_L305
Personal input preferences								
Interesting topic	5	2	1	0	0	0	6	"The topic of the audio should be something interesting and that students like. For example, an informative video so that we get to learn something new from it." Nsp_Carl_S3_Form_Bastian
Entertaining topics	0	1	0	7	3	4	3	"I think that the listening should be more entertaining because it usually gets monotonous and repetitive. It should also have fun things like memes, or things that entertain us while we learn." Sp_Peter_S3_FG_L172
Meaningful/engaging topics	2	5	0	10	2	0	3	"There are topics that are not meaningful to us and a 5-minute audio about something that doesn't grab our attention is boring." Csp_Gaby_S3_FG_L89

Group input preferences								
Current topics	0	3	2	2	2	0	0	"It should be about current trends in music or movies… or that address kids' preferences." Csp_Alexa_S3_FG_L49
Class-related topics	2	4	1	0	3	1	0	"It should contain information related to the unit we are working on. It could be the topic or vocabulary that we are studying in class." Csp_Anton_S3_Form_Tamara
Topics of general interest or familiar topics	1	4	0	1	3	3	1	"The topic should address our preferences as a group, not like something too specific, because some students might not pay attention, so I believe that it should be about something common to us all, such as nature or things like that." Nsp_Carl_S3_FG_L81
Varied topics	1	0	7	7	0	0	0	"I think that the listening should have a little bit of everything and be more varied." Np_Paul_S3_FG_L39**

*C=Central; sp=semi-private; S3=Session 3; Form=Google forms. ** N=North; p=private, S3=Session 3; FG=Focus group.

Of **Input components**, *input quality* is defined as all those aspects of the input that interfere with comprehension processes. For instance, background noise, at times, can be found as distracting (Csp_Gaby_S3_Form_Olivia), or can complement the message nicely (Sp_Peter_S3_FG_L194). *Length* refers to the ideal duration of input texts. Across contexts, participants noted that 2-3-minute texts are ideal for comprehension. Longer segments may tire them (Csp_Anton_S3_Form_Romina), and shorter segments may not allow them to tune in (Csp_Gaby_S3_FG_L64) and/or provide much information (Csp_Alexa_S3_FG_L217). *Varied input* describes the different genres listeners expect to be exposed to. An overuse of inauthentic "dialogues" causes boredom and disengagement (Nsp_Carl_S3_Form_Jafari). Data shows a preference for movie segments and documentaries (Csp_Alexa_S3_FG_L109), short films (Nsp_Carl_S3_FG_L98), songs and audiobooks (Nsp_Carl_S3_Form_Katie).

Potential for learning describes input characteristics that L2 listeners perceive as aiding language development. These should contain *everyday language* for 'real' communication purposes, i.e., with native speakers

(Csp_Anton_S2_Form_Fiona). *Repetition* is the number of times an aural text should be played. Most participants across schools acknowledge the need to have audio/video segments played a minimum of two times (Np_Paul_S3_Form_Amara) and up to five times (Nsp_Carl_S3_Form_Katie). Interestingly, although listening exercises are mostly individual, students are aware of classmates' struggles with English and that repetition may aid comprehension. Input should also *address proficiency level*. Input should not be too easy, with no effort for comprehension (Csp_Anton_S3_FG_L2), or too difficult to cause frustration (Csp_Anton_S3_FG_L63). Finally, *speaker characteristics* refers to preference for speakers that clearly articulate ideas, i.e., with a juvenile and friendly attitude (Csp_Gaby_S3_FG_L6) or whose voices listeners can tell apart (Csp_Gaby_S3_Form_ Matilde). Although our focus was on one-way listening, inevitably, as we explored listeners' goals, students also referred to their preference for their classroom teachers to speak clearly and slowly (Csp_Gaby_S2_Form_Raul).

The third characteristic of the input is its **Linguistic complexity**. *Phonological complexity* describes aspects to do with pronunciation, accent, and speakers' tendency to run-on words. In this regard, participants used adjectives such as clear, paused, and well-articulated to describe pronunciation, and expressed a need to understand every single word. Also, most participants acknowledged feeling more comfortable with American English (Nsp_Carl_S3_FG_L39) over British accents. For *lexical complexity*, texts should contain vocabulary they have studied in class or used in real life (Np_Paul_S2_Form_Cloe), avoiding technical words (Csp_Alexa_S2_Form_Santiago). For *speed of delivery*, while fast speech is much more difficult to comprehend (Csp_Therese_S2_FG_L305), they want more "natural" or "real" speech; however, slow speech seems to be a greater need.

Finally, **Personal input preferences** acknowledge individual preferences and interests for input topics. These should be *interesting* (Csp_Alexa_S3_Form_Alex), *entertaining* (Np_Paul_S2_Form_Isabella), *meaningful and engaging* (Np_Paul_S2_Form_Joe). The data also shows listener awareness of the **Group preferences**, where individual interests cannot be fully addressed at all times. Therefore, the data shows a preference for topics that depict *current trends or events* (Nsp_Paul_S3_Form_Iker), that have been discussed in their own *language class* (Csp_Gaby_S3_Form_Marcela) or in other school subjects

(Csp_Gaby_S3_Form_Emma), or that address *general interests* such as nature (Nsp_Carl_S3_FG_L81). The last aspect of input preferences as a group is *variety*. Participants are constantly exposed to topics of daily routines or casual conversations (Csp_Alexa_S3_FG_L40), and would prefer topics such as English history (Csp_Alexa_S3_FG_L9) or scientific matters (Nsp_Carl_S3_FG_L66).

Task Structure

This is understood as a system in which task components, task difficulty and personal task preferences are sequenced and organized to ensure comprehension of listening materials (Table 11.3).

Table 11.3 *Task structure.*

	Nsp_Carl	Csp_Gaby	Csp_Alexa	Np_Paul	Csp_Anton	Sp_Peter	Csp_Therese	Sample quotes
Task components								
Pre-listening	9	4	5	2	0	8	3	E: "Ok, before listening, you want to review the vocabulary to be used in class and that will appear in the listening - why? N: Because there are words that we don't understand the first time we hear them, and I think they should be explained beforehand." Csp_Therese_S3_FG_L195-196
Post-listening	10	0	6	2	0	5	4	"From my point of view, in the post-listening we should check understanding, clarify doubts, and identify the most common mistakes or where students struggled the most and try to review from there. The teacher could also explain the listening and as a group we should be checking each answer." Csp_Alexa_S3_FG_L291-293
Task difficulty								
Type of exercises	5	10	3	6	0	10	3	"True or false, gap filling exercises... avoid the usual things we do because we always have to answer questions." Sp_Peter_S3_FG_L119

Response difficulty	7	5	4	1	1	0	1	"The exercises should range from less to more difficult. To me, the easiest is multiple choice, and then a more complex one would be open-ended questions. But I rather prefer True or False for my own learning." Csp_Gaby_S3_Form_Britney
Task control	8	1	0	1	4	0	10	"It should be done individually so that I can understand and answer the questions at my own pace." Nsp_Carl_S3_Form_Jafari
Personal task preferences								
Varied tasks	4	0	5	2	1	0	0	"The exercises should be more varied, not the same as always." Csp_Alexa_S3_Form_Flo

*C=Central; sp=semi-private; S3=Session 3; Form=Google forms. ** N=North; p=private, S3=Session 3; FG=Focus group.

Task components describe the individual elements participants expect to find in a listening task, structured into pre-, while-, and post-listening exercises. *Pre-listening* describes all the schemata activation exercises, i.e., vocabulary previewing (Csp_Anton_S3_FG_L11-15), contextualization of the listening text (Csp_Alexa_S2_Form_Vicente), explanation of key concepts (Nsp_Carl_S3_Form_Jafari), exercises to raise awareness of pronunciation of key words (Nsp_Carl_S2_Form_Mary), and tips for them to better approach the exercises ahead. Although participants acknowledged while-listening exercises to be part of task components, we discussed them in the cluster *task difficulty* as it comprises all types of exercises expected to be developed in the while-listening section. *Post-listening* refers to all those activities developed once participants have interacted with the input texts. That is, reviewing key concepts (Nsp_Carl_S3_Form_Angel), making summaries (Sp_Peter_S3_FG_L42) and sharing their opinions about text-related issues and content (Nsp_Carl_S3_Form_Jafari).

Task difficulty comes from student assessments of an exercise, and includes type of exercises, response difficulty, and task control. *Type of exercises* lists specific exercise types, for instance, true/false, multiple choice questions, comprehension questions, that participants expect to find in a listening task. *Response difficulty* acknowledges participant's preference of exercises based on their level of difficulty, i.e., for true/false exercises, since the chances of being wrong are lower (Csp_Alexa_S3_FG_L53-54); for multiple choice questions, due to given choices (Csp_Gaby_S3_FG_

L137-141); text completion, because it allows text analysis (Csp_Gaby_S3_FG_L121-123); and neglect exercises which require writing a full sentence or explaining the reason for their selection (Np_Paul_S3_FG_L264-267). *Task control* refers to the interactional factors that allow learners to work at their own pace or that promote a variety of grouping options. The analysis shows that participants expect to interact with tasks where no time pressure is imposed and where there are no limitations in the number of times an exercise can be completed (Csp_Therese_S3_FG_L384). Also, although participants expressed a preference to first work individually in listening tasks (Np_Paul_S3_FG_L290), they value tasks that are flexible enough that allows different grouping configurations (Nsp_Carl_S2_Form_Jafari) where listeners can re-construct text meaning together (Csp_Anton_S3_FG_L176).

The third factor of task structure is **personal task preferences**. Participants wish these to be interesting (Nsp_Carl_S2_Form_Katie), entertaining (Np_Paul_S3_Form_Syria), and more varied rather than repetitive (Nsp_Carl_S3_FG_L207).

Task Guidance and Support

This third macro-component entails advice and suggestions given to listeners as they experience breakdowns in comprehension, in both, blended learning and self-access environments (Table 11.4).

Task guidance refers to the support provided by teachers as students develop listening tasks in blended learning environments, such as *vocabulary explanations* (Csp_Therese_S3_FG_L321); *exposure to different accents* (Np_Paul_S3_FG_L90); preference for listening to complete and uninterrupted text *–input continuity–* (Nsp_Carl_S3_Form_Javiera); and the reliance on *L1 support* seen as having word meaning explanations (Np_Paul_S2_Form_Cloe), including a combination of English and Spanish sentences in the text, or checking comprehension using the L1. Finally, *feedback* refers to the direct assessment of participants' performance (Csp_Therese_S3_FG_L288-289) and/or the gain of better text comprehension (Csp_Anton_S3_Form_Josefa).

Table 11.4 *Task guidance and support*

	Nsp_Carl	Csp_Gaby	Csp_Alexa	Np_Paul	Csp_Anton	Sp_Peter	Csp_Therese	Sample quotes
Task guidance								
Vocabulary explanations	7	6	4	2	9	4	6	E1: "Would you like the teacher to provide you with the explanation of the vocabulary or you having to search for the words on your own? G: That the teacher gives me the vocabulary" Csp_Therese_S3_FG_L270-271
Exposure to different accents	4	8	0	4	0	0	1	"It should have different accents, like American, British... so that our brain gets used to listening to different types of accents." Csp_Gaby_S3_Form_Britney
Input continuity	5	2	0	0	5	0	0	"I think that pausing the audio would help a lot, especially if it is a long audio that has a lot of new information" Csp_Anton_S3_FG_L211
L1 support	1	0	1	3	2	2	0	"The teacher should explain the listening scenario in Spanish, because if it's just in English, it would be the same as just listening to the audio and we wouldn't understand anyway." Csp_Alexa_S3_FG_L312
Feedback	4	0	2	8	7	14	1	"Written feedback to be able to correct on my own and understand why I was wrong. Also, oral feedback from the teacher pointing out the mistakes and talking about it." Np_Paul_S3_Form_Andrea
Help options								
Textual support	9	7	3	14	9	5	8	"Sometimes there are words that sound the same and I get confused. I would like to have access to subtitles in English to differentiate them." Nsp_Carl_S3_Form_Katie
Visual support	5	1	0	4	0	11	4	"We should watch videos... A video that has animation, that shows us the actions that the characters are doing, in that way I would understand a lot more." Np_Paul_S3_FG_L259

Audio control buttons	3	5	2	2	1	0	14	"When I don't understand the words, I would like to have a tool to be able to pause, change speed, or rewind the audio." Csp_Therese_S3_FG_L390
Meaning technologies	6	3	2	4	4	1	4	"It should include a dictionary or a list of the most complex words to better understand the audio." Sp_Peter_S2_Form_Nicole
Pronunciation aids	15	1	0	6	1	4	1	"I would like a tool that provides the written version of the audio and that provides the pronunciation of the words." Csp_Gaby_S3_FG_L183
Immersion technologies	0	0	0	2	0	2	0	"With the 8D audio, it feels like the person is talking to me directly and I can place myself in the situation which I think will help me understand better." Np_Paul_S3_FG_L312-L313

*C=Central; sp=semi-private; S3=Session 3; Form=Google forms. ** N=North; p=private, S3=Session 3; FG=Focus group.

Help options refers to the features of computer-based listening tasks that participants expect to resort to as they develop listening tasks in self-access environments. In their view, these could take the form of *textual support* such as subtitles, captions, and transcripts/translation to ease comprehension of materials (Csp_Anton_S3_FG_L241) and to view and reinforce pronunciation (Csp_Alexa_S2_Form_Karina). Here, the extant debate on textual support was also apparent in our data; at times, listeners suggested not using textual support at all, since it shifted the goal of listening to reading (Np_Paul_S2_Form_Syria). V*isual support,* in the form of static and moving pictures (Nsp_Carl_S3_Form_Camila) with a preference for pictures or animation that represent what is being said. *Audio control buttons* to pause (Csp_Alexa_S3_FG_L212-213), slow speed (Np_Paul_S3_Form_ Andrea), and rewind. *Meaning technologies,* such as glossaries (Csp_Alexa_S2_Form_Vicente), dictionaries, and translators to identify word meanings (Nsp_Carl_S3_Form_Brax). Moreover, participants consensually expect to find features for p*ronunciation practice* (Nsp_Carl_ S3_Form_Goliat), and to have *total immersion* experience through the use of 8D audio (Np_Paul_S3_FG_L312-L313).

Application to Smart CALL

Two applications to Smart CALL derive from this study: contextualization and personalization. The reported characteristics of computer-based listening tasks clearly reflect the specific context in which they arise. While we cannot claim that these characteristics represent all Chilean high-school learners of English, they do to some extent permeate learners from public and semi-private schools. Participant preferences for speakers with American accents might be explained by exposure to and familiarity with texts in the media. Also, a preference for textual support may be the result of a long tradition of reading skills development (Cárdenas-Claros & Campos-Ibaceta, 2018). In fact, until 1998 teachers were instructed to develop reading and grammar (Lizasoain, 2017). Similarly, a preference for teacher's slow speech and L1 support might be a transference from teachers' classroom practices to the computer-based listening environment in which L1 support is still strong in Chilean classrooms (Cancino & Díaz, 2020). Surprisingly, in an era where students have access to an array of input texts through the Internet, we still found student preferences for teachers as the main source of input. Because playing one-way input necessarily relies on some sort of technology, perhaps teachers find it much easier to read text out loud rather than face poor quality equipment and associated difficulties (Cárdenas-Claros & Oyanedel, 2016). Next, student advocacy for varied input topics, varied input genres, and varied task exercises also seem to reflect the widespread reliance of language teachers on input texts presented in the textbooks from which learners are expected to report comprehension of literal information (Cárcamo, 2018). Here, the long tradition of testing, rather than teaching listening is also apparent –some participants would rather stay in their comfort zones and opt for true/false and multiple-choice exercises to more likely ensure a higher grade (Ramírez, 2020).

Personalization in this study is seen as the participants suggested features of computer-based listening tasks that address their specific profiles and desired levels of performance in listening comprehension. Thus, through the provision of textual support in the form of transcripts, captions, subtitles and translations, our participants envision that they will be able to ease comprehension, differentiate words that sound similar, and address issues with pronunciation; similar reasons are reported by Cárdenas-Claros and Campos-Ibaceta (2018). By including meaning technologies in the form of dictionaries, translators, and glossaries in task design, participants expect to increase the potential for word meaning understanding and comprehension; which aligns with Hubbard (2017) suggestions. Our participants also expect to include visual support in computer-based listening task designs with a special preference for animated videos to compensate for misunderstandings arising from a long tradition of audio-only materials exposure. Interaction with audio control buttons are requested for learners to decide if, when, and how many times a text can be listened to which may attend their short term-memory capacity and preference for global viewing and analytical viewing (Cárdenas-Claros, 2021). Lastly, acknowledging the link between listening and pronunciation, participants too expect computer-based listening tasks to include pronunciation aids not only to be consulted but also to enable them to make stronger links between spoken and written words. Although we acknowledge that features like this do exist, it is the first time these are highly demanded for computer-based listening environments.

Conclusion

This study investigated task characteristics from the perception of 68 high school learners of English in Chile using established personal goal elicitation techniques following Colpaert (2010). We presented findings on input task characteristics, task structure, and task guidance and support components. The dilemma that remains is to design tasks that truly fit the context of – or capitalize on – learner experiences to expand their horizons and show them new alternatives.

This study further advances understanding of task design characteristics in computer-based listening environments from the student's perspective. In our view, the reported characteristics offer the backbone for future guidelines of the components that need to be further investigated for the design of tasks in computer-based listening, an area ripe for future research.

References

Alm, A. (2015, July 6-8). Technology-mediated task-based listening: From authentic input to authentic response. *Proceedings of the XVII International Conference on CALL-Research Conference*, 39–44. Universitat Rovira I Virgili, Tarragona, Spain. https://wwwa.fundacio.urv.cat/congressos/public/usr_docs/call_2015_conference_proceedings.pdf

Brown, S. (2018). Task-based approach to listening. In J.I. Liontas (Ed.), *The TESOL encyclopedia of English language teaching*. Hoboken, NJ: John Wiley & Sons. https://doi.org/10.1002/9781118784235.eelt0613

Brunfaut, T., & Révész, A. (2015). The role of task and listener characteristics in second language listening. *TESOL Quarterly, 49*(1), 141-168. https://doi.org/10.1002/tesq.168

Cancino, M., & Díaz, G. (2020). Exploring the code-switching behaviours of Chilean EFL high school teachers: A function-focused approach. *Profile Issues in Teachers Professional Development, 22*(2), 115–130. https://doi.org/10.15446/profile.v22n2.81152

Cárcamo, B. (2018). Types of listening comprehension promoted in the Chilean EFL textbook Global English. *Colombian Applied Linguistics Journal, 20*(1), 49–61. https://doi.org/10.14483/22487085.12313

Cárdenas-Claros, M.S. (2011). A preliminary framework of help options in computer-based second language listening [Doctoral dissertation]. University of Melbourne. https://minervaaccess.unimelb.edu.au/handle/11343/36232

Cárdenas-Claros, M. S. (2015). Design considerations of help options in computer-based L2 listening materials informed by participatory design. *Computer Assisted Language Learning*, 28(5), 429–449. https://doi.org/10.1080/09588221.2014.881385

Cárdenas-Claros, M.S. (2020). Spontaneous links between help option use and input features that hinder second language listening comprehension. *System*, 93, 102308.

Cárdenas-Claros, M.S. (2021). Computer-based second language listening. In H. Mohebbi & C. Coombe (Eds.), *Research questions in language education and applied linguistics*. Cham: Springer. https://doi.org/10.1007/978-3-030-79143-8_107

Cárdenas-Claros, M.S. (2022, January 13). A research agenda to investigate (computer-based) listening in EFL settings. Keynote address. *Segundas Jornada de Investigación*. Universidad Católica del Maule. Chile.

Cárdenas-Claros, M.S., & Campos-Ibaceta, A. (2018). L2 listeners' use of transcripts: from reasons to practice. *ELT Journal, 72*(2), 151–161. https://doi.org/10.1093/elt/ccx047

Cárdenas-Claros, M.S., Campos-Ibaceta, A., & Vera-Saavedra, J. (2021). Listeners' patterns of interaction with help options: Towards empirically-based pedagogy. *Language Learning & Technology*, 25(2), 111–134.

Cárdenas-Claros, M.S., & Gruba, P.A. (2010). Bridging CALL & HCI: Input from participatory design. *CALICO Journal*, 27(3), 576–591.

Cárdenas-Claros, M.S., & Gruba, P.A. (2013). Decoding the "CoDe": a framework for conceptualizing and designing help options in computer-based second language listening. *ReCALL*, 25(2), 250–271.https://doi.org/10.1017/S0958344013000049

Cárdenas-Claros, M.S., & Gruba, P.A. (2014). Listeners' interactions with help options in CALL. *Computer Assisted Language Learning*, 27(3), 228–245. https://doi.org/10.1080/09588221.2012.724425

Cárdenas-Claros, M., & Oyanedel, M. (2016). Teachers' implicit theories and use of ICTs in the language classroom. *Technology, Pedagogy and Education*, 25(2), 207–225.

Chong S.W., & Reinders, H. (2020). Technology-mediated task-based language teaching: A qualitative research synthesis. *Language Learning & Technology, 24*(3), 70–86.

Colpaert, J., Spruyt E., Gijsen, L. & Vermeiren, A. (2019). Report TECOLA project. Output 5 report. *Toward a methodological framework for task design*. Retrieved from www.tecola.eu

Colpaert, J., & Spruyt, E. (2018). Toward a task design model for mental acceptance and motivation: A transdisciplinary approach. In M. Simons & T.F.H. Smits (Eds.), *Language education and emotions. Proceedings of the third international conference on language education and testing* (pp. 138–145). Antwerp: University of Antwerp.

Colpaert, J., & Gijsen, L. (2017). Ontological specification of tele- collaborative tasks in language teaching. In C. Ludwig & K. Van de Poel (Eds.), *Collaborative learning and new media: New insights into an evolving field*, (pp. 27–44). Frankfurt am Main: Peter Lang.

Colpaert, J. (2010). Elicitation of language learners' personal goals as design concepts. *Innovation in Language Learning and Teaching*, 4(3), 259–274. https://doi.org/10.1080/17501229.2010.513447

Cross, J. (2017). Help options for L2 listening in CALL: A research agenda. *Language Teaching, 50*(4), 544–560. https://doi.org/10.1017/S0261 444817000209

de la Fuente, M.J. (2014). Learners' attention to input during focus on form listening tasks: the role of mobile technology in the second language classroom. *Computer Assisted Language*, 27(3), 261–276. https://doi.org/10.1080/09588221.2012.733710

Duong, P.T., Montero-Perez, M., Desmet, P., & Peters, E. (2021). Learning vocabulary in spoken input-and output-based tasks. *TASK, 1*(1), 100–126. https://doi.org/10.1075/task.00005.duo

Eckert, P. (2013). Ethics in linguistic research. In R.J. Podesva (Ed.), *Research methods in linguistics* (pp. 11–26). Cambridge: Cambridge University Press. https://doi.org/10.1017/cbo9781139013734.003

Ellis, R. (2003). *Task-based language learning and teaching*. Oxford University Press.

Ellis, R. (2009). Task-based language teaching: Sorting out the misunderstandings. *International Journal of Applied Linguistics, 19*(3), 221–246. https://doi.org/10.1111/j.1473-4192.2009.00231.x

Ellis, R. (2013). Task-based language teaching: Responding to the critics. *University of Sydney Papers in TESOL, 8*(1), 1–27.

Ellis, R., & Shintani, N. (2013). *Exploring language pedagogy through second language acquisition research*. London: Routledge. https://doi.org/10.4324/9780203796580

Erlam, R. (2015). "New tricks": Teachers talk about task-based language teaching. *Babel, 50*(1), 4–11.

Esterberg, K. (2002). *Qualitative methods in social research*. New York: McGraw-Hill Higher Education.

Field, J. (2013). Cognitive validity. In A. Geranpayeh & L. Taylor (Eds.), *Examining listening: Research and practice in assessing second language listening* (pp. 77--151). Cambridge: Cambridge University Press.

González-Lloret, M., & Ortega, L. (2014). *Technology-mediated TBLT: Researching technology and tasks*. Amsterdam: John Benjamins Publishing Company. https://doi.org/10.1075/tblt.6

Hubbard, P. (2015, July 6-8). Training learners for self-directed listening tasks. *Proceedings of the XVII international conference on CALL Research Conference*, 289-296. Universitat Rovira I Virgili, Tarragona, Spain. https://wwwa.fundacio.urv.cat/congressos/public/usr_docs/call_2015_conference_proceedings.pdf

Hubbard, P. (2017). *Technologies for teaching and learning L2 listening*. In C.A. Chapelle & S. Sauro (Eds.), The handbook of technology and second language teaching and learning. (pp. 93–106). Hoboken, NJ: Wiley Blackwell. https://doi.org/10.1002/9781118914069.ch7

Lizasoain, A. (2017). El lugar del inglés como lengua extranjera en las políticas y planificación lingüísticas chilenas: ¿De dónde venimos y hacia dónde vamos? *Lenguas Modernas*, (49), 121–136. https://lenguas modernas.uchile.cl/index.php/LM/article/view/49229

Nunan, D. (1989). *Designing tasks for the communicative classroom*. Cambridge University Press. https://doi.org/10.1017/S0272263100009578

Otaif, F.A. (2021). Towards evaluating interactivity in video-based task design: a perspective from computer-based L2 listening. *Saudi Journal of Language Studies, 1*(1), 26–39. https://doi.org/10.1108/SJLS-03-2021-0008

Park, M., & Slater, T. (2014). A typology of tasks for mobile-assisted language learning: Recommendations from a small-scale needs analysis. *TESL Canada Journal, 31*(8), 93–115. https://doi.org/10.18806/tesl.v31i0.1188

Ramirez, D. (2020). *Middle school teachers' practices and perceptions of teaching L2 listening comprehension in an EFL context* [Unpublished MA thesis]. School of English. University of Nottingham.

Rost, M. (2005). L2 listening. In E. Hinkel (Ed.), *Handbook of research in second language teaching and learning* (pp. 503–527). Mahwah, NJ: Lawrence Erlbaum Associates.

Rubin, J. (1994). A review of second language listening comprehension research. *The Modern Language Journal, 78*(2), 199–221.

Samuda, V., & Bygate, M. (2008). *Tasks in second language learning*. Springer. https://doi.org/10.1057/9780230596429

Sun, S.Y. (2020). Using patterns-based learning design for CALL tasks. *Computer Assisted Language Learning*, 1-24. https://doi.org/10.1080/09588221.2019.1657902

TBLT Conference. (2019, August 19-21). Conference Program [PDF]. *8th International Conference on Task-Based Language Teaching "TBLT: Insight, Instruction, Outcomes*. Ottawa, Canada. Retrieved from https://carleton.ca/tblt/wp-content/uploads/TBLT-2019-Ottawa-Conference-Program-August-18.pdf

Vandergrift, L., & Goh, C.C. (2012). *Teaching and learning second language listening: Metacognition in action*. New York: Routledge. https://doi.org/ 10.4324/9780203843376

13
F-Lingo: Leveraging Smart CALL for massive open online courses

Jemma König
Shaoqun Wu
Alannah Fitzgerald
Margaret Franken
Ian Witten

Introduction

CALL centres on the use of technology in language teaching and learning, and among others, CALL applications can include virtual learning environments, web-based distance learning, and mobile-based language teaching and learning. *Smart CALL* provides an additional layer to this, using contextualization, personalization, and socialization to produce CALL techniques that adapt or adjust to a learner's profile, to the specific context of the learner, or that afford meaningful social interactions. In this chapter, we introduce an application of Smart CALL, leveraging customization and personalization alongside Massive Open Online Courses (MOOCs) to provide learners with smart language and vocabulary resources.

MOOCs are a recent development in distance education that have the potential to revolutionize academic learning (Kaplan & Haenlein, 2016). They provide open access, allow unlimited enrolment, and operate internationally. They offer filmed lectures, readings, assignments, quizzes, and user forums. Three prominent examples are Coursera with 35 million learners, edX with 18 million learners, and FutureLearn with 7.9 million learners. They are generally offered by English-speaking universities in the

US and UK, and proponents often express an explicit desire to reach out to other countries and cultures. Clearly, many MOOC students will encounter a language barrier during their study (Alcorn, Christensen, & Kapur, 2015; Shapiro *et al.*, 2017). In response to the problem of language, the Translation MOOC (TraMOOC) project (Castilho, Gaspari, Moorkens, & Way, 2017; Sosoni, 2017), for example, demonstrates research into support reading and listening skills that can be targeted with innovative translation methods. However, the majority of online course providers rarely address this problem, as Colpaert (2014, p. 165) asks, "how many tools for creating MOOCs (such as Moodle, Coursera, Wiziq, Elgg, Udacity and Edx) contain features specifically designed for language learning and teaching?" Moreover, despite the plethora of CALL applications that are available at the time of writing—some of which provide language resources for written content—none specifically addresses online MOOC platforms.

This chapter presents a system called F-Lingo, a browser plug-in, that works on top of an online MOOC platform and facilitates contextualized and personalized domain-specific vocabulary learning. F-Lingo holds two main advantages over other systems: it works within the existing MOOC course platform, seamlessly integrating itself into course content without disrupting learners' subject learning experiences, and it tracks learners' interaction with the platform, enabling the provision of personalised language components. F-Lingo is comprised of three components: *Material Gathering*, *Vocabulary Identification*, and *Progress Tracking*. The Material Gathering component crawls the web pages of a MOOC course, traversing each page and gathering the textual content. The Vocabulary Identification component identifies and hyperlinks the key words, phrases, and concepts from the textual content of a MOOC page. The Progress Tracking component records any interaction the student has made with the system, which allows us to build the student's vocabulary learning profile and provides follow-up vocabulary tests or language activities.

The design of F-Lingo is principled and underpinned by three theories: the noticing hypothesis (Robinson, 1995; Schmidt, 1990), enhanced input, and data-driven learning (Johns, 1991). Noticing is facilitated through input enhancement and enrichment that has been proven to be effective in students' recognition and recall of vocabulary (Sonbul & Schmitt, 2013; Szudarski & Carter, 2016). Johns (1991) used the term "data-driven learning" (DDL) to describe an approach that centres on fostering learners' skills in becoming a "language researcher." Corpus-based data-driven learning has been explored by many researchers and teachers to facilitate vocabulary learning with promising results as demonstrated in the literature (Boulton & Cobb, 2017; Daskalovska, 2015; Vyatkina, 2017).

Although F-Lingo could be ported to any platform, we use the FutureLearn platform, founded in 2013 by the UK's Open University, to demonstrate the concepts that underpin F-Lingo and language learning components that F-Lingo facilitates. All FutureLearn courses are structured similarly. They are often between five and ten weeks long and include a selection of videos, articles, discussions, and quizzes, plus online assessments for those who pay to upgrade their enrolment. F-Lingo can be applied to any FutureLearn course. However, this chapter uses as examples three 5-week courses on data mining: *Data Mining with Weka*, *More Data Mining with Weka*, and *Advanced Data Mining with Weka*. The *Data Mining with Weka* courses are aimed at anyone who deals with data and is interested in obtaining information from it. They are a set of practical data mining courses that teach learners how to use the Weka workbench to mine their own data. The courses consist of both written English, in the form of articles and discussions, and spoken English, in the form of video tutorials. The chapter also reports the results of an initial study in which 109 MOOC students used F-Lingo while taking three 5-week courses.

Literature Review

The affordances of MOOCs for domain specific vocabulary learning

We argue that the MOOCs texts constitute what Godwin-Jones (2011, p. 6) describes as "pedagogically assisted authentic content" in that they have been designed for teaching purposes, albeit for content learning, not language learning. MOOCs texts typically includes:

- a substantial number of texts,
- a sequence of texts.
- a variety of types of texts, and
- a close relationship between the different textual modalities

The grouping and sequencing of MOOCs texts in terms of a thematic progression supports the learning of vocabulary because of the recycling of words, particularly the less frequent and "technical vocabulary" (Coxhead & Nation, 2001) related to the topic. As Gardner explains this is particularly useful in academic language learning. "The power of themes to draw together and recycle the specialized vocabulary of expository materials should . . . be duly noted in many areas of English language education, especially in content-based instruction and English for academic purposes" (Gardner, 2008, p. 5).

Kyongho and Nation (1989) investigated the effect of reading topic related newspaper texts. They claim that in related texts such as these, learners are more likely to be exposed to less frequent words on a frequent basis. "Proceeding through a sequence of stories will reduce the number of words unfamiliar to [the] learners and will help [the] learners . . . to read more efficiently without being interrupted too often by unknown words" (Kyongho & Nation, 1989, p. 325). In other words related texts provide for recycling of vocabulary, and "repeated encounters with an unknown word play an important role in establishing the complete meaning of the word" (Kyongho & Nation, 1989, p. 325).

Domain specific words, phrases and concepts

F-Lingo targets three aspects of domain specific vocabulary learning: domain specific words, phrases, and concepts. F-Lingo uses a simple approach to identify the domain specific words that are not among the most frequent 2000 English words. This criteria was outlined because the most frequent 2000 English words are often held to be sufficient for beginning to comprehend the English language (Milton, 2009; Nation, 2001), and we assume MOOC students have acquired these most frequent words in order to take MOOC courses that are presented in English.

Phrases are formulaic sequences that exhibit typical patterns in academic texts, and serve as "points of fixation" or "islands of reliability" for developing academic writing (Dechert, 1984). We use the term "phrases" to denote two types of formulaic sequences: collocations and lexical bundles because MOOC students are more likely familiar with the concept of phrases. The term *collocation* has different definitions in the literature. We take a syntax-oriented approach in this paper that emphasizes the grammatical structure of a collocation (Firth, 1951; Nation, 2013; Nattinger & DeCarrico, 1992; Nesselhauf, 2004; Sinclair, 1991) and identifies collocations by syntactic structures (e.g., *verb + noun, adjective + noun, noun + verb*). Lexical bundles are common in academic texts, both oral and written. They have distinctive syntactic patterns which include but are not limited to: prepositional phrase + *of,* noun phrase + *of, it +*

verb/adjective phrase, *be* + noun/adjective phrase, and verb phrase + *that*. But perhaps more importantly, they have distinct discourse functions such as for referential expression (framing, quantifying, and place/time/text deictics), for expression of stance (epistemic, directive, ability) and for discourse organization (topic introduction and elaboration) (see Biber and Barbieri, 2007; Biber, Conrad, & Cortes, 2003, 2004).

F-Lingo uses a tool, Wikipedia Miner, to identify the concepts in a MOOC course text. Milne and Witten (2013) describe the method and the tool. It has three steps. First, sequences of words in the text that may correspond with Wikipedia articles are identified using the names of the articles, as well as their redirects and every referring anchor text used anywhere in Wikipedia. Second, situations where multiple articles correspond to a single word or phrase are disambiguated. For example, the word *kiwi* may refer to a bird, a fruit, a person from New Zealand, or the New Zealand national rugby league team, all of which have distinct Wikipedia entries. A machine learning classifier is used to make the appropriate choice, taking into account the prior probability of the mapping, semantic relatedness to other concepts in the same document, and some contextual information. The third step selects the most salient linked (and disambiguated) concepts to include in the output.

The principles that underpin the design of F-Lingo

F-Lingo is designed based on three effective language learning principles: the noticing hypothesis, enhanced input, and data-driven learning, and like other systems that make use of corpora or corpus-like resources (e.g. online concordancers), it represents an *input-based* rather than *output-based* approach (Rott, 2004). Input-based interventions are concerned with exposing learners to linguistic data and providing the conditions under which they attend to linguistic form in that data. In contrast, output-based interventions focus on providing learners with opportunities to put previously presented language items to use. Input-based approaches allow for incidental vocabulary learning to take place by providing for multiple exposures to a word, or a word sequence. Incidental learning of vocabulary has been supported by research, as Gu (2003) states, "Research seems to indicate that incidental vocabulary learning through reading and listening is not only possible but also a plausible strategy for vocabulary development. However, this strategy seems more effective for . . . intermediate to advanced L2 learners" (Gu, 2003, p. 5). More strongly asserted claims associated with input-based approaches include the raising of language awareness, and noticing, with the latter in particular being a condition that potentially supports language acquisition (Lindgren & Sullivan, 2003).

The "noticing hypothesis," proposed by Schmidt (1990), claims that noticing through conscious attention is a necessary prerequisite for second language acquisition. The necessity of noticing has received criticism from some researchers (Carroll, 1999; Gass, 2017; Truscott, 1998). Some have produced L2 data that dispute it (Izumi, 2002; Leow, 2001), while others have produced L2 data that support it, but as a facilitator rather than a necessary prerequisite (Alanen, 1995; Jourdenais, Ota, Stauffer, Boyson, & Doughty, 1995). Thus, the common understanding today is that noticing and awareness facilitate, but are not essential to, language learning (Gass, Svetics, & Lemelin, 2003; Izumi, 2002; Uggen, 2012).

Noticing in written language involves visual input enhancement, such as italics, bolding, or highlighting. Alanen (1995) used italics and found that it had a facilitating effect on learners' recall and use. Jourdenais *et al.* (1995) used highlighting and found that learners who were exposed to the highlighted text used more of the target forms than those who were not. This has led us to explore the notion of enhancing online course content by highlighting vocabulary within the text that learners are reading and providing supplementary materials, such as definitions, sentences examples, and extended collocations retrieved from external language resources.

The term *data-driven* has been widely debated and critiqued because of its technicist connotations by those not always aware of the centrality of student autonomy and self-directed learning to the approach (Boulton, 2011). In reviewing Johns' coining of the term, data-driven learning, and expanding on his views of it, Boulton (2011) explains that Johns was of the view that it would help students to "learn how to learn" and hence to "become better language learners outside the classroom" (Johns, as cited in Boulton, 2011, p. 566). So, while data generated by corpus analysis assumes a central position in the learning process, language learners are seen as "research workers" (Johns, 1994) or become "language detectives to explore language data themselves" (Boulton, 2011, p. 1). Indeed, corpus based data-driven approaches have been proven particularly useful for learners to examine lexico-grammatical patterns from authentic texts, for example, finding correct word combinations (Chen, 2011; Daskalovska, 2015; Vyatkina, 2017; Yoon, 2008), understanding the subtle meaning of certain verbs that lack direct L1 equivalents (Chan & Liou, 2005), and identifying common word choice errors in writing (Chambers & O'Sullivan, 2004).

Application to Smart CALL

Here, we introduce F-Lingo, a Smart CALL application that leverages contextualization and personalization for acquiring domain-specific vocabulary in MOOCs. First, we discuss contextualization, using the development of F-Lingo as a practical example. Next, we discuss personalization, again using F-Lingo as an example, illustrating how Smart CALL techniques can be applied to a real-world system. Finally, we describe a usability study that we conducted to evaluate learners' interactions with the Smart CALL application.

Contextualization: Integrating F-Lingo into the FutureLearn MOOC consortium

Contextualization involves the use of technologies to adapt the learning environment to the specific context of the learner. This can include techniques such as adapting the space or time to that of the learner, or adapting to the cultural context of the learner. F-Lingo leverages these contextualization techniques to provide learners with vocabulary and language resources that are applicable to the environment they are in—specifically the context and content of a specific Massive Open Online Course. Here, we describe the integration of F-Lingo into the FutureLearn MOOC platform, as an example of Smart CALL contextualization.

Integrating F-Lingo into the FutureLearn MOOC platform involves three main components: Material Gathering, Vocabulary Identification, and Progress Tracking, as shown in Figure 13.1.

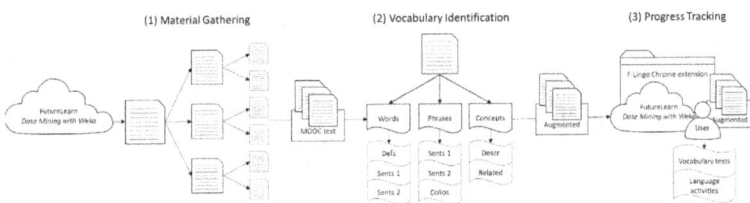

Figure 13.1 *Integrating F-Lingo into the FutureLearn MOOC consortium.*

First, in order for F-Lingo to work within the existing course platform and seamlessly integrate itself into course content, it must first gather information about the content of a course. The Material Gathering component crawls the web pages of a MOOC course, traversing each page and gathering the textual content. The Material Gathering portion of Figure 13.1 illustrates the process involved, traversing the web pages of a MOOC course to extract course content. This content is then processed to extract sentences, which are stored for later use by the Chrome extension.

The second component, Vocabulary Identification, takes the textual content that was collected by the Material Gathering component and identifies and hyperlinks keywords, phrases, and concepts. Once F-Lingo has identified and hyperlinked these items, the hyperlinks can be clicked to open a dialog window providing additional language resources. As shown in the Vocabulary Identification portion of Figure 13.1, F-Lingo provides language resources such as definitions and example sentences for keywords, both from within the course content and from an external source; related phrases and example sentences for phrases, again both from within the course content and from an external source; and disambiguated description and a selection of related links for concepts.

The last component, the Progress Tracking component, takes the textual content that has been augmented with hyperlinks and re-displays it in the FutureLearn MOOC course, as shown in the Progress Tracking portion of Figure 13.1. Once F-Lingo has re-displayed a FutureLearn page, it then begins recording any interactions that students make with the system, including clicking words, phrases, and concepts, and the time that students spend on the corresponding dialog windows. This allows us to build the student's vocabulary learning profile under the assumption that the more time the student pays attention to an item, the more worthy the item to be included in a follow-up vocabulary test or language activity. These statistical data provide evidence and reasoning in our current and ongoing work on automatically generating personalized language activities and vocabulary tests at the end of the MOOC course, as shown in the Progress Tracking portion of Figure 13.1.

Learners can download F-Lingo from the Chrome Web Store. Once it has been installed, the "F-Lingo" navigation bar appears at the top of the page, as shown in Figure 13.2. Learners click on the navigation bar to open the F-Lingo menu on the right, then select whether they want to highlight words, phrases, or concepts, or do a vocabulary test or language activity.

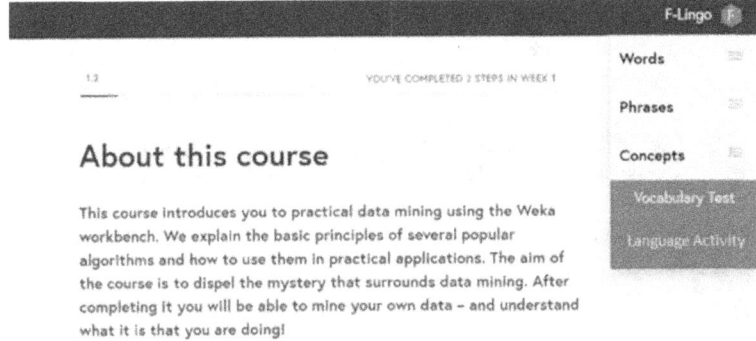

Figure 13.2 *A FutureLearn page with F-Lingo installed and the drop-down menu open.*

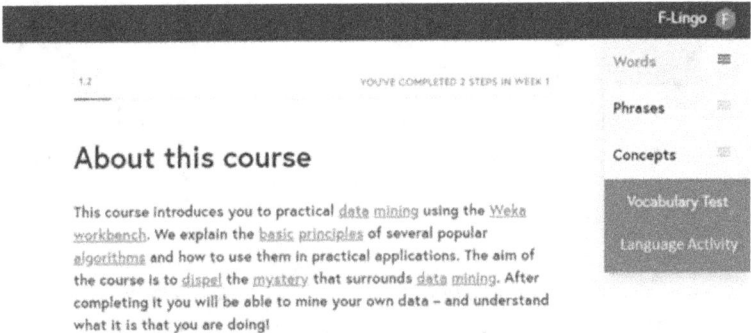

Figure 13.3 *The topic words are highlighted on the "About this course" page.*

When a learner selects the *words* menu item, F-Lingo displays hyperlinks for keywords on the page. Learners can click these hyperlinks to open a pop up window. Figure 13.3 shows the "About this course" page where the keywords are highlighted and underscored. Clicking a word, say *algorithms*, brings up a window, shown in Figure 13.4, that displays the definition of *algorithms* retrieved from Wiktionary[1], sentence examples that contain the word *algorithms* from the course, and sentence examples from the PhD abstracts collection on the FLAX[2] website. FLAX is an online language learning application. It contains collections of digitized text from a variety of sources, including PhD abstracts from the British Library's E-Theses

Online Service, online course material from edX and Coursera, and a selection of texts created by their users.

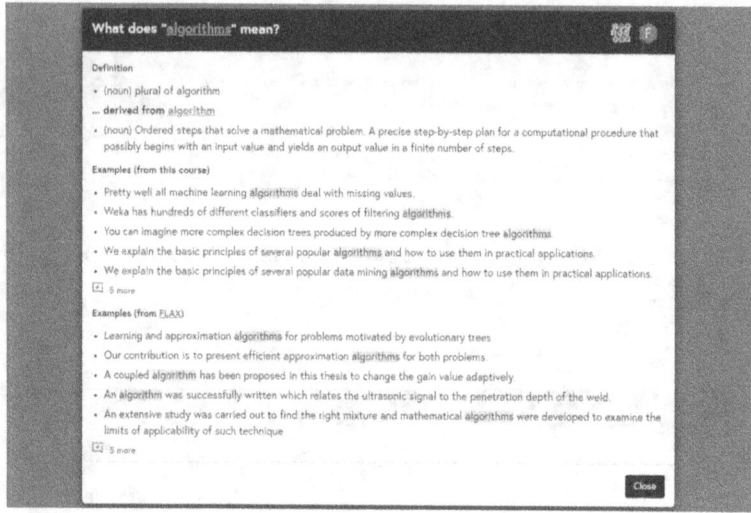

Figure 13.4 *The Wiktionary definition and sentence examples for the word algorithms.*

When a learner selects the *phrases* menu item, F-Lingo displays hyperlinks for collocations and lexical bundles. Like words, learners can click the hyperlinked phrases to open a pop up window. Figure 13.4 shows the "About this course" page where the phrases are highlighted and underscored. Clicking a phrase, say *data mining*, brings up a window, shown in Figure 13.6, that displays sentence examples from the course and from FLAX, along with a selection of expanded collocations. Expanded collocations can be used to expand and enrich learners' vocabulary. For example, the collocations *data mining*, *data types*, and *data structures* illustrate how the word *data* is used in a phrase; the collocations *data mining algorithms* and *data mining models* illustrate how the collocation *data mining* can be expanded. Wu (2010) explored the use of related collocations to expand and enrich a learner's knowledge when reading, and developed a system that highlights collocations in text and provides learners with related lexical information. F-Lingo uses this system to retrieve expanded collocations from Wikipedia. F-Lingo provides expanded collocations for collocational phrases.

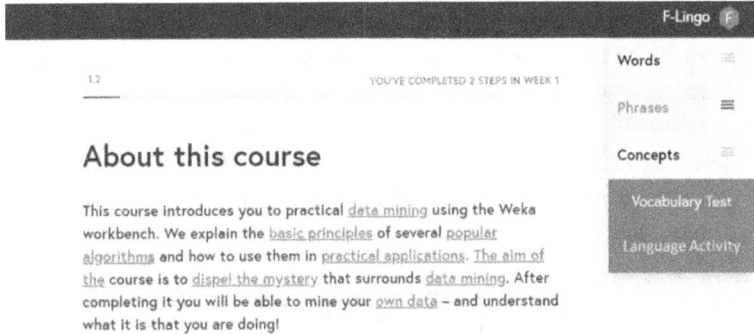

Figure 13.5 *The phrases (collocations and lexical bundles) are highlighted on the "About this course" page.*

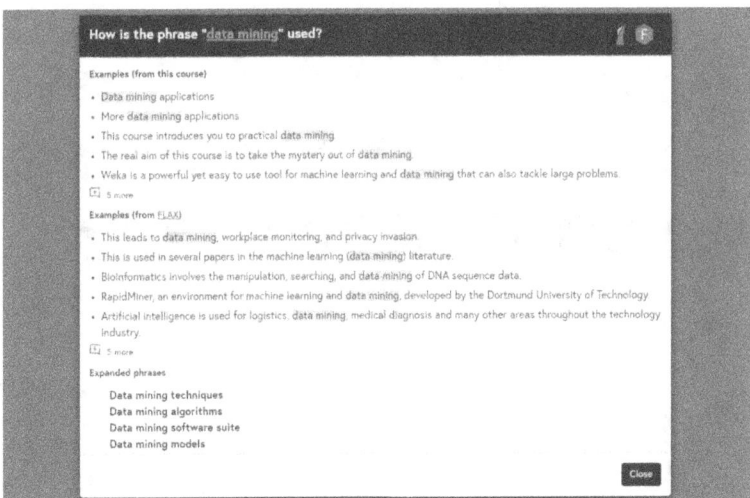

Figure 13.6 *The sentence examples and expanded collocations for the phrase* data mining.

When a learner selects the *concepts* menu item, F-Lingo displays hyperlinks for concepts. We have coined the term "concept" to refer to any single or multi-word lexical item that has been disambiguated. Both single and multi-word lexical items can be ambiguous when seen outside of context. The word *Weka* can refer to the flightless New Zealand bird, or a suite of machine learning software. The phrase *Big Data* can refer to large collections of data, or an electronic music project. F-Lingo uses a tool called Wikipedia Miner to identify and disambiguate concepts within course content. Like words and phrases, learners can click the hyperlinked concepts to open a pop up window. Figure 7 shows the "About this course" page where the concepts are highlighted and underscored. Clicking a concept, say *big data*, brings up a window, shown in Figure 13.7, that displays a disambiguated description and a list of related Wikipedia articles.

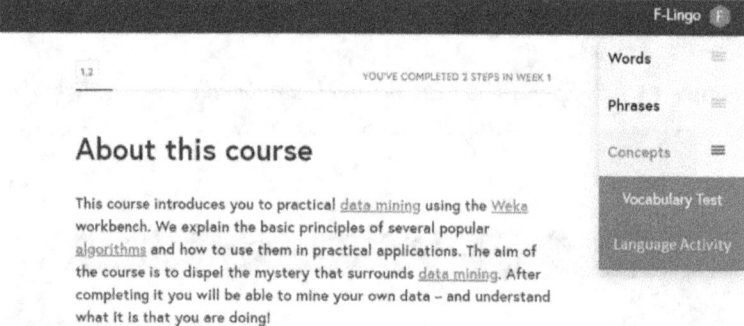

Figure 13.7 *The concepts are highlighted on the "About this course" page.*

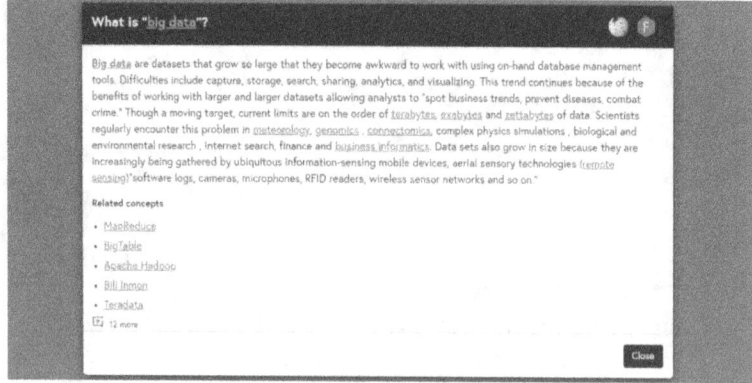

Figure 13.8 *The Wikipedia description and related concepts for the concept* big data.

Personalization: providing learners with personalized vocabulary testing and activities

Personalization involves the use of computing to adapt a system to reflect a learner's profile or performance. This can include techniques such as adaptive language testing and intelligent tutoring. F-Lingo leverages these personalization techniques to provide learners with vocabulary tests and language activities that have been adapted to an individual learner's language profile. Here, we describe the F-Lingo interface for vocabulary testing and vocabulary activities, as an example of Smart CALL personalization.

Vocabulary testing

As shown earlier in the Progress Tracking portion of Figure 13.1, F-Lingo provides learners with vocabulary tests. Although this work is still ongoing, F-Lingo currently provides vocabulary testing that uses contextualised vocabulary, that is, provides vocabulary tests that have been created from the content of a FutureLearn course.

Figure 13.9 shows an example vocabulary test, which a student can navigate to by selecting the *vocabulary test* menu item in F-Lingo's menu bar. As shown in the instructions in Figure 9, to conduct the test, students are asked to read through the list of words carefully and check the box next to any words that they "know." If they do not know what a word means, if they are not sure, or if they do not think the word is a real word, they are asked to leave the box unchecked. This type of test is called a "Yes/No" vocabulary test. It is simple to administer and measures receptive vocabulary. The test includes 40 real words and 20 pseudowords. A pseudoword has the form of a word and is spelled in a predictable way, but does not exist in the lexicon (Groff, 2003), for example, *punit*, *dathm*, or *injusting*.

F-Lingo generates a new version of the vocabulary test each time a student selects the *vocabulary test* menu item in F-Lingo's menu bar. It randomly selects 40 keywords from within the current course content, then uses the list of all keywords to generate a set of 20 pseudowords. Pseudowords are generated using an algorithm that breaks a list of words into character-grams then chains them back together to form pseudowords (König, Calude, & Coxhead, 2019). As an example, the pseudoword *dathm* is created by chaining the character-grams *dat* from *data*, *ath* from *mathematics*, and *thm* from *algorithm*.

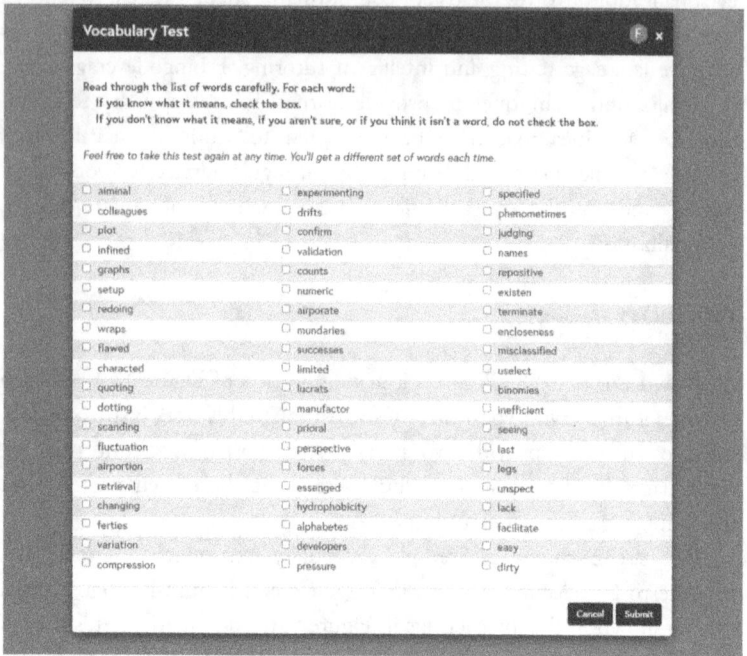

Figure 13.9 *F-Lingo vocabulary test.*

The example vocabulary test shown in Figure 13.9 was created using content from the Data Mining with Weka course. It includes words such as *graphs*, *misclassified*, and *numeric*, and pseudowords such as *existen*, *infined*, and *characted*. This illustrates how the course content can be used to create contextualised vocabulary tests.

Further work is currently being undertaken to extend the vocabulary tests to also consider a learner's interaction with the words on a page. As already mentioned, F-Lingo records interactions that students make with the system. This includes both the date that the interaction occurred, and the duration that the subsequent dialog window was open. We are currently investigating the meaningfulness of these timed interactions. For example, if a learner clicked on the word *algorithm* three weeks ago, then clicked it again one week ago, and again today, we may infer that they are struggling with this word. Likewise, we can make assumptions from the duration of time that additional language resource dialog windows are left open. If a learner clicked on the word *algorithm* and left the dialog window open for only a short period of time, we may infer that they already hold some knowledge of the word and simply needed a reminder. If they left the dialog window open for a much longer duration, we may infer that they were not at all familiar with the word and are now using the additional language resources to come to grasps with its meaning. While student interaction has been implemented in the Progress Tracking component of F-Lingo, these inference calculations are part of our ongoing and future work.

Vocabulary activities

This final section proposes the use of personalised language activities within the F-Lingo Chrome extension. While this has not yet been implemented, the majority of the pieces are already in place. Since this feature will be made available for learners shortly, and because it is an elegant example of smart personalisation, we have decided to include it in this chapter.

Language learning activities are a fun way to cement the process of learning a second language. Personalised activities take this a step further, putting the focus on individual learners and adapting materials to suit their needs. Though not personalised, FLAX has been using language activities for several years, and includes eleven different versions. We will utilize a selection of these, personalising them to work with individual learners, starting with one called Fill-in-Blanks. Fill-in-Blanks exercises involve a set of collocations and their associated sentences. Constituents of the collocations are selectively removed from the text, and the learner is asked to choose the word that completes each collocation.

Figure 13.10 shows an example of one such exercise, which focuses on finding the right verb for a noun. The missing verbs are given at the top of the exercise panel. When chosen, they disappear from this list—except for words that occur more than once, in which case the occurrence count (in parentheses) is decremented. Below is a sentence, or list of sentences, with target verbs omitted and the remainder of the collocation highlighted. The learner completes a collocation by dragging a word from the top and dropping it into place, where it appears in blue; the move can be undone by clicking the word. When the Check button at the lower right is clicked, correctly formed collocations remain, but the offending word is removed from incorrect ones and reinstated at the top of the panel.

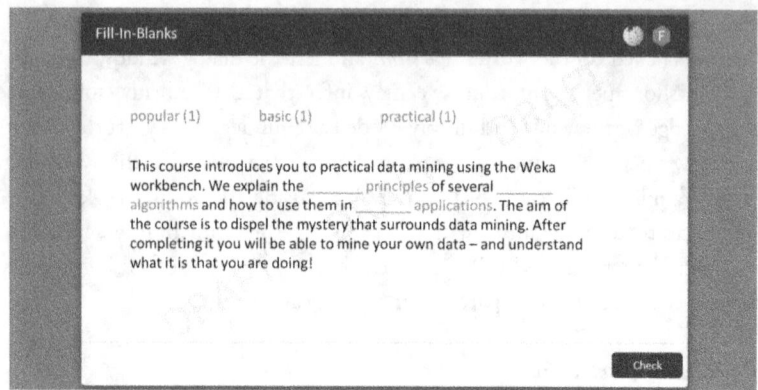

Figure 13.10 *Collocation Fill-in-Blanks example activity.*

This activity works well for sets of words that share similar meanings but have different usage. Learners are frequently confused by words with similar meaning—*basic* and *fundamental*, *dispel* and *disperse*, *principle* and *rule*—and find it difficult to understand their differences by consulting dictionaries. Studying collocations is an effective way to help learners distinguish a word's various shades of meaning.

F-Lingo will select collocations that a student has interacted with, taking into account the amount of time that has passed since the collocation was clicked, and the duration of time that the subsequent dialog window was open, as was outlined for our future work on vocabulary testing. Selected collocations, and their surrounding sentences, will be used to generate Fill-in-Blanks activities, which will be integrated into F-Lingo. F-Lingo currently includes a *language activity* menu item. When the student selects this item from the F-Lingo menu bar, a dialog window will open that displays the activity for them to play. This will allow learners to play the activities through F-Lingo, without navigating away from the FutureLearn page. Figure 13.10 shows a mock-up of what this might look like. In this case, we have used the introductory text from the "About this course" page from Data Mining with Weka. Three collocations have been used to generate this activity: *basic principles*, *popular algorithms*, and *practical applications*.

Initial study and results

An evaluation has been conducted on user data logged by F-Lingo, analysing learner behaviour in relation to their use of the Smart CALL application. F-Lingo has been made available for three FutureLearn courses, Data Mining with Weka, More Data Mining with Weka, and Advanced Data Mining with Weka.

The participant pool for this study was comprised of learners enrolled in one of three Data Mining courses on FutureLearn. Once a learner downloaded F-Lingo, they were given a prompt with information about the study and the option to join it. Learners who consented to F-Lingo logging their data were also asked to enter their first language (L1), and any other languages that they know (L2). Once a learner gave their consent, they were marked as a *consenting user* and any future interactions with F-Lingo were logged. There were 251 consenting users in this study.

Once a learner has given their consent, F-Lingo begins logging any interaction that the learner has with words, phrases, and concepts. Each time a learner clicks on a word, phrase, or concept, F-Lingo opens a dialog with additional lexical information. Once the learner has closed this dialog, the following is logged in a database: a unique ID given to the user (*userID*), the item clicked (*item*), the type of item (word, phrase, or concept) (*type*), the amount of time that the dialog window remained open (*duration*), the course the learner was on when they clicked the item (*course*), the course step they were on (*step*), and the date and time when the interaction occurred (*datetime*).

Participant interaction

Table 13.1 shows the number of participants that downloaded F-Lingo, and the number who used it. Of the 251 participants who downloaded it, 109 used it to click words, phrases, or concepts within the text. These *active users* are the focus of the rest of this evaluation. Table 13.1 also shows the distribution of users whose first language (L1) is English, versus those whose second language (L2) is English. Of the 109 active users, 18% were L1 English speakers and 82% were L2.

Table 13.2 and Table 13.3 show the distribution of L1 and L2 languages. There were 35 L1 languages in total, the most common of which, excluding English, were Spanish, Chinese, Arabic, and Portuguese. L2 language variation was smaller, with only 14 different L2 languages spoken. However, of those, English was by far the most common, with 83% speaking it as a second language. This was followed by French, German, and Spanish. It is not surprising that English was the most common L2 language, given that F-Lingo is directed towards L2 English learners.

Table 13.1 *Participant distribution.*

	L1 English	L2 English	Both
Installed F-Lingo	58	193	251
Used F-Lingo	20	89	109
Percentage	35%	46%	43%

Table 13.2 *Distribution of L1 languages.*

Afrikaans	Dutch (6)	Indonesian	Nepali	Slovenian
Arabic (8)	English (20)	Italian (2)	Odia	Spanish (16)
Bengali	Farsi	Japanese	Persian (3)	Tamil
Brazilian	French	Korean	polish (2)	Turkish (3)
Cantonese	German (3)	Malay	Portuguese (7)	Ukrainian (3)
Chinese (9)	Hindi (2)	Marathi	Russian (5)	Uzbek
Danish	Hungarian	Nederland	Serbian	Vietnamese

Table 13.3 *Distribution of L2 languages.*

Catalan (3)	English (90)	Korean	Romanian	Spanish (5)
Croatian (2)	French (11)	Marathi	Russian (2)	Ukrainian
Czech	German (9)	Polish	Serbian	

Course participation

F-Lingo documents which course a learner is in when words, phrases, or concepts are clicked. As shown in Table 13.4, most learners used F-Lingo while participating in *Data Mining with Weka*, followed by *More Data Mining with Weka*, and *Advanced Data Mining with Weka*. However, there were also a significantly larger number of learners enrolled in Data Mining than the other two courses. Of those enrolled in each course, 2.6%

became active users of F-Lingo in Data Mining, 1.2% in More Data Mining, and 1.2% in Advanced Data Mining.

Table 13.4 *Course distribution.*

	DMwW	MDMwW	ADMwW
Active F-Lingo users	92 (of 109)	12 (of 109)	9 (of 109)
Enrolled in course	3542	966	647
Percentage	2.6%	1.2%	1.3%

Some learners interacted with F-Lingo in more than one course, shown in Figure 11a. Two used F-Lingo in both Data Mining and More Data Mining, two used it in Data Mining and Advanced Data Mining, two used it in More Data Mining and Advanced Data Mining, and one used F-Lingo in all three courses.

Table 13.5 *Words, phrases, and concepts.*

	Words	Phrases	Concepts
Interactions	308 (519) (59%)	83 (519) (16%)	128 (519) (26%)
F-Lingo users	92 (109) (84%)	30 (109) (28%)	37 (109) (34%)

a) Courses   b) Words, phrases, and concepts

Figure 13.11 *Overlap in participation.*

Words, phrases, and concepts

Table 13.5 shows the total number of interactions that were logged, and whether each interaction was with a word, phrase, or concept (row 1).

There were 519 interactions in total. Words were clicked the most (58%), followed by concepts (26%), and phrases (16%). Table 5 also shows the number of users who interacted with words, phrases, and concepts (row 2). More users interacted with words (84%) than concepts (34%) or phrases (28%). However, as with course distribution, some users interacted with a combination of each. As shown in Figure 11b. 22% of users interacted with words and phrases, 20% with words and concepts, 13% with concepts and phrases, and 10% interacted with all three.

Time-based analysis

Each time a learner clicks a word, phrase, or concept a dialog window opens that provides them with additional information. After a learner clicks an item, F-Lingo keeps track of how long the corresponding dialog window was open.

Table 13.6 *Time-based analysis for words, phrases, and concepts.*

	Words	Phrases	Concepts
Mean duration	22.1 s	20.3 s	41.4 s
Mean word count	164	134	94
Words per minute	445 wpm	398 wpm	136 wpm

Table 13.6 shows the mean duration (in seconds) that learners kept dialog windows open, for words, phrases, and concepts. Extreme outliers were removed using the lower and upper quartiles +− three times the inner-quartile range. Concept-dialogs stayed open for the longest period of time, followed by word-dialogs, then phrase-dialogs. This table also shows the mean word counts for dialogs opened by learners. Although concept-dialogs were open longest, they also contained significantly less words than both word-dialogs and phrase-dialogs. To conduct a fair comparison between them, we have calculated the average words-per-minute, as follows:

$$wpm = \frac{wordcount}{duration} \times 60$$

Although we have calculated the words-per-minute (wpm), we do not assume that users always, or ever, read every word in the dialog. However, producing wpm rates gives an indication of how long users spend looking at the dialog in relation to how large, or how many words, were shown.

L2 reading speeds can vary considerably, but the average reading speed for a native speaker (L1) is between 200-250 wpm. All, except one, of the dialogs resulted in a wpm rate approximately one and a half to two times faster than this, suggesting that learners rarely read all the text in a dialog. The one exception to this was concept-dialogs, which had a rate of 136 wpm. This suggests that learners spend more time reading concept-dialogs than word-dialogs or phrase-dialogs.

Conclusion

We have turned our attention to the possibilities of leveraging Smart CALL techniques and Massive Open Online Courses (MOOCs) for academic language learning in general and for supporting academic writing in particular. This is because Smart CALL and MOOCs potentially can contribute a large amount of multimedia language learning material in a particular domain and topic area that serves as rich input. This chapter described the development of F-Lingo, a Chrome extension that leverages Smart CALL techniques; integrating itself into an existing MOOC platform, highlighting lexical items, and providing online learners with language resources.

Part 1 of this chapter explored the use of MOOCs for language learning. First, we discussed the affordances of MOOCs for domain specific vocabulary learning, and the use of domain-specific words, phrases, and concepts. Next, we outlined the principles that inspired the creation of F-Lingo, our Smart CALL application. These include the noticing hypothesis, enhanced input, and data-driven learning. Part 2 of this chapter introduced F-Lingo and outlined its interface and functionalities. First, we introduced the novel idea of working within an online course platform (FutureLearn) to augment original course content with additional information. Next, we introduced F-Lingo's vocabulary testing feature, discussed tracking learners' clicks to determine the importance of different learner interactions for use with language learning, and proposed future work on personalised language activities. Finally, we outlined an evaluation where learners' interaction with F-Lingo was recorded and their behaviours were analysed.

One of F-Lingo's main advantages over other systems is that it works within the existing MOOC platform, seamlessly integrating itself into course content without disrupting learners' subject learning experiences. However, this can also be seen as a limitation. F-Lingo is currently only available for use with FutureLearn, and because of this seamless integration, it cannot currently be applied to any other MOOC platforms. This is because some aspects of its design have been tailored specifically to FutureLearn. It has been developed to only highlight words, phrases, and concepts on particular pages, such as articles and discussions, and it only highlights items in particular parts of each page. The visual feel of F-Lingo has also been developed around FutureLearn. For example, the highlighting colour (teal) was chosen because it gives enough of a contrast with FutureLearn colours to stand out, but does not clash in a way that would disturb the original feel of the site. F-Lingo could be developed for other MOOC platforms, such as Coursera and EdX. However, in order to achieve this same seamless integration, we would need to tailor individual versions of F-Lingo to the look and feel of each platform. While possible, this would involve a significant amount of research, design, and development.

Finally, we have already discussed some of our ongoing and future work. Mainly, our current investigation into the meaningfulness of learners' interactions with F-Lingo, the extension of F-Lingo's vocabulary tests to include these interactions, and the addition of personalised language activities. Further future directions for this research include a more extensive evaluation, and the expansion of F-Lingo into other FutureLearn courses. The study outlined in this chapter focused on learners' behaviour when interacting with F-Lingo. The next step would be to study whether long-term use of F-Lingo improves learners' vocabulary. This could be achieved through longitudinal studies where the vocabulary growth of learners who use F-Lingo is compared with those who do not. This could provide some insight into whether enriching online courses with language resources influences language acquisition. Finally, F-Lingo is currently only available for use with three courses on the FutureLearn MOOC platform. The next step here would be to make F-Lingo available for other courses on FutureLearn. F-Lingo was developed to be applied to any FutureLearn course with very little effort. However, although not technically required, we feel it is important to seek permission from course creators before applying F-Lingo to any of their courses. As such, we are in the process of building relationships with other institutions so that we may extend F-Lingo to encompass a greater variety of courses.

Ethical statement

This chapter describes a participant-based evaluation of F-Lingo. All potential participants were informed that F-Lingo would record what they clicked, but without any personal identifying information. Only participants that accepted the terms had their clicks recorded, and all recorded clicks were used solely for research purposes. Ethical consent was applied for, through the University of Waikato, and approved prior to the start date for the study.

References

Alanen, R. (1995). Input enhancement and rule presentation in second language acquisition. In R. Schmidt (Ed.), *Attention and awareness in foreign language learning. Technical Report #9* (pp. 259–302). Honolulu, HI: University of Hawaii, Second Language Teaching & Curriculum Center.

Alcorn, B., Christensen, G., & Kapur, D. (2015). Higher education and MOOCs in India and the Global South. *Change: The Magazine of Higher Learning, 47*(3), 42–49.

Biber, D., & Barbieri, F. (2007). Lexical bundles in university spoken and written registers. *English for specific purposes, 26*(3), 263–286.

Biber, D., Conrad, S., & Cortes, V. (2003). Lexical bundles in speech and writing: An initial taxonomy. In A. Wilson, P. Rayson, & T. McEnery (Eds.), *Corpus linguistics by the lune: A festschrift for Geoffrey Leech* (pp. 71–92). Frankfurt/Main: Peter Lang.

Biber, D., Conrad, S., & Cortes, V. (2004). If you look at...: Lexical bundles in university teaching and textbooks. *Applied Linguistics, 25*(3), 371–405.

Boulton, A. (2011). Data-driven learning: the perpetual enigma. In S. Goźdź-Roszkowski (Ed.), *Explorations across languages and corpora* (pp. 563–580). Frankfurt: Peter Lang.

Boulton, A., & Cobb, T. (2017). Corpus use in language learning: A meta-analysis. *Language Learning, 67*(2), 348-393.

Carroll, S.E. (1999). Putting "input" in its proper place. *Second Language Research, 15*(4), 337–388.

Castilho, S., Gaspari, F., Moorkens, J., & Way, A. (2017). Integrating machine translation into MOOCs. In *Proceedings of the 9th International Conference on Education and New Learning Technologies (EDULEARN17), Barcelona, Spain. 3-5 July, 2017* (pp. 9360–9365). Valencia: IATED.

Chambers, A., & O'Sullivan, Í. (2004). Corpus consultation and advanced learners' writing skills in French. *ReCALL, 16*(1), 158–172.

Chan, T.-p., & Liou, H.-C. (2005). Effects of web-based concordancing instruction on EFL students' learning of verb-noun collocations. *Computer Assisted Language Learning, 18*(3), 231–251.

Chen, H.-J.H. (2011). Developing and evaluating a web-based collocation retrieval tool for EFL students and teachers. *Computer Assisted Language Learning, 24*(1), 59–76.

Colpaert, J. (2014). 10 Conclusion. Reflections on present and future: Towards an ontological approach to LMOOCs. In E. Martin-Monje & E. Barcena (Eds.), *Language MOOCs: Providing learning, transcending boundaries* (pp. 1–15). Berlin: Walter de Gruyter.

Coxhead, A., & Nation, I.S.P. (2001). The specialised vocabulary of English for academic purposes. In J. Flowerdew & M. Peacock (Eds.), *Research perspectives on English for academic purposes* (pp. 252–267). Cambridge: Cambridge University Press.

Daskalovska, N. (2015). Corpus-based versus traditional learning of collocations. *Computer Assisted Language Learning, 28*(2), 130–144.

Dechert, H. W. (1984). Second language production: Six hypotheses. In H. W. Dechert, D. Mohle, & M. Raupach (Eds.), *Second language productions* (pp. 211–230). Tübingen, Germany: Gunter Narr Verlag.

Firth, J. (1951). Modes of meaning. In J. Firth (Ed.), *Papers in Linguistics 1934-1951* (pp. 190–215). London: Oxford University Press.

Gardner, D. (2008). Vocabulary recycling in children's authentic reading materials: A corpus-based investigation of narrow reading. *Reading in a Foreign Language, 20*(1), 92–122.

Gass, S. (2017). *Input, interaction, and the second language learner*: New York: Routledge.

Gass, S., Svetics, I., & Lemelin, S. (2003). Differential effects of attention. *Language Learning, 53*(3), 497–546.

Godwin-Jones, R. (2011). Emerging technologies: Autonomous language learning. *Language Learning & Technology, 15*(3), 4–11.

Groff, P. (2003). The usefulness of pseudowords. Retrieved from http://www.nrrf.org/old/essay_pseudowords.html

Gu, P. Y. (2003). Vocabulary learning in a second language: Person, task, context and strategies. *TESL-EJ, 7*(2), 1–25.

Izumi, S. (2002). Output, input enhancement, and the noticing hypothesis: An experimental study on ESL relativization. *Studies in Second Language Acquisition, 24*(4), 541–577.

Johns, T. (1991). Should you be persuaded: Two examples of data-driven learning. *English Language Research Journal, 4*, 1–16.

Johns, T. (1994). From printout to handout: Grammar and vocabulary teaching in the context of data-driven learning. In T. Odlin (Ed.), *Perspectives on pedagogical grammar* (pp. 293–313). New York: Cambridge University Press.

Jourdenais, R., Ota, M., Stauffer, S., Boyson, B., & Doughty, C. (1995). Does textual enhancement promote noticing? A think-aloud protocol analysis. *Attention and awareness in foreign language learning. Technical Report #9,* (pp. 183–216). Honolulu, HI: University of Hawaii, Second Language Teaching & Curriculum Center.

Kaplan, A.M., & Haenlein, M. (2016). Higher education and the digital revolution: About MOOCs, SPOCs, social media, and the Cookie Monster. *Business Horizons, 59*(4), 441–450.

König, J. L., Calude, A. S., & Coxhead, A. (2019). Using character-grams to automatically generate pseudowords and how to evaluate them. *Applied Linguistics*, 41(6), 878-900.

Kyongho, H., & Nation, I.S.P. (1989). Reducing the vocabulary load and encouraging vocabulary learning through reading newspapers. *Reading in a Foreign Language, 6*(1), 323–325

Leow, R.P. (2001). Do learners notice enhanced forms while interacting with the L2?: An online and offline study of the role of written input enhancement in L2 reading. *Hispania, 84*(3), 496–509.

Lindgren, E., & Sullivan, K.P. (2003). Stimulated recall as a trigger for increasing noticing and language awareness in the L2 writing classroom: A case study of two young female writers. *Language Awareness, 12*(3–4), 172–186.

Milne, D., & Witten, I. H. (2013). An open-source toolkit for mining Wikipedia. *Artificial Intelligence, 194*, 222-239.

Milton, J. (2009). *Measuring second language vocabulary acquisition.* Bristol, UK: Multilingual Matters.

Nation, I.S.P. (2001). *Learning vocabulary in another language.* Cambridge: Cambridge University Press. https://doi.org/10.1017/CBO9781139524759

Nation, I.S.P. (2013). *Learning vocabulary in another language* (2nd ed.). Cambridge: Cambridge University Press.

Nattinger, J.R., & DeCarrico, J.S. (1992). *Lexical phrases and language teaching*: Oxford: Oxford University Press.

Nesselhauf, N. (2004). What are collocations? In D.J. Allerton, N. Nesselhauf, & P. Skandera (Eds.), *Phraseological units: Basic concepts and their application* (pp. 1–21). Basel, Switzerland: Schwabe.

Robinson, P. (1995). Attention, memory, and the "noticing" hypothesis. *Language Learning, 45*(2), 283–331.

Rott, S. (2004). A comparison of output interventions and un-enhanced reading conditions on vocabulary acquisition and text comprehension. *Canadian Modern Language Review, 61*(2), 169–202.

Schmidt, R.W. (1990). The role of consciousness in second language learning. *Applied Linguistics, 11*(2), 129–158.

Shapiro, H.B., Lee, C.H., Roth, N.E.W., Li, K., Çetinkaya-Rundel, M., & Canelas, D.A. (2017). Understanding the massive open online course (MOOC) student experience: An examination of attitudes, motivations, and barriers. *Computers & Education, 110*, 35–50.

Sinclair, J. (1991). *Corpus, concordance, collocation*: Oxford: Oxford University Press.

Sonbul, S., & Schmitt, N. (2013). Explicit and implicit lexical knowledge: Acquisition of collocations under different input conditions. *Language Learning, 63*(1), 121–159.

Sosoni, V. (2017). Casting some light on experts' experience with translation crowdsourcing. *Journal of Specialised Translation, 28*, 362–384.

Szudarski, P., & Carter, R. (2016). The role of input flood and input enhancement in EFL learners' acquisition of collocations. *International Journal of Applied Linguistics, 26*(2), 245–265.

Truscott, J. (1998). Noticing in second language acquisition: A critical review. *Second Language Research, 14*(2), 103–135.

Uggen, M. S. (2012). Reinvestigating the noticing function of output. *Language Learning, 62*(2), 506–540.

Vyatkina, N. (2017). Data-driven learning of collocations: Learner performance, proficiency, and perceptions. *Language Learning & Technology, 20*(3), 159–179. https://doi.org/10125/44487

Wu, S. (2010). Supporting collocation learning. (Doctor of Philosophy in Computer Science), The University of Waikato.

Yoon, H. (2008). More than a linguistic reference: The influence of corpus technology on L2 academic writing. *Language Learning & Technology, 12*(2), 31–48. https://dx.doi.org/10125/44142

---

1. https://en.wiktionary.org/wiki/algorithm
2. http://flax.nzdl.org/greenstone3/flax

Index

7 Survival Skills, 106
accent, 96, 119
Affordance-Actualization
 Theory, 9
affordances, 10-15
agency, 3, 5, 30
AI, 1, 2, 82-85, 101
artificial intelligence. *See* AI
assessment, 20, 42, 86, 128, 166,
 167, 239, 283, 295
ASR, 55
Automatic Speech Recognition.
 See ASR
autonomy, 3, 14, 120, 145, 152,
 164, 165, 168, 208, 298
blended learning, 8, 9, 101
CLIL, 19, 106, 168
CMC, 30-31, 160
cognitive presence, 127
CoI, 127
Community of Inquiry. *See* CoI
computer-mediated
 communication. *See* CMC
contextualization, 4, 74, 93, 94,
 102, 208, 210, 222, 223, 234,
 235, 283, 287, 293, 299
Content and Language
 Integrated Learning. *See* CLIL
constructivist
 approach, 114
 learning environment, 153
corpus, 33, 34, 186, 191, 199,
 294, 297, 298

Coursera, 293
COVID-19, 1, 84
edX, 293
Educational Engineering, 274,
 275, 276
EMI, 86
English as the medium of
 instruction. *See* EMI
Facebook, 2, 107, 108, 111, 116,
 117, 153, 154, 166
F-Lingo, 293, 294
FutureLearn, 293, 299
goals
 elicitation, 272, 274, 277, 288
 learning, 46
Google Classroom, 30, 35, 36,
 37, 49, 104
Google Docs, 210, 212, 214
grammar, 84, 186
 accuracy, 95
help options, 266, 273, 286
IELTS, 85
IMLL, 271
Instructor-manipulated
 Language Learning. *See* IMLL
Intelligent Personal Assistants.
 See IPA
IPA, 55, 102
 Amazon Alexa, 55, 57, 58, 102,
  103, 104, 113
 Amazon Echo, 103, 105, 108
 Cortana, 102

Index

Google Assistant, 55, 56, 57, 58, 59, 102
Google Home Mini, 106, 108, 113
Google Nest Hub, 57
Siri, 55, 57, 102
learning community, 127
linguistic networks, 34
listening, 160, 266, 268, 270, 273, 282, 286, 287
  comprehension, 63
  computer-based, 267
machine translation. See MT
MALL, 9, 19, 84, 88, 90, 106, 109, 117, 165, 271
MAXQDA, 190, 213, 214
MIM, 126, 128, 143, 145, 146
mobile assisted language learning. See MALL
Mobile Instant Messaging. See MIM
mobile learning. See MALL
MOOC, 4, 19, 20, 293, 294, 295, 296, 297, 299, 300, 313, 314
motivation, 3, 58, 59, 61, 63, 64, 71, 84, 87, 90, 94, 95, 107, 129, 152, 160, 164, 169, 203, 208, 256, 257, 274
MT, 184-188, 190-203
natural language processing. See NLP
neural machine translation. See NMT
NLP, 102
NMT, 185, 186
noticing hypothesis, 294, 298

OERs, 233, 234, 235, 237, 238, 241, 243, 244, 245, 257
Open Data, 4
Open Educational Resources. See OERs
PeerEval, 110
personal assistants. See IPA
personalization, 4, 85, 93, 94, 102, 105, 106, 145, 171, 287, 293, 299, 305
pronunciation, 58, 67, 84, 120, 160
quantitative text analytics, 32
rapport, 128, 135, 136, 138, 143, 144, 146
  management, 127
reading, 58, 59, 116, 184, 233, 234, 241
  aloud, 87
  comprehension, 237
  to-write, 235, 236, 243
second language acquisition. See SLA
self-regulation, 3, 35, 169
SLA, 7, 8, 12, 14, 16, 151, 152, 163, 167, 168, 170, 267, 271, 272
SMART, 2
smart speaker, 102
SNS, 15, 153,
social constructivist theory, 242
social media, 151, 160, 166
social networking sites. See SNS
social network analysis, 34, 35, 49
social presence, 127, 133, 134, 142, 144

socialization, 4, 48, 49, 94, 151, 152, 153, 208
speaking, 55, 57, 59, 63, 67, 71, 82-86, 89, 91, 93, 94, 105, 108, 112, 116, 117, 118, 120, 128, 164, 266, 272
strategies
  learning, 35, 37, 42, 113, 169, 185, 187, 188, 190, 192, 197, 200, 237, 243, 251
  linguistic, 128, 131
  listening, 269
  reading, 242, 249
  scaffolding, 209
  teaching, 13, 172, 234, 242, 244
  writing, 247
task-based language teaching. *See* TBLT
tasks, 271
  assessment, 270
  difficulty, 283, 283
  guidance, 284
  input characteristics, 278
  design, 266, 267, 272
  structure, 282
  unfocused, 270
TBLT, 266, 270, 272, 273
teaching presence, 127
telecollaboration, 126, 129
temporality, 38
TOEIC, 107, 109, 119
Twitter, 107, 111, 116
vocabulary, 22, 58, 63, 64, 67, 84, 104, 108, 116, 128, 132, 141, 160, 170, 184, 186, 195-197, 236, 237, 270, 278, 280, 282, 285, 295-298, 300
  activities, 307

testing, 305
voice assistants, 102
WhatsApp, 128, 129, 130, 131, 132, 133, 134, 140, 141, 142, 143, 144, 145, 146
Wikipedia, 104, 297, 303, 304
wikis, 160
writing, 111, 112, 128, 165, 166, 169, 184, 190-192, 195-202, 207
  collaborative, 209, 210, 238

www.ingramcontent.com/pod-product-compliance
Lightning Source LLC
Chambersburg PA
CBHW071726080526
44588CB00013B/1906